AMERICAN POLITICS AND CULTURE WAR
AN INTERACTIVE LOOK AT THE FUTURE

Larry Tomlinson   Earnest Bracey   Albert Johns

Community College of Southern Nevada

KENDALL/HUNT PUBLISHING COMPANY
4050 Westmark Drive   Dubuque, Iowa 52002

Copyright © 1997, 2002 by Larry K. Tomlinson

Library of Congress Control Number: 2001096167

ISBN 0-7872-9056-4

Printed in the United States of America
10 9 8 7 6 5 4 3 2

Contents

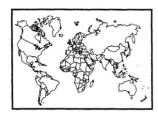 Chapter 1

Politics and Clear Thinking

Sunday morning, December 7, 1941, six aircraft carriers carrying 360 planes reached their destination. The carriers turned east into a brisk wind, increased speed to 24 knots, and launched half their planes. These planes carried a rising sun emblem on the fuselage and red balls on the wings, all symbolizing the Japanese empire. Mitsuo Fuchida led this first wave of Japanese planes. On this day, Navy commander Fuchida wore red underwear and red shorts. Unlike Americans who wear their school colors, Fuchida had a practical reason for the color red. He did not want his men to see his blood if the Americans wounded him. Fuchida had celebrated his 39th birthday a few days earlier. Now on December 7, he was leading a flight of bombers and fighter planes flying 275 miles to destroy the U.S. Pacific Fleet at Pearl Harbor.

Three weeks earlier, Fuchida had stood proudly among the 100 Japanese Navy officers on the flight deck of the carrier *Akagi* and listened to a pep talk by the man who had planned the Pearl Harbor attack. In an informal speech, Admiral Isoroku Yamamoto had told the gathered pilots that they could expect terrific resistance from the Americans stationed at Pearl Harbor. He said: "Japan has faced many worthy opponents in her glorious history—Mongol, Chinese, Russians—but in this operation we shall meet the strongest and most resourceful."

As his "horizontal bomber" flew toward Pearl Harbor at 200 miles per hour, Fuchida remembered fondly how Admiral Yamamoto had shook his hand at the farewell party where he and the other pilots toasted Emperor Hirohito and yelled *Banzai! Banzai! Banzai!* At this memory, Fuchida smiled with warm brown eyes and lips partially covered with a toothbrush shaped mustache grown so that he might look like Germany's admired leader Adolf Hitler.

Flying at 9,800 feet, Fuchida's pilot had his radio tuned to music coming from Honolulu's soft music station KGMB. At 7:00 a.m., Fuchida's planes were picked up as blips at the Opana Mobile Radar Station. The two U.S. Army privates at the radar site decided that more than 50 planes were flying toward the island of Oahu. One private telephoned the Fort Shafter Information Center. After a conversation that lasted about eight minutes, the duty officer told him that the incoming planes were B-17's flying in from California.

About forty minutes after being detected on radar, Fuchida's plane was within sighting distance of Pearl Harbor. Peering through high powered binoculars, he saw seven battleships lined up at their moorings. The American carrier's *Lexington* and *Enterprise* were missing, however. This bothered Fuchida, who knew his primary mission was to destroy the two carriers and as many battleships as possible. Ignoring this disappointment, Fuchida grew excited as he realized that the Americans were caught napping. As Pearl Harbor loomed closer, he fired flares to signal the attack. Then he had his radioman send the code words which meant that the Japanese had caught the entire U.S. Pacific Fleet unaware, *Tora! Tora! Tora!* (Tiger! Tiger! Tiger!).

Except for the two missing American aircraft carriers, the Pearl Harbor attack went according to Admiral Yamamoto's plans. When Fuchida's bombers attacked, the U.S. Pacific Fleet's battleships were lined up off Ford Island, and looked like carnival-game targets. In the first wave, Aichi D3A *Val* dive bombers screamed down and unloaded specially designed armor-piercing shells. B5N *Kate* torpedo bombers followed the dive bombers, flying a few hundred feet above the harbor to drop special shallow water torpedoes. Meanwhile, the famous Mitsubishi A6M *Zero* fighters shredded grounded American planes lined up wing tips to wing tips to discourage saboteurs at nearby Ford, Hickam, Wheeler, Barbers Point, and Kaneohe air bases. In two waves, the 360 Japanese planes turned Pearl Harbor into a smoking ruin.

When the skies cleared of gray, brown, white, lemon yellow, and black smoke, the Americans counted their casualties. Their losses included 2,403 people dead, 18 ships sunk, capsized, or damaged, and nearly 150 lost planes. In contrast, the Japanese attack force lost about 100 men, no surface ships, five midget subs, and 29 planes.

Flying back to the *Akagi*, Fuchida imagined his planes soaring back to Pearl Harbor to bomb fuel tanks and repair facilities. He also expected the carriers, *Akagi, Kaga, Soryu, Hiryu, Shokaku, Zuikaku*, and his First Air Fleet planes would engage in search and destroy hunts for the two missing American carriers. Admiral Chuichi Nagumo who was field commander for the attack did not share Fuchida's enthusiasm for a carrier hunt, however. Nagumo decided to withdraw his fleet from the scene before the American carriers learned about the attack and launched a counterstrike. According to historian Gordon Prange, Nagumo "felt like a gambler who has staked his life's savings on the turn of a card and won. His only idea was to cash in and go home as quickly as possible."[1]

Before Pearl Harbor, Americans tried to ignore Hitler, Mussolini, Tojo and the other evil men who helped start World War II. The December 7 sneak attack, however, aroused Americans from their isolationism and the "die was cast." Now Americans were united as never before in a common hatred for a common enemy. After the attack, President Roosevelt referred to December 7, 1941 as a "date which will live in infamy," and asked Congress to declare war on Japan. On December 8, the Senate voted 82 to zero for war and the House voted 388 to one.

About four months after Pearl Harbor, the Japanese committed another outrageous insult against the American people. After destroying the power of the U.S. Pacific fleet, Japan sent forces against American, British and Dutch facilities in the Philippines, Wake Island, Guam, Dutch East Indies, Malaya, Burma, and Hong Kong. During the invasion of the Philippines, Japanese forces trapped

> Some Americans believe President Roosevelt knew about the Pearl Harbor attack in advance, but let it happen so he could take isolationist Americans to war against the Japanese. Is this a valid criticism of FDR? Use your computer to get the "facts" about this Pearl Harbor conspiracy.

American-Filipino resisters on the Bataan peninsula. Forced to eat monkeys and lizards, the "Battling Bastards of Bataan" held out until April 1942, and then surrendered. The captives were marched 100 miles to a Japanese prison camp. During the forced march, the guards denied the prisoners food and water. The guards also brutally clubbed or bayoneted prisoners who were unable to walk.

This "Bataan Death March" outraged Americans. To exploit this anger, Hollywood went to war and produced several propaganda movies designed to provoke hatred of the Japanese. These movies skillfully stereotyped the enemy soldiers as buck toothed, near-sighted, and blindly obedient to orders. Americans, on the other hand, were portrayed as simple, sincere plain folks drawn into an unwanted war with a devious enemy. Soon after the Bataan Death March, Hollywood released the 1942 movie "Bataan," which showed the fate of an American squad fighting against overwhelming numbers to stop the Japanese conquest of the Philippines. For nearly two hours American audiences saw faceless Japanese soldiers committing every possible atrocity against a multicultural American squad, whose names were Dane, Feingold, Ramirez, Matowski, Malloy, Lassiter, and Epps (a black man). By the end of the movie, every American but one had been killed by the treacherous Japanese. Expecting to die also, the lone survivor Sergeant Bill Dane tries to stay awake as Japanese soldiers in jungle gear sneak up. At the last second, Sergeant Dane awakens, grabs two machine guns and mows down charging Japanese soldiers. The movie ends with Sergeant Dane mouthing obscenities at the oncharging Japanese, and the screen reminds the audience that the Americans who died in the Philippines were martyrs for freedom.

The anger toward Japan was unfairly directed at Japanese Americans. Soon after Pearl Harbor, small businesses began to hang out signs that said, "Jap Hunting Licenses Issued Here." The anti-Japanese feelings caused President Franklin D. Roosevelt to issue the infamous Executive Order 9066, which sent about 120,000 innocent Japanese-Americans to 36 "relocation camps" throughout the United States. This decision was justified by the 1942 movie, "December 7th: the Movie," which suggests that the Japanese living in Hawaii were a dangerous internal threat to national security. Fifty-seven years later, however, the movie, "Snow Falling on Cedars" takes a much more sympathetic view of the relocated Japanese-Americans.

Why did Japan's leaders plan a sneak attack on Pearl Harbor and risk arousing the sleeping American giant? In her book *The March of Folly* (1984), historian Barbara Tuchman offered a common sense explanation for the Japanese miscalculation. She argued that the Japanese leaders were guilty of judging Americans by their own standards. According to Tuchman, the Japanese wrongly assumed that the Pearl Harbor attack would humble Roosevelt and the American government would sue for peace. This was a strange miscalculation, noted Tuchman:

> At a time when at least half the United States was strongly isolationist, the Japanese did the one thing that could have united the American people and motivated the whole nation for war . . . Japan seems never to have considered that the effect of an attack on Pearl Harbor might be not to crush morale but to unite the nation for combat. This curious vacuum of understanding came from what might be called cultural ignorance, a frequent component of folly.[2]

The Japanese leaders who planned the Pearl Harbor attack were guilty of **Intentional Thinking**. This occurs when people have already decided what they want to do and ignore the possibility of disaster. Have you ever been guilty of intentional thinking?

What does Tuchman mean when she refers to "cultural ignorance"? Can you think of any other wars where one nation misjudged the character of another and ended up in a "bad" war?

Have you ever driven a car recklessly, cheated in school on a test, or gone on a "rave" to get some of the illegal drug known as "Ecstasy"? Did you know that this "feel-good" drug can produce serious health problems?

In 1953 Professor Howard Dean suggested a practical way for Americans to avoid tragedies like Pearl Harbor and the Vietnam War. Dean said people should evaluate political issues by using a process which he called "reflective thinking." Reflective thinking requires that we work together in small groups where we can exchange reliable information, listen to moral-value arguments, consider the opinions and ideas. In small groups, wrote Dean, we can "hear all points of view, reflect on them, and work toward a decision."[3]

To understand politics, we need a simple game plan. In this interactive textbook we'll be using a five-stage approach, as described below:

① **Try to state the appropriate policy issue and avoid bad questions.**
② **Gather facts from reliable sources.**
③ **Watch for misused words, i.e., Double Speak.**
④ **Try to recognize the Moral-Value arguments.**
⑤ **Always ask the prediction question, "what will be the future consequence of what we do here today?"**

Stating the Issue

Most political controversies end up being settled by arbitration, policies, rules, laws, judicial decisions or war. When an issue has to be settled by government, it is called a **Policy Issue**. Since 1973, for example, Americans have debated the following policy issue: "Should the Supreme Court's abortion decision be reversed, or changed by an act of Congress?" This is a policy issue because it suggests a solution by a law or policy change. In stating the issue, students should be aware that good questions are fair minded and not loaded, rhetorical, or dichotomous:

❶ **Loaded Questions:** In 1941 Japan made a big mistake because its leaders asked, "How can we humiliate the Americans so that they will agree to our demands?" This is a typical "loaded question" because it is framed to produce a certain answer. Any question that suggests the answer by its wording is loaded. People who have a passionate commitment to one side of a controversial issue like to ask questions that require reasonable people to give the "right" answer. The sincere opponent of abortion rights asks, "Should family planning clinics—which cost millions and are run by bureaucrats—pander to promiscuous women who want government to subsidize their sins?" The sincere proponent of abortion rights asks, "Should pregnant women be deprived of their inalienable right to choose for themselves whether or not to have an abortion?" Why are these loaded questions?

❷ **Rhetorical Questions:** Running for office, the politician asks, "Why are we spending all that money to provide abortions for welfare mothers?" This question is designed to send the message "elect me and I'll end welfare." Rhetorical questions are designed to "send a message" and to manipulate, but they aren't of much use for getting to the truth.

4

❸ False Dichotomous Questions: Pro-life and pro-choice groups like to argue. So they divide the abortion issue into pros and cons by asking, "Do you favor the right of the fetus to grow into a child, or the right of the mother to control her own body?" When a question offers only two possibilities, it is dichotomous and therefore misleading.

What type of question is being asked when a teenager dressed to rave asks himself, "How can Ecstasy be bad for you if it makes you feel good?"

According to newspaper columnist Judy Markey, American men on dates like to talk about themselves, but rarely ask questions about their partners. To support her argument that men don't ask questions, Markey cites the case of a friend—married for three years—whose husband still doesn't know where she attended college because he has never asked.

> **Are women better at asking questions than men? Does Markey offer sufficient proof to prove her argument? Why or why not?**

> **Judy Markey, "Guys Just Don't Ask Questions," Las Vegas *Review Journal* (June 29, 1988), p. 6AA.**

How do we know that Judy Markey's opinions about men are accurately reported? To learn the full contents of her column, we need to know where the authors found the information. This means having a footnote that gives enough information to show us where to look. The example to the left is a simple footnote for a newspaper article. It shows the author, the newspaper source, the date and page number. This information would be needed if you decide to research a question like, "Why do pollsters prefer to hire women to do their survey research?" Is this a good question?

Asking good questions has become an important skill. Schools are now training medical technicians, nurses and doctors in clinical ethics. This new field prepares medical workers to ask new questions, such as, "What should be done about a mother who is 22-weeks pregnant and suffers from brain death?" "Should her body be kept alive until the baby is born?" "Who will pay to keep her body alive?" Since the in-hospital care for the new born baby costs about half a million dollars, medical workers also need to ask, "Who will pay for the baby?"

Now that scientists have broken the genetic code of life, a whole host of new questions will confront your children and grandchildren. What will you say to a child who asks, "Is my hair going to fall out like grandpa's when I get older?"

When pro-life and pro-choice factions debate abortion, they usually divide the issue by asking, "Do you favor the right of the fetus to grow into a child, or the right of the mother to control her own body?" Is there a third possibility?

In Nevada we now have a law which lets doctors prescribe controlled substances for some patients. A fair question to ask might be, "Do such laws encourage drug addicts to seek effective treatments?" Some overly ambitious politicians would rather ask rhetorically, "how can we justify giving illegal drugs to a bunch of criminals?"

On the death penalty, some of us would ask, "How can we justify killing criminals when the Constitution bans cruel and unusual punishment?" Others might ask, "How can a man who killed 186 innocent people be spared the harshest legal punishment allowed by the laws?"

When students do poorly on a test, college professors will ask, "Did anyone study for this exam?" Good study habits develop when we ask good questions. A good question for this chapter would be, "What have we learned from studying the Japanese attack on Pearl Harbor?"

Now that scientists have solved the complete genetic code, a new born baby will leave the hospital with a copy of a form explaining possible defects which will occur as the baby grows into a child, then a teenager, and finally an adult. This means that most future children will someday know how long they can expect to live and what ailment they will suffer as the genes do their job. How about you? Do you want to know your genetic future?

President George W. Bush has been pushing Congress to fund a national defense system geared to destroying incoming enemy missiles. This "Star Wars" idea was rejected when President Ronald Reagan first proposed it in the 1980's. Should the missile defense idea be re-examined in the light of contemporary world politics?

"Why would a sane person use cocaine?" This sounds like a rhetorical question, but there are enough deadly "facts" about cocaine to justify the question. According to *Time's* "Bad News," June 14, 1999, p. 246, "the odds of having a heart attack jump 24-fold during the first hour after taking the drug. That's true even for folks who don't seem to be at risk for heart disease. Apparently the white powder constricts coronary arteries and sends blood pressure soaring."

▲ **Remember:** When an issue requires action by government, it is a **Policy Issue**. Abortion is a policy issue because in 1973 the Supreme Court legalized the right to have an abortion in every state. Later, abortion was debated around the question, "Should Congress pass a law which defines life as beginning at conception?" The question by April 1996 became, "Should President Clinton veto a proposed law to make partial-birth abortions illegal?"

▼ **Beware:** Watch for questions that are **Loaded**, **Rhetorical**, or **Dichotomous**.

Getting the Facts

In the 1960's a popular television show featured actor Jack Webb as Los Angeles police Sergeant Joe Friday. In episode after episode of *Dragnet*, Sgt. Friday or his partner said, "We just want the facts, Ma'am. Just the facts." What are facts? Facts are those things that exist, such as history, batting averages, death or an IRS audit. Americans have a fact fetish. They want to know how often the Los Angeles Lakers have covered

Calvin Klein commercials suggest to young viewers that wearing perfume and skimpy clothes is cool. To offset these ads, should we have a little girl warn us that wearing perfume and skimpy clothes leads to sex, and sex could result in AIDS?

the point spread, how the IRS determines who gets audited, how serial killers choose their victims, and whether or not Madonna plans to play the Virgin Mary in an upcoming movie.

To be educated means to be **Culturally Literate**. How do you know if you qualify? E. D. Hirsch, Jr., in 1987, published a bestseller entitled *Cultural Literacy: What Every American*

6

Needs to Know. Hirsch identifies 5,000 essential names, phrases, dates, and concepts that literate Americans should know. We have listed eight examples below—how many do you know?

① **Hank Aaron**	**Yes**	**No**	
② ***Animal Farm***	**Yes**	**No**	
③ **chromosomes**	**Yes**	**No**	
④ **FDA**	**Yes**	**No**	
⑤ **Big Brother**	**Yes**	**No**	
⑥ **Pearl Harbor**	**Yes**	**No**	
⑦ **Brave New World**	**Yes**	**No**	
⑧ **Hitler**	**Yes**	**No**	

Some Americans believe that public schools should not let students in class discuss questions like, "Was it wrong to drop atomic bombs on Japan in 1945?" They want schools to avoid teaching controversial issues and just stick to the facts. Nevertheless, is that possible? The more controversial the issue, the more necessary the facts. That's why every college offers classes where students learn to use the library and the Internet.

What are facts? Try words taken from the *Oxford Dictionary and Thesaurus*: occurrence, event, happening, incident, experience, truth, reality, actuality, certainty, data, information, particular, detail, point, item, inside information, and "poop."

> Premise: Typical retail price for one Ecstasy pill is about $30. Some call it the hug drug because it makes you feel all warm and cuddly.
> Conclusion: It won't hurt to try it.
> Is this logical? Why or why not?

To be safe, let's define "fact" simply as things that have actually happened and that have been carefully described and evaluated by trustworthy observers; like Gordon Prange's history of the Pearl Harbor attack. Facts are also needed to help shape our attitudes toward important policy issues. To debate abortion, for example, we need to know that in 1997 over one million abortions were performed in the United States. How do we know this? *Time* magazine in its February 28, 2000 edition reported this figure from a report by the Centers for Disease Control and Prevention. To verify the reliability of this figure we need to research the Centers for Disease Control and Prevention on the Internet to determine if this is a reliable source of information about abortions.

> **Who would you hire to write ad copy for your hotel/casino? The job applicant who writes "The MGM Grand Casino Hotel in Las Vegas is a virtual city within a city. With 5,034 rooms, a 17,157-seat arena, 15 restaurants, a 3,800,000 square foot conference center and a stand-alone theme park." Or would you choose the applicant who writes "The MGM Hotel is one big mother?"**

Conventional Wisdom

Getting the facts can be time consuming, and is not glamorous work. Most Americans have no spare time for library or computer research, so they rely on so-called experts to explain how the world works. What we often hear from some experts is merely **Conventional Wisdom**. What is conventional wisdom? In a word, "orthodox." What is orthodox? It means "holding correct or currently accepted opinions." For our purposes, let's define conventional wisdom as meaning those ideals that we accept as true, without asking for proof. They are universal assumptions that we take for granted. Americans live by these assumptions, and if you listen carefully you'll hear people say, "You can't change human nature," "That government is best which governs least," "If you don't like what is on TV, then change the channel," or "Guns don't kill people, people kill people."

Americans believe in conventional wisdom because it sounds logical and is easy to understand. Nevertheless, CW isn't always true or even logical. If we can't change human nature, why have laws that regulate traffic speed and punish drunk drivers? If government shouldn't govern, who's going to stop us from polluting our water and air beyond repair? If TV offers extreme violence during prime time when 15-year-old Christina is babysitting Chad, who is going to be home to turn off the channel? Maybe people do kill people, but a crazy man armed with an AK-47 is more likely to slaughter a school yard of kids than one armed with a baseball bat.

When it comes to politicians, conventional wisdom usually condemns them for being greedy demagogues. Each of the comments below has been made about politicians. Read them and decide which statements are accurate and which are merely empty opinions:

- ☹ "Politics, as a practice, whatever its professions, has always been the systematic organization of hatreds." (Henry Adams)
- ☹ "An honest politician is one who, when he is bought, will stay bought." (Simon Cameron)
- ☹ "A politician is an arse upon which every one has sat except a man." (e.e.cummings)
- ☹ "Spare me the sight of this thankless breed, these politicians who cringe for favors from a screaming mob and do not care what harm they do their friends, providing they can please a crowd!" (Euripides)
- ☹ "If experience teaches us anything at all, it teaches us this: that a good politician, under democracy, is quite as unthinkable as an honest burglar." (H.L. Mencken)
- ☹ "Get thee glass eyes; And, like a scurvy politician, seem To see the thing thou dost not." (William Shakespeare)

Where do these quotes come from? In a scholarly paper, we would have a footnote following the word "not." This footnote would let the reader know that the source of these quotes is Nat Shapiro (ed.), *Whatever It Is, I'm Against It* (New York: Simon & Schuster, 1984), pp. 211-214. Since they are time-consuming, why have footnotes?

Conventional wisdom is hard to resist because parents, teachers and political leaders use it always. Parents dish it up with the baby food. "Drink this milk, and you'll grow up with strong bones." They forget to mention that too much high-fat milk can be unhealthy to some people.

8

Take the common egg. For many years, Americans were told that eggs clogged their arteries and caused heart attacks. Until about 1999 conventional wisdom held that eggs were a food to be avoided; especially for people at risk for heart problems. In July, 1999, however, *Time* published a lengthy health article with the following headline words: "EAT YOUR HEART OUT. Forget what you know about eggs, margarine and salt. The conventional wisdom has been overturned—repeatedly—by surprising new research." The article went on to defend eggs with these words: "EGGS aren't nearly as bad for the heart as doctors used to think. Sure, they're packed with cholesterol. But scientists now know that eating cholesterol doesn't necessarily result in high levels of harmful cholesterol in the blood, where the damage is done."

Media Sources

If you don't have time for library or Internet research, buy a good news magazine or newspaper. News magazines like *Time*, *Newsweek*, and *U.S. News & World Reports* are readable and useful information sources. These media sources are also available on the Internet.

If you want information that comes cheap, then subscribe to your daily newspaper. On any Sunday they fill the combined Las Vegas *Review Journal* and *Sun* with useful information on real estate, health, sports, politics, and the latest murders.

Fortunately, newspapers soften the bad news with the comics, which range from Dilbert's experiences with his sadistic boss to Norman Drabble's troubles with his father Ralph.

> **If you have America On Line and want to learn about current issues, plug into the keyword "Politics."**

Mark Twain once wrote to an old friend, William Dean Howells, complaining that they so filled his morning newspaper with accounts of human depravities that it caused him to spend all day "pleading for the damnation of the human race." However, viewers shocked by these depravities can always turn on TV and watch "Survivors" on a China Sea island struggle to cut throat and come home with a million dollars: Thus adding to the conventional wisdom which says, "Americans will do anything for a buck or fifteen minutes of TV fame."

For many years now, TV journalists have improved ratings and enriched their networks with "real life" shows where average Americans parade their dysfunctions to the cheers of rabid fans. When journalists decide to become part of the event, they change reality by their presence. This happened on a Geraldo show when the host showed how he attended a "hate rally" of white racists and ended in a fight with an obnoxious hater. When this happens, we call it a **pseudo event**. This happens when the media both *creates* and covers the story. This is what happened on the very popular "Survivors" when TV moguls chose a few average Americans and offered them a chance at one million dollars for eating rats and dumping their colleagues.

Sometimes, TV provides viewers with serious events that are treated with restraint and dignity. In May 1989, NBC showed the controversial docudrama *Roe v. Wade*. This TV movie told the story of the famous abortion decision from the perspective of Norma McCorvey—the anonymous "Jane Roe" plaintiff who sued Dallas District Attorney Henry Wade to stop him from enforcing a 1856 Texas anti-abortion law. In her role of McCorvey, actress Holly Hunter dramatically showed the agony and pain of a pregnant woman who could not afford to raise a child and did not want to give it up for adoption. Despite threats of a boycott of advertisers by pro-life groups, NBC showed the docudrama. Defenders argued that TV has a responsibility to dramatize an important constitutional issue. Critics of the movie argued, however, that TV dramas like *Roe v. Wade* cannot be objective.

In his book *Cultural Literacy*, E.D. Hirsch, Jr. says that all Americans should be familiar with events like TV, Elvis, birth control, and the Kennedy Assassination.

Are TV docudramas useful sources of factual information, or merely disguised propaganda?

Without common understanding, argues Hirsch, we have no shared culture. This means knowing the meaning of slogans like, "Remember Pearl Harbor." The Japanese, in contrast, prefer to forget Pearl Harbor. They think bad memories are "water under the bridge" and therefore unproductive. So the Japanese media simply won't print articles that resurrect the memories of World War II.

The American media, however, likes to remind us of shocking and sinister events because these appeal to the inquisitive and morbid side of human nature. The assassination of John F. Kennedy still fascinates Americans, especially those of us who were alive when it happened on November 22, 1963. Nearly thirty years after the Kennedy assassination, Oliver Stone released his highly controversial movie *JFK*. Rejecting **conventional wisdom** that Lee Harvey Oswald was a lone assassin, Stone argues through the film media that Kennedy was the victim of a conspiracy involving the CIA, FBI, and President Johnson. Critics called Stone's movie a "paranoid fantasy," but viewers thought it fascinating entertainment.

In May 2001, American movie goers were entertained by a three hour Hollywood version of the Pearl Harbor attack. Unlike other Pearl Harbor movies, the 2001 version had more romance than action. This fact bothered some critics who thought movies should contain more facts and less romance. What do you think?

Understanding the Importance of Words

As Humpty Dumpty told Alice in Wonderland, "words are what I want them to mean, no more, no less." Former major league umpire Bill Klem often said of balls and strikes, "It ain't nuthin till I call it."

Some advocates of women's rights believe that the male bias in the English language should be completely eliminated. This means replacing the words "manhole," "freshman," and "woman" with "personhole," "freshperson" and "womyn." Is this a good idea? Why or why not?

Modern women have argued for the right to call themselves **Ms.** instead of **Mrs.** or **Miss**. Why? In the *Miracle of Language* (1991), Richard Lederer has a plausible explanation. He suggests that a Mr. John Smith be either married or single. A Mrs. John Smith, however, is definitely married and has her husband's last name. A Miss Mary Jones is still available. According to Lederer, the label Ms. confers equalities by making a woman appear either married or single, like men.

The United States Supreme Court is responsible for deciding when a state law banning obscenity violates the First Amendment. Trying to define what is **"obscene,"** U.S. courts have ended up using uncertain words to define an uncertain condition. In the 1973 words of Justice William O. Douglas dissenting in *Miller v. California*, 413 U.S. 15, "The Court has worked hard to define obscenity and concededly has failed." Former Justice Potter Stewart admitted he couldn't define obscenity, but "I know it when I see it."

Words are not merely useful symbols for communication purposes. They are the chief weapons in the culture war over abortion that is now nearly 30 years old. The abortion controversy has raged around a single definition issue, "Does life begin at conception, later in the pregnancy, or at birth?" In *Roe v. Wade* the Supreme Court majority assumed life was not *viable* during the first three months of pregnancy. Harry Blackmun, who wrote the majority opinion, and his colleagues defined viability as meaning "the capability of meaningful life outside the mother's womb." By deciding that viability was not possible during the first trimester, the justices could justify striking down the state laws that made abortion illegal anytime. Nevertheless, critics thought the definition of viability too uncertain and vague:

> **Presumably, it means that if you take the baby out of the womb, it will live on its own. But there is ambiguity in that notion of viability. In a certain sense no newborn baby is viable. It cannot forage for food or protect itself against the cold. Premature babies need even more elaborate support in order to live. They are not viable on their own, yet we all recognize the states' compelling interest in keeping them alive.[4]**

Philosopher Charles Kelbley argues that the facts alone may never decide the abortion issue because no answer seems forthcoming to the "Quintessential Question: Is the fetus a person? Is it endowed with a 'soul' from the moment of conception?"[5]

Should Congress override the Supreme Court and pass a law which defines life as beginning at conception? What could happen if Congress approves a proposed law to give citizenship rights to the unborn fetus? Is it wrong for the government to decide whether a woman will have the final choice on whether or not to have an abortion? Are these good questions?

Moral-Value Issues

> **How should we define life? Does it begin at conception, viability, quickening, brain waves, or at birth?**

With over a million abortions being performed every year, should Congress define life as beginning at conception, therefore making abortion a form of murder? Those who oppose abortion on moral grounds argue that ending the life of an unborn child is indeed murder. On the other side of this moral-value issue are the pro-choice advocates who believe only the mother is qualified to decide the fate of "her" body.

The abortion controversy has provoked a related debate: "Should public schools teach values and, if so, whose values." Make a list of six essential values that you would like your children to learn by the time they graduate from high school.

Americans define *terrorism* as criminal acts that are outside the accepted rules of diplomacy and war. The people in many other nations, however, view terrorism as merely another form of armed conflict. They see no moral difference between dropping bombs from a

B-52 flying high over a city in North Vietnam or planting a bomb inside a commercial airplane containing hundreds of passengers.

Moral-Value Issues are hard to identify because they involve the question, "Is this wrong?" and because they differ from culture to culture. In the United States, many moral-value issues revolve around our technology. Take the case of a lad who came to librarian Mary Jo Levy and asked for help using the Internet to find information about the humpback whale. The search, according to a newspaper account written by Joanne Jacobs, "turned out to be educational, but not in the way intended."[6] Children using library computers can surf for data and end up with smut. Thus a simple trip to the library may become a major moral-value issue. What possible unintended consequences can we expect to the "smut computer" issue?

Moral-value issues usually begin with the question, "Is it wrong . . . ?" They raise problems that require a decision based on judgments about what is right or wrong. When analyzing facts the student should ask, "What is or was the case?" Definition issues require that we ask, "How are these words used?" When discussing a controversial issue, students need to be aware that all sides will invoke moral judgments. To uphold their arguments, moralists usually engage in five strategies, namely:

❶ **Use value-laden language.** In the case of the abortion controversy, this type of language occurs when pickets carry signs outside abortion clinics that read, "abortion is murder."

❷ **Quote reputable sources.** This happens when pro-choice lawyers say, "The Constitution supports my rights over my own body."

❸ **Predict good or bad consequences.** "If the abortion holocaust is not soon ended, we'll have a civil war on our hands."

❹ **Emphasize inherent value conflicts.** This means accusing your opponents of being inconsistent hypocrites: "How can you claim the right over your own body while an abortion doctor is killing your baby?"

❺ **Using the empathetic appeal.** "How would you feel if your mother had decided to have an abortion when she was pregnant with you?"

So far, we have used abortion to show the importance of having an open mind and using a logical process to discuss and evaluate controversial issues. In any political controversy, be sure to get accurate information, insist on using words accurately, and watch for the moral-value arguments. Be careful. Skillful word manipulators often make moral-value judgments sound like statements of fact

> Would you like your children to visit a library where a computer search for the humpback whale ends up in an ocean of obscenity?

by asking, "How would you feel if your 12-year-old daughter was reading pornography?" or predicting, "if we censor *Playboy* today we'll end up censoring the *Bible*."

Predicting Consequences

About 10 months before the attack on Pearl Harbor, Admiral Yamamoto predicted in a letter that the only way Japan could win a war with the United States would be to "march into Washington and dictate the terms of peace in the White House." Then he added sarcastically, "I wonder if our politicians, among whom armchair arguments about war are being glibly bandied about in the name of state politics, have confidence as to the final outcome and are prepared to make the necessary sacrifices."[7]

Yamamoto's words suggest that he was aware an attack on Pearl Harbor or elsewhere would arouse the American giant and a desperate struggle would follow. His remarks suggest that the only way Japan could win such a war would be a complete victory, not just a successful attack on a naval base. Like most good leaders, Yamamoto had asked the ultimate prediction question, "What will be the future consequence of what we do here today?"

When *Roe v. Wade* was being considered, the justices had a general concern for pregnant women who had to use "abortion mills" in the past. The nine men on the Supreme Court knew that rigid state laws forced women to have abortions at the hands of unqualified doctors working in rooms which were unsanitary. In his majority opinion, Justice Blackmun noted the "prevalence of high mortality rates at illegal abortion mills." Consequently, the court majority decided to allow abortion when it was safe, during the first three months of pregnancy. Though never directly stated in the decision, Blackmun's underlying tone suggested that the court majority felt legal abortions would be safer. Although this was accurate, the court failed to anticipate a significant increase in abortions. Unfortunately, since 1973 the number of abortions has climbed to more than one million yearly, leading to complaints that the court unleashed a "biological holocaust" of the unborn.

Even the best laid plans of mice and men go astray. The Supreme Court in 1973 thought it had a reasonable abortion compromise. However, the Court failed to account for the **Rule of Unintended Consequences**. This happens when government officials make decisions that seem logical, but fail to anticipate serious problems or even disaster. The Pearl Harbor attack, for example, had the unintended consequence of rallying isolationist Americans behind President Roosevelt and a fight to the finish against Japan. No doubt a few reflective Japanese leaders like Admiral Yamamoto thought, "Is this a big mistake?"

Would there be any serious unintended consequences if Congress decided to define life as beginning at the moment of conception? Would we go back to the dark ages when illegal abortions costing $650 were performed by unqualified doctors smelling of booze in a room smelling of Clorox?

Writer Brett Harvey predicts a **worst case scenario**. She says the anti-abortionists are too fanatical and well-organized to accept an abortion compromise. In the past, most Americans had a hands off attitude, and did not take any strong personal interest in

How many abortions were there last year? To get this information, check your local newspapers, call the Census Bureau, or get on your computers and try these groups: National Right to Life [http://www.nrlc.org/], and Parenthood Federation of America [http://www.ppfa.org/ppfa/index.html]. What did you learn about the abortion issue from your computer search?

identifying the women who sought abortions. Today, however, considerable political power is held by the "militant anti choice movement with its underpinnings of fetal life ideology." These militants, says Harvey, no longer believe abortion to be a private affair. They consider abortion so evil that they will line up and scream at a poor woman trying to get a legal abortion. This militancy, predicts Harvey, will lead to demands that state law enforcement officials enforce the morality of the militant anti abortion factions. Harvey ends her worst case scenario by suggesting that in the future state police will end up searching for evidence that women are having abortions illegally. To make her point clear, Harvey asks rhetorically, "Could we expect police officers searching hospital emergency rooms for victims of incomplete abortions? SWAT teams bursting into college dorm rooms where women are performing menstrual extractions?"[8]

The Founding Fathers hoped **Federalism** would prevent controversies like abortion from becoming divisive national issues. In *Federalist 10*, James Madison wrote, "The influence of factious leaders may kindle a flame within their particular States, but will be unable to spread a general conflagration through the other States." In *Roe v. Wade*, however, the Supreme Court elevated abortion from a state controversy to a federal case. Now, we can't go back. The issue is no longer appropriate for states to solve, so we have to wait for either a congressional law or a reversal of *Roe v. Wade* by the Supreme Court. Meanwhile the abortions and protests go on and on . . . .

> When Christian missionaries settled in Australia during the last century, they discovered the Yir Yiront. The Yir Yiront had an entire social system built around stone axcs. Stone to make the axes came from a quarry several miles away. To get the stone the Yir Yiront traded spears to other tribes. The axes were also the exclusive property of the Yiront males; women might borrow an axe, but never own one. The stone axe was also part of the Yir Yiront religion. Members of the Sunlit Cloud Iquana Clan were responsible for carrying out certain religious rituals that required use of the axes.
>
> When they saw the stone axes, the Christian missionaries decided to help the Yir Yiront by giving them better tools. So they gave steel axes to everyone, including the women and children.
>
> Was this a good idea?

The rule of unintended consequences comes to mind every time Congress decides to reform taxes. On January 1, 1991, a typical tax "reform" went into effect. Congress designed it to raise money while forcing rich people to pay their "fair" share. The reform imposed a 10% excise tax on luxury boats that sold for more than $100,000. When they learned of the new tax, rich Americans escaped payment by purchasing their boats overseas. Meanwhile, American boat builders had to lay off more than 20,000 workers because sales of their luxury boats dropped drastically.

After winning the presidency in November 2000, George W. Bush managed to get Congress to reduce the tax bite so that the average family would get a $600 refund. Did this "generous" reform work as intended, or did it have unintended consequences?

The Partial Birth Abortion Ban

After nearly 25 years of arguing, the pro-life and pro-choice factions seem just as unwilling to compromise as ever. The abortion controversy continues through protests, abortion clinic bombings, movies, TV talk shows, and on the Internet. Internet resources include home pages for both pro-life and pro-choice advocates. These home pages include such topics as, "The Abortion Rights Web" and "The Pro-Life News." If you don't have a PC, use the college library and its electronic programs for finding articles and books or go to the college computer center and browse through all the search engines available.

By researching issues like abortion, you become computer wise and culturally literate; and that could mean a good job. Otherwise, you'll have to settle for slinging hamburgers, or playing in a local rock band for minimum wages. Try this question on for size: "Are you going to graduate from college and make us proud of you? Or are you going to keep playing sleazy music with that going nowhere rock band?"

Since a healthy young man can produce in a week or two enough spermatozoa to double the human population of the earth, don't expect abortion to go away without some help from technology or the government. Or we could end the abortion controversy by having a taboo that prohibits sex between couples who are fertile.

Technology, however, usually forces a decision—for better or worse. In 1983, Supreme Court Justice Sandra Day O'Connor recognized this fact when she wrote, "Recent studies have demonstrated increasingly earlier fetal viability. It is certainly reasonable to believe that fetal viability in the first trimester of pregnancy may be possible in the not-too-distant future. The *Roe* framework is clearly on a collision course with itself."

> Now that a female egg can be fertilized by a male sperm *in vitro*, is there any reason to continue the practice of abortion since the fertilized egg is viable almost at conception? Should Congress recognize this fact by passing a law that defines **Life** as beginning at conception? What about a law that gives citizenship status to the "unborn?"

In April 1996, President Bill Clinton had to do some reflective thinking. He had on his desk a politically dangerous bill known as the **Partial Birth Abortion Act (HR 1833)**. Florida House Republican Charles Canady (R-Florida) designed HR 1833 to stop abortions done for "health" reasons during the third trimester of pregnancy. The proposed ban stated that, "Any physician who, in or affecting interstate or foreign commerce, knowingly performs a partial-birth abortion and thereby kills a human fetus shall be fined under this title or imprisoned not more than two years or both."

> **What does interstate commerce have to do with abortion? To get the answer to this question, use your information sources and look up the definition of Implied Powers. Then ask your teacher for help. Describe what you learned in the space below:**

Those who would ban late term abortions describe the operation as a "grisly procedure" in which the doctor pulls the unborn child out legs first through the birth canal; then its skull is punctured and its brain removed. They then crush the empty skull to ease passage out of the mother's body. Those who support a woman's right to have a late term abortion say there are sometimes unusual, but compelling reasons to have an abortion during the last three months of pregnancy. These reasons, according to the National Abortion Federation, include undiagnosed pregnancy, medical complications, severe fetal abnormalities, tragic events, teenage pregnancies, delay caused by parental notification laws, lack of money, physician shortages, and waiting period requirements. The NAF claims that third trimester abortions are very rare. According to NAF statistics, fewer than 1% of abortions are done after twenty weeks and they are "extremely rare" after 26 weeks of pregnancy.

Throughout the controversy, opponents of the partial birth abortion procedure complained that **doublespeak** was disguising the grisly nature of the operation. Physicians who performed the operation liked to soften its gruesome nature with medical **Euphemisms** like "D and X," "dilation and extraction," "intact dilation and extraction," "intrauterine cranial decompression," and "partial birth abortion."

With his usual flair for singling out the gut issue, columnist Thomas Sowell told his readers that the partial birth abortions were being done not for medical reasons but for legal technicalities. Because the baby's head is still inside the mother's body when this happens, argued Sowell, "this can legally be called an abortion rather than the murder of a newborn baby."[9]

Despite the persuasive arguments made by the National Abortion Federation and other pro-choice groups, the Senate on December 7, 1995 passed HR 1833 by a 54 to 44 majority vote. Then on March 27, 1996, the House passed the proposed ban law by a more decisive 286 to 129 majority.

> **Partial Birth Abortions: Should They Be Banned?**

Bill Clinton had to make a tough call. HR 1833 was the first time Congress had acted to outlaw a specific abortion procedure since *Roe v. Wade* declared that states could not prevent a woman from having an abortion in the first three months of pregnancy. If Clinton signed HR 1833, feminist groups could defect and cost him important electoral votes in the upcoming November Presidential election. If Clinton vetoed HR 1833, he would be vulnerable to criticism that he favored a procedure being called "infanticide" by its critics.

Before making his final decision, President Clinton wrote Senate Judiciary Committee Chairperson Orrin Hatch (R-Utah) saying he would sign HR 1833 if Congress amended it to allow the procedure when it is "necessary to preserve the life of the woman or avert serious health consequences to the woman."

> **The words "avert serious health consequences for the woman" would, according to Senator Dole, leave the door open for all kinds of reasons to have late term abortions. Why is this a "definition" issue?**

Soon after, Republican Senate Majority Leader Bob Dole, in a February 28, 1996 letter to the President, argued that an exception for medical reasons would allow abortions for a wide range of reasons. In his letter, Dole argued that "health" was being defined by those "with the most extreme abortion agenda in many ways that would ensure that this exception swallows the rule."

The proposed law, he wrote, already allows exemptions for mothers with physical illness, disorders, and injuries. A broader exemption, he concluded, "would simply defeat the purpose of the bill, which is to stop this grisly procedure."

Despite the anti abortion criticism, President Clinton vetoed the Partial Birth Abortion Ban Act on April 10, 1996 with these words: "I have always believed that the decision to have an abortion should be between a woman, her conscience, her doctor and her God."

Like most **moral-value** conflicts, the abortion ban issue unleashed a torrent of **value laden words**—mostly aimed at President Clinton. One Vatican spokesperson called the veto "shameful . . . an incredibly brutal act of aggression against innocent human life."

One of the most effective moral-value strategies is **empathetic appeal**. This means asking your opponent to *feel* for the victim of a perceived injustice. While they were arguing the partial-birth abortion ban bill, both sides invoked the empathetic appeal. Attacking abortion, Rep. Henry Hyde (R-Illinois) said it's not the end of a pregnancy, "it's the termination of a defenseless little life." On the pro-choice side, the Religious Coalition for Productive Choice urged Congress in a letter dated April 29, 1996, to have compassion for a fetus, who if born would "inevitably suffer or die."

Newspaper columnist Christopher Matthews defended the Presidential veto by describing the agony of a college classmate whose wife chose to have a partial birth

Is Matthews asking a **rhetorical question**?

abortion because she was carrying a child with severe health disabilities. To emphasize his empathetic appeal, Matthews asked, "What do we, the people of the United States want our government to do in cases where a woman learns late in pregnancy that her child will be born with a severe handicap and decides to end the pregnancy?"[10]

Both pro-life and pro-choice factions predicted bad consequences to argue their case. Pro-life groups predicted the veto would come back to haunt Clinton in November and cause him to lose his bid for reelection. Pro-choice groups predicted Bob Dole's support for HR 1833 would cost him the votes of women and cause him to lose his bid to replace Bill Clinton. During the November 2000 presidential election, Republican George Bush had to defend his pro-life position on the abortion issue. What position did Democrat Al Gore take on the abortion controversy?

Michael Ferguson, Executive Director of the Catholic Campaign for America, told a reporter: "President Clinton is defending the killing of live, kicking babies who feel pain and are a mere three inches from birth."

While the House of Representatives was considering HR 1833, sponsor Canady responded to pro-choice advocates who were arguing that the fetus feels no pain because anesthesia administered to the mother during the procedure kills the child. In response, Canady said there was no proof to support that argument.

On September 21, 1996 the House overturned the Clinton veto by a two-thirds majority 285 to 137 but the abortion ban supporters in the Senate were unable to muster enough votes to override the veto, and thus the **checks and balances system** continued to frustrate those Americans who want decisions made by a legislative majority, not one President or five judges.

After the April 10th veto, the Religion News Service reported that ban supporters including Bob Dole intended to make Clinton's veto a key issue in the 1996 election campaign. Despite the opportunity, Bob Dole did not exploit the partial birth abortion issue as his pro-life supporters hoped. During Dole's first TV debate with Clinton on October 6, 1996 the

> **What do you think about an operation in which the doctor partially delivers a live baby feet first until all but the baby's head is exposed, then stabs the baby in the base of the skull, and uses a catheter to suck out its brains? Do these words bother you? Why?**

issue was never directly mentioned. And though "profoundly disappointed" with the April 10 veto, Dole seemed six months later to have lost his enthusiasm for a fight with the President on the issue. This Dole reluctance frustrated columnist Ben Wattenberg who on October 9 accused Dole of "pussy footing" on the morality issue. Wattenberg predicted sarcastically that Dole was in danger of "standing as the candidate of a renamed GOP—The Gutless Old Party."[11] That same day, the Dole campaign released a radio commercial attacking Clinton for supporting "ninth month abortions . . . gays in the military and condoms for school kids." But by election campaign standards, the radio commercial was bland and lacked details describing the "grisly procedure." In the children's story *Alice's Adventures in Wonderland* (1865), Alice arrives at the house where the March Hare, Mad Hatter, and the Dormouse are seated outside at one corner of a large table. As Alice approaches, the Hatter says, "Your hair needs cutting." Before Alice can reply, the Mad Hatter asks, "Why is a raven like a writing desk?" When Alice says, "I believe I can guess that," then the March Hare asks, "Do you mean you can find the answer to it?" Before Alice can speak again, the Hatter asks, "What day of the month is it?" This question sends Alice and her tormentors into a rambling conversation about whether clocks should tell the time of day, the day of the month or the year.

During a December 1985 monologue, *Tonight Show* host Johnny Carson asked, "What is the difference between a woman from Nevada and a parrot?" Getting no response from the studio audience, Carson answered, "You can teach a parrot to say 'no'."

> **Are TV talk shows a good example of critical thinking, or more like the "Mad Hatter's Tea Party"?**

If you listen to talk show hosts and their guests, you'll hear these "Logical Fallacies."

❶ **Faulty Generalization: "All men are scum."**

❷ **False Analogy: "Politicians act like criminals."**

❸ **Cause and Effect Fallacy: "Cigarettes make me feel good, so they must be healthful."**

❹ **False Dilemma: "If you want to protect pornography, you can't be on the side of women."**

❺ **Slippery Slope: "If we allow rock bands to be satanic today, all our children will end up serial killers in the future."**

The Lie Exposed

■ Gruesome abortion procedure far more common than claimed.

Recall, if you will, President Clinton's veto last spring of the partial-birth abortion ban. Mr. Clinton asserted he had "studied and prayed" on the subject, and determined that it is used only on "a few hundred women every year" whose fetuses are "about to be born with terrible deformities."

Well, Mr. Clinton must not have studied or prayed hard enough. Even though pro-choice organizations were bolstering his claim that "only" about 500 such infantici ... er, abortions, took place each year, the Centers for Disease Control put the number at 13,300. Plus, anti-abortion forces produced proof—later confirmed in The Wall Street Journal and in an investigative report by The Record of Hanckesak, N.J. —that the procedure was common and most often performed on healthy babies of healthy mothers.

One of the key advocates of the procedure was Ron Fitzsimmons, the executive director of the National Coalition of Abortion Providers. He went on "Nightline" in 1995 to proclaim that the procedure was rare and performed only when the mother faced dire medical consequences if she carried the pregnancy to term.

But Mr. Fitzsimmons lied—"lied through his teeth," as he now admits. In an upcoming article in Medical News, Mr. Fitzsimmons confirms what his opponents in the anti-abortion movement say: Partial-Birth abortions are common and routinely done on the healthy fetuses of healthy women who just don't want the child. "The abortion rights folks know it, the anti-abortion folks know it, and so, probably, does everyone else," he told The New York Times this week.

And what is this procedure politely characterized as "partial-birth abortion" but condemned as infanticide even by the likes of liberal Sen. Daniel Patrick Moynihan? What is it that Pope John Paul II has dubbed an "incredibly brutal act of aggression"? Well, here's how Medical News describes it: "Extraction of an intact fetus, feet first through the birth canal, with all but the head delivered. The surgeon forces scissors into the base of the skull, spreads them to enlarge the opening and uses suction to remove the brain>"

Bill Clinton ought to do more praying with that image in his mind.

Congress stands ready to outlaw partial-birth abortion (with an exception for women whose lives would be endangered without one). Indeed large, bipartisan majorities in both houses voted for the partial-birth abortion ban in 1996—the House favored it 286-129—only to be overruled by Mr. Clinton's veto. Even stalwart, pro-choice liberals such as Minority Leader Dick Gephardt supported the prohibition.

It is Bill Clinton and Bill Clinton alone who allows the gruesome practice to continue unchecked.

Now that you've learned a few skills, let's analyze a Las Vegas *Review Journal* editorial: This editorial appeared in the Las Vegas *Review Journal* January 28, 1997 on page 14B. Prepare a footnote on a 5 x 8 card, and then analyze the editorial by the criteria suggested below.

❑ To help you successfully complete the study questions, the authors have generously listed below some important clues:

    ✌ "Partial-birth abortions are common and routinely done on the healthy fetuses of healthy women who just don't want the child."
    ✌ 500 or 13,300?
    ✌ "infantici ...er, abortions."
    ✌ Look for value-laden words, etc.
    ✌ You're on your own matey!

Let's practice your critical thinking skills, using the editorial.

■ Is the writer pro-choice or pro-life? How do we know this?

■ What facts does the writer use to support his position?

■ Why does the writer use the word "infanticide"?

■ Describe the different moral-value issues raised in the editorial.

■ Has Congress tried yet to override President Clinton's 1996 veto?

Notes

1. Gordon W. Prange, *At Dawn We Slept: The Untold Story of Pearl Harbor* (New York: McGraw-Hill Book Company, 1981), pp. 22, 195-201, 258-260, 265-272, 322, 338, 344, 351, 366-368, 374-379, 392, 415, 419, 426, 480, 543, 578, 737.

2. Barbara W. Tuchman, *The March of Folly* (New York: Alfred A. Knopf, 1984), p. 31.

3. Howard Dean, *Effective Communication: A Guide to Reading, Writing, Speaking and Listening* (New York: Prentice-Hall Inc., 1953), p. 263.

4. George McKenna, *A Guide to the Constitution: That Delicate Balance* (New York: Random House, 1984), p. 317.

5. Charles Kelbley, "Abortion: Agreeing to Disagree," *Newsweek* (December 16, 1985), p. 9.

6. Joanne Jacobs, "Libraries are being pressured to serve as Internet nannies," Las Vegas *Review Journal* and *Las Vegas Sun* (December 15, 1996), p. 6D.

7. Prange, *At Dawn We Slept*, p. 11

8. Brett Harvey, "The Morning After," *Mother Jones* (May, 1989), pp. 21-27, 43.

9. Thomas Sowell, "Slippery Talk Clouds Abortion Issue," Las Vegas *Review Journal* (April 28, 1996), p. 2C.

10. Christopher Matthews, "Partial Birth Abortions are Hard to Defend," Las Vegas *Review Journal* (April 12, 1996), p. 11B.

11. Ben Wattenberg, "GOP: The Gutless Ooze Party?" Las Vegas *Review Journal* (October 9, 1996), p. 11B.

 # Chapter 2

Political Culture

The Pledge of Allegiance is just words: "I pledge allegiance to the flag of the United States of America and to the republic for which it stands, one nation under God, indivisible, with liberty and justice for all." These 31 words once gave Americans a

Cultural Literacy Break: Can you think of any logical reason why the open hand, stiff armed salute to the American flag was stopped during World War II?

tingling sensation known as patriotism. Now, however, this simple pledge has become a controversial **symbol**. The original pledge, written in 1892 by Francis Bellamy, did not contain the words "under God," but instead said "my flag." The phrase "under God" was added to the pledge by an Act of Congress in 1954. Before World War II Americans said the pledge and extended an open hand stiff arm salute to the flag. This Nazi-like salute disappeared, however, after Pearl Harbor.

During the 1988 presidential contest between Vice President George Bush and Massachusetts Governor Michael Dukakis, the Pledge of Allegiance became the focus of a controversy. Bush raised the pledge issue in New Orleans after Republican delegates had nominated him to be their candidate for president. In his acceptance speech, Bush asked, "Should public school teachers lead our children in the Pledge of Allegiance?" During the campaign, Bush tried to provoke Dukakis by invoking the memory of three American revolutionaries from Massachusetts who fought against British tyranny more than two hundred years ago. At every opportunity, Bush would say to his audiences, "It's hard for me to imagine that the Founding Fathers—Samuel Adams, John Adams, and John Hancock—would have objected to teachers leading students in the Pledge of Allegiance to the flag of the United States."

Jeopardy Break: Formulate a correct question for the name of the Massachusetts revolutionary who signed the Declaration of Independence first with notably large handwriting [P.S. He might sell you some insurance today].

As the campaign rolled into its final two months, the pledge issue had taken the spotlight from more pressing issues. This fact caused *Time* to observe sardonically that "while the national debt was topping $2.5 trillion, while a growing number of beggars wandered urban streets, and America's overburdened school systems prepared for the return of classes, the electorate was treated to the spectacle of George Bush forcing Michael Dukakis to debate whether elementary school children should be compelled to recite a loyalty oath before they rattle off their ABCs."[1]

Was the pledge important enough to be a serious debate topic? Let's look at the **facts**. In 1977 while governor of Massachusetts, Dukakis had vetoed a legislative bill that required public school teachers to lead their students in the Pledge of Allegiance. He vetoed the bill when the state's Attorney General told him it was unconstitutional because of a precedent set in 1943.

In *West Virginia State Board of Education v. Barnette,* 319 U.S. 624 (1943), the United States Supreme Court had invalidated a similar Virginia law because it forced Jehovah's Witnesses to worship a "graven image," denying them freedom of religion. By signing the 1977 legislative bill, Governor Dukakis would have opened the door to similar lawsuits. In support of Dukakis, New York *Times* columnist Tom Wicker posed a **rhetorical question**: "Would George Bush have approved the same bill under the same circumstances? Would he think it *more* patriotic to defy and disobey the Constitution as interpreted by the highest court in the land?"[2]

Chicago *Tribune* columnist Mike Royko tried to put the controversy in perspective by telling his many readers that the Pledge of Allegiance was written to sell flags for the Boston magazine *Youth's Companion.* Royko chided Bush for failing to tell his audiences that Bellamy was a radical preacher whose favorite sermon was "Jesus the Socialist."

> To find the Barnette case in a traditional law library, you need to use 319 U.S. 624 (1943). To find Supreme Court decisions on the Internet, you'll need to use "Supreme Court Decisions" and the following code: [http://www.law.cornell.edu/supct.] Use the Internet and see if you can bring up the Barnette case.

Despite all the furor, American voters seemed unconcerned about the pledge issue. On election day ABC polled voters and found only 12% were concerned. It was important, however, as proof that political candidates like to use **symbols** to embarrass their opponents. Most of the 46 million Americans who voted for George Bush saw him as the candidate who symbolized law, order, and patriotism. Republicans aimed the pledge issue at those Americans who felt public schools ought to be teaching more patriotism and less evolution. In their minds, Michael Dukakis was a dangerous "liberal" whose concern for civil liberties was greater than his love of country.

> Which presidential candidate would you have preferred in 1988—Bush and his pledge or Dukakis and his support for religious diversity? Is this a fair question?

Culture Symbols

During the 1988 election, George Bush used the Pledge of Allegiance controversy to defeat his Democratic opponent. Eleven years later, the **symbol** controversy had switched from the pledge to desecration of the flag.

On December 12, 1995, the Senate by a 63 to 36 majority fell three votes short of the two-thirds necessary to amend the Constitution. President Clinton opposed the desecration amendment because it would alter the Bill of Rights, which contains the First Amendment's guarantee of freedom of speech. Though opposed, Clinton could only criticize the proposed amendment because the President cannot veto a constitutional amendment. Challenging Clinton's criticism of the proposed amendment, Senate Majority Leader Bob Dole argued that burning the flag is not "protected" speech and that the First Amendment is "not absolute."

Supporting Bob Dole's position, Las Vegas *Sun* columnist and former Nevada Governor Mike O'Callaghan wrote, "Burning or stomping Old Glory is beyond freedom of speech—and isn't speech at all."[3]

☺ Would you vote for a state referendum banning flag desecration in this state if artistic students at this college used nude models draped in the U.S. flag?

It takes a two-thirds majority in both the House and Senate to propose a constitutional amendment. Under the Constitution, who has the power to ratify an amendment?

Quarrels over political symbols like the flag are what make us human. In his *Study of Culture* (1949), cultural anthropologist Leslie A. White defined a **symbol** as a "thing the value or meaning of which is bestowed upon it by those who use it." In other words, humans can make the flag an honored symbol and salute it, or they can burn it to protest. The red ball on Japanese planes attacking Pearl Harbor was meant to symbolize the rising sun of the Japanese empire. American pilots, however, used the word "meat-ball" to describe the red ball symbols.

This capacity to bestow symbolic meaning seems to be unique to humans. A dog might sleep on a warm rising sun flag, but has no capacity to give it abstract meaning. This capacity to create meaning is what makes humans unique and very different from animals. Like most of us, Animals can reason, calculate and learn from experience. Nevertheless, they don't write dictionaries, produce mathematical formulas or have a multitude of definitions for the simple words "freedom of speech." No animal ever marched off to fight a holy crusade carrying the *Bible*, pledging allegiance to a cross or singing "Remember Pearl Harbor," "Praise the Lord and Pass the Ammunition." No animal has ever complained about a word being racist, sexist, or ageist. Only humans, it seems, have words that are politically correct or incorrect.

The latest fighting symbol is the Confederate battle flag that has flown over southern states since the Civil War. Should states be banned from displaying flags that some Americans find objectionable?

Professor White believed it impossible "for a dog, bird, or even the ape, to have any understanding of the meaning of the cross to a Christian, or of the fact that black (white among the Chinese) is the color of mourning."

The trait that separates humans from animals is our preoccupation with symbols, with flags that represent patriotism, or with trench coats that symbolize power.

On April 20, 1999 to celebrate Adolf Hitler's birthday, Eric Harris, 18, and Dyland Klebold, 17, shot and killed 14 fellow students and one teacher at the Columbine High School in Littleton, Colorado. The two killers were apparently "outraged" that athletes and others at the school teased and tormented them. To get even, Harris and Klebold planted more than 50 explosive devices at the school and armed themselves with carbine rifles and a semiautomatic TEC-DE 9 pistol. In a frightening display of rage, Harris and Klebold fired over 900 rounds at helpless students, shot a young girl for professing a belief in God, and then committed suicide.

Judging from news reports, Harris and Klebold belonged to a faction of Columbine students known as the "Trench Coat Mafia." They were also obsessed with violent video games, Adolf Hitler, and Marilyn Manson. And they were fascinated by the movie "Basketball Diaries," which has an alienated student dressed in a trench coat and shooting fellow classmates who have been guilty of teasing him.

How could trench coats be responsible for the Columbine massacre?

In June 2001 Timothy McVeigh was legally executed for blowing up the federal building in Oklahoma City. In McVeigh's mind the 168 victims of his huge bomb symbolized government agents who took part in the burning of the Branch Davidian compound near Waco, Texas. Was McVeigh insane or merely a product of intentional thinking?

Although animals lack the power to create meaning, they sometimes seem more humane than humans. In 1996 a gorilla named Binti Jua (Daughter of Sunshine) living at Chicago's Brookfield Zoo did an act of kindness that would shame many humans. She rescued a three-year-old human toddler who had fallen 18 feet into her enclosure and was unconscious. While five other gorillas stood nearby, Binti carried the child to a door where other humans could rescue him. This unusual act of kindness and intelligence made Binti a national celebrity, and *Time* featured her as "The Gorilla of American Dreams."

Do chimps have culture? In Tanzania, chimps at Gombe routinely use sticks to probe the ground for termites, but chimps one hundred miles away in the Mahale Mountains do not. This fact has been used by anthropologists to argue that some animals, like the Gombe chimps, have the capacity to create culture. Is "culture" the power to think or the capacity to create meaning? Is there a difference?

In the 1996 movie *Congo*, a gorilla uses sign language which becomes words through a translator-amplifier gadget. Could such a gorilla be said to be using "symbolic language"?

In her novel *Lives of the Monster Dogs* (1997), Kirsten Bakis plays with that notion in a fascinating story about the year 2008 when a tribe of large dogs, surgically and genetically altered, with prosthetic hands, voice boxes, and human intelligence arrive in Manhattan. The dogs are the creation of a German surgeon who tries to develop unstoppable soldiers by transforming dogs into soldiers who walk upright.

The capacity to create meaning for symbols seems so far to be limited to humans. Even computers that play chess have to be programmed with symbols created by humans. Until we discover a library for gorillas, we'll have to be satisfied that only humans use dictionaries and build computers. Some researchers have taught chimpanzees to use sign language. We also know that chimps teach their offspring how to find food. Some researchers argue that apes have culture because they can learn to communicate. What do you think? Do apes have culture?

Language is the crucial element in human culture. If you don't want to be fired at work, be sure you understand words like "unwelcome sexual conduct," and "hostile environment." If you happen to be in the military, you had better avoid "fraternization" with a person of the other gender.

Suppose a company employs you and your job is to develop advertising copy for a new product. What words should you avoid? Somebody at Reebok decided to use the word "Incubus" as the label for a woman's running shoe. According to *The Encyclopedia of the Occult, the Esoteric, and Supernatural* (1977), however, an Incubus is a mythical demon that corrupts sleeping women by

Will the expanded meaning of the words "Incubus" and "Docker" influence what you wear? Why or why not?

having intercourse with them. Another advertising *faux pas* is the Levi label "Dockers." According to the *Dictionary of Slang and Unconventional English* (1984), a docker could be a dock worker, a reused cigarette butt, a rude peasant blowing his nose, or the angry sailor who cuts off the clothes of a prostitute who has given him a venereal disease, and chased her into the streets.

Words are important because they shape our values. During a 1863 speech at Gettysburg, Civil War President Abraham Lincoln used 272 words that are now part of the national conscience. He said, "Fourscore and seven years ago our fathers brought forth upon this continent a new nation, conceived in liberty, and dedicated to the proposition that all men are created equal." What if Lincoln had said, "A long time ago some wrinkled old dudes decided all us persons are the same?" or "go ezy on the xtasi baby!"

In his book *Lincoln at Gettysburg*, historian Garry Wills argued that Lincoln's words changed the shape of the nation's history by making freedom and equality the reasons for fighting the Civil War. Should we go to war over words like "freedom" and "equality?"

Words are important because they expose our prejudices. When different groups want to change our feelings, they start by changing our words. When used to describe males, the word "burly" was a compliment. It meant being sturdy and masculine, not scrawny and weak. Now, however, burly means something else. In other words, using the word "burly" now is racist. So don't use it! When used to describe females, the word "buxom" means healthy, plump, cheerful and full-bosomed. Currently, buxom is **politically incorrect** because it is an "offensive reference to a woman's chest." ✩ If we stop using words like "buxom" will we also stop having buxom thoughts? Other current bad words include "airhead," "gyp," "jock," "senior citizen" and "sweetie." After reading the banned list put out by the University of Missouri School of Journalist, Chicago *Tribune* columnist Mike Royko wrote: "Maybe it's time to wave the white flag. The age of supersensitivity is crushing me."[4]

Ever met a gorilla (nonhuman) who ambled into a post office and sprayed his fellow workers with gunfire? Know any gorilla dictionary that uses the phrase "going

Going Postal, BAM! BAM!

postal" to mean "being totally stressed out?" Know any gorillas whose language contains such words as DOS, user friendly, mung, MIPS, FLOPS, big streaming, bogosity, modem, defenestrate, klug, SPAM?

This computer jargon is symbolic of the language of technology. In the world today there are about 6,800 languages. Our schools require a basic understanding of computer language, but few of us know any language but English. Why?

Human DNA is 98.4 percent identical to the DNA of chimps. Does that fact mean humans and chimps are members of the same species? Chimps can be taught to give the "finger." Does that mean we are cousins to a bunch of monkeys.

Chimpanzees usually draw large crowds at the Zoo. Is that because they seem so human, or because they are playful? What about human entertainers who perform by grabbing their private parts? Isn't crotch grabbing monkey business?

> **What about computer programs that convey unpopular words? In 1996 a $40 million libel lawsuit was filed by a man offended by the ability of computer software to recognize and respond to a racial slur. The lawsuit was filed by Thomas Wallace of Omaha, Nebraska who discovered the infamous "N" word in an encyclopedia software from Compton's New Media of Carlsbad, California. Should the "N" word be purged from all movies, books, TV, the Internet, newspapers, etc.**

Popular entertainer Madonna made a career by wearing men's clothes and grabbing her crotch. Was this merely a childish ritual, or does Madonna symbolize women who have "power?" Has crotch grabbing become a symbolic protest that has become part of our culture? Will Madonna be remembered like the ✌peace sign, the finger ☜ and the ace of ♠ spades? Since the crotch is merely some human anatomy where the legs come together, the grabbing has no health or therapeutic value, so it must be some kind of **symbolic** message understood only by the fans who like contemporary music. Is crotch grabbing serious business or should it go in the history books as just another fad, like leapfrog, Flossie Flirt, Lincoln Logs, Mah-Jongg, Mousketeers, "Kilroy was here," Silly Putty, Day-Glo Colors, and Pet Rocks.

Symbolic messages like crotch grabbing, the extended middle finger, and the ace of spades are important because they are part of our culture. What is culture? Think of it as the way of life of people. It includes such things as our artifacts, values, rules, customs, and technology. To see how culture works, visit a Las Vegas casino and watch Blackjack. The poker chips are artifacts which anthropologists will someday be using as proof that people who lived in Las Vegas a few thousand years before had coinage of uneven value. In Blackjack, an ace of spades can have a value of one or eleven—which the rules arbitrarily assign. The rules require that the dealer stand on 17. Custom dictates generous tips for the dealer and cocktail server. As for technology, it is symbolized by computerized card games and new games like "Jeopardy." Technology decides if you'll be a winner if you play the right machine.

So then, what is culture? Anthropologist Edward Burnett Tyler once defined it as "the complex whole which includes knowledge, belief, art, morals, law custom, and any other capabilities and habits acquired by man as a member of society."[5] More simply, culture includes our beliefs, institutions, pots, pans, beer and gigabytes.

> **Math Problem: What is a gigabyte? Answer 1,073, 741,824 bytes. How do we get this number?**

While Americans were praising Binti for her near-human behavior, people in Africa were eating infected chimpanzees and dying from the dreaded Ebola virus. Despite space suits and sophisticated maximum containment facilities, world scientists seem unable to prevent outbreaks of Ebola, which is 60 to 90 percent fatal. Most outbreaks occur in underdeveloped countries where epidemics of cholera, dysentery and malaria are spawned by war, poverty, overcrowding and poor sanitation. Though more fortunate, many Americans have poor hygiene habits like failing to wash their hands after using the rest rooms. Should there be a federal law making it a misdemeanor for restaurant employees to work with unwashed hands?

In the summer of 1987, Coors slapped a new "Original Draft" label on its beer, replacing the old "Banquet Beer" labels. Although Coors changed neither the ingredients nor the taste of its beer, sales slumped badly in Texas. Texas drinkers for some reason noticed a difference in the taste of Coors when they changed the labels. Why?

Many career women are not comfortable with traditional gender words. They don't like "Mrs." It stereotypes women as the property of men. They don't like "Miss." It means being available for marriage. "Ms." is the preferred title. Why?

Technology

Any invention that improves on our biological selves is a form of technology. Thus, a pair of eyeglasses with bifocals is technology. So is a Stealth bomber. Technology and its support systems are what humans invent to make life easier, more entertaining, and profitable. These inventions, however, often result in **unintended consequences**. ☆ **Reminder: What is the Rule of Unintended Consequences?**

Soon you can "ring up a coke" by using your cell-phone to buy a soft drink from a machine. Is this a good idea?

In January 1997 Americans were shocked by these headlines: "Researchers Clone Lamb From Single Adult Cell," "Scottish Researchers Successfully Clone Ewe," and "SEND IN THE CLONES." What future unintended consequences can we expect from cloning?

In his 1932 novel *Brave New World* Aldous Huxley predicted that someday our technology would totally control our lifestyles and values. Huxley depicted a society where birth control is perfected to the ultimate. In Huxley's fictional society they decant all babies in test tubes through a process which produces 96 identical twins from each fertilized egg. Later, they educate children in government conditioning centers. Through a procedure called hypnopaedia, children in this brave new world are sleep-taught to believe in the values of their society. Since government has decanted and raised children, parents are useless survivals. So they teach children that "father" and "mother" are obscene words. Since families, with their guilt, jealousies, love and other strong emotional attachments are gone, children and adults are now free to indulge in every form of sex. As described by Huxley, small children play "find the zipper." Young adults engage in group sexual encounters called "an orgy porgy." Adults take sex hormone drugs and enjoy full sex until about 60, when they die on schedule. Every citizen is promiscuous, and without guilt. To stir up the hormones, adults attend erotic movies called

Huxley's fictional world is one where all human values are secondary to technology. Is such a society now possible in the United States? Why not?

"Feelies." At the movies, every sensation shown on screen is felt by the audience. In Huxley's world "Our Ford" has replaced God. Since Henry Ford invented the assembly line for cars, Huxley thought he ought to be the god of a society where people are mass produced. To make sure no woman ever has children naturally, the young women of brave new world take special hormones and birth control drugs contained in a special "Malthusean Belt" that all women wear.

American women, on the other hand, use condoms, birth control pills and abortions to prevent

"O brave new world, That has such people in 't" ---DWEM

unwanted children. During the Clinton years and under President George W. Bush, partial birth abortion has become controversial. Suppose we had a national referendum on the policy issue, "Should Congress grant full citizenship protection for the unborn?" How would you vote on this issue?

Should we use our technology to keep the average person alive for at least one hundred years? Or would it be more appropriate merely to use our scientific knowledge to discover more ways to predict how we will age, and eventually die? Science now can predict who will be afflicted with Alzheimer's disease. Do people really want to know what diseases are in their future? Would knowing how our gene code will eventually unfold make us any happier? Or is there a certain comfort in denying that our bodies will ever let us down?

Remember the **Rule of Unintended Consequences**. In April 2001 the House of Representatives 252 to 172 passed the "Unborn Victims of Violence Act." This proposed law would recognize a fetus six weeks or older as a person. In your opinion, does this act threaten to have serious unintended consequences?

In his book *Why Things Bite Back: Technology and the Revenge of Unintended Consequences* (1996), Edward Tenner reveals how technology has gone awry. Tenner says he was inspired to write an exposé of technology when he discovered that computers, which were supposed to eliminate paperwork, had created more paperwork than anyone could have imagined in the worst bureaucratic nightmares. Tenner also singles out antibiotics which have not eradicated ancient diseases but have left us with "wave after wave of drug-resistant microbes and we are running out of antibiotics to fight them." Tenner has no sacred cows, and disputes the belief that sports equipment has made it safer to play games like football. In his judgment, sports equipment designed to make football safer "encouraged more reckless moves and ended up making the sport more dangerous than unpadded, unhelmeted rugby."

Cultural Lag

Like culture, Blackjack has its own artifacts, symbols, values, customs and rules. Artifacts are objects made by humans for human use. When they excavate Las Vegas, the archaeologists will find rusted beer cans, obsolete slot machines and plastic poker chips. These are artifacts. The symbols are in the cards. The King, Queen, and Jack count 10. The Ace of Spades is one or 11. It also symbolizes death and bad luck, but not in Blackjack. Blackjack rules require the dealer to shuffle the cards, have them cut, bury the top card, and deal to her left. They require players to announce if they have a natural 21, request additional cards or stand. In most casinos, dealers have to hit 16 or less and to stand on 17, 18, 19, or 20. The rules specify that the dealer must take her cards after the players and they require the players to announce "bust" if they exceed 21.

This "dealer take last" rule, according to Blackjack experts, gives the house a 7% advantage. Why? Since the rule is "unfair" to players, why don't the rules allow the players to draw last every other hand?

Elaborate customs supplement Blackjack rules. Experienced players know and follow the rules. To turn down additional cards, players say, "I stand," or "I have enough." They can also do this by signaling "no thanks" with an open palm, which symbolizes pushing the dealer away. If any player wants an additional card, he says "hit me," or uses a sign—beckoning with his finger, scraping his card or bringing his palm toward himself.

It takes intelligence to understand Blackjack rules, and a commitment to conform properly. The players know when to stand or take a hit. They understand the customs and symbols. Like democracy, Blackjack is a game suitable only for players mature enough to learn the rules and willing to be civil.

Do colleges have rules and customs designed to prevent disruptive behavior in the classroom? What would happen to education if every student or faculty decided to do his or her "own thing?"

Technology, however, is changing the nature of the game. Instead of sitting around a table with a dealer and elaborate customs, most players prefer video games. Today, any troglodyte can pay 25 cents, count to 21, and push the correct buttons. Video games require few rules, no customs, and little intelligence. Instead, EPROM (Erasable Programmable Read Only Memory) chips inside the machines make most of the important decisions for the players and pay off randomly. At a traditional game, players play at a pace set by the dealer. Now the electronic shufflers set the pace and in the future lone players will play most of the card games matched against the random mind of the EPROM or its replacement.

When technology races ahead and leaves rules, customs, values and civility in the dust, society suffers from an affliction known as **Cultural Lag**. Sociologist William Fielding Ogburn popularized the notion of a cultural lag in 1922. Ogburn argued that different parts of modern culture change at different speeds. He said all societies consist of component parts like our biological selves, family values, religious beliefs, social groups, economic systems, education, and technology. According to Ogburn these component parts are rarely in harmony. When one element rushes ahead of the others, the society involved has a lag between the dynamic element and those parts which fall or lag behind. In his book *Social Change*, Ogburn described the lag in these words:

The thesis is that the various parts of modern culture are not changing at the same rate, some parts are changing much more rapidly than others; and that since there is a correlation and interdependence of parts, a rapid change in one part of our culture requires readjustments through other changes in the various correlated parts of culture.

Ogburn's thesis of cultural lag can be used to explain how our lives are influenced by the technological miracles which now exist, and will be invented in the future. Human cloning, for example, may someday make it possible for each American to live twice the current life span. In your opinion, what types of cultural lag problems could occur if pigs could be cloned to provide human body parts and enable some people—but not all—to live 145 years?

The most pervasive **cultural lag** in the United States exists between our rapidly expanding technology and our bodies. Cultural lag occurs when automobile companies build powerful "sports utility vehicles" that guzzle gas and are driven by Cro-Magnons who vent their spleens with extended middle finger insults or display their primitive anger by waving a handgun allowed by a constitutional amendment ratified in 1791.

As our technology races ahead, other elements in our cultural mix lag badly. The TV shows us about 20,000 murders during a lifetime, so many Americans demand censorship of TV and registration of all handguns. In the light of contemporary violence these proposals seem to make sense. But then there is that pesky Bill of Rights which prohibits censorship and protects the right to keep and bear arms.

In the past, freedom was celebrated as the best way for scientists to discover the truth about human nature. Since the "age of reason" two hundred years ago, we've used our freedom to rid the world of smallpox. We've also cursed the world with hydrogen bombs, AIDS, and cloned sheep. Now we've broken the gene code but we can't stop road rage.

Although we have very sophisticated technology, many American drivers suffer from a primitive survival known as "road rage." Road rage is a classic case of a cultural lag created by the deadly mixture of primitive emotions and sophisticated machines.

The human body hasn't really changed much since our Cro-Magnon ancestors lived in caves. When faced with danger, our primitive bodies change in ways suitable for living in a hostile environment. Under stress, our hearts speed up, pumping more blood to our muscles and brain. Eye pupils open to let in more light, and we breathe harder. Blood sugar production goes up and our digestion slows so we can fight. We sweat, like animals, scream primitive oaths and "give the bird" to a slow driver who is going 64 mph in a 65 mph zone.

The sympathetic nervous system that produces this "fight-flight" response is a survival of our primitive ancestors' genes. Despite all our electronic gadgets, we are—in Ogburn's words—a "Cro-Magnon in an office." This office dweller no longer clubs his enemies and rapes captive women. Instead, she plays office politics and complains about sexual harassment.

31

"Do we have difficulties in adjusting ourselves to our institution of marriage and a rigid sex code?" asked Ogburn rhetorically in 1922. His answer: "May these difficulties be due to our primitive nature which may have been adjusted in the age of cave dwellers and anthropoids to a more promiscuous expression?" Speaking for the men of his generation, Ogburn continued, "May our wanderlust tendencies be traced to the fact that primitive men were wandering hunters?"

What about a woman who joins the army, is trained at government expense to fly helicopters but decides to leave after she and her husband have a baby. The female pilot asks for a discharge so she can nurse and breast-feed her baby. The Army says no, claiming it spent $500,000 to educate her at West Point. What should be done? Is this a cultural lag? Why?

If we answer Ogburn's questions positively, we doom modern attempts to regulate Cro-Magnon hunters through sexual harassment rules because they go against mans' nature. So let's ask rhetorically, "Are sexual harassment laws merely a belated attempt to regulate the primitive behavior that enabled our male ancestors to spread their genes around and therefore, in a Darwinian sense, to survive and achieve immortality?" In the future, humans won't have to worry about biological survivals like sperm, eggs, and birth control. Why not?

In its March 10, 1997 issue *Time* magazine asked, "Will we follow the sheep?" and added "It will be up to science to determine if it should be." Do you agree?

In 1998 biologists were convinced that complex human behavior could be linked to certain genes. In other words, a thug who ends up in prison for murder would be considered a product of bad genes and a student who excels in a history class would be a product of good genes. This premise is controversial because it suggests that a gay man is more the product of his nature than his nurture. What do you think? Is "Behavior Genetics" a good explanation for the fact that some people in this class will achieve while others fail, and thus sustain the logic of the bell shaped grading curve?

Still confused about cultural lag? Well, you could ask the teacher for more examples, but that might give a grade advantage to students who absorb every detail and are known as "curve busters," and we can't have that now can we?

In 1997, Los Angeles police officers carrying 9 mm weapons had a gun battle with two bank robbers who carried high-powered automatic rifles like the AK-47. After the gun battle, which injured 16 officers and civilians, police officers broke into tears as they described their frustrations at being outgunned by the machine-gun toting would-be bank robbers.

Is this a cultural lag? Explain

To understand cultural lag you need to answer this question: "Why are police officers armed with weapons inferior to those available to would-be bank robbers?"

Will our sophisticated computers replace our primitive brains? Consider that a Pentium II chip can process 500 million instructions every second. If computers can process information faster and better than humans, why require every rowdy teenager to graduate from high school? Currently, scientists are racing to decipher the genetic code. This means we will soon have the capacity to categorize people on the basis of their genes. Thus, a woman with the "right genes" will be encouraged to join the Marines and become a combat killer while a boy child with the "wrong genes" will end up as a biological experiment. This "genetic determinism" will enable society to identify future warriors and assign them to combat without worrying about gender or sexual preferences. Some researchers claim there is a "gay gene" that can be isolated. If so, what would be the consequences of knowing for certain that sexual preference is determined by biological imperatives rather than life experiences?

Cultural Lag: Is It Bad?

Third world countries have difficulty developing the medical technology needed to control diseases like the Ebola virus. Yet, an African Pygmy using sophisticated misty cloud synthesizer has been traveling around the world entertaining people in places like Australia, France, Great Britain, and the United States singing the latest popular song "Deep Forest." Meanwhile, American surgeons doing operations are listening to their favorite classical music while researchers are measuring their blood pressure and pulse rates. Soft music apparently makes people relax and improves job performance.

Researchers, who use word processors to report their findings, may feel tingling in their fingers and end up disabled by RSI (Repetitive Strain Injury). Having learned a stern lesson about the cultural lag between the biological and the technological, the RSI victim ends up hiring a lawyer and suing her employer under the federal Americans with Disabilities Act. Should we hold employers responsible for body injuries suffered by using advanced technology? What happened to the idea that computers would make life easier?

Don't panic, yet. Technology is not going to disappear in the future. It is probably here to stay and to make life easier. Remember, anything that improves on nature is a form of technology—from space shuttles to test tube babies, to cloned ewes, to brave new worlds.

Has the physical coils of the menopause stopped your biological clock? Not to worry. Just head for Rome, Italy where a fertility clinic will implant a fertilized egg and is giving women in their fifties a guaranteed opportunity to have children.

Is a future world filled with grandmothers eating low-fat chocolate yogurt and chasing their very young children around Albertsons, Smiths, Luckys, or Vons a possibility? Yes. However, these menopausal ladies may need to withdraw a deposit from the local sperm bank because a combination of stress, smoking, drugs and pollution has made millions of young men sterile. How do we know this? Research shows that sperm counts, which were about 113 million per ejaculation in 1938, were down to 66 million in 1990.

Studies also show that the sex organs of male alligators living in polluted water are getting smaller. If technology keeps producing all these unintended consequences then future human

Pregnant Mothers - Low Sperm?

males may also lose their sexual drive. That could lead to a decline in male-female sex and a growth industry for CyberSex. Instead of passion, future men may have to use their modem, download, turn on AOL's Net Girl and indulge in fantasy. Computer pornography may gratify some people, but it creates another cultural lag. To quiet protests by religious organizations, state and national lawmakers keep trying to restore obscenity laws controlling when, where, and how this network sex can occur. This creates a lag between religious freedom and freedom of expression, both protected by the First and Fourteenth Amendments.

Nevertheless, surfing the Internet can be more addictive than compulsive gambling. According to University of Pittsburgh researcher Kimberley Young, you're hooked on the net if you spend 38.5 hours a week on chat rooms typing to people who have assumed names so they can be sexy or obnoxious without any repercussions.

Scientific knowledge is dangerous in the wrong hands. Who should decide how cloning will be used: scientists, government, factions or scientists like the famous Dr. Frankenstein?

Roger Shattuck, Professor of Modern Languages at Boston University, says the time has come to consider limits to scientific research. In his book *Forbidden Knowledge* (1996), Shattuck raises this tough question: "Is there any existing or hypothetical knowledge whose mere possession must be considered evil *in and of itself*?" Should society put any limits on the pursuit of knowledge? What about government scientists working on a vaccine who accidentally unleash an incurable virus?

In Huxley's *Brave New World* there is no sin, no guilt, no crime. Citizens play electronic games like Obstacle Golf. Casual sex is encouraged. Soma removes fears. Death is explained away as a necessary way to recycle minerals for the rest of society. Dying people are kept in the "Galloping Senility Ward" where little children see death while they are treated with chocolate milk shakes. In Huxley's fantasy world the only children under any pressure to be good students are the Alpha Pluses, the elites who will someday be the scientists who figure out new ways to control Cro-Magnon impulses and re-direct them toward social purposes rather than let them become random violence.

We know this process in the United States as **Socialization**. In the past teenagers were urged to study their American history so they could become good citizens. Now teens can logically argue that they have genes which make them hate history.

Like the children in *Brave New World*, contemporary American youths seem more determined to pursue pleasure than cultural literacy. This fact was exposed on August 12, 1996 in the San Jose (California) *Mercury News* by columnist Joanne Jacobs, who reported that more school kids today want to be "druggies" than "brains." As her proof, Jacobs cited a three-year survey of 20,000 Wisconsin and California high school students. Researchers Laurence Steinberg and Bradford Brown talked to students in nine urban, suburban and rural high schools. They excluded private schools and very poor inner-city schools. Steinberg and Brown estimated that 40% of teenagers are "disengaged" from school, and are just going through the motions. Fewer than one in five students say their friends think that getting good grades is important. Some students do not try very hard because they fear being singled out as "showing off." According to the researchers, 70% of the students surveyed spent less than four hours a week on homework, which is a fraction of the time spent by European and Japanese students. Why would American students strive to be well-dressed and mediocre?

> **In May 2001 Hollywood released "Pearl Harbor," an exciting movie with lots of romance and some questionable history. Are the kids who saw this movie now more interested in history?**

Political Values

Technology creates miracles, but also mistakes. Frankenstein taught us a lesson. Yet to control technology, we rely on more technology. We exposed this "mad" idea during the Cold War when the Soviet Union and the United States pursued a policy known as "mutually assured destruction,"

> I Love New Clothes, I Love New Clothes....[sleep taught message drummed into the children of Brave New World]

which was a polite way of saying "they have 8,500 nuclear warheads, so we need 10,000." To control their increasingly marvelous technology, Americans need an updated value system suitable for dealing with disruptive inventors who might decide to build a modern Frankenstein monster.

Liberty, justice and equality are the essential American values. These values are expressed through historical documents like *The Declaration of Independence*, the *Constitution*, Lincoln's *Gettysburg Address* and *The Federalist Papers*. All of these sources are more than 300 years old. That means to be educated in American values every student must be socialized to like history. Is this reasonable?

Most Americans are familiar with the Declaration of Independence, although they often get it confused with the Constitution. To avoid being foolish, remember these words by Thomas Jefferson and their source: "We hold these truths to be self-evident, that all men are created equal, that they are endowed by their Creator with certain unalienable Rights, that among these are Life, Liberty and the Pursuit of Happiness."

To secure these rights, argued Jefferson, "governments are instituted among Men, deriving their just powers from the consent of the governed—That whenever any Form of Government becomes destructive of these ends, it is the Right of the People to alter or to abolish it, and to institute new Government . . . " Jefferson wrote these words to justify the American Revolution.

> **What did Jefferson mean by "self-evident" and "unalienable rights"? What about his use of the word "Creator"? Would it violate anyone's freedom of religion if they were required in high school to study the Declaration? Why not?**

The words "consent of the governed" are the basis for democracy. What do the words "created equal" mean?

> **Are poor people living in slums free in the same sense as middle class people living in comfortable homes?**

In 1837, South Carolina Senator John C. Calhoun rejected the idea that anyone had a right to be free or equal. Defending slavery, Calhoun argued, "There never has yet existed a wealthy and civilized society in which a portion of the community did not . . . live on the labor of the other."[6] In Calhoun's South, slaves worked the fields thus giving white gentlemen leisure time to raise horses, gamble and read books. Although black people suffered under slavery, the South's white aristocrats defended plantation life as more cultured and civilized than life in Northern cities.

Calhoun's argument that inequality is necessary for progress was the basis for a popular ideology that emerged after the Civil War freed the slaves. Inspired by Charles Darwin's theory of **natural selection**, philosophers in England and the United States developed an ideological rationale to justify extreme poverty in the midst of extreme wealth. Known as **Social Darwinism**, this ideology justified great accumulations of wealth as a reasonable working out of the idea of natural selection. Instead of complaining about the huge inequalities between rich and poor, the Social Darwinists defended inequality as nature's way of rewarding the talented, hard-working and frugal millionaires.

At Yale University, William Graham Sumner told his students that taxing the rich to help the poor was wrong. No man, said Sumner, was entitled to happiness, only the opportunity to pursue it. Sumner premised that few persons were born to be poor and helpless. This led him to conclude that poor people were those who were "negligent, shiftless, inefficient, silly, and imprudent." Sumner's logic caused him to resist all attempts by governments to help unfortunate people by levying high taxes on those who were ambitious and successful. In Sumner's staunch opinion, any man who could be forced to divert his wealth to aid others was not a free man. As for the welfare state ideas being bandied around in the 1880's, Sumner wrote: "We shall find that all the schemes for producing equality and obliterating the organization of society produce a new differentiation based on the worst possible distinction—the right to claim and the duty to give one man's efforts for another man's satisfaction."[7]

Gambling is one way that people pursue wealth and pleasure. In a way, gambling is a form of happiness. The "pursuit of happiness" specified in *The Declaration of Independence* is no guarantee, however, that you'll emerge from a casino with a full wallet.

Despite the glowing 1776 promise of happiness, the idea that government owes anyone happiness is a very strange idea to most people outside the United States. Until the last century, most Americans expected life to be hard until they died and, as a reward for suffering quietly on earth, went to heaven.

> **Social Darwinism and Adolf Hitler**
>
> The most infamous exponent of Social Darwinism was Germany's World War II dictator Adolf Hitler, who preached the ideology that inferior races should be eliminated because they were unfit to live.

> Should Las Vegas casinos be required by law to guarantee every player at least one jackpot? Why? Why not?

☹ **John Stossel questioned the belief that happiness is a fundamental right on Channel 13, ABC-TV in Las Vegas on April 15, 1996 under the title "The Mystery of Happiness: Who Has It & How to Get It." With his usual skeptical voice, Stossel told TV viewers that the slogan "Don't worry, be happy" was unknown to our ancestors. In contrast, contemporary Americans are told repeatedly they can achieve happiness through control over their lives, a fulfilling job, optimism, strong religious faith and friendships. That idea, however, was never embraced by any society until 1776 when it was declared by the colonies united against England. What do you think? The Constitution in its preamble promises to establish justice, insure domestic tranquility, provide for the common defense, promote the general welfare, and secure the blessings of liberty. Should it be amended to include "the pursuit of happiness." Explain.**

What about factions which interpret the pursuit of happiness as shooting people, blowing up buildings, using drugs, or playing loud thumping music in a parked automobile?

Customs and Politics

When a modern "Ms." marries, she wears a white gown, and is pelted with rice. The white gown symbolizes virginity, and the rice means "be fertile and have lots of children." Many brides, however, are not virgins, and instead of many children, many married women prefer a career. Despite these modern realities, the bridal ceremony is a custom that survives and gets more elaborate and expensive every year. Why?

In one episode of the very popular TV comedy "Seinfeld," the character of George Castanza develops a lust for his cousin, and audiences laughed. In real life, "incest taboos" are very serious business. The taboo bans carnal knowledge between parent and child, and brother and sister.

Like most customs, the incest taboo has a logical function. In biological terms, inbreeding increases the chances of mental and physical defects in offspring. The taboo also has a social purpose, which is to keep family harmony by eliminating potentially disruptive rivalries and jealousies. A third reason stems from the psychological fact that growing up means gradually to separate from your parents and siblings.

Taboos usually exist because they are a practical and inexpensive way to prevent dangerous behavior. In the past we had no antibiotics to cure sexually transmitted diseases, so witch doctors invented customs.

Since sex is now in the open, and we are all entitled to pursue happiness in whatever form it takes, should we repeal all those state laws which make incest a crime? Why? Why not?

Which is a more effective way to control AIDS, a state law that makes it a crime to have sex if you have tested HIV positive, or a death penalty taboo imposed on anyone who knowingly risks giving the virus to his or her bed partner?

Sir James George Frazer tells us that Western African tribes had a custom that when a man returned home from a long absence, they required him to wash his body with a particular fluid and get marked on his forehead by the witch doctor. They required the ritual before the man could have a conjugal visit with his wife. The purpose of the special bath and forehead mark was to protect the man's wife and villagers from any magic spell which "a strange woman may have cast on him in his absence, which might be communicated through him to the women of his village."[8]

Customs often exist to let people know where they belong in the social order. In his *Age of Faith*, Will Durant described how feudal lords made sure their serfs paid taxes. Besides rent, head taxes, fishing fees, sales taxes, and a death tax, they expected every serf to buy his quota of wine from the lord each year. If the serf failed to buy his wine on time, the customary tax law said, "Then the lord shall pour a four-gallon measure over the man's roof; if the wine runs down, the tenant must pay for it; if it runs upward, he shall pay nothing."

In the past, they often blamed women when men were having problems. In 1486 two Dominican Monks published the famous witch-hunting guide known as *Malleus Maleficarum*. This book very seriously

In what sense does this custom let the peasants know their place in society? Is it a fair custom? Is it a logical custom?

blames witches for just about every sexual problem ever suffered by men, even including a loss of feeling in their sexual parts. They usually drowned these suspected witches, or killed them by fire.

In some countries, women are not supposed to enjoy sexual feelings. Young Egyptian women are sometimes subjected to a painful ritual. As described in 1994 on CNN TV, 10-year-old Nagla Hamza had her clitoris cut off with a pair of barbers' scissors. Female circumcision is common in Egypt and other parts of Africa. Experts estimate that about 80% of Egyptian women have undergone this painful operation, which seems to serve no health purpose except to deprive women of sexual pleasure.

Although some customs are cruel and seemingly illogical, others make perfect sense. In Blackjack asking for additional cards with hand signals is customary. And the dealer will ask rude players to behave or be remove from the casino by security.

Social customs operate to keep our natural selfish instincts under control. When customs fail to prevent disruptive behavior, we make laws. According to political scientist A. Lee Brown, social conflicts are "those disagreements, disputes, and conflicting situations capable of being regulated by accepted cultural norms, good manners, and self-restraint."[9] When cultural norms, good manners, and self-restraint fail or are absent our tribal leaders (politicians) start churning out more laws, policies, rules, judicial decisions and the usual suspects are rounded up and punished.

In the past, society protected American women from sexual harassment through elaborate customs. When escorting ladies, gentlemen walked near the street so mud splashed by carriages hit the man, not his lady friend. These Victorian gentlemen rarely swore in a lady's presence, and they always opened doors for the presumed weaker sex. During World War II, however, American women entered the work force in huge numbers and were privileged to hear the male vocabulary in all its embellished strength. They saw men spit tobacco and were the targets of sexual harassment. As on the job sexual bantering increased, many women demanded legal protection. The demands of these "feminists" resulted in written sexual harassment rules, which replaced the old chivalrous customs.

Locate a copy of the sexual harassment policy at your job, or at this college. Should we continue trying to define sexual harassment through formal rules, or try to go back to the old customs?

In 1991 millions of Americans watched the televised Senate hearings on the confirmation of Clarence Thomas to the United States Supreme Court. The hearings were controversial because law professor Anita Hill had accused Thomas of sexual harassment. After the Senate Judiciary Committee confirmed Thomas, the media analyzed the controversy. Thomas Sowell, a senior fellow at Stanford's Hoover Institute, saw the hearings as clear evidence that Americans had gone overboard in their zeal to replace customs with laws. In his newspaper column, Sowell argued that having males inhibited by custom was more logical than formal sexual harassment laws. He reasoned that since men are physically stronger than women, it made sense "to create inhibitions that can restrain men when there is no other restraint around." In other words, customary restraints don't require on the spot enforcement by police or other officials.

Sowell supported his argument by reasoning that men formerly regarded women as special and not simply "persons" with "different plumbing, as our modern rationalists would have it." To illustrate this point, Sowell recalled how in rough neighborhoods a "guy using foul language could often be brought into line quickly when one of his buddies said: 'Hey, man, there's a girl here.'" Sowell concluded his analysis by noting that contemporary women are "liberated" and no longer ladies. "Today, the girls themselves use language that would once have embarrassed a longshoreman."[10]

* The ancient Greeks toasted their dinner host by drinking to his health. This custom was designed to make sure the host had not poisoned the wine. Do contemporary Americans have a similar custom?
* It is a custom among Norwegians never to drive after drinking. As a result, 78% of Norwegians who drive home from a party abstain from drinking while only 17% of American drivers abstain. Why?
* It took the passive smoking issue to alert Americans to the dangers of second hand smoke. Yet some condominium associations still allow smoking in condos where the ventilation systems are joined. Why?
* In the past, public school students were encouraged to walk school halls on the right side. Like driving, this custom minimized collisions. Students now would rather crash than conform. Why?
* Schools used to teach courage, generosity, and honesty through the lives of great leaders like Washington and Lincoln. Now they don't. Why?

One hundred years ago Americans were learning courage, generosity and civility through role models like George Washington. Readers were inspired by the cherry tree incident described by Mason "Parson" Weems in 1806. Weems, a firm moralist but bad historian, told how a youthful Washington hacked up his father's cherry tree with a small axe, and then confessed by saying, "I can't tell a lie, Pa; you know I can't tell a lie. I did cut it with my hatchet." Rather than spank George or take away his car keys, his father opened his arms, smiled and said, "Run to my arms, you dearest boy . . . run to my arms; glad am I, George, that you killed my tree; for you have paid me for it a thousand fold. Such an act of heroism in my son is more worth than a thousand trees, though blossomed with silver, and their fruits of purest gold."[11]

> What would happen to little George today? Would he confess, or stonewall daddy? Would his father accept the confession at face value, or make George take a lie detector test?

Although George Washington was truly a "man among men" he is no longer a role model for the young. Nor is Charles Lindbergh, who flew alone in his airplane "Spirit of St. Louis" from New York to Paris. Without newspaper and radio coverage, the Lindbergh flight would have gone uncelebrated. Now TV decides who will get his or her "15 minutes of fame." The modern celebrity can range all the way from Tiger Woods to a "survivor" who has no athletic skills except the ability to win staged contests.

Some of us attend "Rock and Roll" concerts, but most of us have only a misty grasp on the meaning of the two "R" words. Is "Rock and Roll" the same as Chubby Checkers twisting around the clock, or Elvis wearing his Blue Suede Shoes or the Beatles singing "Yesterday"?

Most of us admired Michael Jordan when he played professional basketball for the Chicago Bulls. A few of us only admire themselves. People who love themselves are compared to Narcissus, the legendary beautiful youth who sat every day looking at his own reflection in a pool of water. Unable to gratify himself just looking, Narcissus reached one day to hug himself, fell into the pool and drowned.

Self-centered men misinterpret friendly female gestures. In a study, Frank Saal of Kansas University discovered the extent to which men and women interpret signals differently. Saal had men and women view tapes of a "getting acquainted" ritual between a man and a woman, and of a female supervisor giving instructions. In both cases, men viewed the behavior of women as more seductive, flirtatious and promiscuous than was intended. Saal concluded that most men simply misread women who are friendly.[12]

In the past men who misread women were slapped in the face, or slugged by the nearby boyfriend. Now they get slapped with sexual harassment lawsuits and—in the case of a few members of Congress—lose their jobs.

Congress used to live by the custom of being able to disagree "without being disagreeable." Folkways that stressed the importance of avoiding "personal" attacks reinforced this principle. As described by political scientist Donald R. Mathews, these "Senate Folkways" included "avoiding personal attacks on colleagues, striving for impersonality by divorcing the self from the office, (and) 'buttering-up' the opposition by extending unsolicited compliments." The stilted formality of the senators sounds ludicrous today, as in this statement once made by Senator Lyndon Johnson of Texas when the Senator from California criticized him: "The Senator from Texas does not have any objection, and the Senator from Texas wishes the Senator from California to know that the Senator from Texas knew the Senator from California did not criticize him . . . "[13]

☹ Are you one of those people who tells sexist or racist jokes? If so, don't use your E-Mail! Experts warn they may preserve your message on the employer's hard drive, and you will be risking an employment-discrimination lawsuit. Gotcha!

> How civil are you? Do you listen carefully when others are talking? Do you wait your turn before commenting? Is your body language accepting, or rejecting?

Rules

Did your E-mail start today with this question, "Why is beer better than a woman?" Don't touch that keyboard, no matter how tempting. E-mail is not a conversation. Civility dictates that racist or sexist jokes are privacy issues, unless we publish them over a company's E-mail. Now we've entered a twilight zone where old rules no longer apply. Does your company have a policy on E-mail? Better find out before mailing your favorite joke. Remember, "Big Browser is Watching You!"

In Blackjack the rules seem to favor the players. They require dealers to stand on 17, and draw extra cards if they have a count less than 17. Players, on the other hand, get to draw as often as they want, unless they exceed 21, and to stand on any count. The crucial rule of Blackjack, however, requires players to draw first and to bust before the dealer takes any additional cards. This rule, according to gambling expert John Scarne, is the real reason casino operators like Blackjack, "and why most players lose at the game."

The Blackjack rule requiring players to draw first and declare if they bust means the dealer collects their bets before she draws out. This gives the casino about a 7% edge over all the players, and is a good demonstration of the political dictum: **The rules are never neutral**. This means, according to political analysts, that all rules favor somebody and penalize others.

Should football be scored like ice skating?

Skeptical? Take football. In that game, teams win by scoring touchdowns, field goals and extra points. To win under this scoring system, professional football teams need big, strong, fast and fearless players. For the sake of argument, assume that the NFL adopted a one to ten point system like those used in figure skating, gymnastics, and platform diving. How would that change the game?

If rules could make everyone equal, women might someday be playing for professional football teams like the Green Bay Packers. Is this likely ever to happen?

In 1972 Congress passed by a two-thirds majority a resolution that "Equality of rights under the law shall not be denied or abridged by the United States or by any State on account of sex." This Equal Rights Amendment then went to 50 state legislatures

Should the rules be changed so that a simple majority vote of Congress would amend the Constitution? Why or why not?

for approval. Under the Constitution, it takes three-fourths of the states to ratify (approve) an amendment. The ERA was killed because it simply could not get more than 33 states to ratify in time. By making it difficult to change the Constitution, the Founding Fathers in 1787 adopted a rule that later proved unfair to women.

The rules make Blackjack players draw before the dealer. Professional football discriminates against slow, small, weak men. No women qualify to play football, but they're being trained as combat soldiers. There is no Equal Rights Amendment because the Constitution is so difficult to amend. These are all examples of this dictum: **The Rules are Never Neutral.** Every rule benefits someone, and works to the disadvantage of others. Consider these examples:

❑ **The United States Supreme Court does not consider a fetus to be a human being with full constitutional rights. As a result, we cannot charge pregnant drug addicts with child abuse or child neglect. Is this fair?**

❑ **Two lesbian couples sued the State of Hawaii in 1991 after being denied a marriage license under state law. In 1996 the state supreme court ruled that "equal protection" of the law means Hawaii must allow homosexual marriages. Under the "full faith and credit" clause in Article IV, Section 1 of the Constitution all the other states will have to recognize homosexual marriages licensed in Hawaii. Is this fair?**

❑ **Members of the Michigan Jural Society Association claim the right to drive without a driver's license and to buy guns illegally without a permit because of a state constitution clause which says "All political power is inherent in the people." Is a driver's license a "right," or a "privilege?" What about guns?**

❑ **Rickover Junior High School in Sauk Village, Illinois has a dress code which prohibits students from cutting symbols in their hair, wearing beads, ornaments, cornrows, dreadlocks, braids or ponytails. Is this dress code fair?**

❑ **While the American military is being shaken by charges of rape, sexual harrassment, and adultery, officials of the British, French, Israeli, Irish and Polish governments say these are rare problems for their military. Why?**

In Nevada, Democrats and Republicans control the state assembly, so they get to make rules that favor a two-party system. Skeptical? Check it out. This fact of life suggests a second important quality of the rules, namely: **Whoever makes the rules controls the game**.

During the Middle Ages (500 A.D. to about 1500), feudal lords practiced *ius primae noctus*, also known as the "right of the first night." This meant that a lord could, if he wanted, call the bride of a lesser ranked man to the castle on the wedding night to be deflowered. The purpose of this rule (or custom) was to let peasants, serfs, and lesser nobles know just who was making the rules. In other words, the right of the first night was a symbolic display of power.

> Among Australian aborigines, there used to be a manhood ritual which required cutting the penis of a young male along its entire length from the glans to the scrotum. This ritual arguably marked the transition from childhood to manhood and was a logical ritual for teaching young males that life was harsh, and manhood required sacrifice. Do young American males have any similar ritual?

In Blackjack, the rules require players who exceed 21 (or bust) to turn over their cards immediately. This rule is enforced by the dealer and the other players; who will frown at the rule breakers. But if any player persists in breaking the rules, security officers may use force to remove the offender. This happens because **rules are often designed to prevent or control disruptive behavior.** In life, as in Blackjack, we try to avoid conflict through smiles, handshakes, and appeasement. When these customs fail, however, then we call in security to enforce the rules.

Back in 1895, Clara Baer of New Orleans Newcomb College published the first set of rules for girls' basketball. As specified by Baer, the typical girls' team would play with six players; three forwards near the offensive basket did the scoring, while three guards stayed on defense. Predictably, for sixty years women played a slow-moving, boring game. Men, on the other hand, could fast break, throw long passes, and play pressure defense from basket to basket. Many Americans defended the separate women's rules by saying that the ladies lacked the endurance to play a full court men's style basketball.

> Lawyers and other successful people try to find out why rules were adopted before they make decisions. Now that sexual harassment rules are well-entrenched, maybe we need to ask "why did we adopt these controversial policies in the first place?"

Eventually someone discovered a slight error made by Clara Baer. She had written for a copy of basketball rules from inventor James Naismith, and he mistakenly sent her a diagram of a play—complete with dotted lines—showing where players stood. Thus Naismith's intended play became a diagram showing where women had to be at all times. As a result of the mistake, women played with six players on what was essentially two separate slow and unexciting half-court games. Fortunately, the ladies now play full court and seem to have no problem with their endurance. They even have a professional basketball league. Since the ladies now play every sport but professional football, has the time arrived to provide a sport that short, 200-pound women can play?

Clara Baer's mistake is a good reminder for the dictum: **Always find out why rules were adopted before you accept them at face value.**

To show this point, take baseball. In a column published in April 1992, Joseph Sobran compared baseball to politics. According to Sobran, baseball has humane but inflexible rules which everyone accepts. Enforced by umpires and obeyed by all concerned, baseball rules combine "fairness, stability, conservatism, tradition." According to Sobran, the players may "fight with each other or argue with the umpires about particulars, but nobody quarrels over the rules themselves." Politics, on the other hand, has become a game where all the players want rules that guarantee they'll win the game, no matter how badly they play. The trouble with politics today, argues Sobran, "is that control of the rule's committee and the umpires has become the game itself." Because everybody wants their own rules, nobody plays by any rules. He thinks that wanting only the rules that work to their advantage is a stupid way for politicians to play the game.[14]

Is the World Series fair? In 1996 the Atlanta Braves scored 26 runs while the New York Yankees had a total of 18. Yet the Yankees won the series four games to two. Should we change the World Series so that the team with the most runs wins?

So far, we have advised you to remember these four dictums whenever you are considering changing, enforcing, ignoring or resisting any rule or law:

➤ **Rules are Never Neutral.**
➤ **Whoever Makes the Rules, Controls the Game.**
➤ **Rules are Designed to Control Disruptive Behavior.**
➤ **Try to learn the Origin of Important Rules.**

We forgot dictum five: ➤ **Rules Differ From Culture to Culture.** In Europe during the Middle Ages, tax collectors required peasants to buy a yearly quota of their lord's wine. If the peasant failed to buy the lord's wine on time, then the lord's men would pour a four-gallon measure over the peasant's roof and if the wine ran up the roof it did not have to be purchased. This wrong-way wine custom also proves how those who make the rules control the tax burden.

The current Electoral College system uses a "winner-take-all" custom that benefits the two major parties. Is this fair?

In his book *The Death of Common Sense* (1994), Philip K. Howard tells how a federal rule banning workers from having a beard under a dust mask led to the firing of an Amish worker, who could not shave his beard for religious reasons. Is this a fair rule?

43

For the most part, it makes sense to limit customs and rules to behavior that is or could be disruptive. Today, however, Americans have tried to impose written rules for just about every behavior that might bother someone, somewhere, somehow.

What should be done about all the rules that are currently designed to help people with special problems, such as the handicapped, the old, the young, the minorities, the oppressed, the victimized, the overtaxed, the drug addicted, the unwed, the poor, the homeless, the dysfunctional, the sad, the angry, the not quite angry, the frustrated, the unhappy, the depressed, the violent, the overworked, the stressed out, kids who use graffiti to hide their despair? What about a Las Vegas 9-year-old who in March, 1997 did $10,000 worth of damage to a newly laid concrete walk? Should he go to jail, or get an ice cream cone to cure his moods?

Political Socialization

In Australia there once was a tribe known as the Yir Yiront. These primitive people had an entire social system build around one item of technology, a stone axe. Owned exclusively by the dominant males, the axes were a symbolic reminder to the women and children that older men were making the rules. To borrow an axe to do her work, a wife had to follow strict custom and certain procedures. Custom required that she must first ask her husband for his axe. If he refused, for any reason, the wife had to next ask her brother for his axe, and then her father and so on. To get their own axes, young males had to be initiated into the world of their elders. The axe, therefore, reinforced the fact that older, more aggressive males were in charge of the social, religious, economic and political values. Consequently, nobody sought sexual harassment, child abuse, or equal rights laws.

Christian missionaries gave steel axes to the Yir Yiront women and children. Was that a tragic mistake or a humanistic gift of social equality?

The stone axe was important because it was a key ingredient in the socialization process among the Yir Yiront.

We socialize people by making them fit for living in groups, tribes, states, countries, etc. **Socialization** is how we get people to conform, cooperate and live together peacefully. Tribal people socialize through such primitive methods as symbolic axes, taboos, customs, magic, rules. Among the Narrinyeri of South Australia, leaving a meal unfinished was taboo. Adults were constantly looking for the bones of beasts, birds, or fish which had been part of a meal. The taboo made everyone careful to eat all the food and to burn remaining bones. Consequently, the Narrinyeri land was free of rotting food, human waste, and other sources of disease. Without a food taboo, the Narrinyeri would have needed waste disposals, sewers, garbage collectors, politicians, and taxes.

Political Socialization, according to political scientist Kenneth P. Langston, "is the process, mediated through various agencies of society by which an individual learns politically relevant attitudinal dispositions and behavior patterns." In other words, children say the pledge of allegiance so they'll grow up to be loyal citizens who respect traffic signals, and vote. In 1989 this process was occurring every morning at Goodsprings Elementary School near Las

Vegas when all the kindergartners started the day with a pledge to the flag. This was followed by reading, writing, arithmetic and how to interpret traffic signals. And in their classes, six-year-olds gave reports completing the sentence, "If I had a lot of money, I'd . . . ."[15]

Most socialization is **Manifest**. This means that it comes in a specifically marked package. To make us better citizens, state legislatures pass laws requiring that we all study courses in American history and politics. We call this "civic education."

Those parents who want school prayers, the pledge of allegiance and more patriotism are essentially demanding more manifest conservative socialization. What type of socialization takes place when parents encourage their children to win by cheating?

Young Americans have played "Monopoly" since they invented it more than 50 years ago. The manifest goal of the game is to get enough play property and money to win. The hidden message, though, is that players with luck, skill and good investments win at life by driving their business opponents into bankruptcy. This is the hidden message of "Monopoly." It is also called **Latent Socialization**.

In 1997 *Dateline* NBC TV viewers saw Marine paratroopers punching a pin with two half-inch protruding points on the back into the chests of other Marines. Is this sadistic ritual merely Marine socialization, or a callous act of barbarism?

Latent socialization occurs when high school students are told to get good grades so they'll succeed by teachers who appear to be on the cutting edge of poverty. Latent socialization occurs when students are told history is a fascinating subject, and given textbooks which are boring. Or incorrect. What happens, for example, when the students are given a science textbook which says that the First World War ended in 1945?

In his book *The Sibling Society*, writer Robert Bly argues that America is a society of "half adults built of technology and affluence." According to Bly we have developed a society of surly teenage siblings in which "Adults regress toward adolescence; and adolescents—seeing that—have no desire to become adults."

These alienated adults have difficulty qualifying for technologically oriented jobs, so they end up victims of worker layoffs. *Time* columnist Lance Morrow blames mass layoffs and the replacement of workers by electronics for the disappearance of traditional loyalties and employees' motivation. This has created a sizable number of Americans who are "passive-aggressive." The alienated U.S. Postal Service employees who shoot their co-workers are symbolic of the type, argues Morrow.[16]

In 2001 a TV commercial showed a Jaguar sports car driven by a young man; with a "voice-over" that said "Your guidance counselor said you would never amount to anything . . . your guidance counselor drives a minivan." What type of socialization is this?

Children need good parents to teach them to love, and survive. Since many Americans are too busy to tutor their children every day, we use technology to keep the little kids out of trouble. Check your home: Does it have outlet plug covers, cabinet latches, nursery monitors, and toilet seat latches? Congratulations, you're a technologically sophisticated caretaker.

Technology alone will not keep children safe, however. They need to internalize safety by hearing words like, "Don't play with fire Bobby, it's dangerous."

High schools that churn out young adults poorly prepared for useful work. Adults who want to remain teenagers forever. Passive-aggressive types running around armed with guns. Do Americans need to reestablish socialization goals, or should we continue to let everyone "do his/her own thing?"

What is meant by "Do your own thing"?

Every society uses its symbols, values, customs, rules, taboos, and technology to ensure that its citizens are loyal consumers, patriotic citizens, good soldiers, and culturally literate. To understand our culture, college students learn ideas of freedom, justice, and equality from Dead White European Males (DWEM's) like Plato and Shakespeare. Is this good?

Education is supposed to make us civil. To be civil we should not offend others with bad words, extended middle fingers or second-hand smoke. This type of civic education requires teachers to warn students that smoking is a dangerous habit, and that it is callous to smoke in enclosed areas. Being civil means to defer immediate gratification. It means self-control. Without self-control, we have to rely on a Big Brother to dictate the meaning of civility.

In 1996 President Clinton signed an executive order to keep cigarettes out of the mouths of teenagers and proudly announced, "Joe Camel and the Marlboro Man will be out of our lives forever." ☆ Why do we need an executive order to ban Joe Camel and Marlboro Man?

Eliminating advertising aimed at teenagers may reduce the number of future smokers, but will it cause any unintended consequences for Nevada casinos? According to University of Nevada Professor John Dobra, Nevada's economy would suffer badly if the federal government goes ahead with a plan to ban smoking in places like casinos. According to Professor Dobra, such a ban would cost Nevadans about 50,000 jobs in the end.[17]

Should gamblers who smoke voluntarily go to a special casino room for smokers only, so that their second-hand smoke does not bother the non-smokers? Would this type of segregation violate any constitutional provisions?

The major agents of socialization are families, friends, churches, schools, and the media. For some, gangs. The super predators who belong to violent gangs are the products of bad socialization. Some Americans believe they can salvage gang members if governments eliminate poverty and improve the home lives of impoverished children. Others believe just as strongly that youthful thugs are beyond hope. These "conservatives" would put all criminals in jail, and throw away the key.

Conventional wisdom, however, ignores the cultural appeal of gangs. According to UCLA sociologists Jack Katz and Daniel Marks, the appeal of gangs is their special clothing, hair styles, music and walk. Gangs also have "semiotics" of graffiti, special hand signals, and a "shared store of historical

If Katz and Marks are accurate, then neither liberals nor conservatives are offering valid solutions to this nation's gang problems. What should we do about violent gangs?

events that may be recounted endlessly." Instead of worshiping George Washington for telling the truth, gang members want to dwell on the day "G.W." shot a rival gang member during a drug war. The gang subculture, according to Katz and Marks, reinforces a "tough-guy image." Heavy penalties do not deter gang members nor necessarily are they the victims of poverty. They rob, rape, or murder for psychological reasons, "sneaky thrills."[18]

Most of us get our "sneaky thrills" vicariously. That is, we identify with the heroes and villains on TV, in the movies, or in computer games. By the age of two most American children are watching violent TV cartoons. In a few years, these children will be playing with toy guns. By adolescence, they'll have about 20,000 hours of TV under their belts and will be watching soap operas and professional wrestling. Most will be culturally literate enough to recognize these people: Michael Jackson, Demi Moore, Marilyn Manson. Some will recognize George Orwell, Big Brother, and the Boston Massacre.

In April, 1989 a total of 696 seniors at 67 four-year American colleges and universities were given an 87-question Gallup survey devised to see what they knew about history. The survey showed that nearly 60% did not know the Korean War started when Harry Truman was president, and 42% could not place the Civil War in the correct half century. Most shocking was the fact that 23% believed that Karl Marx's communist phrase "From each according to his ability, to each according to his need" is part of the U.S. Constitution.[19]

Who is to blame for this ignorance? Parents? Teachers? The Media?

Neil Postman attributes mush brain to a TV culture where "all public discourse takes the form of entertainment." Television, he thinks, has degraded intelligent conversation.

In economics, **Gresham's Law** states simply that "bad money drives out good." When it comes to socializing American youth, the law should read, "violence and sex

> **Certain dates are crucial to American history. With what events do we associate the dates listed below?**
> ❖ 1776
> ❖ 1861-1865
> ❖ 1914-1918
> ❖ 1939-1945

drive out intelligence and learning." In 1984 American children played with 214 "action figures" with names like G.I. Joe, Transformers, GoBots, Voltron and Masters of the Universe. To compete with these exciting toys, all we had then were books. Now the kids have virtual reality computer games, and books. In the battle of action toys versus books, which side is likely to win? Do dogs bark?

To defend selling these mindless toys, manufacturers rely on the **catharsis argument**. This is the claim that playing at war, channels normal aggressions toward harmless activities. The catharsis theory asserts that by letting violent tendencies surface through games, we reduce tension and that makes kids less violent in the end. Psychologists, however, warn that such toys encourage or cause aggressive behavior.

What is the cause of violence by young males? Some psychiatrists would blame society, claiming that social environment is the cause of violence. Others, however, put the blame on our molecules. Studies of rhesus monkeys suggest that human violence is caused by low levels of a substance called serotonin, which acts as a messenger molecule for brain cells. These studies also show that nurturing mothers offsets low levels of serotonin. What can we learn from monkeys? Scientists have also discovered that young rhesus monkeys leave their troop and travel as part of violent gangs until ready to rejoin monkey society. Do humans follow similar behavior? What should we do about youthful criminals?

While socialization by parents, schools, and churches lags behind, American technology is rushing toward the fictional brave new world. This technology is replacing traditional values. The information superhighway lets kids drag the mouse, click on and watch the miracle of the Web and Internet. Can books compete with the sounds and visual excitement of TV and computers?

Instead of going to church and mixing with family and friends, teenagers can now stay home and surf for their religious ideas. They can download on Jesus and Mohammed. Or get a copy of the Atheist Manifesto [http://206.126.103.21/dan/atheist-manifesto.html], American Baptist Churches Mission Center Online [http://www.abc.usa.org/] or Church of the SubGenius BRAIN TOOLKIT [http://sunsite.unc.edu/subgenius].

> Be careful what you download from religious sources: You might end up belonging to a cult that decides to commit mass suicide to join aliens flying behind a comet.

Before radio, TV and computers, Americans traveled all day by stagecoach or wagon to listen to three hour speeches by mostly white male politicians, or the famous black abolitionist Frederick Douglass. Those speeches, combined with partisan newspapers, shaped the political values of Americans in the past. Now, TV, radio, the Web and E-mail make it possible for political candidates to get unfiltered information directly to every voter in Nevada in a few minutes, if the prospective voter is listening. Before all this technology, Americans relied on broadsides, newspapers or the *Congressional Journal* for the voting records of their Senators and Representatives. Now, they broadcast graphics-intensive content-drive pages filled with current legislative information over the Internet. For better or worse, the Internet brings your elected representatives as close as the computer terminals at this college or in your home. In 1992, for example, H. Ross Perot proposed that Americans begin using their computers to hold national referendums on important issues like tax increases.

> Is Perot's techno-democracy a good idea?

Factions

The once mighty Soviet Union now consists of 15 separate republics. Inside each of these republics there are quarreling groups known as **factions**. These factions include Armenian nationalists, ethnic Romanians, Moldovan separatists, Sunni Muslims, and Turks. Each faction is essentially pursuing self-interest at any cost. Factionalism has divided the former communist nation Yugoslavia into warring Bosnian and Serb forces. This civil war has produced incredible savagery, including terrified babies tied to bus seats and starving people in detention camps.

In the 18th century, our Founders had similar problems. They had managed to separate from England, but had no practice running a democratic nation. To avoid a monarchy, the colonists developed the weakest possible central government. This first constitutional government is known as the Articles of Confederation. It consisted of a single-house Congress, whose members were chosen by state legislatures. There was no president, but Congress did have power to wage war, negotiate treaties, and borrow money. Under the Articles, however, Congress had no power to levy direct taxes on citizens, regulate commerce among the several states, or raise a standing army.

The *Articles of Confederation* reflected Thomas Jefferson's noble idea that the government which governs least is best. This weak central government was perfect for those Americans who hated high taxes and the idea of a national army used to put down domestic insurrections in the states. Others, however, agreed with the famous 1651 warning by British monarchist Thomas Hobbes who wrote in his *Leviathan* that where government is too weak there tends to be no knowledge, no arts, no letters, no society and "worst of all, continual fear and danger of violent death; and the life of man, solitary, poor, nasty, brutish and short."

The weakness of Congress under the Articles frightened many conservative Americans. They saw a Congress with no power to regulate commerce, watching helplessly while the states imposed tariffs on everything from cabbage to firewood. These Americans were disgusted by the fact that the new government had no navy, and had to borrow $300,000 from Holland banks to bribe Barbary pirates to release captured American seamen. Creditors panicked when debtors showed up with worthless currency known as "continentals" to settle their debts.

During the Revolution of 1776, Congress had commissioned privateers to raid British ships. These "freedom fighters" were invaluable during the war against England. After the war, however, they kept on fighting and were now attacking American merchant ships. Outnumbered by 500 to 20 ships, the Continental Navy was helpless. These privateers were bandits, debtors, criminals and other social misfits who sailed under names like Captain Blood, Lieutenant Ghost, and Boatswain Butcher—just the sort of fellows to frighten conservative merchants, landowners, bankers, and lawyers. Afraid that their lives might someday become nasty, brutish and short, influential Americans decided they had to do something about the Articles of Confederation. The event which triggered this haste occurred in 1786 and is now known in the history books as Shays' Rebellion. Squeezed by high taxes and debt, western Massachusetts' farmers formed a small army

> Has government at all levels in this country become so inefficient, clumsy and weak that for some Americans life is truly solitary, poor, nasty, brutish and short?

and behind revolutionary war hero Captain Daniel Shays marched through the state harassing judges, tax collectors, and county sheriffs. Though finally defeated by an army raised by Boston merchants, the angry farmers sent fear throughout the new nation, especially among wealthy and conservative men. Shocked by the rebellion, George Washington wrote to his old friend Secretary of War Henry Knox asking "For God's sake, tell me . . . what is the cause of these commotions?" Knox wrote back October 23, 1786 telling Washington that the troublemakers were radicals who had the strange idea that since they had fought the British they ought to share in the confiscated property. These radicals also believe, wrote Knox sarcastically, that anyone who opposed their plans was "an enemy to equity and justice, and ought to be swept from the face of the earth."[20]

The idea that common people should share the wealth was unpopular with George Washington and his friends. They decided the time had come to change the rules, and called for a special convention to write a new constitution. One central thought guided the 55 lawyers, merchants, bankers, land owners,

> Check the footnotes at the end of this chapter, and determine where the authors found the quote from Washington's friend Henry Knox. Is it important to have access to the footnote sources, or should we eliminate footnotes altogether?

and other elites who traveled to Philadelphia in the summer of 1787, namely, "How do we keep rebellious farmers and other factions from destroying this nation?"

> Why were these Americans so concerned about a few thousand rebellious farmers in western Massachusetts? Is it really possible for a small faction to destroy a nation?

Consider the case of Adolph Hitler. He and six followers began the National Socialist Worker's Party in Germany. From these humble beginnings, Hitler's party by 1933 had 288 of the 647 seats in the German Reichstag, and he was chancellor. In March 1933 the Reichstag by 441 to 94 votes passed an enabling act giving Hitler the power of a dictator. With this power, Hitler crushed his political opponents, filled the concentration camps, and launched the frightfully destructive events that led to World War II. Once all powerful, Hitler carried out his "Final Solution," now known as the **Holocaust**. Over six million people died because a neurotic man who looked like a shopkeeper and wore a toothbrush mustache achieved absolute power.

When they met in Philadelphia over two hundred years ago, the Founding Fathers worried that a future demagogue like Hitler might someday arouse enough popular support to become dictator. So they designed a political system specifically aimed at controlling the types of factions considered dangerous in the 18th century.

After the Founders finished their work at Philadelphia, a hand-written copy of the Constitution was sent to each of the 13 states for ratification. During that process, New Yorkers were treated to a newspaper debate over the new rules. This debate included James Madison, John Jay, and Alexander Hamilton. All three supported ratification. They explained their reasons in 85 brilliant essays known as *The Federalist Papers*.

> **Try always to understand the origin of rules. In the case of the Constitution, your best sources for understanding that famous document are *The Federalist Papers*.**

In Federalist 10, Madison revealed a Hobbesian view that people often pursue self-interest at the expense of others. Most citizens, wrote Madison, are driven by "fallible" reason to embrace wild schemes involving religion, politics and property. To secure an advantage, people join factions. Madison defined factions as ". . . a number of citizens, whether amounting to a

Judging by Madison's words, both pro-choice and pro-life factions fit his definition of a faction. Do you agree? What about the National Rifle Association?

majority or minority of the whole, who are united and actuated by some impulse of passion or of interest, adverse to the rights of other citizens, or to the permanent or aggregate interests of the community." In *Federalist 10*, Madison said governments had two ways to deal with factions: Either remove the causes or control the effects. Then he suggested **two ways to remove the causes** of factions, namely: ➡ Destroy the liberty necessary for their existence or ➡ give every citizen the same opinions, passions, interests.

Like most of his contemporaries, Madison understood that freedom and factionalism went together like air and fire. In his wildest dreams, however, Madison never envisioned a time when Hitler and Stalin would use fear and technology to achieve absolute conformity. Nor did Madison foresee how technology could provide so much comfort that citizens would gladly give up their individuality. These themes come later in the works of George Orwell and Aldous Huxley. ❤ Cultural literacy check: Who wrote *1984*? Who wrote *Brave New World*?

Madison, however, wanted nothing to do with either a harsh dictatorship led by Big Brother, or a benign utopia where everyone could take Soma and watch Feelies. He argued logically that the new Constitution would **control the effects of factions** without destroying liberty or freedom of conscience.

If you're having difficulty understanding Madison's argument, put it in the form of an outline or box. Let it look something like this:
Removing the Causes of Factions:
  ① **Destroy Liberty**
  ② **Give Everyone the Same Opinion, Passions, and Interests**
Controlling the Effects of Factions:
  ① **Republicanism**
  ② **Federalism**
  ③ **Separation of Powers**
  ④ **Checks and Balances**

Controlling the Effects of Factions

Why was Saddam Hussein allowed to remain as military ruler of Iraq after the United States and its friends in the 1991 Persian Gulf War defeated his military forces? President George Bush decided to let the Iraqi dictator remain in power because other nations were afraid Hussein's removal would lead to a dangerous war among all the factions in Iraq, namely Shiites, Kurds, and Sunni Arabs. Thus, the power of factions.

In Madison's day, factions frequently organized around two issues, religion and property. The most common and durable sources of factions, wrote Madison, "has been the various and unequal distribution of property." Like any sensible man with property, Madison and the Founding Fathers worried that radicals might get power and then pass laws that would redistribute the wealth by taxing the rich and giving to the poor. On this point, Madison noted in Federalist 10 that legislative majorities are prone to overburden the rich with taxes so that they would have more "shillings saved to their own pockets."

Today, however, we fight most battles around issues like crime, education, women's rights, hate crimes, and abortion. These battles are part of larger conflict, now known as the **Culture Wars**. Thus we have pro-choice and pro-life locked in a daily battle over the right of a woman to have an abortion and thus end a potential life. Neither side seems willing at this point to compromise. To control the effects of battling factions, the men who wrote the Constitution used an intricate system based on republicanism, federalism, separation of powers, and checks and balances.

> ❏ **A republican form of government** is one in which the people elect others to represent them and make the laws.

Under such a system, argued Madison, "No man is allowed to be a judge in his own cause, because his interest would certainly bias his judgment, and, not improbably, corrupt his integrity." To remove these biased citizens from the legislative process, Madison and the others created a complicated system. They had members of the House of Representatives directly elected by voters from congressional districts. Senators, however, were to be chosen two from each state by their state legislatures. To remove the President from the masses, the Founders created a special selection body known now as the Electoral College.

Madison justified indirect representative government by arguing that it was the most logical way to govern a large population spread out over a huge land mass. Despite Madison's plan, many Americans seem ready to abandon republicanism. Ethnic minorities in particular complain that Congress over represents white men. Feminist factions complain that women, who comprise about half the population, are under represented in Congress. In 1992 only 31% of the 535 Senators and Representatives were women. Occasionally, someone speaking for ethnic groups and feminists suggests that we replace the current "winner-take-all" election system with proportional representation. Is this a good idea?

> ❏ **Federalism**. This is a political system where we divide power between a central government and states.

Federalism controls factions by limiting their harmful effects to individual states. The influence of factious leaders might, noted Madison, "kindle a flame within their particular States, but will be unable to spread a general conflagration through the other States." To emphasize this point, Madison noted how a religious sect "may degenerate into a political faction in a part of the Confederacy; but the variety of sects dispersed over the entire face of it must secure the national councils against any danger from that source."

> **Many traditional women are satisfied with republicanism. They feel that the men they vote for are just as concerned with women's rights issues as any woman. Moreover, women in a traditional marriage are often satisfied with their husband's politics and worry that feminists are playing around with the rule of unintended consequences. What do you think?**

When the Supreme Court in 1973 decided to override state laws and make abortion a national issue they ignored Madison's advice in *Federalist 10*. The decision may have pleased pro-choice advocates, but it ignited passions that had been much quieter when abortion was an issue decided by every state.

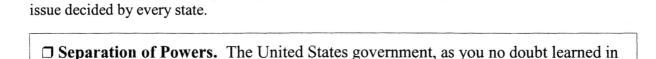

❐ **Separation of Powers.** The United States government, as you no doubt learned in high school, consists of three separate branches, the legislative, judicial, and executive.

Separation of powers is a powerful rule, and affects how we play politics in this nation. It means that members of Congress have no compelling reason to hide the mistakes of a President. It means an independent judiciary able to rule decisively—and sometimes wrongly—on such momentous issues as abortion rights. It means a President who can act decisively in a national emergency without waiting for Congress to convene, but it also means that Congress can impeach him/her for abusing his/her powers. Above all, separation of powers means that no branch of our government may conspire to have its own way legally without the advice, support, or intrusion of others. The Founding Fathers defined tyranny as "The accumulation of all powers, legislative, executive, and judicial, in the same hands, whether of one, a few, or many, and whether hereditary, self-appointed or elective . . . ."[21]

❐ **Checks and Balances.** To check ambitious officials, the Founding Fathers designed the Constitution with a "fail-safe" backup known as checks and balances.

Dubbed "auxiliary precautions" by Madison, Jay and Hamilton, this fail-safe system is marbled throughout the Constitution and includes the following provisions:

⇨ **Qualifications for Office. For the purpose of checks and balances, ages for each branch differ. Minimum ages are: President 35, Senators 30, and Representatives 25. Why have this age difference?**

⇨ **Staggered Terms of Office. Terms of office are staggered so that the President serves four years, a Senator six, members of the House two and Supreme Court Justices for life. Why?**

⇨ **Differing Constituencies. The original system required Electors to select the President, District voters to elect House members, state legislatures to decide how to choose Senators, and the President to nominate Justices, with senatorial advice and consent. Why?**

⇨ **Shared Powers. Each branch shares power. Though the President is Commander in Chief, Congress has to declare war. Article I, Section 8 delegates considerable law making power to Congress. Yet in Article I, Section 7 the President is given the power to veto these laws.**

George W. Bush was elected President in 2000 by 537 popular votes in Florida. Four months after the election, Congress was debating an end to the Electoral College. Has that much favored reform become a reality? Why? Why not?

Notes

1. "Taking the Pledge," *Time* (September 5, 1988), pp. 14-15.

2. Tom Wicker, "Bush League Charges," Las Vegas *Review Journal* (June 27, 1988), p. 7B.

3. Mike O'Callaghan, "Flag Amendment Loses by 3 Votes," Las Vegas *Sun* (December 23, 1995), p. 8B.

4. Mike Royko, "A Nose Rub of Sorts for Ditzy Word Jocks," The Daily *Spectrum* (June 3, 1990), p. 5A.

5. Edward B. Tyler, "Primitive Culture," in Paul Bohannon and Mark Glazer (eds.), *High Points in Anthropology*, 2d ed., (New York: Alfred A. Knopf, 1988), p. 64.

6. John C. Calhoun, "Speech on the Reception of Abolition Petitions, Feb. 6, 1837," in Michael B. Levy (ed.), *Political Thought in America* (Homewood, Illinois: The Dorsey Press, 1982), p. 245.

7. William Graham Sumner, "What Social Classes Owe to Each Other," *Ibid.*, p. 261

8. James George Frazer, *The Golden Bough: A Study in Magic and Religion*, I, abridged ed., (New York: Macmillan Publishing Co., Inc., 1922), p. 229.

9. A. Lee Brown, Jr., *Rules and Conflict: An Introduction to Political Life and Its Study* (Englewood Cliffs, New Jersey: Prentice-Hall, Inc., 1981), p. 197.

10. Thomas Sowell, "Could it be that Courtship Traditions Developed for a Reason," Las Vegas *Review Journal* (January 14, 1992), p. 7B.

11. Dixon Wecter, *The Hero in America* (Ann Arbor Paperbacks: The University of Michigan Press, 1941), pp. 134-135.

12. *USA Today* (July 8, 1986).

13. Donald R. Mathews, *U.S. Senators & Their World* (New York: Random House, 1960), pp. 97-98.

14. Joseph Sobran, "Two Different Ideas About the Rules," Las Vegas *Review Journal* (April 12, 1992), p. 2C.

15. Kenneth P. Langston, *Political Socialization* (New York: Oxford University Press, 1969), p. 5. "Making the Grade in Goodsprings," Las Vegas *Sun* (January 15, 1989), p. 1AA.

16. Lance Morrow, "Guerillas in Our Midst," *Time* (March 18, 1996), p. 102.

17.Sean Whaley, "Smoking Ban May Hit Hard," Las Vegas *Review Journal* (December 5, 1996), pp. 1A, 3A.

18.Jack Katz and Daniel Marks, "Swinging Back and Forth in Gangs," Las Vegas *Review Journal* (January 26, 1989), p. 11B.

19. "Poll Reveals Ignorance of History," Las Vegas *Review Journal* (October 9, 1989), p. 3A.

20. Henry Knox to George Washington (October 23, 1786), Washington Papers, Library of Congress.

21.Roy P. Fairchild (ed.), *The Federalist Papers*, 2d ed., (Garden City, New York: Doubleday & Company, Inc., 1966), p. 139.

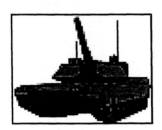

Chapter 3

Power

Americans love big trucks, big dogs, and big guns. They also wear the logos of successful athletic teams like the Yankees, the Lakers, and the 1991 NCAA basketball championship UNLV Rebels.

In Las Vegas, high rollers have "juice," which is another way of saying influence, money, or power. People with juice get all the perquisites of power, known as the "perks." Las Vegas perks include extensive casino credit, magnificent four bedroom suites at Caesar's Palace, and lots of free drinks.

Where did the idea of power come from? Scottish anthropologist James George Frazer offered a plausible explanation in his classic study of primitive cultures, *The Golden Bough* (1922). According to Frazer, the primitive peoples of Africa, Asia and America attributed power to the doctors,

> **Who now has power in Las Vegas, and how can we pick them out? Do they throw money around making wild bets at sports books? Do they wear their baseball caps with the bill turned back? Do they carry guns?**

shamans, or sorcerers who worked magic for the benefit of the entire community. These medicine men, according to Frazer, worked **public magic**. By public magic, he meant they used charms, spells, and rituals to bring food, good weather, health and blessings to everyone in the tribe or village. By casting spells, these early medicine men became celebrities. Their ability to work public magic made them logical candidates to become chief or king.

Eventually, the most intelligent and resourceful members of the tribe were drawn toward careers in working public magic. One important quality for a future leader was to be a persuasive liar. According to Frazer, since the average medicine man did not always deliver good weather or good luck, he needed plausible excuses. Otherwise, he faced the wrath of angry people. This possibility produced a natural selection process which worked against sincere medicine men, who were unable to lie convincingly if their spells failed. The unscrupulous liars survived, according to Frazer, because they always had a plausible explanation when the magic failed. Frazer ended his narrative by suggesting that the supreme power in most tribal communities thus fell into the hands of "men of the keenest intelligence and the most unscrupulous character."

After describing how witch doctors became political leaders, Frazer went on to suggest that primitive people were better off being ruled by **intelligent scoundrels** than by **sincere fools**. "In the field of politics," he wrote, "the wily intriguer, the ruthless victor, may end up being a wise and magnanimous ruler, blessed in his lifetime, lamented at his death, admired and applauded by posterity." In comparison, noted Frazer, "once a fool always a fool, and the greater the power in his hands the more disastrous is likely to be the use he makes of it."[1]

In Europe, city states eventually replaced primitive tribes. Unlike tribes, city states did not need medicine men or witch doctors to work public magic. This task was taken over by kings, queens, and princes.

In his famous book *The Prince* (1513), Niccolo Machiavelli offered a brutally candid game plan for leaders who want to keep their power. Giving advice to the prince of an Italian city-state, Machiavelli laid down the rules for staying in power without doing any public magic. Typical was Machiavelli's discussion of the question, "Is it better to be loved or feared?" To Machiavelli the choice was obvious. It was "much safer to be feared than loved . . . [because] men are ungrateful, fickle, false, cowardly, covetous, and as long as you succeed they are yours entirely; they will offer you their blood, property, life, and children . . . when the need is far distance; but when it approaches they turn against you." Machiavelli concluded the ruler should not rely on good faith. Instead, fear is more effective since men are less likely to offend a ruler if they fear him than if they love him. ✰ Is this good advice today?

Thomas Hobbes had a very pessimistic world view, and in 1651 he warned the people of England that they needed a strong monarch; otherwise their lives would be nasty, brutish and short. Machiavelli, however, was not interested in making life safe. He was merely telling his prince how to stay in power. When you hear the words Hobbesian or Machiavellian, what do they now mean?

Leaders who have followed Machiavelli's advice have learned to be unscrupulous without seeming too cruel. Abraham Lincoln, for example, had some **Machiavellian** qualities. Although many loved him, Lincoln could be devious and he was not afraid to be harsh when it mattered. When he declared the 1863 Emancipation Proclamation, Lincoln freed only the slaves in the rebel states. Those enslaved in loyal states were not freed. Lincoln's often inconsistent, but perfectly logical decisions, inspired former President Richard Nixon to refer to the "Great Emancipator" as a "cold pragmatist and a total politician." ✰ Why would Nixon refer to Lincoln as a cold, pragmatic politician?

Politicians need more than cold pragmatism, and Machiavellian charm. They need to appear warm, thoughtful, charismatic. In other words, they need to appear lovable because TV projects them into millions of homes. Like tribal witch doctors, modern political leaders have to look into the camera eye and lie convincingly about magic spells that failed to produce good weather, or slow the inflation pace. In his 1967 book, *The Medium is the Massage,* Canadian culture analyst Marshall McLuhan suggested that TV is so pervasive that to be elected today a politician must somehow disguise his/her quest for power under a blanket of innocent charm. Charming people look cool on TV, and win. Eager candidates look frantic on TV; they sweat and lose.

By 2020 advertisers will be touting products like the General Motors' Generals, the Microsoft Mustangs and the Texaco Terrors. These companies will be represented by celebrities whose masculine voices and rugged features can be used to sell beer, perfume, and computers.

People who have charm, charisma and style are not called witch doctors or politicians anymore. Today's key word is **celebrity**, and it can be anyone from a "voice over" by Joe Namath to Martin Sheen playing president on the "West Wing."

Celebrities have power because they can get us to buy cars, deodorant, life insurance or an ideology. Unlike Machiavelli's prince, modern celebrities are loved, not feared. Some are worshipped as Saints, given names like "The King" and featured as postage stamp icons.

Madonna is famous because she combines vulgarity and shrewdness. For these qualities, she is now an entry in *The Cambridge Dictionary of American Biography* (1995). That's why Time Warner Inc., paid $60 million for her talents. Madonna also has two children born out of wedlock. Should we admire women who have children without being married?

> **Trivia Jeopardy: This dead "King" was popular in Las Vegas, and his image helped sell over one million postage stamps in 1992.**

> Why do we worship outrageous celebrities? Sigmund Freud called this **"need completion." To feel good about ourselves, we need to identify with popular, powerful personalities.** Need completion gives us the chance to live out fantasies without taking any risks. ☆ Does Freud's theory apply today?

In 1927 Americans fell in love with a risk taker named Charles "Lucky" Lindbergh. Lindbergh became famous by flying his plane *Spirit of St. Louis* nonstop from New York to Paris. Lindbergh's brave deed inspired people around the world. He was praised by newspapers, radios and in movie news. Eleven years after his heroic flight, Lindbergh visited Nazi Germany to see if the air force put together by Herman Goerring was powerful enough to support Hitler's plan to conquer Europe. Lindbergh came away convinced the Luftwaffe was more powerful than the combined air power of the European nations that opposed Hitler. Lindbergh's superficial analysis of German air power influenced the leaders of Great Britain and France, who agreed at Munich in 1938 to let Hitler carve up Czechoslovakia. This appeasement at Munich eventually led to World War II because it reaffirmed Hitler's belief that democratic nations were afraid to fight.

Several years later, writer William Shirer claimed that Lindbergh was responsible for the myth of German air supremacy. According to Shirer, the combined air forces of Great Britain, France, Czechoslovakia and Russia had the capacity to defeat Germany.

> **Munich is the capital city of Bavaria, and also a symbol meaning a dishonourable appeasement. How can the same word mean both a location and a feeling?**

Nevertheless, Lindbergh's reputation and celebrity status were so immense that "his dire warnings to the French and British were taken very seriously and no doubt played a considerable part in inducing Chamberlain and Daladier to capitulate so shamefully at Munich."[2]

By 1941 President Roosevelt had decided that Great Britain and the rest of Europe would fall to Hitler, unless helped by the United States. Thus Roosevelt pushed Congress to let him sell, transfer, exchange, lend or lease military supplies or equipment if necessary for national defense. In the long-run, **Lend-lease** helped defeat Hitler's plans for world conquest and was also responsible for the ultimate defeat of Japan. While Roosevelt, however, was trying to get reluctant Americans to fight Hitler, popular celebrity Lindbergh was spearheading an isolationist movement that might have kept Americans neutral if the Japanese had not bombed Pearl Harbor.

By 1984 the gap between media fantasy and reality had closed to the point where actor Ronald Reagan was elected President of the United States. Historian Garry Wills thought the celebrity game had finally gone too far, and accused Americans of having the fantasy that

Reagan was their "Amiable Rambo, a nonthreatening avenger on reassuring terms with Armageddon." This Amiable Rambo, suggested Wills, was elected so that he could insult the Soviets, yet not plunge the world in a world-ending nuclear war.[3]

Popular celebrities like Ronald Reagan get to be President because they have charm, good writers and very good body language. In his influential book *Politics: Who Gets What, When, How* (1958), political scientist Harold Lasswell predicted that someday most power would be in the hands of the **symbol manipulators** like lawyers, artists, writers, and actors.

> During the Vietnam War, American public opinion was split between hawks willing to escalate the war and doves who wanted to withdraw. Several Hollywood and other celebrities took sides and used their status to argue either for or against the war. Use your research abilities, and identify one prominent Vietnam war hawk and one dove.

> If anyone ever calls you a "buffoon" you need to know if this is an insult, or a compliment. Locate a reliable information source, and look up the word and list three other words that are synonymous.

Newspaper reporters and historians made Lincoln lovable by portraying him as "Honest Abe," a man who educated himself by reading books by candlelight in a log cabin. In contrast, Ronald Reagan's reputation as a "nice guy" was established when he made movies like *Kings Row* (1942) and *Knute Rockne—All American* (1940), and *Bedtime for Bonzo* (1951).

When Reagan made a mistake the media was rarely able to make the people believe their leader was a scoundrel. This fact caused frustrated reporters to invent the term "Teflon President" for Reagan because criticism never tarnished his popularity with the masses.

Reagan demonstrated his charm in the 1980 TV debates against incumbent Jimmy Carter. During the debates, Carter starred directly at the camera and appeared tense and stiff. Reagan, according to political scientist Roger D. Masters, "exhibited a high frequency of relaxed appeasement, and—in speech patterns—hesitated. Reagan also made a highly symbolic gesture when he crossed the space between the two candidates to initiate hand-shaking."[4]

During his presidency, Ronald Reagan dressed for power. On the job he wore impeccable suits, but relaxed on his California ranch wearing riding boots and chopping wood. Young men now relax by wearing bulky jeans. Would you vote for a politician in baggy pants?

In the 1960's young Americans were waging symbolic protests, so they wore faded jeans, army fatigues, and hiking boots. Now, they rebel through backward baseball caps, gunnysack clothes, tatoos, nose rings, tongue rings, earrings, purple hair, and other nonconformist symbols.

> ☆ One Las Vegas tatoo parlor in April 1997 advertised that it would help customers pass their drug tests. What might that suggest?

Modern celebrities cultivate a careless look in the way they dress. Men appear on TV talk shows dressed in casual shoes, wearing half-open shirts and scruffy ties. Many ladies appear on TV dressed like hookers.

Cultivating a sloppy look is an effective way to display a certain "careless" power. During the 17th century, French nobles spent hours achieving a look of careless chic; like they had just left a lady's bedchamber. The swashbucklers then wore high soft battlefield boots to formal balls, placed bright ostrich plumes in their hats, and smeared their hair with rouge. Had he lived in France four hundred years ago, former Chicago Bulls celebrity rebounder Dennis Rodman would have been a swashbuckler. If he had lived in Puritan Massachusetts four hundred years ago, however, Dennis would have been hanged as a male witch.

> In his *Encyclopedia of Word and Phrase Origins* (1987), Robert Hendrickson says the word "hooker" has three different origins. One theory comes from the way a prostitute "hooked" prospective customers by linking arms with them. Since the word may demean women, should it be banned from use—especially in college textbooks.

> Like women who prefer Ms., male witches had a preferred name. Look it up.

In his classic *The Theory of the Leisure Class* (1899), economist Thorstein Veblen exposed how Americans dealt with power one hundred years ago. Instead of high soft boots, Americans wore plain suits but they spent the rest of their money on items like huge homes with too many rooms, and consumed conspicuously—just like the middle class today. They also kept dogs as pets, a luxury which Veblen considered too excessive given the low character of most dogs.

Modern day rulers usually keep a dog around to prove they are mere mortals, like the rest of us. Adolph Hitler had a dog, and a mistress. Hitler knew what the common people wanted, so he made Jews the scapegoats for Germany's World War I defeat. He also knew the power of symbols, and adopted the hooked cross set in a circle and surrounded by black, red and white. Most Americans recognize Hitler's **swastika**. After becoming President of Haiti, Francois (Papa Doc) Duvalier used voodoo symbols to keep his people cowed. To enforce the peasants' belief that he represented the voodoo god Baron Samedia (the spirit of death), Papa Doc often dressed in black suits since that color symbolized death. He also changed the colors of the Haitian flag to red and black, the colors of voodoo secret societies. Hitler's colors were also red and black.

> Hitler's swastika is also known by the word *Hakenkreuz*. It has been called the crooked cross by the many historians who believe Hitler corrupted Christian symbolism for his own purposes. Jump on your Internet and WWW, and pull up the origins of Hitler's swastika. Thank you.

☆ Do these colors have any political significance today?

Getting bald is a symbolic loss of power. Primitive societies believe in sympathetic magic—which means that any part of the body that gets separated still remains in sympathetic union with the body. Thus, anyone who gets possession of your hair, nails, or teeth can work black magic and make you suffer. Remember Samson? He was the famous strongman who could kill a lion barehanded and slaughter 30 Philistines at one time. Samson's power came from the fact that he never cut his hair. After Delilah learned the secret of Samson's strength, she clipped his hair while he slept and turned him over to her Philistine friends. They gouged out Samson's eyes and humiliated him. Although Samson got some revenge, we tell the story to remind readers of the *Bible* that exposing the source of your power is dangerous.

> **Can you think of anything Americans might do today to obtain hair, clothing, a signature, or other celebrity items that might produce a little sympathetic magic?**

Every President he served under always treated Former FBI Chief J. Edgar Hoover (1895-1972) very carefully. The source of Hoover's power was a substantial file of private, and often embarrassing, information on most of the nation's leaders. The files, destroyed by Hoover's faithful secretary after his death, were not as derogatory as most people believed. Yet the files served their purpose. They made Hoover powerful by the very fact of their existence. ☆ Hoover had power because he could "blackmail" people. What does it mean to blackmail?

To achieve in life, young Americans must become **culturally literate**. This means knowing that "FBI" means Federal Bureau of Investigation. The FBI is one agency under the Justice Department. Hoover headed the FBI for almost half a century, and is even today considered the "consummate bureaucrat." ☆ Why?

By the time you read this, the U.S. Army will have investigated charges made in 1996 that drill instructors at the Aberdeen Proving Ground sexually harassed female recruits. Throughout history men and women have associated sexual prowess with political power. In the Middle Ages, impotent men blamed witches for their problem. So they hunted down women, called them witches and hanged, drowned or burned them at the stake.

If living today these witch hunters could get a witch doctor to prescribe Viagra.

Men who feel sexually inadequate

> **To empower women, the U.S. Army has been training them for combat. By integrating military units, the Army may have opened a Pandora's Box of woes. Has the time arrived to reconsider the role of women in combat? Or do the men who sexually harass need to find new careers?**

often compensate by trying to manipulate women. Judging by most accounts, Hitler was ordinary in the bedroom but a powerful speaker who aroused female passions. When he gained power in Germany, Hitler pushed through laws that required German women to bear children for the glory of the Third Reich and punished them for having abortions, using contraceptives, getting divorces, and believing feminist ideas. They made Jewish women scapegoats for "sex democracy," which were Hitler's words for feminism. Nazi propagandists urged Young Germans to slay the dragon of sex democracy "so that we may again attain the most holy thing in the world, the woman as maid and servant." Hitler and his followers were, according to feminist Kate Millett, typical of men who use rape and forced sex to prove their power over women.

.

Is the U.S. Army a patriarchal culture where rape is a sanctioned way to keep women unequal?

Advertisers often use sex to sell products, and power. In 1989 Camels was singled out for a perfectly awful ad which appeared in such magazines as *Rolling Stone* and *National Lampoon*. They designed the ad for young men who planned to spend the summer at the beach. It showed some "smooth moves" for young males, and said "Run into the water, grab someone and drag her back to shore, as if you've saved her from drowning. The more she kicks and screams, the better."

Rough sex is a power game. They exploited this fact in the S&M fantasy movie *Love Crimes* in which Sean Young plays Atlanta attorney Dana Greenway, who tracks and traps a serial rapist played by Patrick

Do you agree with Lizzie Borden?

Bergin. Then Greenway falls in love with the serial killer and they make mad passionate love. Defending this fantasy, director Lizzie Borden said, "All sex is a power thing. I'm a feminist, but I believe a strong woman wants someone stronger than her to allow her to act out her sexual impulses."[5] ☆ Do strong women need to be dominated in order to act out sexual impulses?

In October 1996 President Clinton signed a bill outlawing Rohypnol and other "date rape drugs" used by would-be rapists in what he called a "sick attempt to facilitate their violent crimes." The new law provides for a 20-year sentence for anyone using the drug; which is odorless, tasteless and 10 to 20 times more powerful than Valium. Date rape drugs are dropped into the drink of unknowing victims. When the victim falls asleep, her date rapes her. The victim has little memory of the rape. This drug and another date rape chemical named GHB (gamma hydroxy butyrate) has American women wondering just how far some men will go to achieve sexual power. ☆ Is date rape the same as "statutory rape"?

Meanwhile, women are trying to figure out what types of clothing will give them "power" in an era of unsafe sex. One recent approach is the wearing of thigh-highs which, according to fashion writer Martha Duffy, is an "attempt to look as tarty as possible in an impossibly safe sex world." What about teen age women celebrities who wear low cut gowns?

Women who have executive careers usually don't wear tarty thigh-highs. But they do have to play office politics, and beat men at their own game. When it comes to office games, women may have a real advantage. In a 1985 survey of office strategies, *Newsweek* argued that women "can be especially good office politicians, because they have always had to rely on persuasion rather than intimidation."[6]

Many men, in comparison, remain office Cro-Magnons. They storm around giving orders, flirting with co-workers and telling gross jokes. ☆ Are obnoxious office playboys a cultural lag, or merely having fun?

Cro-Magnon men often learn their power games in places like the handball court,

Have you ever seen a female tennis pro throw a tantrum during a televised match?

the tennis court, or the golf course. They know that on the golf course the boss gets a "gimmie" although he has a six-foot putt. They recognize the power game being played when a losing tennis player throws a tantrum, and uses anger to improve his performance and ruin the timing of his opponents. What about a player who smashes three rackets during a match?

Young women [we used "little girls" but Word Perfect prefers "young women"] would rather play with dolls than with a baseball bat. We used to teach them to be motherly and lovable. In sports women may have smiled once, but now the better athletes attack the game with all the ferocity of high testosterone males. This facial expression is known as the **paranoid scowl**, which includes a down-turned mouth, clenched teeth, and narrowed eyes. When a big dog likes a person, it wages its tail and rolls its tongue. When the dog is ready to attack it gets a canine paranoid scowl. This dog sign consists of laid back ears and curled lips exposing the fangs, like young gang members who think a glance means they're being dissd.

As a rule, most women know the smile is more effective than the paranoid scowl, and they've learned that asking good questions is an effective way to deal with people.

But some women feel so helpless and weak that they will do almost anything to take control of their bodies. This helplessness led to an eating disorder known as *Anorexia Nervosa*. To gain control, some young women have starved themselves. As for young men who lack a feeling of power, they might get drunk and abuse their significant others.

When people lack power, they rationalize their plight by drinking beer or vomiting to lose weight. Or they lie. According to psychologist Sam Keen, children feel inferior so they lie to their parents. For the same reasons, workers lie to the boss.[7] Other Americans fantasize that someday they'll tell their Cro-Magnon boss "where to go." Most of us are content, however, to rebel vicariously. We encourage the office troublemaker to insult the boss, and then disappear when the purging starts.

In the future, computer-communications services like America Online will challenge newspapers, magazines, radio, TV and comic books for full control of our values.

> **In the past, purge meant to be spiritually clean. Later, the communist party purged itself of unreliable elements. Then young women purged themselves to lose weight. Now, we "purge" our computer files.**

Values are shaped by propaganda. In dictatorships, most propaganda is controlled by the government, and is political. American propaganda, on the other hand, is controlled mostly by private groups with money and power. Corporations usually don't try to openly gain political control. Instead these companies use "sociological propaganda" to convince us that the American way of life is good because we have jobs, consumer goods, and technology.

> **Remember, sociological propaganda is designed to convince us that our way of life and technology is marvelous, simply marvelous!**

"Extreme Power" is now offered by Think Pad 770, "the only family of notebooks in the world with a huge 14.1"screen, a 233 Mhz' Pentium processor with MMX technology, DVD, Dolby' digital audio and enough support for up to 10.2GB' storage capacity.

Power means being able to work public magic, lie persuasively, be fearsome, use good body language, exploit sex, master technology, have inside information, and hold a good job. Money helps.

The framers of the Constitution made the President commander-in-chief, but gave Congress the power to declare war. Many of the Founding Fathers remembered how the English kings often taxed the people to pay for wars fought over imagined insults from other country's leaders. Thus the Constitution stipulates that Congress have the power "To declare War." Yet in January 1991, President George Bush made war on Iraq without a formal declaration by Congress.

The President also has "inherent powers." Define the word inherent and give an example of this type of power.

By the time Congress was ready to debate whether to allow an attack on Iraqi forces, President Bush already had an army ready to strike and was portraying Saddam Hussein as a mad dictator, like Adolph Hitler. ☆ Why was President Bush able to fight this "unofficial" war?

President Bush was able to send Americans against Iraq because under the Constitution, Article II, Section 2 it says "The President shall be Commander in Chief of the Army and Navy of the United States . . . . " As Commander in Chief, President Bush was in a position to use all the technology and fire power possessed by the U.S. military. Under Article I, Section 8, Congress is delegated the power "To declare War. . . ." The same Article makes Congress responsible to "provide for the common Defense. . . .To raise and support Armies . . . . To provide and maintain a Navy . . . . To make Rules for the Government and Regulation of the land and naval Forces." ❑ When it comes to war, Congress and the President each has a role. In past wars, have they always worked together? When the Civil War began in 1861 did President Lincoln wait for Congress to act, or did he act on his own power?

In her book, *The Gentle Art of Self Defense*, Suzette Haden stressed the importance of knowing how to ask good questions. The ambitious office worker doesn't merely ask, "how many cars did we sell this week?" Instead, she asks, "What have we learned about public taste from the types of cars we sold this month?"

☺ Suppose you were teaching your little brother how to ride a bicycle, and he kept whining, "Why do I have to learn this, it's boring?" How would you answer that question?

"Whiners" ask, "Why do we have to study the Vietnam War? It's boring!" However, "Winners" ask, "What can we learn from studying the Vietnam War?"

The Vietnam War caused Americans to lose faith in their leaders. Nevertheless, somebody has to make decisions and use power. One hundred years ago the United States led the world in production. Despite economic ups and downs, our workers are still among the most productive in the world.

To get things done somebody has to have and use power. Many Americans, however, fear power and agree with these words once spoken by British Lord Acton: "Power tends to corrupt and absolute power corrupts absolutely."

Joseph Stalin is a good example of a leader absolutely corrupted by power. For 23 years he terrorized the Soviet people with purges, death camps, and secret police. Since the USSR had no official tyrant removal system during that time, the Soviet people had to wait until their paranoid leader died in 1953. After Stalin died, his body was entombed next to Lenin's in the mausoleum in Moscow's Red Square. At the 20th Party Congress in 1956, Nikita Khrushchev and other Soviet leaders attacked the *cult of personality*, and accused Stalin of being a self-centered tyrant who falsified history and glorified himself.

Unlike modern governments, tribal societies have simple and expedient ways to eliminate a powerless leader. Seventy-five years ago one African tribe required its king to appear every day to listen to the popular complaints, and settle disputes by administering justice. This was usually done by the king holding court daily under a special tree. If the king was ever too sick to work, however, the Fazoql tribe had a custom that kept would-be leaders on their toes. According to James George Frazer, the king was hanged "on the tree in a noose, which contained two razors so arranged that when the noose was drawn tight by the weight of the king's body they cut his throat." More humane, but more humiliating was a custom practiced by the Shilluk of the White Nile. The Shilluk were deathly afraid a king afflicted by sickness or senility would lose his magic and cause their cattle to die and their crops to rot in the field. So they were constantly looking for symptoms of approaching powerlessness. One of the fatal symptoms, according to Frazer, was the king's incapacity to satisfy the sexual passions of his many wives. When this happened, the wives immediately notified the tribal chiefs. As soon as they learned of the king's impotence, the chiefs locked the old man in a hut with a young virgin and left him there to starve to death. After the king's death, however, the Shilluk remembered him fondly and rarely spoke of his mistakes.[8]

In the United States we neither kill our leaders (at least, not legally) when they lose power nor do we leave them to die in a hut with a virgin. Americans are civilized. We use an Electoral College to select a President. Then if the President screws up, the House of Representatives has the power to draw up impeachment charges, and the Senate acts as the trial jury to determine guilt.

> **How does our Constitution provide for the selection and removal of the President. Use your copy of the document and look up impeachment, Electoral College, and the 22nd Amendment. Has any U.S. President ever been impeached?**

> **When the President's public magic goes, we can't rely on his wife to expose his impotence, nor can we expect him to stand every day under a tree making judgments to prove his good health. Instead, we rely on his opposition in Congress and the media to keep us informed. Whose judgment is more trustworthy, several wives or the media?**

Mass Psychology

Modern rulers get power by appealing to the hopes and prejudices of the masses. Though a leader may get bad advice, have many enemies, or be the target of a media frenzy, he or she can survive by knowing how to manipulate the masses. This means being able to combine knowledge, intuition and technology to convince the public its leader has delivered on all the promises of jobs, profits, glory and impeccable ethics. In other words, a "Wizard of Oz" who hides behind a curtain of smoke and noise.

Adolph Hitler was a skillful user of mass psychology. In his brief (1933-1945) reign as German Chancellor, Hitler was responsible for the deaths of millions of innocent people. Yet, he aroused powerful loyalties. How did he do it?

Hitler was a masterful, extemporaneous speaker, moved by a magic that made him able to select the right words for his audience. His contemporary Otto Strasser said Hitler had an instinctive flare. His words, wrote Strasser, touched each private wound, "liberating the mass unconscious, expressing its innermost aspirations, telling it what it most wanted to hear."[9]

Hitler could use mass psychology on the German people because he had little respect for their intelligence and strength. He often compared mass audiences to women because he thought both lacked will power. Consistent with his contempt for the masses, Hitler gave them spectacle, excitement, focused hatred and a terrible war.

Hitler and his aides organized huge rallies to arouse mass support for his megalomanic plans for national glory and military prowess. After he came to power in 1933, Hitler turned the city of Nuremberg into a national shrine for yearly rallies of the National Socialist Party. During these rallies, hundreds of thousands of uniformed party leaders and gullible Germans listened spellbound while Hitler shouted. Thousands of men wearing brown uniforms marched in perfect order led by young boys beating their drums. They covered every building with swastika flags. Ordinary Germans cried and had a crazed look that reminded American journalist William L. Shirer of the Holy Rollers he had once seen in the back country of Louisiana, "with the same crazed expressions on their faces."[10]

Hitler's party staged rallies at a 7,400 acre site known as Zeppelin Field on Nuremberg's southern outskirts, where 150 spotlights beamed toward the sky. There on a raised platform Hitler spoke to 1,600,000 people, convincing them the German nation could restore its former glory by building a huge military machine and destroying their enemies.

What did Huxley mean by "herd poison?"

Hitler succeeded with his mass psychology by using what Aldous Huxley called **herd poison**. This occurs when we bring people together en masse to hear speeches that appeal to their lowest instincts. Rather than engage in reflective thinking, people listen to their prejudices and subconscious fears. In a mass audience, according to Huxley, the individual escapes from responsibility, intelligence and morality "into a kind of frantic, animal mindlessness."[11]

In *The Myth of the Machine* (1970), writer Lewis Mumford tried to explain the meaning of youthful rebellion in the 1960s. He wondered why young Americans were protesting technology, but would travel long distances in motor cars to attend rock festivals where they magnified their egos through TV happenings and obliterated their consciousness with a drug like music played on electrically amplified guitars. Such inconsistent behavior bothered Mumford, and he called it "megatechnic primitivism." The people who cheered Hitler showed this primitive emotionalism. In a 1967 movie "Privilege," British film makers show how wild crowds and a popular young singer enable fascists to take over England's popular culture, church, and government. In "Privilege," phony police beat up the popular singer on stage and are themselves attacked by the crowd. Eventually, this scenario of police brutality and helpless "victim" is used to turn the people against their democratically elected leaders. Is there any possibility that any real or phony police brutality could turn Americans against their government?

Hitler's use of mass psychology was mostly for political reasons. American advertisers also use mass psychology, but their goal is to sell products. The people who write advertisements are trained in psychology, sociology, and anthropology. They usually sell erotism by convincing us that their products will make us attractive, exciting and popular.

The hucksters who sell political candidates depend too much on negative messages aimed at the opposition. During the 1992 primary elections, they filled TV with negative ads devised by the **symbol manipulators** and **image masters**. One ad for Republican hopeful Patrick Buchanan tried to embarrass former President Bush by showing gay men cavorting in skin-tight leather, a scene from a film produced with federal money provided by the National Endowment for the Arts. While they were showing the cavorting gay men, the ad's narrator said, "Even after good people protested, Bush continued to fund this kind of art."

Such ads aim at subconscious fears and hatreds. These ads work because people who design them know how to get inside your mind. An early pioneer of mass psychology was Ernest Dichter, President of the Institute of Motivational Research. Dichter and his staff took several hundred Americans and thoroughly examined their emotional make-up to decide their fears, ambitions and hopes. They compiled these subconscious feelings on a card-index system which they organized to decide how to sell products to future consumers. Dichter used the free association techniques employed by Sigmund Freud, who popularized the use of psychoanalysis to treat people suffering from mental disorders. Dichter's consumers were shown drawings of intricate patterns and asked what they saw. In his study of the techniques of persuasion, J.A.C. Brown said Dichter and his associates used their research to determine such subconscious feelings as latent homosexuality, paranoid trends, and emotional insecurity. They later turned this information into advertising campaigns aimed at exploiting customers.[12]

User-tracking software is now being used to find out if you have children, buy big vans, or watch HBO. This technology will be used to sell you children's car seats, an SUV, and Cable TV. It might also someday be used to introduce your 16-year-old single daughter to an internet dating service, which means she has a 19% chance of being contacted by a sex offender.

Since obscenity laws were relaxed, movies show a great deal of nudity and sex. Many contemporary celebrities take their clothes off to gain power. This is unusual since expensive clothing has always symbolized power. Yet celebrities like Madonna have discovered that some nudity and suggested sex are very profitable. They now study Madonna, in fact, at some universities as an icon for her era. She is a favorite of many feminists for openly flaunting an ancient phenomenon known as the "whore's rule over men." Like nude dancers in Las Vegas, Madonna teases and controls her audience by bringing out the wild and erotic side of people. Sigmund Freud had a word for this type of behavior. He theorized that normal people have three components to their personalities, namely the **Id**, **Ego**, and **Superego.** To put Freud's theory in modern perspective, consider the **Id** as that part of our subconscious personality that impels men to do illogical,

Since the time of William Shakespeare, the word "strumpet" has been used as the ultimate insult word for promiscuous women. **Under pressure from feminist groups, the word has been replaced by the euphemism "sexually active." Was it a good idea to abandon strumpet and replace it with sexually active.**

impulsive, childish things like making sexist jokes to a feminist boss. While the Id is having fun, the **Ego** is quietly thinking "these jokes could get us sued for sexual harassment." Meanwhile, the **Superego** is screaming "stop these jokes right now, they are sinful!"

Is the Id out of the Bag?

Does television let the Id out of the bag by encouraging viewers to believe that silly and dangerous behavior is exciting and there are no bad consequences?

Each of the following is an actual advertisement. Read each one, and decide if there is a hidden Freudian message:

✳ In 1996 a Saab convertible ad urged drivers to "peel off" their inhibitions and have a good time.

✳ Calvin Klein ads show very young models posed half undressed in casual attire, and wearing casually erotic expressions.

✳ In a 1996 ad, Levi showed a handsome man and attractive woman on an elevator. She is wearing jeans that bulge slightly open at the point below her navel. The man then fantasizes about having erotic love with his elevator companion. The sexual fantasy is followed by images of marriage. This fantasy ends suddenly, however, when a baby is born.

In *Brave New World*, Huxley showed that people can be controlled through their childish impulses. He invented a fictional world where everyone takes a mild euphoric called Soma, and engages in casual sex. Huxley's Id-driven people attend "Feelie" movies, listen to electronic music, and dance the "Orgy Porgy." In this sensual dance, the participants go round and round grabbing the buttocks ahead of them, shouting slogans like "twelve as one, twelve as one. I hear Him, I hear Him coming," and "Orgy-Porgy, Ford and fun, Kiss the girls and make them One." Eventually, all the dancers end on the floor in prone and supine positions.

Huxley's novel is even more relevant today than it was in 1932, when they published the first edition. More than any other writer of his era, Huxley asked, "If people seek only pleasure, will they give up their freedom for self-gratification?"

Techniques of Mass Psychology

The most common mass psychology techniques include:
① Band Wagon, ② Plain Folks, ③ Heroes, ④ Martyrs, ⑤ Villains, ⑥ Scapegoats, and ⑦ Stereotypes.

---

❶ Whether aimed at an audience gathered to hear rock music or political harangues, the basic technique for getting people to conform without thinking is the **Band Wagon**. The word bandwagon comes from a custom in the old South of having a band play on a wagon pulled through the streets of small towns advertising a favorite candidate. As the band passed, they urged bystanders to jump aboard. The bandwagon is another way of saying, "Hey, everyone is having fun but you, so jump aboard and get with it!"

Television has eliminated the need to have an actual wagon. Now we can all get on the bandwagon by drinking Pepsi-Cola like our favorite celebrity or voting for the political candidate who is ahead in the polls, or who has the most popular athletes on her side.

Do Americans advertise their political candidates as effectively as we advertise Pepsi Cola? Using any of our Presidents, write a jingle that would be a good advertisement. Example: "George, he's our guy; cut down the tree and made Dad cry; but he got honest, and made money buy and buy." So it's bad. See what you can do, smart guy.

For nearly one hundred years, Americans have been drinking Pepsi-Cola, a soft drink invented by Caleb Bradham. When the Japanese attacked Pearl Harbor, Americans were singing "Pepsi-Cola hits the spot/twelve full ounces, that's a lot/Twice as much for a nickel, too/Pepsi-Cola is the drink for you." They wrote this jingle in 1939 when the United States was in the midst of the Great Depression, and it was effective because it promised a bargain. By 1949 Americans had more money to spend, and they were concerned about the health benefits of soft drinks filled with sugar. So they advertised Pepsi as "the light refreshment," which meant it contained less sugar than Coke.

A few years ago TV ads showed crowds of fun loving Americans who called themselves the "Pepsi Generation" and urged viewers to join them on the soda pop bandwagon.

Later, Pepsi moved into the China market with this advertisement: "**Come alive with the Pepsi Generation.**" This message fizzled, however, because it came out as "**Pepsi brings back your dead ancestors.**"

The bandwagon is alive and well today. Rock and roll bands encourage spectators sometimes to join them on the bandstand, and jump into the frenzied crowd. Bandwagon appeal comes alive, electronically, every Sunday when football fans crowd into their favorite Las Vegas bar and talk the language of true believers, namely "long bomb," "penetration," "tight ends," "flex defense," and they are winning "this game in the trenches." Now your children can get on the bandwagon by learning to play Internet games with friends and "preverts."

While Green Bay's ferocious Packers were winning the Super Bowl in 1997, their rabid fans were calling themselves the "Cheese Heads." Then in 2001 the Lakers won the NBA with a star player who dances on his toes in a TV commercial and is not afraid to have some fun. This is our second mass psychology technique, known as **Plain Folks**.

❷ When propagandists or symbol manipulators play upon our pride in being ordinary and simple, they use the plain folks appeal. The American political culture reinforces a form of leveling which we proudly call "equality." This political value encourages politicians to figure out ways to hide their wealth, power and sophisticated charm by trying to appear ordinary and down-to-earth. So they kiss babies, wear casual clothes, admit once smoking marijuana [without inhaling, of course], and in the old days kept a log cabin around as their alleged place of birth.

By any standard, George Washington was a snob. His friends made bets to see who had the guts to place an unwelcome arm around George's broad shoulders. When he became a politician, however, dignified George had to become "good old boy" George. After being defeated twice for the Virginia House of Burgesses, the future President figured out what he had to do to win. Instead of lofty speeches, Washington filled Virginia voters with rum, wine, beer, and brandy. Then he won, by 310 votes to 45. According to historian Herbert Agar, the aloof Washington came down to the level of ordinary people long enough to bribe them with "about forty gallons of rum punch, twenty-eight gallons of wine, twenty-six gallons of rum, forty-six gallons of beer, six gallons of Madeira, and three and a half pints of brandy." "Having learned the secret of success," wrote Agar sardonically, "Washington remained in the House of Burgesses until he left Virginia to head the Army of the Revolution."[13]

❸ Because Washington was a revolutionary war hero and our first President, he was the new nation's first genuine hero. **Hero Worship**, however, requires more than good deeds. It means having a good press agent or, as they might say today, an "image consultant." Washington's image consultant was the writer Mason Locke Weems, known to his contemporaries as "Parson." Weems invented the famous story of Washington chopping his father's cherry tree with an axe, and proudly confessing. Hitler's followers in the United States adopted Washington as their hero. When the German-American Bund held a Madison Square Garden rally in New York City on February 20, 1939, a thirty-foot picture of George Washington served as a backdrop. The National Socialists admired Washington because he enjoyed a reputation for stern discipline. This was George's big appeal. He was a man of character, who always kept his emotions under control.

After the assassinations of John F. Kennedy, Robert Kennedy, and Martin Luther King, Jr., Americans were wary of idolizing high profile political figures. So they turned to sports heros as their primary heroes. Probably the greatest current sports celebrity is the professional golfer Tiger Woods. Like Washington, Tiger is stoic but carries an overwhelming desire to win. Like George W., Tiger W. has a proud father.

For their heroes, Americans prefer macho men like George Washington. And we prefer heroes who have the capacity to take a joke. That includes a 350-pound Laker center who dances on his toes.

Hero worship has undergone a metamorphosis, and emerged from the groins of mass culture as the modern **Celebrity**. Beat painter Andy Worhol once predicted 15 minutes of fame for everyone. This flippant prediction may be coming true, as Americans do their worst to get invited to a TV talk show or get to "survive" on an island.

What do Debree Murphee, Jessica Hahn and Donna Rice have in common? All three are ordinary women who became celebrities. Hahn reportedly earned one million dollars for her *Playboy* layout seven years after an encounter with TV preacher Jim Bakker. Rice made a few appearances touting jeans after allegedly having an affair with Presidential hopeful Gary Hart. Murphee got six figures for appearing in a *Penthouse* spread celebrating her motel meetings with televangelist Jimmy Swaggert.

> In recent years, Americans have discovered that many popular heroes are non-conforming exhibitionists. Imagine a painting of George Washington with orange hair, tatoos, and a nose ring. Would a Washington make-over diminish his reputation in your eyes? Why or why not?

During the Clinton presidency, Paula Jones has been a celebrity for her sexual harassment suit claiming that Bill Clinton once exposed himself to impress her. How did that issue end up? Are there any other "celebrities" whose sexual adventures have put them in the headlines?

By qualifying to travel into space on the NASA Challenger in 1986, Wyoming science teacher Christa McAullife was a sure candidate to be a genuine national hero, not a shallow celebrity. Instead, she became a national **martyr**.

❹ The **Martyr** is a person who chooses to suffer or die rather than change a belief or surrender to the enemy. They clearly made this point in the World War II movie "Bataan," which shows the deaths of heroic Americans who refuse to surrender to the Japanese. During the American Revolution, Nathan Hale spied on the British, was captured and executed. When he was to be hanged, Hale uttered these famous words, "I only regret that I have but one life to lose for my country" and became a symbol of the Revolutionary spirit.

Nathan Hale died a war hero. Christa McAullife, in contrast, died helping to promote our space program. Have we created a new brand of hero-martyr who sacrifices, not for religion or a political ideology but for technology?

Christa McAuliffe was the school teacher astronaut who died in the tragic explosion of the Challenger space shuttle in 1986. If the space shuttle had completed its mission, we would remember McAullife as a trivia question. However, her shocking death made her a martyr, of sorts. The soldiers on Bataan died rather than surrender. Nathan Hale remained a patriot to the end. Christa McAullife died promoting the NASA space program. Her death inspired an Evanston, Wyoming science teacher to proclaim proudly that Christa had died in the line of duty; "her duty as a teacher."

American historians martyred Nathan Hale because he believed in a cause. Another famous martyr, Joan of Arc, died for her religious beliefs. Christa McAullife, on the other hand, died trying to show that our space program was important enough to risk lives.

❺ The flip side of hero and martyr is the **Villain**. In the past, we portrayed male villains in the stage plays as sneaky jerks who wore curled mustaches and were always trying to seduce the heroine. Occasionally, a melodrama like "Love Rides the Rails" shows villainous Snidely Whiplash lust after Penelope. Or it shows a woman of easy virtue [active sex life] trying to seduce uptight virtuous hero Dudley Doright.

In mass societies, villains are useful. They give audiences an opportunity to hate vicariously without feeling strong emotions like anger or guilt. In his novel *1984*, George Orwell has the people of Oceania engage daily in two minute "hates," during which their leaders encourage them to curse the televised faces of national enemies. In Orwell's novel the chief scapegoat is Emmanuel Goldstein, a renegade backslider who presumably deserted socialism and disappeared. Somewhere he is alive and hiding. As portrayed in *1984*, the mention of Goldstein causes people's stomachs to tighten and they get sick to their stomachs. So the two minute hates are the equivalent of taking Tums after a bad date.

❻ Having a single villain for an entire society to hate is an old custom. Among the Hebrews, the **Scapegoat** gave the people an opportunity to blame one person for the collective feelings of guilt, sin, or inadequacy. On the Day of Atonement a high priest would transfer to a goat all the transgressions which had occurred during the previous year. They would then drive the goat out of the village and kill it. The ancient Greeks had a similar ritual. If a city was suffering plague or famine or losing a war, the Greek leaders would single out an ugly or deformed person to suffer all the afflictions. They took this human scapegoat,

During World War II, American movie audiences watched Bugs Bunny and Popeye cartoons which portrayed Japanese soldiers as stupid, cruel and clumsy stereotypes. These cartoons are still available, but the U.S. is no longer at war with Japan. Should such "racist" cartoons be banned?

according to Frazer, to a central location, and gave him figs, bread and cheese. After eating, the scapegoat was beaten with branches while flute players piped a particular song. After the ceremony, the unfortunate person was burned alive and his ashes cast into the sea.

The most brutal use of scapegoating was by Hitler, who blamed Jews for Germany's loss of World War I and had millions killed in the holocaust. Josef Stalin, leader of the former Soviet Union, was another ruthless user of the scapegoat technique. After the assassination of his sidekick S.M. Kirov in 1934, Stalin conducted a purge of top communists and made them scapegoats for every ailment that afflicted Soviet society.

In his play *The Crucible* (1955), Arthur Miller showed the mind set of an accused witch. Events of 1692 inspired the play when the people of Salem Village, Massachusetts executed witches to purge themselves of evil spirts thought to have caused bad luck.

Miller's play was designed to show that the Salem witch trials were similar to the communist witch hunts going on in the United States a few years after World War II ended. During the late 1940's actors, directors and writers became scapegoats for America's apparent inability to stem communism around the world. The House Un-American Activities Committee accused the scapegoats of making movies sympathetic to the Soviet Union and communism during World War II. This witch hunt continued into the 1950's under Wisconsin Senator Joseph R. McCarthy, who accused the U.S. State Department of being filled with Communists.

❼When we describe all white men as rich and greedy, the mass psychology technique used is **Stereotyping**. They have aimed most stereotypes in our society at minorities, like African Americans whom they portrayed in old movies as lazy, ignorant and afraid of ghosts. Two movies come to mind. The first,

During one of his comedy routines broadcast over HBO, George Carlin blamed the corruption of American language on rich, greedy, white men. Are white men becoming the current scapegoats?

released in 1915, was entitled, "Birth of a Nation" and was designed by director D. W. Griffith to show what happened under carpet bag rule after the Civil War. The second, "Guess Who's Coming to Dinner?" (1967), features handsome black actor Sidney Poitier meeting for the first time the parents of his white woman friend. The movie stereotypes Poitier as a highly successful, perfect gentleman who has to persuade parents Spencer Tracey and Katharine Hepburn that he deserves their shallow, but virtuous daughter.

Stereotypes are fixed or conventional notions about one's nationality, gender, or religion. In the past Italian peddlers were portrayed on stage as agitated, Jewish pawnbrokers rubbed their hands in selfish glee. Male Negro characters turned white with fright when they heard ghosts. And women were always portrayed in the past as helpless screamers.

Current stereotypes show Italians as mob bosses and women as just as aggressive and violent as men. Someday, perhaps, we'll see TV dramas where white men scream when frightened and have to be rescued by muscular feminists. Or will we?

> To gain "empowerment," many Americans want to ban those words which are racist, sexist, and otherwise hurtful. Many advocates of women's rights want to eliminate sexist language from the national vocabulary. This has led to new words like "firefighter" replacing the old gender-limiting "fireman." Like any social movement of true believers, the advocates of language change went too far. They decided to abandon descriptive words like "disabled" and replaced them with unclear euphemisms like "differently abled." Critics call these new words "politically correct" and make fun of the people who use them. In 1992 writers Henry Beard and Christopher Cerf satirized the new words in their $10 book *The Official Politically Correct Dictionary and Handbook*. In this best seller, Beard and Cerf showed how silly abstractions like "chemically inconvenienced" had replaced traditional words like "drunk."
>
> Myrne Roe, editorial writer for the Wichita (Kansas) *Eagle*, saw nothing funny in the satire aimed at politically correct words. Roe defended the new words as the best way to stop hurtful speech. Moreover, she thinks changing fireman to firefighter has increased the number of women who work as firefighters. Roe defended being politically correct, and argued that people who insist on using "hateful words" are arrogant and insensitive. (Source: Myrne Roe, "The Arrogance of the Anti-Politically Correct," Las Vegas *Review Journal* (August 31, 1992), p. 9B.
>
> What do you think? Should we poke fun at these new words, or take them seriously as a sincere attempt to end insensitivity?

Techniques of Manipulation

In *Through the Looking Glass*, Lewis Carroll has Alice arguing with Humpty Dumpty over the meaning of the word "glory." Eventually, Humpty Dumpty scornfully ends the argument by proclaiming that a word "means just what I choose it to mean—neither more nor less."

> The four major techniques of manipulation are:
> ① using words to control,
> ② seeing conspiracies everywhere,
> ③ association, and
> ④ the subliminal messages and the subconscious.

❶ We fight most political controversies over **Words**. Pro-Life and Pro-Choice can't seem to agree when the fetus becomes a "child," or when "life begins," or when it becomes "viable," or what the mother's "freedom of choice" should mean.

We learned earlier that humans are unique in their capacity to give arbitrary meaning to a series of letters or figures. Every human civilization possesses this capacity to symbolize, from tribes to bureaucracies. The savage Kenyahs of Borneo have a poison which they pour in rivers to kill the fish. While planning their deadly task, the Kenyahs talk in loud voices about their "fish leaves," which means the deadly tuba root they use to poison the fish. The Kenyah use the words "fish leaves" instead of "poison" because they don't want the cats, birds or insects to hear their poison scheme and warn the fish.[14]

During the Persian Gulf War, American military spokespersons used special jargon to describe the action. When we bombed military targets, the Pentagon officials used words like "suppress their assets," "degraded," "eliminated," or "neutralized." When American planes bombed anti-aircraft batteries, we described them as engaging in "airborne sanitation."

British novelist George Orwell was always bitter about the way politicians and military leaders manipulated words. Orwell noted how the word "pacification" meant bombing defenseless villages, machine gunning cattle, and torching village huts. When Orwell made these observations more than forty years ago, Soviet people were being imprisoned for years without trial, or shot in the back of the neck, or sent to die of scurvy in Arctic lumber camps. All this was done, said Orwell, because Soviet leaders wanted to eliminate "undesirable elements."[15]

During the Vietnam War, American military leaders tried to eliminate communist influence in the Mekong Delta by bombing villages, defoliating crops, and forcing peasants to leave their land. Rather than admit we were conducting a policy of terror, American spokespersons called it an "Accelerated Pacification Campaign."

When the Nevada Department of Wildlife issues permits to kill excess deer, they call it "game management." We know game managers as "sportsmen." Sportsmen like to "hunt," which means to kill deer.

Such words as "fish leaves," "accelerated pacification campaign," and "game management" are called **Euphemisms**. These are words and phrases invented to hide grim reality. In his book *A Dictionary of Euphemisms & Other Doubletalk,* (1983), Hugh Rawson, who is a recognized expert on euphemisms, says they come in six shapes, namely:

☆ **Foreign Words**: Afraid to use the naughty American word that means the lower rear part of the human trunk? Use the British word "arse" or the French "derriere."

☆ **Abbreviations**: Stuck for a gentle put-down? Try SOB.

☆ **Abstractions**: Stuck for a way to describe your best friend's malady, without being totally insulting? Don't call him a drunk, try the abstraction "problem drinker."

☆ **Indirection**: When generals order a "retreat," they say, "We are breaking off contact with the enemy at 0815 hours." This makes a humiliating situation sound well planned and logical.

☆ **Understatement**: Nuclear officials have mastered the art of understatement, largely because they deal with the grim reality of annihilation. So when a nuclear reactor is out of control, nuclear officials call it, "above critical." When teachers mean, "you're in danger of flunking," they understate: "You may need to study harder."

☆ **Long Words**: Long titles to describe small jobs are rampant. If you decide to pump gas for a living, you can call yourself a "petroleum transfer engineer." If you drive a truck delivering potato chips expect your customers to refer to you respectfully as their "Executive Snack Route Consultant."

Why are euphemisms so popular? As Orwell suggested, many government leaders have a special interest in hiding what they are doing. Moreover, people who share these special meanings feel they belong to an elite group. Military officers, for example, develop a common bond when they share in the special knowledge that "ballistically induced aperture in the subcutaneous environment" means a bullet hole in a human target. Teachers also have a special language. We don't teach you "how to think" anymore. Now, we are "enhancing your ability to process concepts." Teenagers have always had special words like bad, cute, cool, devastating, mean, keen, marvelous, swell, terrific, etc. Many now have special sign language that says, "I'm in a gang, and I'm gonna waste you if you 'dis' me."

We pay professional athletes for their speed, agility and strength, not their vocabularies. Some are "vocabularies impaired" so they have to fall back on the ubiquitous "you know" during interviews that last more than one sentence. Some athletes, however, are "verbally talented," and they end making millions—much more than college professors—as TV analysts. We can hear them every day on TV describing games in the special jargon of sports. Golf analysts, for example, use words like, "killing snakes" and "yips." Know what these words mean? Congratulations, you're a member of that special elite known as the weekend hacker.

Doctors spend lots of time on the golf course, hoping to escape the pressure of their medical practice and all the lawsuits. With liability insurance soaring, doctors have learned that vague language is safer than honesty. When a patient has an adverse reaction to a drug, doctors now say, "Your biochemistry differs from most." They used to say, "I guess I should have given you a different drug."

The American Psychiatric Association in 1952 published the first edition of their desk manual, known as the "Diagnostic and Statistical Manual of Mental Disorders," or DSM. This first edition listed 60 categories of mental diseases that included such favorites as paranoia and schizophrenia. By the time the fourth edition was published 42 years later, there were more than 350 mental diseases listed. Among these new mental diseases is "Paraphillic Coercive Disorder." This exotic sounding mental disease is sometimes used to give a label to men who rape. It is described as being preoccupied with intense urges and sexually arousing fantasies that involve forced sexual conduct. Feminists are outraged that rape is being defined as a mental disorder, and want psychiatrists to stop using euphemisms like PCD.

❷ **Conspiracy Theories.** In 1905 Russian Serge Nilus published forged documents known now as "The Protocols of the Elders of Zion." This document purported to outline secret Jewish plans for achieving world power by controlling the world's banks and undermining the morality, family life and health of gentiles. Hitler read the forgeries, believed they were true and had millions of Jews killed after he became the leader of Germany. Many Americans, however, believe such documents are real and believe the world is in danger of being taken over by an international conspiracy, sometimes called the New World Order. These Americans worry about the IRS, Secular Humanists, the Trilateral Commission, the FBI, and the United Nations.

Feminists are angry with words like "Paraphillic Coercive Disorder" because PCD sounds like a disease while, in their opinion, "rape" should be considered morally wrong, and a crime against

One conspiracy theory blames high-ranking U.S. officials and Dallas oil men for the assassination of President John F. Kennedy on November 22, 1963. Kennedy was shot and killed by bullets that came from the sixth floor of the Texas School Book Depository. Dallas police later arrested a 24-year-old former U.S. Marine named Lee Harvey Oswald, who had lived in the Soviet Union, married the daughter of a colonel in the Soviet KGB, and handed out literature for the Fair Play for Cuba Committee at New Orleans. Two days later, Oswald was shot to death by Dallas nightclub owner Jack Ruby. After investigating the assassination, a special commission headed by Chief Justice Earl Warren announced in September 1964 that Oswald acting alone had killed Kennedy. Although they criticized the Warren Commission Report, its conclusions became conventional wisdom.

> Interested in conspiracy theories? Get on the World Wide Web and try this address: http://w3one.net/~conspira for the Kennedy Assassination. And if interested in UFO's, try http://medianet.nbnet.nb.ca/ufo/index.htm

In 1991, however, movie audiences saw a different version of the truth. Using mind-boggling special effects, director Oliver Stone's movie *JFK* argued strongly that Kennedy was the victim of a conspiracy among top ranking U.S. government officials. They drummed this message into the movie audiences by new wave editing effects popularized by MTV. During an interview, Stone admitted that he purposely reached for the subconscious minds of his audience. He told the reporter, "We want to get to the subconscious . . . and certainly seduce the viewer into a new perception of reality."[16]

In recent years, some African Americans have jumped on the conspiracy bandwagon. For three days in August 1996 the San Jose *Mercury* published a series of articles alleging that federal agents used millions of dollars from the sale of cocaine in the ghettos of Los Angeles to finance the CIA-backed Nicaraguan rebel army during the Reagan administration. Though unproven, the *Mercury* story gave African Americans a plausible explanation for the prevalence of "crack" in their neighborhoods. Other popular conspiracy theories include:

> △ **AIDS is a genocidal federal plot to eliminate the black race.** △ **In the 1960s the FBI employed illegal tactics to disrupt the civil rights movement.** △ **Over a 40-year period black men with syphilis were allowed to die.**

> In 1997 President Clinton formally apologized because the Public Health Service in the 1930's let black men with syphilis die without treatment so they could study the long-term effects of the disease. Was this apology justified?

❸ **Association**. When TV viewers see young models wearing T-shirts and jeans draped erotically around their bodies, the name Calvin Klein comes to mind. This is the power of **association**, which is a very simple and effective way to manipulate the masses. When the propagandist brings in **negative** symbols to slander opponents, he is using **guilt by association**. During the 1988 Presidential campaign, Republican George Bush used this tactic by suggesting that Democrat Michael Dukakis was responsible for a Massachusetts weekend furlough program that allowed Willie Horton to escape and rape a woman. Since Horton was black and the raped woman was white, the ad made Dukakis look bad.

Hitler is a favorite hate symbol. Whenever there is an anti-abortion rally, someone shows up with a picket sign proclaiming "Hitler was pro-abortion too!" Since Hitler's government gave bonuses to women who bore children for his master race, perhaps we should give him a pro-life label.

Should the infamous "N" word be banned from literature? Chicago educator John H. Wallace was shocked when as a high school student they required him to read *The Adventures of Huckleberry Finn*. According to Wallace, the "N" word appears in the novel more than 200 times. To protect other African-Americans, Wallace published a new

> Should the "N" word be removed from all its sources? Should the word be judged obscene, and banished from all proper usage? Should verbal use of the "N" word be considered a "hate crime" and suitably punished?

edition of Mark Twain's classic. In this modern update, the "N" word has been replaced by the euphemisms "slave," "black man," or "Jim." The update also removes other offensive references to African-Americans. Judith Krug, Director of the American Library Association's Office for Intellectual Freedom, criticized the changes saying Wallace's rewrite stripped the original book of its irony.

❹ **Subliminal Messages and the Subconscious Mind.** The most startling treatment of "brainwashing" is the 1962 movie "The Manchurian Candidate." With the Korean War as its background, the movie shows a squad of captured American soldiers brainwashed by the enemy. The soldiers are then sent back to the United States, unaware that they have been programmed to help the communists take over the United States. Although 35 years old, the movie effectively demonstrates the power of subliminal messages on the subconscious mind. This type of brainwashing supposedly goes on all the time in advertising.

In 1982 Bill Gillespie, a candidate for the doctoral degree at the University of Kentucky, accused large, national advertising agencies of intentionally hiding words and images in their ads. During an interview with writer Jim Jordan, Gillespie said he found the word "sex" hidden in a T-shirt decal, a phallic symbol in a restaurant ad, and a four-letter obscenity in a cigarette ad. Gillespie said the most common themes hidden in these ads were love, sex and death. These hidden words, according to Gillespie, register in the subconscious and cause people's hearts to beat faster, their blood pressure to increase, and deeper breathing.[17]

Two retail stores operated by the Seattle-based Jay Jacobs chain in 1985 were using a series of barely audible spoken messages played on recorded soundtracks, which told shoppers, "We arrest shoplifters . . . stay honest . . . don't steal."

Some men are using subliminal messages to take control of the mating game these days. The Mephisto Metamorphics Company sells a cassette which carries a subliminal message designed to arouse a woman and focus her attention on one man. The 60-minute tape—which can be popped into a car stereo on a date—combines music and subconscious commands telling the woman that her date is a good, faithful man who is attractive and a great lover.

Russian physiologist Ivan Petrovich Pavlov earned an international reputation by conditioning his dog to associate the sound of a bell with food. Eventually, the brainwashed dog drooled whenever it heard the bell. In his novel *Brave New World*, Aldous Huxley uses Pavlovian conditioning to make lower caste children afraid to read books and pick flowers. They bring tiny children into a room where they are encouraged to crawl toward flowers and books. Just as the children touch the objects, they are blasted with loud noises and shocked with electricity. For the rest of their lives, these children will associate flowers and books with unpleasant memories.

They also program Huxley's citizens through a form of sleep teaching known as *hypnopaedia*. While they sleep, the citizens of brave new world repeatedly hear these phrases: "I love new clothes, I love new clothes," "ending is better than mending,

What would be the purpose of burying these words in the subconscious of young Americans, "I love new clothes, I love new clothes."

ending is better than mending," and "the more stitches, the less riches, the more stitches, the less riches."

The World According to Orwell

Imagine living in a world where TV watches you, sex is an act of treason, and people with the wrong facial expression go to the Ministry of Love to be tortured and executed. British novelist George Orwell imagined such a world in 1948 and described it in his famous novel *1984*.

The novel has a simple story. It describes a few weeks in the life of Winston Smith, a 39-year-old bureaucrat who works for the government of Oceania, forging history in the Ministry of Truth. Smith lives in a drab apartment where he is forced daily to do Jane Fonda-like exercises under the supervision of a female gymnast, who watches him through the TV set. During his free time, Smith drinks synthetic "Victory Coffee" and "Victory Gin," both of which are tasteless.

Eventually, Smith has an affair with a young woman, Julia. Julia also works for the Ministry of Truth, and her job in Pornsec is to write dirty books for the lower classes. Julia is a member of the Anti-Sex League, and helps monitor party members who might have lust on their minds. Smith and Julia do their lovemaking in woods outside London, where they can't be overheard by hidden microphones, nor seen by Thoughtpolice helicopters.

Later, Smith is befriended by O'Brien, a member of Oceania's ruling Inner Party. By mistake, Smith thinks O'Brien is part of a conspiracy to overthrow Oceania's dictator, known as "Big Brother." To entrap Smith, O'Brien gives him a subversive history book which explains how an atomic war destroyed the world in the 1950s, and the Inner Party gained control of Oceania.

After reading this taboo account of English Socialism (Ingsoc), Smith returns to Julia. To get some pleasure from their dull lives, Winston and Julia set up a love nest above a curio shop in the slums of London. However, at the height of their happiness, they are arrested by the Thoughtpolice—who have been watching them from the start.

At the Ministry of Love, Winston is tortured and interrogated by O'Brien in Room 101. In this room, everyone's worst fears are exploited. Winston is afraid of rats. So they placed a cage of hungry rats over his head. The only barrier between Smith's eyes and the hungry rats is a small door. As the door begins to open, Smith screams, "Do it to Julia! Do it to Julia! Not me! Julia!! Not me!!"

After the rat cage, Smith will do whatever Big Brother wants. There is no love left for either Smith or Julia; they have betrayed each other. By the end of the novel, Smith is sitting at the Chestnut Tree Bar in London, swilling Victory Gin and blubbering out his hopes that Oceania wins its latest war. Smith will eventually be shot and become an "unperson."

The words "Big Brother," "Thought crime," and Orwellian are very much a part of our national vocabulary. These words refer to an oppressive government that uses technology and fear to give every citizen the same opinions, passions and interests. In his book *Cultural Literacy: What Every American Needs to Know*, E. D. Hirsch has an extensive appendix that lists "what every literate American should know." The Hirsch list includes "George Orwell" and "Big Brother is Watching You." Are these Orwellian words important enough to be learned in high school?

Orwell's *1984* is not merely a love story about Winston Smith and Julia. It is a cautionary tale about what can happen if any ruling faction achieves the power to:

✠ Make citizens fight perpetual war against real or imagined enemies.
✠ Repress all political dissent.
✠ Suppress all natural instincts, like sex.
✠ Create a special language designed to limit thought.
✠ Manipulate history.

In *1984*, Oceania is constantly at war with the other two world powers, Eurasia and Eastasia. These wars are used by Oceania's ruling elite to justify the scarcity of consumer products and to mobilize hatred against real and imagined enemies. Since the enemy on some days is Eurasia and at other times is Eastasia, the Inner Party has to keep changing the facts of the past to convince Oceania's people that yesterday's evil empire is today's friendly and helpful ally.

Political repression is a way of life in Oceania. The Thoughtpolice are everywhere looking for people guilty of face crime, thought crime or own life. Adults are controlled through the children, who scurry through the streets dressed in the snappy blue uniforms and red neckerchiefs of the Youth Leagues. Youth League members are rewarded for informing on any adult who looks suspicious. Everyone is expected to participate in the daily two-minute hates and the week long hate rallies. Citizens who avoid the rallies are guilty of "own life," hunted down and sent to the Ministry of Love.

To control the masses, the ruling elite has Oceania's scientists dedicate their talents to finding ways to make people conform. Instead of finding ways to cure disease, Oceania's scientists work on truth drugs, shock therapy and electronic spying.

Orwell envisioned sex being used in the future to control political behavior. To keep party members loyal, the government of Oceania prohibits all casual sex. To make sure the rules are followed, young women are recruited for the Anti-Sex League and spend their time looking for signs of love or lust—both banned behavior. At party meetings the favorite lecture topic is how to abolish the orgasm.

The lower classes, however, are not controlled through the sex ban. Instead, they are free to live normal sex lives, but enhanced by a steady diet of pornography and electronic music fed to them through the Ministry of Truth.

Orwell's greatest contribution to our understanding of power is his portrayal of the way governments manipulate language. In Oceania traditional English has been replaced by a new language called **Newspeak**. Oceania's coffee, for example, is never tasty, tangy or cold. The proper Newspeak words are "plusgood," "good" or "ungood."

During the 1930's in the Soviet Union, people who were good at appearing to accept the "party line" without question were sarcastically called "politically correct" by those Russians who opposed Stalin and communism. In the United States, "PC" has emerged to label people who want to eliminate insensitive language. The politically correct movement ranges from Native Americans who want to ban the Cleveland Indians' mascot "Chief Wahoo" to Feminists who would replace "woman" with "womyn." Is the PC movement a reasonable way to deal with controversial symbols and words, or has it become a serious threat to freedom of expression? Is there a third possibility?

In his book *Doublespeak* (1981), William Lutz demonstrates how government bureaucracies create long titles and tongue twisting acronyms. His favorite is the federal agency known as the "Federal Insurance Administration, Office of Risk Assessment, Technical Operations Division, Production Control Branch of the Federal Emergency Management Agency," also known as "FIA/ORA/TOD/PCB/FEMA." Government agencies in Orwell's nightmare world are not funny, however. The "Ministry of Truth" is where lies are invented. War is planned by the "Ministry of Peace." The "Ministry of Plenty" provides statistics to prove that Oceania's hungry people have plenty of food. People are tortured in the "Ministry of Love." If they escape death, Oceania's "traitors" are sent to forced labor camps known as "joycamps." The walls of Oceania are plastered with slogans that suggest doublethink, namely "War is Peace," "Ignorance is Strength," "Love is Hate," and the admired leader Big Brother is "Watching You."

By manipulating words and meanings, the government of Oceania promotes *doublethink*. This means the mental capacity of having contradictory beliefs simultaneously. Oceania's citizens, for example, see nothing wrong with loving a Big Brother who tortures them. Nor does it bother them to shout "War is Peace." Through fear, brain washing, and propaganda, the government of Oceania has created citizens whose minds are scrambled. The result of all the manipulation is **crimestop**. The people of Oceania are simply incapable of thinking any heretical thoughts. Before any skeptical thoughts can enter their minds, these people stop it. Moreover, their minds are so confused that they are simply unable to grasp analogies, recognize logical errors, or understand even simple arguments. Whenever they are asked to think, they get bored. **Orwellian**, then, means any practice that destroys human dignity, perpetuates war, suppresses natural instincts, or encourages collective stupidity.

Mutability of the Past

The Japanese people would like to forget Pearl Harbor, Bataan, and Midway. They consider these events to be *mizu ni nagasu*, which means "water under the bridge." So the facts about these events are kept out of Japanese school textbooks, popular literature, films, and TV. Americans, on the other hand, would like to forget an executive order signed by President Franklin D. Roosevelt on

On March 20, 1997 the House of Representatives voted 295 to 136 to ban "partial-birth abortions" except in cases in which the mother's life is in danger. The vote came nearly one year after President Clinton vetoed a similar law. If the Senate approves the ban by a two-thirds majority, it can go into effect without Presidential approval. Throughout, the partial-birth abortion issue has been debated around the question "What is a partial-birth abortion, and what does 'freedom of choice' mean?"

February 19, 1942 giving the Secretary of War sweeping powers to remove "any or all" persons from specified "military areas." Under this order, about 120,000 Japanese Americans were rounded up and forced to move to tar paper barracks built in places like California's deserts and the swamps of Arkansas. These Americans were forced into relocation camps because U.S. officials were afraid they would sabotage the country's war effort against Japan. History shows, however, that none of these relocated Japanese Americans was ever convicted of sabotage.

Henry Ford liked to say "history is bunk." He always hated books; they were a waste of time. In *Brave New World*, Aldous Huxley has his pragmatic and pleasure seeking hedonists worshiping Ford's assembly line and whispering the words "Our Ford" when they felt in a sacred mood. George Orwell, however, shows just how far governments will go to destroy history and make heroes out of a Big Brother who controls people by controlling their past.

In Oceania, the ruling elite understood the power of history, and lived by the dictum: "Who controls the past controls the future; who controls the present controls the past." Winston Smith's job, as a forger in the Ministry of Truth, was to change history when Big Brother made any mistakes. On a typical day, Smith might get a message in Newspeak that says "times 17, 3, 84 bb speech malreported africa rectify." He then dialed the telescreen for a copy of the London *Times* for March 17, 1984, which reported on that day that Big Brother had predicted the South Indian front would remain quiet, but an Eurasian offensive would be launched soon in North Africa. Big Brother was wrong, however. The Eurasian offensive was launched in South Africa and the armies of Oceania had suffered a humiliating defeat. To cover Big Brother's mistake, Smith rewrites the speech to make him predict what actually happened.

Orwell's "Ministry of Truth" was his way of showing how history can be manipulated by governments. In the former Soviet Union, for example, school children learned through their history books that John F. Kennedy was assassinated by "ultrarightists linked to the CIA and FBI who were carrying out the will of the oil magnates of Texas."

Orwell's Big Brother government used a "memory hole" in Winston Smith's office to dispose of embarrassing facts. Hollywood movie makers, on the other hand, can change history without worrying about hiding embarrassing distortions. In their book *Past Imperfect: History According to the Movies* (1995), the Society of American Historians singles out 59 movies as examples of historical distortion. In the recent movie *JFK*, for example, director Oliver Stone reenacted the Kennedy assassination by placing a gunman behind the stockade fence on the famous "grassy knoll" in Dealey Plaza. According to reviewer Stanley Karnow, railway signalman Sam Holland had told the Warren Commission of a "puff of smoke" he had seen just after the shots. Many conspiracy theorists believe Holland's story to be evidence of a second assassin. While filming the scene, however, Stone had difficulty finding a rifle that would produce enough smoke for a puff to be seen on film. To produce the necessary visual effect, Stone had a prop man pump smoke from a bellows.

If you want to verify Karnow's account of Oliver Stone's movie JFK, you need the following footnote: Stanley Karnow, "JFK" in Mark C. Carnes (ed.), *Past Imperfect: History According to the Movies*, (New York: Henry Holt and Company, 1995), pp. 270-273.

There were no women among the 55 delegates to the 1787 Constitutional Convention. So when Meussel School of South Bend, Indiana did a play about the Convention only boys were cast. In protest, 10-year-old Meussel student Sarah Rosen led 14 girls and four boys in a protest singing

"We Shall Overcome" and "The Star Spangled Banner." The demonstration caused one boy to drop out of the play. The protest, however, made Sarah Rosen a celebrity, and she was named by *Ms Magazine* as one of the publication's "Women of the Year" in 1987. ☆ In your opinion, did Sarah Rosen deserve to be named a woman of the year? Was her protest justified?

The following news story appeared in the April 29, 1997 sports section of the Las Vegas *Review Journal* under the headline "Zoeller trades racial quips with black golfer."

GREENVILLE, S.C. — Fuzzy Zeoller, trying to joke his way out of trouble over racially insensitive remarks, traded quips with a black golfer Monday about "fried chicken" and "watermelon." Playing at the Thornblade Classic, his first outing since his comments about Tiger Woods, Zoeller had an exchange this time with his friend, Victor McBryde. "Hey, Fuzzy," yelled McBryde, on the tee box two holes ahead of Zoeller. He shouted to McBryde about getting "you some fried chicken." McBryde told Zoeller not to forget the "cornbread." And Zoeller replied, "How about some watermelon?" Later Monday, Zoeller read a statement to CNN/Sl. "I've had a lot of time to think over the past several days. Race has been a serious issue in this country for years. But it still seems to me that we have to stop being so sensitive about things. I'm white, Vic McBryde is black, so what? I kidded him, he kidded me back. If we don't learn to laugh at each other and ourselves, we're not ever going to get along." Last week, Zoeller apologized for calling Woods "that little boy" and for asking the Masters champion not to order friend chicken or collard greens for next year's champions dinner.

When the Chicago Bulls played the Utah Jazz for the 1997 NBA title in Salt Lake City Dennis Rodman made derogatory remarks about Mormons and was fined $50,000. Was this fair?

Do you agree with Fuzzy Zeoller's statement "we have to stop being so sensitive about things?"

Notes

1. Frazer, *The Golden Bough,* pp. 52-55.

2. William L. Shirer, *20ᵗʰ Century Journey: A Memoir of the Life and Times II, The Nightmare, 1930-1940* (Boston: Little, Brown and Company, 1984), pp. 367-368.

3. Garry Wills, "A Fantasy Breeds a Scandal," *Newsweek* (December 29, 1986), p. 22.

4. Roger D. Masters, "Nice Guys Don't Finish Last: Aggressive and Appeasement Gestures in Media Images of Politicians," paper delivered at 1982 Annual Meeting of the American Association for the Advancement of Science.

5. Glenn Lovell, "Film Stirs Discussion of Sex and Brutality in the Age of AIDS," Las Vegas *Review Journal* (February 6, 1992), p. 8D.

6. "Playing Office Politics," *Newsweek* (September 16, 1985), pp. 54-59.

7. Sam Keen, "Why Americans Love to Lie," *Family Weekly* (December 5, 1982), pp. 4-9.

8. Frazer, *The Golden Bough*, pp. 309-319.

9. Allan Bullock, *Hitler: A Study in Tyranny*, rev. ed. (New York: Harper & Row Publishers, 1962), pp. 373-374.

10. Shirer, *Twentieth Century Journey*, p. 119.

11. Aldous Huxley, *Brave New World Revisited* (New York: Harper & Row Publishers, 1958), p. 42.

12. Brown, *Techniques of Persuasion*, pp. 179-180.

13. Herbert Agar, *The Price of Union* (Boston: Houghton Mifflin Company, 1950), p. 26.

14. Mario Pei, *The Story of Language*, rev. ed. (Philadelphia: J. B. Lippincott Company, 1965), p. 253.

15. George Orwell, "Politics and the English Language," in Charles Muscantine and Marlene Griffith (eds.), *The Borzoi College Reader* (New York: Alfred A. Knopf, 1966), pp. 74-85.

16. Richard D. Heffner, "War Against 'JFK' Acknowledge Triumph of Visual Media Over Print," Las Vegas *Review Journal-Sun/Sunday* (February 23, 1992), p. 3D.

17. Las Vegas *Review Journal* (March 7, 1982).

Chapter 4

The Decision Makers

Locate a computer and ask to see a chart showing how the federal bureaucracy is organized. If you're good at surfing the net, you'll locate an organization chart of the federal government. That chart will show that the Constitution is at the top of the pyramid. Under the Constitution are the three major branches, the legislative, the executive, and the judicial. Under these three branches is a network of 14 departments titled agriculture, interior, commerce, justice, defense, labor, education, state, energy, transportation, health and human services, treasury, veterans affairs, and housing and urban development. Under these 14 departments you'll see 50 independent establishments and government corporations. At the bottom of this pyramid is the U.S. Postal Service with its 40,000 branches, 780,000 employees and $50 billion annual budget. At the top of the organization chart is the Constitution, a document that delegates to Congress limited powers that somehow have been stretched to create this vast and powerful bureaucracy.

Why do Americans have so many huge federal agencies? The U.S. Postal Service has 40,000 branches, 780,000 employees and a $50 billion annual budget. Does it take that much money and personnel to deliver the mail? Why can't we get by with fax machines, E-mail, and electronic fund transfers?

Consider the possible unintended consequences if the federal bureaucracy was completely destroyed by terrorists.

① We could eliminate the IRS and stop paying income taxes and an estate tax that now goes as high as 55% of the savings you've left your children.

② The Food and Drug Administration can be dismantled, but who's going to warn you about biotech industry food products that have genetically engineered ingredients.

③ The Centers for Disease Control and Prevention will not be around to warn American travelers the dangers of visiting nations where malaria and tuberculosis are rampant and very contagious.

④ Young Americans will continue drinking potentially dangerous high energy drinks like Red Bull, Adrenaline Rush, and Jones Whoop-Ass.

The FDA could experiment by using a double blind study in which one group drinks Red Bull, a second group is given a relatively harmless soda pop, and the third group gets flavored water which they think is "Adrenaline Rush." But is this right? Should government agencies like the FDA and the U.S. Marines get to experiment on volunteer citizens?

Back in 1932 the United States Public Health Service accepted the responsibility of medical treatment for nearly four hundred Macon County, Alabama black men who had syphilis. Instead of warning the men that they had the deadly disease, PHS doctors told them they had "bad blood." Rather than treat the men with medicine then being used, the doctors waited for them to die. After the black men died, the doctors performed autopsies and evaluated the damage. Doctors participated in this deadly experiment because they were curious to see if black people reacted any differently than whites to the ravages of syphilis.

Even after penicillin was developed in the 1940's, the PHS doctors continued to withhold treatment from the men and their families. In 1972 the cruel business in Alabama was exposed by Associated Press reporter Jean Heller. Nine years after the exposé, history professor James H. Jones told the complete story in his book *Bad Blood* (1981). Like any good historian, Jones tried to explain why for four decades PHS doctors had let their human guinea pigs die.

Between 1973 and 1996, the national government had paid over $10 million to a total of 6,000 victims of the Tuskegee experiment. In February 1997, HBO dramatized the cruel business in Alabama under the title "Miss Evers Boys." Then in May 1997, President Bill Clinton issued a formal apology to the survivors of the Tuskegee experiment.

In 1960 an American company tried to get Food and Drug Administration approval to market a tranquilizer under the brand name Kevadon. The tranquilizer was already being sold in West Germany and Great Britain under the name Thalidomide. It was being prescribed for sleeplessness, nervous tension, asthma, and relief of nausea in early pregnancy.

> **How could a bureaucracy in a democracy use humans as guinea pigs for such a cruel experiment? Do you know any other similar cases where a "sealed bureaucracy" conducted experiments on humans, or let them die of neglect?**

Dr. Frances Kelsey, a researcher for the FDA, would not certify that Thalidomide was safe. She had doubts because reports said it caused numbness in the hands and feet of some patients. As a result, the drug was not marketed in the United States. Because they had taken Thalidomide during pregnancy, several hundred West German and British women gave birth to deformed babies; and because Dr. Kelsey did her job, thousands of American babies were spared.

Thirty-six years later, however, the Food and Drug Administration was being criticized for allowing a potentially dangerous drug to be sold by prescription to Americans. The possibly dangerous drug is the popular anti-depressant Prozac, which had been singled out in 56 criminal cases as the reason for sudden violent behavior. The FDA was taking heat over Prozac because in 1991 it denied a petition filed by the Citizens Commission on Human Rights to take the drug off the market.

For the most part, the FDA is a friendly Big Brother agency that tries to protect ordinary Americans. It employs about 2,100 scientists who work in 40 laboratories in the Washington, D.C. area and around the country. These scientists analyze products for contamination by illegal substances and review test results of companies seeking approval for drugs, vaccines, food additives, coloring agents, and medical devices. FDA scientists also test food samples to see if unacceptable amounts of pesticides are present. Other FDA responsibilities include labeling standards for foods, blood bank operations, medical devices and cosmetic safety. To protect consumers, the FDA has some 1,100 investigators and inspectors who cover the country's almost 95,000 FDA-regulated businesses. These agents visit more than 15,000 facilities a year checking out about 80,000 product labels. In sum, the FDA regulates over $1 trillion worth of products, has approximately 9,000 employees to see that the cosmetics we use are harmless, the medicine safe, and the food healthy.

During 1996, FDA workers bought 300 of the nation's most consumed groceries and tested them for fat, salt, vitamins and other ingredients on the food labels. According to then FDA Commissioner David Kessler, the product labels were correct about 90% of the time. But if you like the Hostess Ding Dong, be careful. It contains more calories and grams of fat by about 30% than the nutrition label suggests. And if you like pizza, you'll have to wait until the Agriculture Department finishes its study of meat products, such as pepperoni pizzas.

Established in 1931, the FDA is one of about 80 regulatory services, commissions, agencies, and administrations that keep Americans safe from bad products, misleading advertising, environmental hazards, unsafe products, and dangerous working conditions.

> **Why is the Department of Agriculture responsible for pepperoni pizza, while the FDA regulates non-meat pizzas?**

> **Alphabet Soup, Trivia Contest: Identify each of the following government regulatory agencies and describe their missions:**
> ① **FTC**
> ② **FCC**
> ③ **EPA**
> ④ **OSHA**
> ⑤ **CPSC**

We have government agencies because modern life requires large scale organizations. To work, these organizations need hierarchies, written rules, expertise, accountability, formal ways to communicate, and the inevitable **Red Tape**. In the past, government officials wrapped their documents in special red tape. Today, red tape means waiting in a long line while a government clerk slowly processes all the paperwork necessary to register your automobile, or to graduate from college. Red tape means the FDA and the Department of Agriculture trying to regulate the over eight hundred million pieces of pizza sold in public school cafeterias every year. Under the rules, students can buy cheese pizza in their school lunchroom from a local pizzeria. They also can purchase pepperoni pizza that was bought frozen elsewhere and reheated in the cafeteria. Until 1992, however, the rules banned sale of meat-topped pizza slices from Pizza Hut or any other nearby pizza joint. Why?

In primitive societies, the rules are usually much easier to understand. If a husband is too brutal to his wife, in some tribal communities, the chief and witch doctor threaten to put a curse or spell on the abusing husband. When the spells fail to work, abused wives may take the law into their own hands. In ancient Assyria, wives retaliated by squeezing their husband's testicles. This ancient form of self-defense eventually led to laws that if a woman crushed one testicle she had one finger cut off, and if she crushed two her breasts were cut off.

This type of "eye for an eye," "tooth for a tooth," and "finger for a testicle" justice is common in primitive cultures. Now we have many, many laws and we need armies of bureaucrats to create, interpret, and enforce the laws. That's progress.

In this country, we used to rely heavily on custom to keep men from abusing their wives and "significant others." Customs that required gentlemen to open doors for ladies had a compelling purpose; they reminded men that women had a special status. This special status presumably kept women safe from aggressive men. By the 1970's, however, these customs were replaced by rules aimed at legally punishing men for codified improprieties like sexual harassment. Now instead of a few customs, Americans need laws, rules, memorandums, lawyers, special boards, and lots of red tape; all designed to make sure men behave like gentlemen.

In Vietnam a peasant buying a pig needs approval from five different government officials. In America, a worker buying a new automobile only needs money, good credit, a driver's license, registration papers, insurance, smog checks, etc. All this red tape associated with car ownership makes us frequent guests of bureaucracies like the Nevada Department of Motor Vehicles and Public Safety. Now, we have health maintenance organizations and a trip to the doctor generates considerable paperwork.

⌂ Will the "dating game" someday require agreed upon written rules and red tape like the infamous Antioch College policy?

> **In her book *Who Stole Feminism* (1994), Christina Hoff Sommers tells the story of a University of Michigan sophomore who describes tongue-in-cheek how a political opinion poll would be unreliable if the pollsters tried to interview Dave [the] Stud when he was entertaining three beautiful women in his penthouse. The female graduate teaching assistant who read the sophomore's corny attempt at humor was angered and warned him in writing that she considered his remarks to be "sexual harassment." What do you think?**

While government bureaucrats strive to protect Americans from dangerous medicines, killer viruses, and sexual harassment, those who see conspiracies around every corner spread scare sheets blaming AIDS on government scientists. They argue that Americans are not getting the truth about AIDS, and on the Internet they have warned us that:

✚ Between 7 and 8 million Americans are infected with the HIV virus.
✚ The AIDS virus burst upon the scene in 1978 with the introduction of the Hepatitis B vaccine which "exhibits the exact epidemiology of AIDS."
✚ Contrary to government assurances, AIDS is transmitted in your saliva.
✚ There are at least six different AIDS viruses loose in the world.
✚ Condoms will not prevent AIDS.

The HIV pandemic has infected about 50 million people and killed 16 million or more. How did this deadly mutating virus cast its plague on the world? According to British author Edward Hooper in his book *The River,* AIDS is the unintended consequence of two American scientists who developed polio vaccines using chimp kidney cells as their medium at laboratories in the African Congo and in Philadelphia. This controversial theory is backed up by the fact that modern travelers can go to far away lands carrying along deadly diseases without realizing it. This fact of modern travel is a good example of cultural lag: Our technology carries us to places where nature has created deadly diseases that our immune systems can't handle.

So why don't we just use condoms and wait for the HIV virus to disappear? If condoms were perfect devices they might work but we'd have to overcome primitive customs that reinforce the idea that a "real" man would be insulting his partner if he wore protection.

We could try the approach used on American servicemen in World War II and produce educational movies showing all the dire consequences of unsafe sex. Such "scare" movies have been replaced by commercial TV warnings. The TV warnings are more sophisticated than the old "raw reality" movies, but have they stopped people from practicing "unsafe" sex? Moreover, any anti-AIDS campaign sponsored by the national government is grist for conspiracy theorists looking for evidence that the "feds" are trying to control our lives.

If AIDS is defeated, it will not be by trying to convince people there is a conspiracy somewhere out there. Instead, the applause will go to scientists working at places like the FDA, U.S. Centers for Disease Control, the University of California (San Francisco) Center for AIDS research, National Cancer Institute, United Nations, Merck Drug Company, Duke University, Center for AIDS Research at the University of California (San Diego), and the Aaron Diamond AIDS Research Center in New York City.

In 1996, Dr. David Ho was named *Time's* "Man of the Year" for his work treating AIDS patients with protease inhibitors and standard antiviral medications at the Aaron Diamond Research Center. The new treatments are working, but they cost about $20,000 a year, and are now too expensive for the 90% of AIDS victims who live in Africa, India, Thailand, and to a growing extent Central and Eastern Europe.

It takes a lot of money to fund all the scientific research that makes our technology possible. Today, more than 700 federal laboratories, hundreds of university research facilities, over two million scientists and engineers, and a national research budget of $76 billion make the U.S. the world's leading scientific power. And to pay for all this, we need taxes.

The Tax Collector

> **How Much Does It Cost to Treat One AIDS Patient?**

In the Middle Ages, laws and customs were designed to let serfs know who made the rules. Part of their tax burden was a law that required serfs to buy wine from their lord's vineyard each year. The law stated that if a serf didn't buy his share of wine on time then, "the lord shall pour a four-gallon measure over the man's roof; if the wine runs down, the tenant must pay for it; if it runs upward, he shall pay nothing."

In this nation, the IRS has never had to rely on custom or the laws of gravity to collect taxes. Armed with laws, computers, and agents, the IRS relies on complicated tax laws, a regular filing date, random audits, stiff penalties and fines, and public fear to make sure every eligible American gets to pay "voluntary" taxes.

> **Big Brother Is Taxing You!**

When it comes to tax collecting, knowledge is power. In 1086 William the Conqueror sent tax agents to every village in England, where they counted everything from family members to the number of plows. This information was eventually compiled in a *Domesday Book*, which got its name from the fact there was no more appeal from its findings than the Last Judgment.

Instead of a *Domesday Book*, the Internal Revenue Service has a massive computer complex centered in Martinsburg, West Virginia. IRS computers process about 100 million tax returns every year. Over the years, IRS agents have collected nearly 300,000 computer discs filled with data. These computers are now capable of comparing your tax returns with information sent by banks, credit unions, and employers. Because of this technology, the IRS now knows all your bank accounts, dividends, interest rates, property investments, sales taxes, and personal checks. And someday it will know if you have a genetic defect which could limit your ability to buy health insurance.

Because the IRS has all this information, many Americans compare it to Orwell's "Big Brother." If so, this is a Big Brother with an insatiable appetite for information and not much sympathy for taxpayers. In 1989, for example, the IRS asked title companies and escrow officers in Las Vegas to "blow the whistle" on questionable customers. Justifying its request, the IRS said it wanted to keep drug money from being "laundered" through the purchase of real estate.

> **Should the IRS be a combination tax collector, law enforcement agency that encourages title companies and escrow agents to "blow the whistle" on suspicious customers?**

When the IRS isn't compiling data, its agents are busy catching tax cheats and levying penalties. About 12 of every one thousand tax payers are audited. Delinquent taxpayers are punished with penalties and tax taxes, plus interest. The taxpayer can appeal, however, most appeals are handled by the IRS. This practice seems unfair, like having the lord pour wine on a roof that always slants down to the ground. A taxpayer determined to get "impartial justice" may be able to get a final decision rendered by a federal court or by the Tax Court in Washington, D.C. Despite the audits and agents, about 2,500 filers with incomes over $200,000 in 2000 paid no federal income tax.

Since the IRS makes about 10 million errors every year, the possibility exists that you could be audited by mistake. Like Damocles, every taxpayer has a "sword" hanging by a thread over his or her head. The threat of an audit exists for every taxpayer, but especially for those who file long forms and take exemptions or who make a mistake in arithmetic. If you make a small mistake, the auditors may not catch it for several months. They will, however, charge you both a penalty and back interest on the unpaid balance. This is done so that taxpayers will be careful not to make mistakes.

> **Does a tax bill for $212.46 to pay off a 54 cent shortage make sense? Why or why not?**

In 1989 Gordon and Sandra Allred of Sandy, Utah ended up owing the IRS 54 cents. Two years later in December 1991, the Allreds received a notice that they owed a tax bill of $212.46. How was this calculated? The penalty for late payment was $94.60, which figures out to 25 percent of the late tax. Interest on the late payment had reached $117.32 by 1991. If you add it all up, it equals $212.46.

The IRS also has the "100 percent penalty rule," which allows it to try to collect unpaid payroll taxes from officers and employees of companies when it is unable to collect taxes from the company itself. Confused? Suppose you worked as a secretary and signed checks for a boss who failed to pay her payroll taxes to the IRS. In that case, the IRS might come after you for the unpaid taxes. Not fair, you say? Well, it makes more sense than hoping for wine to run uphill.

Many Americans are uncomfortable with the power of the IRS. In 1980 they filed 13,390 protest returns. In 1981 a group calling itself the Second Continental Congress paid for a television commercial which showed IRS agents armed with shotguns grabbing the land of a hapless farmer and his family. In 1984, 8,200 Americans filed "frivolous returns" and were each fined $500. And the experts estimate that over 35% of taxpayers now cheat on their taxes.

These tax protesters risk jail and stiff penalties. In order to justify their behavior, the tax protesters usually use these three arguments:

☹ The requirement that financial records be kept to verify tax forms is a form of slavery prohibited by the Constitution.

☹ The government can't tax income because the currency has been worthless since the nation went off the gold standard in 1933.

☹ The 16th Amendment, which allows a direct income tax, was never properly ratified.

Are these arguments realistic? Not really. From 1989 to 1991 a total of 571 tax protesters were sentenced to jail. And those who won acquittals were socked with a 75% penalty plus interest from the date their taxes were due. Yet some "experts" still argue that the income tax is not legal.

> In Chapter two we learned that governments where all power is concentrated in one body is the essence of tyranny. Is the power of the IRS checked in any way? We also learned that "whoever controls the rules controls the game," and "rules are never neutral." Do these two dictums describe in any way how the IRS currently functions? Explain.

Most Americans have learned to laugh off taxes. They create jokes like the "Simplified 1040" which says "(1) How much money did you make last year? (2) Send it in."

But taxes are not funny. The tax code now consists of over seven thousand pages of complicated rules. The original 1040 had three schedules and one page of instructions. Now 1040 has nine schedules and 36 pages of instructions. Complex rules and complicated tax forms lead to mistakes, and place every taxpayer at the mercy of red tape and tax agents.

Like Big Brother watching Winston Smith on the telescreen, IRS agents can snoop into our private lives. This unpleasant possibility was exposed July 20, 1994 by a *USA Today* story which said, "Big Brother may not be watching, but he might be snooping. Internal Revenue Service officials said at a Senate hearing Tuesday that more than 1,300 IRS employees have been investigated the past five years on suspicion of improperly snooping through private taxpayers files—information that is supposed to be for official use only and strictly confidential. Those probes resulted in disciplinary action against 420 IRS workers."

Even more scary is the fact that some Presidents have used the IRS to punish their political enemies. According to recently released tapes, President Richard Nixon on May 13, 1971, told his top aides that he wanted a "ruthless son of a bitch" to be the new commissioner of internal revenue. By "SOB," Nixon meant an IRS commissioner who would "go after our enemies and not go after our friends." Translated, this means Nixon wanted to use the IRS to punish his opponents. The "enemies list" compiled by Nixon and his aides included hundreds of people whose chief sin was contributing to the campaign fund of Democratic Presidential candidate George McGovern, who ran against Nixon in 1972.

Unfair tax codes, Big Brother snooping, and enemies lists have combined to make the IRS a favorite target of congressional tax cutters. In July 1996, the House approved a spending bill that cut the IRS budget by 11% to $6.6 billion and would eliminate roughly 2,000 jobs.

In 1819 the U.S. Supreme Court struck down a Maryland tax levied on a branch of the national bank created by Congress. In the majority opinion of Chief Justice John Marshall, "the power to tax involves the power to destroy. . . ." By 1996, the U.S. Bank was gone but the power of taxes to destroy was still being used by state governments. In California, for example, there is a state tax of 35 cents on each package of cigarettes. The extra tax money is spent in California for state anti-smoking campaigns, including TV and radio public service announcements, hotlines and school programs. As a consequence, cigarette smoking in California is down from 26% in 1984 to 15.5% in 1996.

Learn more about the IRS and the executive branch through the Internet. For starters, try these sources: [http://www.fedworld.gov/] and [http://www.yahoo.com/Government/ Executive Branch_/Branch/].

Is it fair to tax smokers and use the revenues to harangue them about their nasty habit? What name should we give to such taxes? What about "Sin Tax," or "Health Enhancement Revenue Services"? Which would you prefer?

Bureaucrats and Newspeak

Although government employees protect us from bad drugs and AIDS, they bombard us daily with questionable words. Bureaucratic Newspeak and Politically Correct Words are now merging to form **BNPCW**, which means simplified language for simple and overly sensitive minds. This merger can be seen in all its grotesque glory in what is happening to the *Holy Bible*. Two versions of the Bible compete for readers these days. Since 1611 most Protestants have read the King James version. In the summer of 1996, however, the King James version was being challenged by the New Living Translation. To fully understand how words convey feelings, compare the two versions now being published:

✟ King James version: "And the LORD God said unto the woman, What is this that thou hast done?" The New Living Translation: "Then the LORD God asked the woman, 'How could you do such a thing?'"

✟ King James version: "The LORD is my shepherd; I shall not want." The New Living Translation: "The LORD is my shepherd; I have everything I need."

✟ King James version: "After this manner therefore pray ye: Our Father which art in heaven, Hallowed be thy name. Thy Kingdom come . . ." The New Living Translation: "Pray then in this way: Our Father-Mother in heaven, hallowed be your name. Your dominion come."

What do you think? Is The New Living Translation an improvement over the King James version of the Bible?

91

When a citizen of Oceania was packed off to a forced labor camp, he was told he was being sent to a **joycamp**. Using the word "joycamp" as the name for a place where people are beaten and starved is a form of language manipulation which George Orwell called **Newspeak**. When bureaucrats invent new words to manipulate the public, they are guilty of newspeak. We also use the terms "doublespeak" and "doubletalk" to label this invented language.

Most propaganda is used in the United States to convince us that our technology is helpful and safe. To make it easier for Americans to live with the dangers of nuclear power, our bureaucratic symbol manipulators have created words that hide the danger. When a reactor is out of control, for example, nuclear officials say it is merely "above critical." When members of the Nuclear Regulatory Commission gathered to discuss

> To find out just what happens when radiation escapes from a nuclear facility, use your World Wide Web to contact the Radiation Effects Research Foundation [http://www.rerf.or.jp/] which is dedicated to studying the effects of the atomic bombing of Hiroshima and Nagasaki during World War II.

Three Mile Island, they knew that when oxygen and hydrogen combined in a certain way at a reactor accident, it could cause an explosion powerful enough to make parts of Pennsylvania unlivable for hundreds of years. And the word they used for this horror? "Blip."

The nation has nearly 100 nuclear power plants that annually use more than one thousand tons of uranium. The spent uranium is radioactive and highly deadly. Since the Nuclear Waste Policy Act was passed in 1982, the Department of Energy has been searching for a permanent place to deposit nuclear waste. The sites considered so far include Hanford, Washington; Deaf Smith County, Texas; or Yucca Mountain, Nevada. Until a permanent site is selected the DOE is storing nuclear waste in temporary locations under its "Monitored Retrievable Storage" (MRS) program. Essentially MRS means transporting tons of radioactive spent fuel rods to temporary sites, until the permanent sites are ready.

When the deadly material is moved, there may be accidents. When you read about the possible explosions or radiation leaks in your newspapers, look for the Department of Energy people to use words like "incidents" or "events" to describe potential disasters.

> Now that traditional dating customs are being replaced by formal rules, the meaning of words like "unwanted touching," or "hostile environment" can lead to a sexual harassment suit that could ruin your reputation and career. Locate a copy of this college's sexual harassment policy and decide if, in your opinion, it is a reasonable policy.

The Regulators

The Sudanese tribes along the borders of Ethiopia had a special "leopard-skin chief." He settled feuds and disputes that could not be solved by the families involved. The chief was a neutral third party who determined if any rules or customs were violated. His job was to make a just decision and threaten a curse for either party who violated his judgments. Since the Sudanese considered a leopard skin to have a human soul, they took the threat of a curse seriously.

Having neutral third parties render judgments and enforce the rules helps us avoid blood feuds and lawsuits. We have courts where neutral justice is handed down, and we have independent regulatory agencies which protect us from unsafe products like Thalidomide. These federal regulatory agencies are known by their acronyms, namely the ICC, SEC, FCC, FDA, FTC, NLRB, EEPOC and EPA. They were established by Congress to ensure that ordinary Americans are not the victims of fraud, misleading advertising, or dangerous foods.

For over 30 years, millions of American women have welcomed the boost in self-esteem that comes with silicone breast implants. In 1992, however, FDA chief David Kessler declared a moratorium on silicone implants. Kessler urged manufacturers to stop marketing the devices and surgeons to stop inserting them in women. The decision stunned millions of women who rightly wanted to know what was going on.

Judging by media accounts, Kessler's decision was made because the largest U.S. implant manufacturer, Dow Corning Wright, may have concealed evidence that its product was unsafe. Moreover, Kessler had also received reports from rheumatologists who linked the device to autoimmune disorders.

☆ Should regulatory agencies like the FDA be empowered to dictate what products Americans can sell or buy? Why don't we go back to the custom known as *Caveat emptor, quia ignorare non debuit quod ius alienum emit* which is Latin for "Let the purchaser beware, for he ought not to be ignorant of the nature of the property which he is buying from another party."

Having regulators warn us about unsafe products and misleading food labels is not a total blessing. It means that we will be bombarded with bad news. In 1986, for example, Congress considered a bill to force fast food companies to list all the ingredients in their products.

> **What about Americans who bought automobiles with air bags and have since discovered that the bags expand at 200 mph and are capable of killing a young child in the front seat?**

☆ Would you like to know how much saturated fat there is in your favorite fast food hamburger? Would it change your eating habits to know this fact?

Would you like to know all the ingredients in that Big Mac you had for lunch? According to a study conducted in 1980 by Colorado State University, the humble hamburger is the subject of 41,000 federal and state regulations carried out in accordance with 200 statutes and 111,000 court cases. The bureaucrats are on the job, making sure your favorite hamburger has at least 1.8 milligrams of thiamine in the bun, no more than 30% fat, nor more than 5 parts DDT per million parts meat fat, a pickle three-eighths of an inch thick, and ketchup that must flow no more than 9 centimeters in 30 seconds.

Americans may moan and groan about all the red tape associated with big government, but they keep demanding more and more regulations. In 1990, Congress responded with the Nutrition Labeling and Education Act which provides for mandatory nutrition labeling for most processed food. The law required that by 1993, we'd finally have uniform definitions for the nine descriptive terms that appear on our food products. Now we'll know what advertisers mean by the words "free," "low," "reduced," "high," "light or lite," "fresh," "less," "source of," and "lean" and "extra lean."

Want to know how much fat and cholesterol there is in your favorite foods? Check the nutrition facts on the label. Want a free source of information that describes the different types of fats and cholesterol and their effects on your health? Use your Internet World Wide Web [http://www.pueblo.gsa.gov] and ask for free FDA pamphlet 527D "A Consumer's Guide to Fats."

In 1996 the Food and Drug Administration warned Americans not to buy a product known as "Herbal Ecstacy" and other dietary supplements which contain the stimulant ephedrine because it had caused 15 deaths and 400 reports of side effects, ranging from heart attacks to seizures and psychosis. Herbal Ecstacy has been popular among young Americans because it promises euphoria, heightened sexual awareness and enhanced athletic performance.

In Brave New World every citizen is encouraged to take Soma, a mild euphoric drug. They are sleep-taught to believe in the drug's mood altering capabilities by listening to the slogan "a gram is better than a damn."

On New Year's Eve, December 31, 1996, young partygoers in Los Angeles gathered at the Olympic Auditorium to hear a concert by "In 7th Heaven." During the concert, about 50 people got sick from drinking liquid vials passed around by partygoers. According to Los Angeles police, the vials contained a high concentration of caffeine. Labels indicated a plant extract called "kava kava," which police described as a nervous system depressant.

One day after the concert was canceled, FDA officials pointed out in their defense that many of the teenagers drank more than five times the recommended dosage despite a warning label on the vials which were distributed.

Others at the concert were reportedly also consuming "Herbal Ecstacy." Since contemporary Americans seem to be suffering the unintended consequences of all the "free love" being promoted in the late 1960's, why are companies selling products like Herbal Ecstacy and, more importantly, why are young Americans using these potentially dangerous products?

☆ If you are too young to remember the "good old days," the unintended consequences of "free love" and drug use include AIDS, Unmarried Mothers, One Million Abortions Yearly, Children Born Out of Wedlock, Skyrocketing Divorce Rates, STD, Spouse Abuse, Sexual Harassment Laws, etc.

In the past, women who slept around were called "promiscuous" and worse. To be politically correct, Americans replaced the judgmental word promiscuous with the more gentle words "sexually active." In an age of AIDS, abortions, and children born out of wedlock, is it a good idea to replace judgmental words with merely descriptive words?

According to a Joyce Brothers column published in the Las Vegas *Review Journal* January 2, 1997, "Doctors have reported that young men seem to be having somewhat more problems with impotency than they did in the past." The popular Dr. Brothers theorized that stress, drinking, and drugs are causing the increase in impotence.

In his fascinating book, *The Encyclopedia of the Occult, the Esoteric, and the Supernatural* (1977), Benjamin Walker argued under the category of "Ear" that "the constant repetition of strident, harsh, metallic and penetrating noises is injurious to body and mind. "Many patients in mental hospitals are the victims of noise." Walker then proceeded to point out that loud "pop music" causes long term damage to the body. This damage includes impaired brain activity, damage to the heart, and in the long run "this continuous assault on the senses raises the reflex level of the nervous system and leads to progressive impotence." To clinch this last argument, Walker writes that contrary to popular belief, "many pop stars are sexually subnormal. Furthermore, following the need for the strong sensory stimulus to which they are accustomed, many pop addicts inevitably drift into drug addiction."

Television is regulated by the Federal Communications Commission, which is responsible for prohibiting indecent language. In the past when TV went "too far," Americans protested to the FCC. Today TV is controlled by a rating system that warns viewers when a movie or program contains violence, "adult" language, and sexual content.

> If scientific studies discovered truth behind the theories of Dr. Brothers and Benjamin Walker, would you favor an FDA ban on rock music until its long term effects could be tested further? Why, or why not?

While the morality police worry about adult language on TV, scientists are developing new drugs and we are now entering an era in which the genetic code has been deciphered. Now that scientists have broken the genome, the FDA will have to monitor all the miracle drugs that will be produced by what *Time* magazine (January 15, 2001) calls the "Brave New Pharmacy."

> Scientists now can use genetics to improve our future children. What new rules will be needed now?

The Major Malfunction

On January 28, 1986, 73 seconds after being launched from Cape Kennedy, the Challenger shuttle exploded, killing all seven crew members. After the tragedy, President Reagan appointed William P. Rogers to head a commission to inquire into the way NASA conducted its shuttle program. After four months of hearing testimony and investigating the facts, the Rogers Commission filed a 256 page report blaming the shuttle explosion on "flawed judgment."

What happened? As the 100 ton Challenger lifted off, O-rings which were supposed to seal joints on the 149 foot booster rockets failed. As a result, extremely hot gases leaked from the right booster and caused it to swing into the external fuel

> My God, Thiokol, when do you want me to launch? Next April?

tank, which exploded. NASA had launched 26 previous shuttle flights without an explosion, but there had been other problems. The Rogers Commission heard one testimony that there had previously been 748 serious problems on various shuttle launchings and flights. The commission was also told of "engineering anomalies" that bothered NASA engineers. And the Rogers Commission also learned that in July, 1985 a NASA budget analyst warned by memorandum that O-rings had shown significant signs of erosion in previous firings.

On the day before the Challenger was launched, NASA officials called a last minute meeting to consider objections raised by an engineer for Morton Thiokol, the company that built the boosters. The engineer warned that temperatures at Cape Kennedy would be too cold on launch day and could cause the O-rings to fail. Faced with the request from Morton Thiokol to delay the launch, the head of NASA's Solid Rocket Booster program asked in frustration, "My God, Thiokol, when do you want me to launch? Next April?"

This **rhetorical question** had the intended effect, and the launch was made on a cold day. After the seven "recovered components" were buried, critics had a field day condemning the way NASA made decisions. One described the process as so vague that nobody felt responsible for the final decisions. This vagueness, however, may have been a "subconscious goal of the NASA system," since no one wanted the ultimate responsibility of making decisions that might result in the astronauts' deaths.[1]

> **In primitive societies, a king who mistakenly ordered his warriors to their deaths might be locked in a hut and left to die with a virgin. Modern bureaucracies, however, are not supposed to make mistakes because they require decisions by several well-trained and educated persons at various levels. So what went wrong on January 28, 1986?**

Bureaucrats are expected to follow logical and rational steps before making decisions. Politicians supposedly are elected for demonstrating the same qualities. When elected officials and career government workers make mistakes, look for a phenomenon known as **Groupthink**. Groupthink occurs when our elected and appointed officials meet together in small groups and make huge errors.

The Groupthink Hypothesis

On April 17, 1961 some 1,400 Cuban exiles stormed ashore at the Bay of Pigs in southern Cuba, determined to overthrow the communist government of Fidel Castro. The brigade had been recruited, trained and financed by our Central Intelligence Agency. Only 135 of the exiles were soldiers. The rest were students, businessmen, lawyers, doctors, former landowners, and a few criminals. Most were from Florida where the exiles lived. They trained in Guatemala, where the CIA had built a $1.8 million base to train exile pilots to fly World War II B-26 bombers and provide air cover for the invasion. The Cuban brigade was carried to the Bay of Pigs in seven old freighters leased by the CIA, and loaded into landing barges for the invasion. Because U.S. Navy ships and planes escorted them to the invasion site, the Cuba exiles thought they were merely the vanguard of a much larger invasion force. The CIA had encouraged the Cuban exiles during their training to believe this. But once on the beaches at the Bay of Pigs, the exiles learned they were on their own.

Although they fought valiantly, the Cuban exiles were defeated in three days. Castro had better planes, more tanks and a small army of 20,000 to throw at the 1,400 exiles. Most of the Cuban exiles were captured and later had to be ransomed by the United States for food and medical supplies.

After his election in November, 1960, John F. Kennedy learned of the proposed CIA invasion for the first time. It had been initiated under President Eisenhower, who had not been all that eager to approve the Cuba invasion in the first place. But Kennedy was eager to make a show of force against Castro. Moreover, the plan was described to him by two men he respected, CIA director Allen Dulles and his assistant for covert operations, Richard M. Bissell, Jr. In order to get advice, Kennedy consulted with his Joint Chiefs of Staff, his Secretary of State, his Secretary of Defense, certain Latin American specialists, his special assistant Arthur M. Schlesinger, Jr., Senate Foreign Relations Committee Chairman William F. Fulbright, and others. By March, 1961 Kennedy and his advisory group were meeting three and four times a week to discuss the proposed invasion of Cuba. And in April, Kennedy finally gave the go ahead.

In retrospect, the Bay of Pigs invasion was a bad idea. But Kennedy had been persuaded by three major arguments:

① The first argument, based on incomplete CIA intelligence information, was that the Cuban people were just waiting for the opportunity to overthrow Castro and would rise up to join the exiles as soon as the invasion force had established a beachhead. This did not happen.

② Secondly, even if the invaders were not able to push Castro's forces aside, they would be close enough to the nearby Escambray Mountains where they could disappear and organize guerilla operations against the Castro regime. Since the mountains were 80 miles from the Bay of Pigs, through a tangle of swamps and jungle, the invaders could not disappear and were easily captured.

③ CIA officials told Kennedy he would be viewed as indecisive and weak if he failed to launch an invasion which was all primed and ready to go.

In his book *Victims of Groupthink* (1972), Yale psychology professor Irving Janis invented the concept **Groupthink** and used it to describe what when wrong with the 1961 Bay of Pigs invasion. Groupthink, according to Janis, occurs in five distinct stages, namely:

❶ **Suppression of Personal Doubts**. This happened in 1961 to Kennedy's special assistant Harvard history professor Arthur M. Schlesinger, Jr. In his biography *A Thousand Days: John F. Kennedy in the White House* (1965), Schlesinger admits that he had serious doubts about the Bay of Pigs invasion, but suppressed them because he was so awed by the presence of the charismatic Kennedy and the cabinet heads, the CIA people, and three generals covered with medals in the staff room. The sight was so over-whelming that Schlesinger shrank into a chair at the far end of the table and listened in silence.

❷ The second stage of groupthink occurs when some group members decide to become **Mindguards**. Mindguards are people who try to prevent other group members from asking embarrassing questions like "Why is the Emperor wearing no clothes?" During the Bay of Pigs invasion talks, Secretary of State Dean Rusk assumed this role. While Rusk was away at a SEATO conference, his assistant Chester Bowles attended a few meetings of the Kennedy advisory group. Bowles was clearly shocked by the invasion plans, but didn't voice any objections because he wanted to express his concerns with Rusk first (like any good bureaucrat). When Rusk returned Bowles asked him in a memorandum if they could discuss the

CIA plan with the President. Rusk, however, told Bowles not to worry since the invasion plan had already been reduced to a guerilla action. After reassuring Bowles, Secretary Rusk then filed the memorandum.

❸ Once the mindguards discourage dissent, group members begin to believe that all participants in the planning stage agree. In groupthink terms, this is known as developing an **Illusion of Unanimity.** This phase was noticed by Schlesinger, who later wrote that the invasion plans took place "in a curious atmosphere of assumed consensus."

❹ In the planning stage of any decisive action, group members develop an **Illusion of Invulnerability.** Sports teams have a similar problem, known as being "over-confident" or "cocky." In 1961 the Kennedy people reached that point when they wrongly assumed Cuba's supposedly rebellious population would rise up and overthrow Castro when the invasion started. CIA estimates of popular dissatisfaction with Castro were undoubtedly inflated by over-confident CIA agents. Assuming the exile army could melt away into the mountains if the invasion failed was another symptom of invulnerability. Behind the final decision was the assumption that Castro's Cuban militia would not be able to defeat even a small army of exiles if it was backed by U.S. brains. This is what happened in Vietnam when U.S. officials decided we could win a war against North Vietnam because our technology was superior.

❺ The final stage of groupthink is **Leadership Fostered Docility.** This happens when leaders discourage disagreement, foster self-censorship, and encourage mindguarding. Kennedy learned from the Bay of Pigs and later during the Cuban Missile Crisis and remained away from staff meetings so that his presence would not discourage dissent. During the Vietnam War, President Lyndon Johnson often made fun of staff members who opposed escalating American involvement in that fateful war. Too bad he didn't listen.

On the night of December 6, 1941, the Navy admirals responsible for defending the Pearl Harbor fleet held a dinner party. During the festivities, the wife of Admiral William Halsey said she was certain the Japanese were going to attack Pearl Harbor. Though Fanny Halsey was considered a brilliant woman, the officers at the dinner table dismissed the notion that a third rate power like Japan would attack the mighty U.S. fleet docked in a harbor that was too shallow for torpedo warfare to work. Groupthink stage?

British writer Edward Hooper in his book "The River" argues that American scientists used chimp kidney cells to develop polio vaccines as their medium at a laboratory in the Congo. Were the Americans guilty of an illusion of invulnerability?

So far the HIV pandemic has infected 50 million people and killed 16 million. Judging by some sources, HIV was spread by scientific mistakes. What were these mistakes?

Presidential Character

On January 20, 1981 Ronald Reagan was sworn in as President of the United States. While the inauguration ceremonies were proceeding in Washington, D.C., the Washington *Post* carried an article by political scientist James David Barber, who predicted of Reagan, "as President, he will be dangerous."

Professor Barber based his prediction on a **Presidential character model** which he had developed. This model is based on three major components, namely **Style**, **World View**, and **Character**.

Presidential character has always fascinated Americans. Although most of us won't admit it, we are often strongly attracted to the "intelligent scoundrels" who lie persuasively and are repelled by "naive fools" who have a compulsion to always tell the truth. Don't agree? Then consider this example: You're wearing an attractive, but flimsy dress outside on a cold, windy day in Las Vegas. Male friend One comes up and says, with a sunny smile, "hey you look really great in that dress!" Female friend Two comes up, and asks with a worried look "Aren't you cold?" Case closed.

① By style Barber meant the way a President habitually performs his political roles. The key roles include **rhetoric**, **personal relations**, and **homework**. In the case of Reagan, his major style was rhetorical and had earned him the label of the "great communicator." John F. Kennedy also communicated in a grand manner, and used heroic words like "man holds in his mortal hands the power to abolish all forms of human poverty and all forms of human life."

② World View means how a President views human nature, the causes of social change, and important moral conflicts. Reagan, according to Barber, came to the presidency with a world view that made him feel comfortable with wealthy people, but not sympathetic to people who are poor. This world view, according to Barber, led Reagan to support social welfare cuts and tax policies beneficial to rich Americans. In his *The Presidential Character* (1985), Barber wrote the "bottom line" for Reagan was "soak the poor, feed the rich."

③ By character Barber meant, "the way the President orients himself toward life." In this regard, Barber classified Reagan as the type of leader who would delegate too much responsibility and not be willing to take charge.

After his original prediction in 1981 that Reagan would be dangerous, Barber followed with a comprehensive evaluation in his 1985 book. In this account, Barber classified Reagan as a "passive-positive" who would be controlled too much by events and his aides.

The best Presidents, according to Barber, are the "active-positives," like John F. Kennedy. They have high energy, enjoy the job, have high self-esteem, are flexible and grow in office. The most dangerous personality types are the "active-negatives" who, like Richard Nixon, lack self-esteem and are driven to work hard as a way to escape feelings of personal inadequacy. Active-negatives see life as a struggle, and have only a vague self-image. In Nixon's world most people "were weak, and lazy, and uninspired—a world in which a man with the will to win and a driving dream could, if he tried very hard, make his way out."[2]

What do you know about the current President's Style, World View, and Character? How does he perform his key roles? Does he have a high energy level, i.e., active or a low energy level, i.e., passive? Does he have high self-esteem, i.e., positive, or low self-esteem, i.e., negative? When President George W. Bush was campaigning for President he vigorously opposed the federal estate tax. What does that tell you about his character?

For pure excitement, Theodore Roosevelt (1858-1919) was probably the most fascinating personality to occupy the White House. A sickly youth, Teddy built up his body and ended up on Harvard's wrestling team. Later Roosevelt became a war hero, vice president, and in 1901 he succeeded to the presidency when William McKinley was assassinated. During his career, Theodore Roosevelt so loved the spotlight of popularity that one cynic said of him, "he wants to be the bride at every wedding and the corpse at every funeral."

Unlike popular Teddy, Richard M. Nixon was obsessively hated by most of the liberal media. During the Christmas season of 1995, Oliver Stone released his controversial movie, "Nixon." Starring British actor Anthony Hopkins, "Nixon" suggested that the former President never outgrew a severe rural childhood or his attachment to his stern mother. Since Nixon's resignation, Americans have invented a newspeak word to describe Nixon's sad home life, namely "dysfunctional family." If such a background lowers self-esteem and contributes to active negative traits, has the time arrived to disqualify Presidential candidates from dysfunctional families?

What about a candidate whose wife is unfit to be the "first lady." Abraham Lincoln's wife Mary Todd certainly qualifies for an active-negative label. As first lady, according to *The Cambridge Dictionary of American Biography*, "it seemed as if she could do nothing right; she overspent, was exceedingly jealous of Lincoln's affections, and was accused of Confederate sympathies." Later, Mary Todd had a nervous breakdown. Should Presidential character tests be applied to spouses in the future?

By the election of 2004, you will probably have access to a database now being compiled by industrial psychologists at major universities. The data compares Presidents on traits such as intelligence, conscientious-ness and neuroticism and is designed to shed light on what type of personalities make the best Presidents. The data base ranks Presidents on the basis of five significant characteristics, namely neuroticism, extroversion, openness to experience, agreeableness and conscientiousness. Using these criteria, the industrial psychologists ranked Theodore and Franklin Roosevelt as numbers 1 and 2 in extroversion, with Bill Clinton 3rd. Richard Nixon was rated most neurotic, while Bill Clinton finished 23d in that negative category. As for intelligence, Thomas Jefferson and Theodore Roosevelt ranked 1 and 2, while Clinton ranked 10th. On agreeableness, James Madison and Abraham Lincoln ranked 1 and 2, while Clinton ranked 20th. The psychologists found George Washington to be the most conscientious while Clinton finished 40th.

During his administration Bill Clinton presided over good times. But he also was impeached for bad conduct. How should the history textbooks remember the 42nd President? For national prosperity? For Paula Jones and sexual harassment? For Monica Lewinsky, cigar arrogance and the notorious blue dress DNA?

According to the study, the most successful Presidents tend to score high on IQ, assertiveness and competency. The great Presidents tend, however, to score low on straight forwardness and compliance. Surprisingly, traits such as trust and altruism—both major campaign issues in the election of 1996—didn't seem to matter to the industrial psychologists.[3]

☙In other words, intelligent scoundrels seem to make better leaders than trustworthy fools. If that premise is sound, then perhaps American voters should stop worrying about whether or not their leaders commit sexual harassment and be glad they don't start World War III. On the other hand, perhaps we need to elect leaders whose egos keep their Id under control at all times.

On August 21, 1964, three North Vietnam patrol boats supposedly fired torpedoes at a U.S. destroyer operating 30 miles off the coast of North Vietnam in the Tonkin Gulf. After the alleged attack, President Lyndon Johnson asked Congress to authorize him to retaliate.

Five days after the Tonkin Gulf attack, the Senate 88 to 2 and the House of Representatives 416 to 0 approved a resolution which authorized the President to "take all necessary measures to repel any armed attack against the forces of the United States and to prevent further aggression."

During the 1964 Presidential campaign, American movie audiences were laughing at Stanley Kubrick's outrageous satire *Dr. Strangelove*. Kubrick shows World War III being started by a crazy Air Force general who thinks the communists are fluoridating his drinking water. To stop the commie plot, General Jack Ripper launches his B-52 bombers at Soviet targets. This decision forces President Muffley to the realization that U.S. nuclear policy in the 1960s was perfectly MAD. What does MAD mean?

During the 1964 election campaign incumbent Johnson reassured American voters that he did not intend to get involved in a land war in Asia. On September 25, 1964, Johnson told a TV audience that the United States did not want to get into a war with Vietnam, which could lead down the slippery slope to a war with Red China: "We don't want our American boys to do the fighting for Asian boys. We don't want to get involved with a nation with seven hundred million people and get tied down in a land war in Asia." And a month later in Pittsburgh, he assured a crowd, "There can be and will be, as long as I am President, peace for all Americans."

Most Americans wanted to believe President Johnson because they were frightened by his hawkish opponent Republican Senator Barry Goldwater of Arizona. Goldwater had scared the media during his San Francisco acceptance speech when he said, "I would remind you that extremism in the defense of liberty is no vice. And let me remind you also that moderation in the pursuit of justice is no virtue." During the 1964 campaign, Democrats exploited Goldwater's hawkish reputation. They called him "trigger happy" and ran the famous "Daisy Girl" commercial which showed a small girl picking flowers while a background voice counted down, "Three, two, one....Boom!" The TV screen was filled with a massive nuclear explosion and the audience heard Lyndon Johnson saying, "We must either love each other, or we must die."

In November President Johnson won a landslide victory. He captured over 60% of the popular vote and had a 486 to 52 margin in the Electoral College. Most Americans were relieved. In their minds, they had avoided a possible nuclear war launched by a super patriot.

Dr. Strangelove satirized the nation's military and civilian elites. Should movies that make fun of our leaders be censored?

Three months after the 1964 election, President Johnson ordered American planes to bomb targets in North Vietnam. And in March 1965, 3,500 U.S. Marines landed at Da Nang in the first deployment of U.S. combat troops to Vietnam. By 1968 there were over half a million Americans fighting a land war in Vietnam.

Why did President Johnson ignore his election promises and involve the United States in a full scale land war in Vietnam? In his analysis, James David Barber describes Johnson as destructive and a compulsive liar. Barber classified Johnson as active-negative. "The primary risk in electing an active-negative character to the presidency is the risk of disaster," wrote Barber, "of one man's personal tragedy plunging the nation into massive social tragedy."[4]

The nation might have avoided the worst of Vietnam if voters had known about Johnson's behavior as a college student. In 1928 the future President attended Southwest Texas State Teacher's College at San Marcos where he was known to everyone on campus as "Bull" Johnson. The college yearbook singled out twelve students for special treatment that year. One was Lyndon Baines Johnson. The yearbook had his name and the following caption below the photograph of a Jackass: "As he looks to us on the campus every day . . . From far away, and we sincerely trust he is going back. A member of the 'Sophistry Club.' Master of the gentle art of spoofing the public."

In the *College Star's* humor column, a student writer defined "Bull" as "Greek philosophy in which Lyndon Johnson has an M.B. degree." Everyone on campus knew "M.B." meant "Master of Bullshit." According to one classmate, Johnson got the name "Bull" because he was so full of bullshit, manure that people just didn't believe him . . . he was a man who just could not tell the truth."[5]

> **Interested in getting inside information about American politicians today? Use America Online under keyword: "Politics."**

Before electing a President, American voters should know which of the candidates is an intelligent scoundrel, which is a naive fool, and which was called "Bull" in college.

It is the President, according to political scientist Louis Koenig, who "bears the awesome responsibility to our allies, to his own people, indeed to all mankind, of deciding when if ever to use vast arsenals of American nuclear weaponry. Under law only he, the Commander-in-Chief."[6] This awesome responsibility comes from 22 words in Article II, Section 2 of the U.S. Constitution which says the President "shall be Commander in Chief of the Army and Navy of the United States, and of the militia of the several States . . . ."

Under the checks and balances system, Congress also has war powers. It declares war, taxes and spends for the common defense, sets rules for the military services, and when necessary tries to limit an over-zealous President. After the Pearl Harbor attack, President Roosevelt asked Congress to declare war on Japan. Without this declaration, Congress could have refused to give Roosevelt the funds to fight a full-scale war. A determined President, however, can sometimes circumvent the power of Congress to declare war. He can provoke a war as James K. Polk did in 1846 by sending troops to occupy a disputed border area between Mexico and the new state of Texas, starting fighting that Congress reluctantly formalized with a declaration of war. The President also may commit Americans to fight in a "police action," as did Harry Truman in June 1950, after North Korean soldiers invaded South Korea. Or, like

Lyndon Johnson in 1964, a President can wait for the enemy to provoke an "incident" and then ask Congress for the power to wage an undeclared war.

When George Bush sent Americans against Iraqi forces in January 1992, he was following through on his threat to oust Saddam Hussein's troops from Kuwait. Although Hussein was a dictator in the mold of Adolf Hitler, the Persian Gulf War was fought to preserve American interests, namely oil. Should wars be fought over resources like oil?

During World War II and the Korean War, Americans got most of their news from written sources. The Vietnam War, however, came to Americans every night over television. By showing anti-war protests at home, and atrocities happening in Vietnam, TV made that war the most unpopular in American history. The proximity of TV to modern war signals a new era perhaps best described as "the medium is the massacre."

Abraham Lincoln only had to worry about newspaper reporters who liked to call him everything from "ugly baboon" to "honest Abe." More than any other President, likeable old honest Abe demonstrated the awesome possibilities of being Commander in Chief during wartime. He raised an army, emptied the treasury, and suspended civil liberties without asking for congressional approval. When the South seceded, Lincoln raised an army of 40,000 three year volunteers and then directed the Secretary of the Treasury to spend $2 million for food, uniforms and guns. Concerned about the threat to the national capitol from rebels in Maryland, Lincoln wrote the army commander there to suppress local insurrections even if he had to suspend the *writ of habeas corpus.*

Habeas corpus is a court order telling an official who has a person in custody to bring the prisoner to court and explain why he or she is being detained. It is an important civil liberty because it prevents arbitrary arrest and imprisonment. Without habeas corpus, suspects could be imprisoned and left in jail. The Constitution guarantees the right of habeas corpus, but Congress may suspend it in cases of rebellion or invasion.

Acting on Lincoln's orders, Union soldiers in May, 1861, arrested John Merryman and charged him with conspiring against the United States. Merryman was imprisoned at Ft. McHenry, Maryland. One day after Merryman's arrest, a petition for habeas corpus was presented to Chief Justice Roger Taney, who then ordered Ft. McHenry's commander General Cadwalader to deliver his prisoner. Instead, Cadwalader told Taney that Merryman was charged with treason and the right of habeas corpus had been suspended by President Lincoln. After charging Cadwalader for contempt, Chief Justice Taney issued a judicial ruling that the writ of habeas corpus was exclusively a legislative power and the President could not suspend the privilege or authorize a military officer to do it. Despite Taney's ruling, habeas corpus writs were ignored and suspected traitors and spies were left to rot in federal prisons during the Civil War.

When Congress convened on July 4, 1861, in extraordinary session, Lincoln defended suspending the writ of habeas corpus by asking, "Are all the laws but one to go unexecuted, and the Government itself go to pieces lest that one be violated?" Congress agreed with the logic of this rhetorical question, and on March 3, 1963, authorized the President to suspend the writ when ". . . in his judgment, the public safety may require it."

Suppose a President decides to make war on drug dealers and orders the military to make sweeping, warrantless searches of neighborhoods where drugs are known to be sold. Let's say that these searches violate the Fourth Amendment prohibition against unreasonable search and seizure, but that they are very effective in ending the traffic in drugs. Would you give high marks to a President who broke the drug trade, but violated the Constitution to do so?

Being President

While his role as Commander in Chief gets most of the crisis headlines, the President has several other equally important jobs, namely:

① **Chief Executive**. Article II makes the President responsible for carrying out the laws with these words: "he shall take care that the Laws be faithfully executed." By laws, the Founding Fathers meant the Constitution, acts of Congress, and Supreme Court decisions. Each President is free, however, to determine how much power to

> Despite his questionable bending of the Constitution, Abraham Lincoln always gets high marks from historians who usually rate him among the four "great" Presidents. Should a leader who ignores the Supreme Court and suspends the writ of habeas corpus be ranked among the great Presidents? Why or why not?

use when he enforces the law. Andrew Jackson, for example, hated Indians and Chief Justice John Marshall. So when the Supreme Court in 1832 ruled Georgia had to stop violating the rights of Cherokee Indians, Jackson said sarcastically, "Marshall has made his ruling, now let him enforce it." In 1980 Ronald Reagan was elected because he promised to be a tough "law and order" President. So when 12,000 members of the Professional Air Traffic Controllers (PATC) went on strike and refused to return to work, Reagan fired them.

> Are there any limits to the power to execute the laws? In an 1890 case known as *In re Neagle*, the Supreme Court ruled that a President has unspecified powers that emanate from his very position as chief executive. Similar to a king's royal prerogative this "inherent powers" doctrine was used by President Truman to justify seizing U.S. steel mills during the Korean War. The Supreme Court ruled, however, that Truman had gone too far. How far can a President go under this inherent powers doctrine?

Substantial power requires intelligent maturity. In the corporate world, executives with "Emotional Intelligence" [EQ] get promoted because they have an optimistic view of life and tend to treat obstacles and setbacks as temporary and therefore surmountable. Pessimists tend to take setbacks as personal and permanent; so they don't usually bounce back easily. Former President Franklin Roosevelt had polio and needed a wheelchair most of his adult life. Rather than feel self-pity, "happy warrior" Roosevelt guided the nation through the Great Depression and World War II. Though popular, Roosevelt was often criticized because he was capable of being devious and dishonest. Richard Nixon, in contrast, was also devious and dishonest, but he was overwhelmed by his harsh childhood and political defeats. More revealing, Nixon never forgave an enemy. Is the current President a happy warrior?

Researchers who developed the EQ rated Bill Clinton high on intelligence and ability to establish rapport with the people. Because of his eagerness to please, Clinton was perceived as weak by the industrial psychologists. As for controlling his impulses, Clinton—in the words of Richard Ellis of Oregon's Williamette University—is "terrible."[7]

> **What does it mean when experts refer to a President as impulsive?**

> An impulsive chief executive might decide to send the CIA after drug dealers in the inner cities, and have them imprisoned without the possibility of parole. Perhaps we need to control our Presidents by requiring them to take a drug that brings out their active-positive qualities. What do you think?

In order to see that the laws are faithfully executed, a President must be able to appoint loyal supporters to top government jobs. In Article II, Section 2 the Constitution empowers a President to nominate ambassadors, federal judges, and the heads of departments. The modern President and his department secretaries control about seven thousand jobs. These include positions such as top executive department employees, White House employees, federal judges, U.S. attorneys, U.S. marshals and various board and agency employees. The Senate, in most cases, must give its advice and consent to nominees.

This **Advice and Consent** rule was a hot media topic in July 1991 when President George Bush nominated 43-year-old Clarence Thomas to replace Thurgood Marshall, who was retiring from the Supreme Court. At first, the choice of Thomas seemed ideal. Like Marshall, Thomas was a successful African American. Unlike Marshall, however, Thomas was a conservative who believed equality did not have to include affirmative action and quotas. On the surface, the Thomas nomination seemed a perfect political choice. Senate Democrats who opposed Thomas for his conservatism would be called "racist," and Bush could not be accused of being a racist, even though he did qualify for the title "intelligent scoundrel."

Two months after Thomas was nominated, he was accused by former aide Anita Hill of sexual harassment which had occurred several years before. After televised hearings that kept Americans glued to their sets, the Senate by a 52 to 48 vote reluctantly approved Thomas.

Although many Americans were shocked by the lewd facts brought out during the Clarence Thomas hearings, the process had worked exactly as envisioned by the Founding Fathers. They had given both the

> Checks and Balances at Work, Again

President and the Senate a role in the appointing of federal judges, so that a public debate could be held. From the beginning when the Senate refused to confirm George Washington's first nominee to be chief justice, public debates have been an integral part of the nominating process.

Despite the controversies over Presidential appointments, there is also a custom which makes it easier for a President whose political party controls the Senate. Euphemistically titled **Senatorial Courtesy** this custom requires that a President always confer with his party's senators from the state in which a federal office is filled. This means any federal judges appointed to office by President Clinton in 1997, required him to get a recommendation from

Senators Harry Reid and Richard Bryan. If the President ignores this "courtesy," the Senate invariably rejects his nominee. The practical purpose of senatorial courtesy is to give the senators control over federal patronage in their states. **Patronage** means the power to give special favors to loyal supporters and friends. It is another form of "juice."

In the past, reformers always opposed patronage on the grounds that it gave government jobs to people whose only job qualification was their loyalty to the winning party. This "spoils system" was justified by political boss New York Senator William Learned Marcy who defended the appointment of Martin Van Buren as minister to England as a reasonable application of "the rule that to the victor belongs the spoils of war."

> **Should a winning political party be able to reward its loyal followers with government jobs, contracts, or other forms of juice. Why, or why not?**

During the Civil War, Abraham Lincoln's Republican party controlled both houses of Congress. To save the Union, Lincoln and the Republican majority in the Senate made sure that most high ranking Union officers and federal job holders were loyal party members. When the Civil War began in 1861 most Americans believed in Marcy's dictum. They understood that for government to work there has to be someone willing to do the job. Lincoln was a typical politician and made sure loyal Republicans were appointed major generals, postmasters, mail agents, land office registrars, assessors, tax collectors, Indian agents, customs agents and pension agents.

Critics often wonder why most Americans give so little of their time to political activities. Political scientists doing political surveys usually discover that Americans don't like politics, and use impressive words like **alienation** to explain the indifference. The answer, however, may be economic rather than psychological.

Andrew Jackson used government jobs and other patronage to build a strong political organization. *Spoils* made it possible for ambitious young men with energy but little education to get ahead. Reformers, however, thought the system too corrupt. They didn't like the idea of government employees also being party workers and giving part of their pay to the bosses. As a way to end this "corruption," the reformers pushed through the famous 1883 Pendleton Act. This law placed most federal jobs under a competitive civil service system based on merit, which essentially now means a college degree and the ability to do well on a written government test. In the past, ambitious immigrants could earn government jobs with loyalty to a political party. This meant a payoff for politically active young men. Is that "payoff" still available?

② **Chief Legislator**. In addition to his considerable powers as Commander in Chief and Chief Executive, the President gives Congress considerable advice on the types of laws needed by Americans. In the making of laws, Presidents have the power to influence legislation through their messages to Congress, the veto, and control over sessions. This law-making power also includes the President's personal contacts with members of Congress, the use of patronage, and his ability to deliver votes by appealing to the voters.

✪ **State of the Union Message**. Article II, Section 3 states the President "shall from time to time give to the Congress Information on the State of the Union, and recommend to their Consideration such Measures as he shall judge necessary and expedient." The State of the Union Message is submitted by the President, usually in person at the beginning of a regular session of

Congress. Regular sessions begin during the first week of January of odd-numbered years, with the start of the terms of all Representatives and one-third of the Senators. On Tuesday, February 5, 1997, President Clinton made a typical State of the Union speech to a Republican-controlled Congress. In his speech, President Clinton promised to balance the budget by the year 2002 and opposed a balanced budget amendment. He also outlined a program to increase education spending by 20% to a total of $51 billion for the fiscal year 1998.

Clinton's education budget drew mixed reactions from three political scientists interviewed by the Las Vegas *Sun* reporter Steve Kanigher. Royce Smith, who teaches American politics at CCSN, applauded

> **Have you personally benefitted from the monies spent by the federal government on education?**

Clinton's education package and said, "It's time for someone to address the fact it's much cheaper to educate people than incarcerate them." Larry Tomlinson, another CCSN political scientist, praised Clinton's proposed $1,500 tax credit for the first two years of college . However, Erick Herzik of the University of Nevada, Reno, criticized the Clinton budget saying the proposal to spend $51 billion more was merely a "drop in the bucket" in a $1.5 trillion budget.

Presidents used the State of the Union Message as a convenient way to present a "shopping list" of legislative proposals to Congress and as a way to assure the public the President is doing his job. While the President is speaking, moreover, members of his staff are preparing legislation, testifying before congressional committees, and trying to identify ways to save money.

✪ **The Power of the Veto.** Grover Cleveland always had a narrow view of the presidency. He thought Congress should make laws, and a President should merely execute them. But Cleveland had to modify his attitude because Congress kept passing pension bills that threatened to empty the federal treasury. In 1862, Congress passed a law which said all soldiers and sailors who had suffered any physical disability while serving in the Union Army would be entitled to pensions, and so would their widows, orphans, and other dependents. By the time Cleveland became President in 1884, these pensions were costing the national government over sixty million dollars a year. Under a law approved by President Hayes in 1879, every individual claiming a pension might recover the full amount owed him from the day he left the service. As a result, pension claims agents scurried around the country looking for war veterans who had ailments which could be blamed on their military service. By 1885, the nation had 325,000 pensioners receiving payments for all kinds of disabilities, ranging from missing legs to bad eyesight.

A notorious penny pincher, Cleveland made war on the pensions by vetoing hundreds of bills submitted to him by a generous Congress. Not content to merely veto these bills, President Cleveland liked to add a note of sarcasm to his veto messages. A typical case was his June 23, 1886 veto of House Bill 6688 entitled, "An act for the relief of William Bishop." Bishop was seeking a pension because he caught the measles while on duty as a substitute from March 25, 1865 to May 11, 1865. Though Cleveland himself had hired a substitute to avoid Civil War duty, he went ahead and vetoed HB 6688 and returned it to Congress with typical sarcasm. In his veto message, Cleveland remarked how "fifteen years after the brilliant service and this

107

terrific encounter with the measles" the claimant had discovered that the disease had "settled in his eyes, also affecting his spinal column."

Outraged by Cleveland's insensitivity, Republican newspapers castigated him for his "ridicule, cheap wit, sarcasm, satire, and vituperation of the unfortunates who were so indiscreet as to go into the army and lose their health or lives."

Has any modern President shown Cleveland's stubborn refusal to bow down to a powerful faction like the northern veterans who organized after the Civil War as the Grand Army of the Republic? Has any President in recent history stood up against the National Rifle Association and advocated strong gun laws?

> **Should Presidents avoid sarcasm when they veto a pension for a veteran who served less than two months and is claiming his eyesight was permanently damaged by his war service?**

Despite Cleveland's vetoes of veterans' pensions, other Presidents were more generous. By 1923 (58 years after the Civil War ended), the total cost of Civil War pensions had reached $238,924,872.

Many of these pensions got past Presidential vetoes as riders attached to legislation that the President could not veto. This was possible until 1997 because a President could not veto only a portion of a bill, he had to veto the entire proposed legislation. Thus a rider attached to a government appropriation bill would "piggyback" into existence. Now the President has a **line-item veto** which means he can veto portions of a bill without killing the entire proposal. This means, in practical terms, that the President can now veto what Bill Clinton once called the "special-interest boondoggles, tax loopholes and pure pork."

> **The pork barrel used to be a place on southern plantations where slaves lined up for their daily ration of food. Now the term means government project that benefit incumbent elected officials. A typical pork barrel project might be a useless paved federal road in a congressional district represented by a member of the majority party in Congress.**

Under the new law, President Clinton could sign a bill and then within five days reject a line item. Congress could then pass a separate bill to reinstitute the specific item and the President had the power to veto that bill. Finally, Congress has the power by a two-thirds majority to override the Presidential veto.

✪ **Special Sessions.** Article II, Section 3 grants power to the President to summon Congress into special session on "extraordinary occasions." In 1948 Harry Truman was running for reelection after spending nearly four years quarreling with a Republican Congress. After the 1948 Republican National Convention wrote a platform which attacked Truman's policies, he called a special session and offered to sign any legislation that Congress would approve. After convening, the 80th Congress refused to consider any bills and adjourned after 13 days. Afterwards, Truman used the slogan "the no-account, do-nothing Congress" for his reelection campaign and surprised all the pollsters by winning in 1948.

③ **Chief Diplomat.** The President has the constitutional power to make treaties, provided that two-thirds of the Senators concur. He plays the key role in making and implementing the nation's foreign policy. And he also has access to intelligence information gathered by the Department of State, Pentagon, and the Central Intelligence Agency.

While Article II spells out the Presidential powers in detail, there are also many unwritten customs to guide our leaders. One such custom began in August 1789 when President George Washington went to the Senate for its "advice and consent" to a treaty negotiated with the Southern Indians. Accompanied by Secretary of War Henry Knox, Washington gave a copy of the proposed treaty to the Senate's presiding officer, Vice President John Adams. Adams then tried to summarize the treaty for the Senators. But the carriages bouncing over the cobblestones outside the New York meeting hall were too loud, and Adams could not be heard above the din. The carriage traffic noise was so bad, wrote Senator William Maclay, that he could scarcely hear Adams, but he was sure it was something about "Indians." After reading the first part of the proposed treaty twice, Adams asked the Senators for their advice and consent. At this moment, Senator Maclay suggested that Adams read the entire treaty and the supporting arguments.

By now Washington was very angry and, as described by Senator Maclay, had "an aspect of stern displeasure." The other Senators then started raising minor questions about protocol, which inspired Maclay to ask for a few days to review the treaty and wait

> Washington's attitude is described here by the words "stern displeasure," "violent fret," and "sullen dignity." What contemporary slang words could we use to describe Washington's

for the Georgia delegation, which had not arrived in New York. Maclay later claimed he made the motion to postpone so that the Senators would not be intimidated by the presence of the angry Washington.

A motion was finally made to refer the proposed treaty to a committee of five for its review and recommendations. The motion, however, caused an argument among the Senators over whether such important issues should go to a committee. The rude behavior of the Senators finally enraged Washington and—according to Maclay—the President "started up in a violent fret." After grabbing back his treaty, Washington yelled, "This defeats every purpose of my coming here," and then he left "in sullen dignity."[8]

Although Washington returned two days later for a brief review of the treaty, the damage was done. He never again tried to get the Senate's advice and consent on a treaty until after it was negotiated. Since Washington, Presidents usually send treaties to the Senate only for final approval, and do not get the Senators involved in treaty negotiations.

✪ To avoid the difficulty of getting two-thirds of the Senate to vote "yea," our Presidents now use the **executive agreement**. Usually negotiated with other heads of state, the executive agreement does not have to be approved by the Senate. Unlike a formal treaty, however, the executive agreement is not binding on future Presidents.

> The custom of negotiating treaties without Senate participation had serious unintended consequences in 1920 when the U.S. Senate voted 49 to 35 for the League of Nations, but fell short of the two-thirds majority needed. Locate a reliable source and explain how the custom started by Washington in 1789 had dire consequences in 1920.

While Nazi Germany was threatening to engulf all of Europe, President Franklin Roosevelt used the executive agreement to save England. In September, 1940 Roosevelt gave the British 50 U.S. destroyers in exchange for rights to build air and naval bases in Newfoundland and in the Caribbean. The destroyers for bases deal was made through an executive agreement because

Roosevelt knew that a majority of the Senators did not want to get involved in Europe's war and would not ratify a treaty. Among those who opposed the deal was the famous hero Charles Lindbergh, now an outspoken isolationist.

> Now that the Soviet Union is no longer a communist threat, Reagan's defenders argue that his Cold War policy of building up a strong nuclear deterrent helped hasten the downfall of the USSR. What do you think?

During his administration, President Ronald Reagan used the executive agreement to deploy 108 American Pershing II missiles in West Germany. After the missile agreement was approved by the West German Parliament 286 to 225, critics charged that Reagan had brought the possibility of an accidental nuclear war closer. Defenders, however, argued that Reagan's missile deal was part of a long range plan to get the Soviets to agree on a general reduction of missiles.

How can Congress control a President who happens to be Commander in Chief, Chief Executive, Chief Legislator, and Chief Diplomat? According to James Madison, the Founding Fathers devised a political system in which ambition was made to "counteract ambition." In order to carry out his policies, for example, the President must have the support of a majority in Congress. And by nature the members of Congress are men and women of ambition who will back a President only when it is in their best interests.

In the exercise of his powers then, a President must have congressional cooperation. Consider, for example, **the power of the purse**. The Constitution states, "No money shall be drawn from the Treasury, but in consequence of appropriations made by law." The Constitution also specifies that all bills for raising revenue shall originate in the House of Representatives. This means that a President who wants to conduct an undeclared war will eventually have to rely on Congress for the funds to buy equipment, weapons and food for the soldiers. In 1861 Abraham Lincoln spent the $2 million in the treasury before Congress could act, but to keep fighting the Civil War he had to wait for additional funds to be appropriated legally.

In addition to the traditional checks and balances, the President must also undergo constant scrutiny by the media. Newspaper, radio, television, and the Internet are a contemporary equivalent of checks and balances. Let's refer to them as the **Electronic-Techno-Checks and Balances**.

Bill Clinton, who became a "lame duck" in November, 2000, has been one of our most controversial presidents. Clinton's impulsive sexual escapades seem to symbolize the motto of the 1960's generation which Clinton symbolized, namely "if it feels good, do it!" and "make love, not war!"

Being President is a big job. It includes sending American soldiers to dangerous places, seeing that the FDA does its job, pushing Congress to protect gays in the military, helping bitter foes get along in the Middle East, keeping party bosses happy and avoiding humor that falls flat.

Former President George Bush, during a March 30, 1989 speech at the convention of the American Association of Community and Junior Colleges in Washington, D.C., tried humor and ended up with the following *faux pas*: "It has been said by some cynic, maybe it was a former President, 'If you want a

> Should we laugh at George Bush's faux pas, or demand he be impeached for insulting American women?

110

friend in Washington, get a dog.' We took them literally—that advice—as you know. But I didn't need that, because I have Barbara Bush."

While John F. Kennedy was seeking the Democratic nomination for President he noted the large number of candidates by saying, "I understand there was a survey in which they asked each U.S. Senator about his preference for the Presidency—and 96 Senators each received one vote." Do you see humor in this remark? Why, or why not?

While Franklin Roosevelt was President, Americans crowded into theaters to watch the movie *Abe Lincoln in Illinois* (1940) which has actor Raymond Massey playing Lincoln as a solemn, homespun lawyer pushed into politics by childhood sweetheart Ann Rutledge and by future wife Mary Todd, who forces ambition on the carefree Lincoln. This humble image survives even today. In 1995, for example, Hollywood gave movie goers *The American President* which featured Michael Douglas as friendly Andrew Shepard, a widowed President who spends most of his free time wooing lovable lobbyist Sydney Wade (played by Annette Bening). While movie audiences cheer humble leaders, we also cheer characters like Rambo, who take great delight in killing FBI, CIA, and other government agents who work for those same Presidents. Why?

---

④ **Inherent Powers**. In 1890 the Supreme Court ruled that a President has the power to see that the laws are faithfully executed, and that he was not limited to merely enforcing laws passed by Congress [*In re Neagle*, 135 U.S. 1 (1890)]. In this landmark case, the Supreme Court ruled 6 to 2 that a President has powers that may grow out of the mere necessity of keeping the peace. These powers need not be enumerated in the Constitution, but can be assumed as an obligation to keep the peace. English kings had a similar power, and it was called the **royal prerogative**. This is the type of power exercised by Lincoln in 1861 when he raised an army, emptied the treasury and suspended the *writ of habeas corpus*. It is not unlimited, however. In 1952 President Harry Truman used his inherent powers to take over the nation's steel mills. To avoid a national strike during the Korean War, Truman issued an executive order directing the Secretary of Commerce to take possession of and operate the steel mills. Although the steel companies obeyed the Secretary of Commerce, they sued for an injunction in a Washington, D.C. district court. On April 30, 1952 the district court issued a preliminary injunction stopping seizure of the steel mills. With unusual haste, the Supreme Court reviewed the case and on June 2nd decided six to two against Truman. In 1971 President Nixon tried to keep Vietnam War documents known as the Pentagon Papers from being published by the New York *Times*, and invoked his inherent power to keep classified documents from being published, but lost his battle in the courts.

Did you have trouble understanding the Presidential powers? If so, reduce the essay to an essential outline, which should look like this:
    ① Chief Executive   ② Chief Legislator
    ③ Chief Diplomat   ④ Inherent Powers

The Lawmakers

When the first Congress met on April 1, 1789 in New York City, it had a total membership of 87 men. Most had served in their state legislatures, the Continental Congress, or at the Philadelphia convention. During its two year term, the first Congress created three cabinet offices, established the Northwest Territory, handled hundreds of petitions, enacted over 60 laws, proposed a Bill of Rights, and sat respectfully while a nervous President Washington gave speeches. This Congress met a total of 519 days, and each member was paid $6 a day.

There were no official political parties when the first Congress met. Most of the Founding Fathers feared political parties and thought they were unnecessary. They hoped the new nation could be wisely governed by pressure groups which would form brier

Despite a profound tradition of democracy, the British government has an obsession with secrecy. Under the Official Secrets Act passed by Parliament in 1911, it would be a criminal offense for any government official to publicly disclose a document such as the Pentagon Papers. The official attitude in England is that information belongs to those who rule. If this were the case in the United States, events like the Kennedy Assassination would not be public knowledge. In recent years, Americans have lost considerable faith in their government because of movies which suggest Kennedy was killed by government agents, not a lone gunman. What do you think? Should the U.S. continue its "open" policy on press coverage, or have its own official secrets act?

coalitions around issues that concerned them. This naive belief in government by enlightened factions was crushed by the reality of power. In his analysis of political parties, historian Herbert Agar points out that the growing power of the presidency plus the need to control that office forced the pressure groups to form permanent parties, "each with its own traditions, its own saints and martyrs, its own fierce battle cries."[9] Once established, these permanent coalitions realized their only hope to hold the diverse nation together was to offer the prize of power.

Because an overly ambitious President might organize an interest group coalition strong enough to keep in office too long, the nation needs more than one political party. Since a multiparty system might be too chaotic in a nation of diversity and battling factions, the two party system is a logical option for the United States. Thus the 105th Congress elected in 1996, while Bill Clinton was president, was comprised of a Senate with 55 Republicans and 45 Democrats. The Republicans also controlled the House of Representatives with a 228 to 206 majority: One independent rounded the House total to 435.

Remember, the Constitution did not provide for political parties. It did, however, sanction a system of checks and balances. Faced with Republican majorities in both the House and Senate, Bill Clinton had to veto several bills—including the partial birth abortion ban.

Although their numbers have increased in recent years, the number of women and minorities in Congress remains proportionately low. Check the current Congress. Of a total of 435 members in the House and 100 Senators, how many are female or racial minorities?

No matter what gender or ethnic group, all members of Congress share the perks; and they are substantial. In 1991, for example, each of the 535 members of Congress was paid a salary of $125,100 a year; and by 1995 that amount had increased to $133, 600. By July 2000, the House of Representatives had voted a $3,800 cost-of-living increase to add on their $141,300 annual salaries. This raise for both Democrats and Republicans was the result of an agreement between party leaders not to attack each others' incumbents during the November 2000 elections. In addition to salaries, members of Congress are paid honorariums to give speeches. They also have perks that include free health care, free prescription drugs, free long distance telephone calls, mailing privileges, free parking at National Airport, reserved parking spaces, an inexpensive gym, reasonably priced haircuts, and low cost meals at the 14 Senate and House eating establishments. These range from simple cafeterias to opulent dining rooms, complete with crystal chandeliers and black-tie waiters. Typical cost in 1991: $7.50 for a filet mignon steak.

Use your Internet sources and locate the Almanac of American Politics using the following Web code: [http://www.PoliticsUSA.com/PoliticsUSA/resources/almanac/mas1.htm]. Use this resource to find out the current salaries and perks enjoyed by members of Congress.

Perk-less Americans were shocked in 1991 when the General Accounting Office revealed that in one year alone, members of Congress bounced 8,331 checks worth millions at the lawmakers private bank, now known as B.C.C.I., the "Bank of Corrupt Congressional Incumbents." The perks and bounced checks were clear evidence in 1991 that there existed what writer Nancy Gibbs called a "congressional culture of privilege and protection that is entirely legal because its members make its laws."[10] This **Culture of Privilege** existed in 1991 because the members of Congress employed themselves. It existed because "those who make the rules, control the game." This is reflected in the fact that members of Congress get free health care and have a House pharmacy where free prescription drugs are dispensed.

During the 1992 Presidential election campaign, Democratic candidate Bill Clinton promised Americans a national health care system that would provide every citizen with some of the perks enjoyed by members of Congress. He also promised to cut taxes, halt crime, stop the traffic in illegal drugs, reform welfare, save the environment, provide legal equality for gays, and balance the budget. Two years later the charming President and his Democratic Party were in trouble with the voters. Taxes were still high, drug addicts were still committing crimes to pay for their habit, welfare and the environment still needed saving, gays in the military was a disaster for Clinton's image, and the national debt had not improved much since 1992 when the nation was $4 trillion in debt and going deeper at the rate of $45,662,100 an hour, $1.1 billion a day, $400 billion a year.

Cultural trivia time: Who was Rasputin?

After his election in 1992, President Clinton promised Americans he would reform the national health care system and make it more fair and efficient. To show his determination, the President appointed his wife Hillary to head up health care reform. This was his first mistake. Provoked by conservative radio celebrity Rush Limbaugh, conservative males were angered by the thought that a non-elected feminist who called herself Hillary Rodham-Clinton might be a modern day equivalent of the notorious Rasputin. While conservative columnists were taking shots at Hillary's aggressive management style, the Health Insurance Association of America (HIAA) sponsored a television ad exploiting the **plain folks appeal**. The ad featured a middle aged couple named "Harry and Louise" worrying that under the Clinton plan their taxes would go up, they would lose their personal choice doctor, and another expensive and inefficient government bureaucracy would result. The President then made his second mistake. He publicly denounced the ads, which gave the media a field day.

On November 8, 1994 the voters elected a Republican majority in both the House of Representatives and the Senate for the first time in 40 years. In Washington state, the voters ousted Speaker Tom Foley, a Democrat seeking his 16th consecutive term in the House. Down in Palm Springs, California the voters elected former rock star, Sonny Bono, to represent them in the House.

> **Was Hillary Clinton unfairly criticized by Republicans and Rush Limbaugh?**

For the first time in forty years, Republicans had majorities in both the House of Representatives and the Senate. The Republican victory was attributed to the votes of "angry white males," and on its November 21, 1994 cover *Time* magazine showed a huge Republican elephant stomping a tiny, bug-eyed Democratic donkey under the caption "Stampede."

In American politics there is a **winner-take-all** bias that gives the winning party control of important committees. When the 104th Congress opened on January 4, 1995, the members spent two days electing chairpersons for the 22 House standing committees and the 16 standing committees of the Senate. Among these new chairpersons would be 92-year-old South Carolina Republican Strom Thurmond, who would seek more military spending and use his influence to protect textile manufacturers in his state from foreign competition. Thurmond would also be *President pro tempore* of the Senate, which put him three heart beats away from the presidency of the United States. While the members of the winning Republican party were grabbing the important committee jobs, party members on both sides of the aisle were eating 1,200 pizzas.

The big loser in the off-year election was President Clinton, who had appeared so inept for two years that when voters were asked in November, 1994, "Should the Democratic Party renominate Clinton as its candidate for President?" only 41% said "Yes." When the early exit polls showed the impending disaster, Clinton realized that he had spent too much time trying to cooperate with Congress and not enough setting the agenda for the entire nation. In his book *The Choice* (1996), Bob Woodward describes Clinton as a moody opportunist who saw ways to use the Republican-controlled Congress to his advantage:

> **After hours of talk, fury, disappointment and systematic consideration of the alternative villains, Clinton settled down to feel sorry for himself. But he was accustomed to converting bad news to good, and he eventually began talking about the loss of Congress differently. Could it be an opportunity? Free him of the restraints? Give him a foil?**[11]

Traditionally, the word "foil" means that which sets off something to advantage. It also means to baffle, frustrate or parry. As stated here by Woodward, it meant that Bill Clinton, like a self-obsessed Hamlet, was saying to himself, "I'll let Congress be my foil, and when they slip up I'll do them much harm and it will make me their eventual master."

While the brooding President tried to put a positive spin on the Democratic debacle of '94, the Republicans celebrated their majority hold on the House of Representatives by electing controversial Newt Gingrich (R-Ga.) to be their Speaker; while his parents, wife and daughters watched proudly from the gallery. To elect Gingrich, the House Republicans called for an old-fashioned "roll call" vote. When he was announced the winner by a 228 to 202 party line vote, Republicans chanted "Newt! Newt! Newt!" while the silent Democrats sulked.

As Speaker, Gingrich had the power to recognize speakers, rule on questions of parliamentary procedure, appoint members to select and conference committees; but not to standing committees. Backed by a Republican majority, a confident Gingrich said he would make Congress more accountable, balance the budget and lower taxes through a revolutionary "Contract with America."

> **Specifically, the Gingrich Plan included a constitutional amendment to balance the budget, a line-item veto, a crime bill to speed the death penalty, welfare reform, a family values plan to provide tax credits for children, middle-class tax cuts, slowing military budget cuts, restoration of Star Wars, repealing taxes imposed on Social Security payments to seniors, deregulation of the environment, penalties for frivolous lawsuits, and congressional term limits. Which of these proposals eventually became law? Which did not?**

By the end of 1995, *Time* had featured Newt Gingrich as its "Man of the Year," and justified its decision on the grounds that he had delivered most of his goals and changed the way "Washington sees reality." Gingrich had done this, in the words of columnist Lance Morrow, "ruthlessly, brilliantly, obnoxiously."[12] During 1995 the House passed all but one of the reforms which the Republican "Contract with America" promised. By January 1, 1996, however, only three had been signed into law by President Clinton.

Despite his inability to persuade President Clinton and Senate Republicans to support his proposed contract, House Speaker Gingrich had become a powerful politician—something he dreamed about as a youth. Like Abraham Lincoln, Gingrich had come from humble beginnings and become a powerful figure in American politics. Unlike Lincoln, Gingrich did not come across as a humble leader.

In December 1995, 1,000 adult Americans were contacted by telephone by the Yankelovich Partners Inc., and asked, "Do you have a favorable impression of: Newt Gingrich, Ross Perot, Bob Dole, Hillary Rodham Clinton, Bill Clinton?" The poll showed President Clinton the most popular with 61% favorable, followed by Hillary with 57%. At the bottom of the "Yes" list was Newt Gingrich with only 24% of the respondents saying they had a favorable opinion of him.

For some reason, Newt Gingrich's unpopularity did not seem to hurt Republican candidates for the House and Senate. In November 1996, voters kept Republicans in control of the House by a 228 to 206 majority and in the Senate 55 to 45. Despite Republican victories in a majority of districts and states, Republican Presidential candidate Bob Dole lost.

> Why did Bill Clinton win reelection in 1996? Four reasons seem plausible:

① **The Budget Fiasco:** Late in 1995 President Clinton vetoed two budget bills that originated in the House of Representatives. After each veto, the federal government was shut down and provided only essential services. These shutdowns were featured in media stories

115

showing government workers and others suffering. As a result, Congress was barraged with criticism while the President seemed to be above the turmoil.

② **Crybaby Newt:** In November 1995, Air Force One took off on a 25-hour round-trip flight to Israel with President Clinton, Newt Gingrich and others on board for the funeral of Prime Minister Yitzhak Rabin. During the flight, Gingrich tried to get the President to talk about the budget impasse, but Clinton refused. On the return flight, the Speaker was assigned to a seat in the back of Air Force One. When the plane landed back in Washington, Gingrich and other Republicans exited by a ramp near the back of the plane. Later, when talking to reporters about the budget gridlock, Gingrich complained that he was being tougher during budget negotiations because he felt he had been snubbed during the Air Force One flight. Admitting that his complaints were petty but "human," Gingrich told reporters, "You've been on the plane for 25 hours and nobody has talked to you, and they ask you to get off the plane by the back ramp. You just wonder where is their sense of manners? Where is their sense of courtesy?" These remarks coming from the aggressive Speaker of the House—himself often criticized for being rude—inspired reporters to rush to their word processors and pound out skeptical stories. The New York *Daily News* carried a headline "Cry Baby" with a drawing of Gingrich in a diaper, crying. TV comedian David Letterman described President Clinton telling the Speaker that he was being shifted to the rear to "balance the weight." On the House floor, one Republican asked rhetorically, "Is it parliamentary to call the Speaker of the House a crybaby?" Adding insult to insult, White House press secretary Mike McCurry offered Speaker Gingrich some M&M's that carried the Presidential seal. Bill Clinton had his foil.

During the 1996 election Speaker Newt "Crybaby" Gingrich was reelected from his congressional district. But he had to struggle to be reelected Speaker of the House for the new 105th Congress, that began its term on January 7, 1997. Then after the 2000 general election, Gingrich resigned as Speaker of the House. Why did such a powerful and ambitious politician step down? Surf and let us know what you discovered.

③ **Clinton Moves to the Center:** Like most Republicans and Democrats, Bill Clinton discovered that American voters like moderates and prefer to travel in the middle of the road rather than crash by going too far left or too far right. To get to this "Vital Center," President Clinton had to mute his campaigns for national health insurance, gays in the military, strong gun controls, and abortion rights. Instead, Clinton scrapped traditional Democratic positions and borrowed heavily from the Gingrich agenda. On the crime issue, for example, the President endorsed expanding the federal death penalty, limiting death-row appeals, and spending billions to build more prisons. Instead of supporting liberal crime policies, Clinton took on the cape of fearless crime fighter and praised curfews, uniforms for public school students, and stole Bob Dole's thunder by lecturing to the entertainment industry about the need to control drugs, and to stop showing gratuitous television and movie violence. Instead of portraying the "I never inhaled" hippie, baby boomer, Clinton began sounding like a Republican curmudgeon when he sided with law enforcement conservatives on virtually every crime issue. To cap off his resurrection as a law and order champion, the 1996 Clinton was fully committed to winning the war against drugs. In essence, Bill Clinton underwent a metamorphosis. He changed from charming rogue to intelligent scoundrel. These qualities, and his pro-abortion stance, made

Clinton the favorite of a majority of female voters which offset the angry white males who had made Newt Gingrich their champion.

④ **The Old Grump Factor:** By November 1996, the Presidential issue had narrowed down to a simple question: "Who can we trust? Bill Clinton, who stands before the camera and debates with a benign smile, or that grumpy Bob Dole and his crybaby friend Newt Gingrich?"

In 1995 campaign donors had to pay $20,000 for a personal visit with the Speaker of the House, and considerably more to sleep in the White House.

While donors were buying influence with elected officials, common Americans were more worried about the **national debt** and the **budget deficit**.

> Deciding a President on the basis of personal charm is not always wise. On March 4, 1997 Bill Clinton made a decision that may prove to be wise or dangerously foolish sometime in the future. Declaring the creation of life "a miracle that reaches beyond laboratory science," President Clinton barred spending federal money on human cloning, and also urged a halt to private research until we better understand its ethical impact. Was this a good idea? Could a ban on cloning research have any dangerous unintended consequences?

> Explain what we mean by the "national debt" and the "budget deficit." Now crank up your computer, and ask for "The National Debt Clock http://www.brillig.com/debt clock/" and put the new figures in the space below:

To reduce the budget deficit to manageable levels, Congress could raise taxes, cut defense, eliminate foreign aid, reduce entitlements, freeze spending and stop all entitlements, like medicare, food stamps, or farm subsidies. Or Congress could eliminate some of the "human resources" programs like college loans.

During the Clinton years, Republicans kept trying to amend the Constitution to require Congress and the President to balance the budget. In 1997, the House by a 280 to 153 majority approved the balanced budget amendment. The Senate did the same 66 to 34. Yet the amendment was never adopted. Why not?

> If the House by a 280 to 153 majority approved the balanced budget amendment; and the Senate by 66 to 34 approved, why has it failed to become part of the Constitution?

The failure of Congress to approve the balanced budget amendment in 1997 frustrated Senate Majority leader Trent Lott (R-Miss.), and he complained, "When you give your word to your constituency that you will vote for a balanced-budget amendment and then turn around a few months later and vote against it that raises the question of basic honesty."

There was a time when politicians could stay in Washington and hide from their angry constituents. Modern technology, however, has made it possible for constituents to visit their legislators frequently. Moreover, members of Congress now can fly home to their districts and states every month. Technology has brought members of Congress close to their constituents, perhaps too close.

When they're not back home campaigning for votes, members of Congress are busy making laws. To learn more about current legislation, use Internet sources such as [http://thomas.loc.gov/] or use the keyword "Politics" if you happen to have America OnLine (AOL). From these and other sources, you can learn how legislation gets passed and which members of Congress have the most power. The most powerful members of Congress get their legislation passed. To understand this type of power, we need to look at the leadership, the committees, the filibuster, congressional districts, and the porkbarrel:

① **The leadership** - The Speaker of the House is recognized as the single most powerful individual among the 435 members. If the President and Vice President were both killed in an accident, or assassination, the Speaker becomes President. The Speaker directs floor debate, controls the House agenda, appoints members to select committees and refers bills to committee. Other important House leaders are the majority and minority leaders, the whips and the deputy whips. In the Senate the majority leader has the most power. Bob Dole of Kansas had this position until he decided to run for President. To show his commitment to the task, Dole resigned from the Senate *before* the election. Since Dole was trailing in the polls throughout the campaign, we wonder why he resigned as leader of the Senate.

② **The committees** - In his January, 1961 inaugural speech, John F. Kennedy promised Americans a New Frontier and challenged, "Ask not what America will do for you, but what together we can do for the freedom of man." After giving Kennedy 70% of their votes and his margin of victory in the Electoral College, black Americans expected the President to expand their freedom with a strong civil rights bill. Since Kennedy's Democratic party outnumbered Republicans 64 to 36 in the Senate and 263 to 174 in the House, there seemed to be no logical reason why the President could not get a civil rights bill through Congress. Before a civil rights bill could be passed, however, President Kennedy had to get it through the House Rules Committee. The **Rules Committee** is the traffic cop responsible for regulating the flow of legislative traffic in the House. All bills that emerge from any of the 22 standing committees must receive a "rule" before going to the House floor for final debate and vote. The House Rules Committee, however, can hold a bill, amend it or write a new one. Or it can send the proposed legislation forward with a special "rule," which sets the amount of floor time for debate, and either allows or forbids amendments from the floor. The special rule determines the fate of a bill. If a majority on the Rules Committee wants a bill killed, it may release it under a "wide-open-rule," which allows any minor amendments from the floor. If the majority wants a bill passed in its original form, it is released under a "gag rule" which prohibits amendments from the House floor.

In 1961 the Rules Committee was chaired by 77-year-old Howard W. Smith, a Democrat who had represented Virginia's Eighth District since 1931. Judge Smith chaired the committee because he had **seniority**, which means the most consecutive years in the House and on a particular committee. In the past when Smith wanted to stop passage of a bill before the Rules Committee, he simply went home to Virginia for a few days "to milk the cows." Smith was a conservative, who saw no reason in 1961 to pass any more civil rights legislation. Because he chaired a powerful committee, Judge Smith was able to bottle up Kennedy's proposed civil rights legislation and frustrate the liberals in Congress. The Speaker of the House in 1961 was Texan Sam Rayburn, a pragmatic Democrat whose motto was, "If you want to get along—go along." Aware that Kennedy's legislative agenda was threatened by Judge Smith, Speaker

Rayburn proposed enlarging the Rules Committee from 12 to 15 members. The Rayburn plan would give liberals an 8 to 7 majority. After a bitter fight, the House on January 30, 1961 voted 217 to 212 to add the new members. After this significant victory, Kennedy had a much better chance to get a civil rights bill through the House of Representatives.

③ **The Filibuster** - When the Senate considered the civil rights bill, conservative southern Senators staged a 75 day filibuster. The word comes from a Dutch word meaning "pirate." Filibusteroes were nineteenth century pirates who preyed upon ships off the coasts of Latin and South America. In the Senate, a filibuster means to "talk a bill to death" by debating until the supporters surrender and make concessions. The 1964 filibuster was ended when two-thirds of the Senators present and voting decided to end the debate. To end the filibuster by **cloture** now requires under Senate Rule 22 that three-fifths (60) of the 100 Senators vote to end debate. Though always controversial, the filibuster is a respected custom because Senators have a strong commitment to free speech and minority rights. And it also demonstrates the dictum that "those who know how to play the game, will know how to win the game."

> If you were a member of the Senate and a law banning partial-birth abortions was being considered, would you participate in a filibuster to defeat the bill? Why or why not?

④ **The Single-Member District** - In American politics, job security means power. A Senator from a "safe" state acquires seniority and good committee assignments. Being *safe* means being elected to represent a

> Why do single member districts and winner-take-all favor a two-party system?

district or a state which consistently votes for the same party and its candidates. Each of the 435 members of the House of Representatives is elected from a single-member district. This refers to an electoral district from which a single (that is, one) legislator wins because he/she has more votes than any other candidate. The word for this is "plurality" not "majority." To repeat, to win election to a seat in the House of Representatives, the winning candidate does not need a majority of popular votes, only a plurality. In 1842 Congress sanctified this system by an apportionment law which required that every state entitled to more than one representative be divided into districts of contiguous territory, each one entitled to a single Representative in the House. Since 1929 the number of Representatives has been frozen at 435, and today each district should contain about 575,000 people. How do we get this figure? Simple math. The Census Bureau announced on April 1, 1991 that the U.S. population was 249,632,692. Subtract the number of people living in Washington, D.C., divide this number by 435 congressional districts and you get a figure near 575,000. This single-member district system is winner-take-all and for that reason favors a two-party system. The Electoral College and Senate elections are also based on winner-take-all, and that fact makes it virtually impossible for weak third parties to ever elect anyone and they soon disappear. By now H. Ross Perot, who ran twice for the presidency, is out of the presidential race because his party has failed to elect anyone to Congress.

As Speaker of the House, Newt Gingrich presided over the impeachment of Bill Clinton in 1999. But the Senate did not convict Clinton of high crimes and misdemeanors. Meanwhile Speaker Gingrich's party lost five seats in the House. So Gingrich resigned.

⑤ **Porkbarrel politics** - Besides locking out third parties, the single-member district system also encourages the use of power to reward faithful voters. On plantations in the Old South, slaves used to gather around a barrel every morning for their daily allotment of pork. Today, the "porkbarrel" refers to members of Congress using their power to get special benefits for their state or district. Instead of getting pork from a barrel, American politicians get votes and contributions from people who benefit from military bases, federal highways, post offices, and dams in their state. To make sure the pork is distributed to everyone, there is a lot of logrolling in Congress. This is an old custom which means, "You scratch my back and I'll scratch yourn." In the past, the President could not stop the pork tide because he lacked an "item veto" and that allowed members of Congress to slide their favorite projects through by attaching them as "riders" to important legislation, like appropriations bills. Today, the President has a **line-item veto**, and this is supposed to end the most wasteful porkbarrel projects.

> Is the line-item veto working as expected, or is Congress still spending too much on porkbarrel projects? Have there been any unintended consequences of the line-item veto?

Members of Congress are now debating where the pork will go on a $96 billion space station that will spread the "space pork" to 15 states.

Judicial Review

In 1965 the Supreme Court had to decide if Estelle Griswold had been denied any liberty protected by the due process clause of the Fourteenth Amendment. Griswold was Executive Director of the Planned Parenthood League of Connecticut. In November, 1961, Griswold and a physician who worked at the League's New Haven Center had given birth control advice to a married couple. The physician, Dr. Charles L. Buxton, had examined the wife, prescribed a contraceptive device for her use, and charged a small fee. At the time, Connecticut had a law which provided "any person who uses any drug, medicinal articles or instrument for the purpose of preventing conception shall be fined not less than fifty dollars or imprisoned not less than sixty days nor more than one year or be both fined and imprisoned." Another section of the law provided that any person who counsels the use of contraceptives "may be prosecuted and punished as if he were the principal offender." Griswold and Buxton were arrested for counseling the use of contraceptives and fined $100 each. They appealed, arguing that the Connecticut law had denied them the liberty protected by the due process clause of the Fourteenth Amendment.

After the Supreme Court of Errors of Connecticut upheld the $100 fine, Griswold and Buxton appealed to the United States Supreme Court. By a 7 to 2 decision, the Court ruled in 1965 that the Connecticut birth control law was unconstitutional. The Court's opinion was delivered by Justice William O. Douglas and its judgment of reversal of the defendants' conviction was agreed to by Chief Justice Earl Warren and Associate Justices Clark, Harlan, Brennan, White, and Goldberg. In his opinion, Justice Douglas broadened the meaning of the Constitution by arguing that specific guarantees in the Bill of Rights have **penumbras** formed by "emanations from those guarantees that help give them life and substance." These include the

120

First Amendment's right of association, the Third's prohibiting of quartering soldiers in homes, the Fourth's guarantee against unreasonable searches and seizures, the Fifth's guarantee against compulsory self-incrimination, and the Ninth's guarantee that "the enumeration in the Constitution of certain rights, shall not be construed to deny or disparage others retained by the people." These guarantees, according to Justice Douglas, created a zone of privacy large enough to encompass the use of contraceptives by married people.

What did Justice Douglas mean by "penumbras"?

Douglas also asked, rhetorically, "Would we allow the police to search the sacred precincts of marital bedrooms for telltale signs of the use of contraceptives?" The very idea, he concluded, "is repulsive to the notions of privacy surrounding the marriage relationship."

In his dissenting opinion, Justice Hugo Black said Douglas had stretched the meaning of the Constitution too far. Agreeing that the state birth control law was silly, Black said he could see no justification, however, for creating a zone of privacy on the basis of "an emanation from one or more constitutional provisions." "I like my privacy as well as the next one," wrote Black, "but I am nevertheless compelled to admit that government has a right to invade unless specifically prohibited by some specific constitutional provision."

After taking this "narrow view" of the Constitution, Black warned that the precedent set in *Griswold v. Connecticut,* 381 U.S. 479 (1965) would give the "federal judiciary the power to invalidate any legislative act which the judges find irrational, unreasonable or offensive."

Eight years after Griswold, the Supreme Court majority in *Roe v. Wade* invalidated Texas anti-abortion statutes by

Eight years after the Griswold case, the Supreme Court expanded the meaning of "privacy" to include a woman's right to have an abortion? By then, Justice Black was dead. Judging by Black's opinion in Griswold, would he have upheld a woman's right to an abortion? Justify.

holding that a woman has the right to end an unwanted pregnancy. In his opinion for the majority, Justice Harry Blackmun used history, medical facts, and logic to argue that a right of privacy exists in the Ninth and Fourteenth Amendments. Justice White disagreed, calling the majority opinion "an improvident and extravagant exercise in the power of judicial review which the Constitution extends to this Court . . ."

In footnotes, you will see this case cited as *Roe v. Wade*, 410 U.S. 113 (1973). What does this citation mean?

In the two cases described above, the Supreme Court exercised its power of **Judicial Review**. As defined by political scientist Howard Dean, judicial review means "that whenever it becomes necessary for the settlement of litigation before it, a court may scrutinize state and federal legislation and the acts of state and federal executive officers and courts in order to determine whether or not they are in conflict with the Constitution."[13]

The power to declare a federal law unconstitutional was decided in the famous 1803 case known as *Marbury v. Madison*. This fascinating case involves a lame duck President and Congress, an absent minded Secretary of State who ends up as Chief Justice, and an obscure Federalist denied a judicial commission but immortalized as the catalyst for judicial review. To get all the facts about this important case, use your computer skills. *Marbury v. Madison* is still the law of the land. It empowers the Supreme Court to decide the constitutionality of a federal law designed to balance the budget, define life as beginning at conception, or pay reparations to African Americans whose ancestors suffered at the hands of whites.

Locating Supreme Court Decisions? Try this Internet Source: [http://www.law.cornell.edu/supct]. This source will give you the complete text of Supreme Court decisions, including opinions of the Court, concurring opinions, and dissenting opinions.

Judicial Review is a formidable power, and in our system it is in the hands of nine persons who hold their jobs for life, or good behavior.

In the past, the Supreme Court was referred to as "Nine Old Men." Now the Court has nine persons of mixed gender, and comfortable age. If they blunder the entire nation could be in trouble. There are, however, three legal ways to limit the Court's power.

① The President and Congress can increase the number of justices. This was tried by President Franklin Roosevelt, who tried to increase the number of Justices from nine to 15. Roosevelt's "Court packing plan" failed, however.

② The House of Representatives can impeach a sitting Justice. The most famous impeachment attempt occurred in 1804 when the Republican-controlled House voted articles of impeachment against Federalist Justice Samuel Chase and needed 23 votes in the Senate to convict. Since the Republicans had 25 Senators and the Federalists nine in 1804, the odds were against Justice Chase. However, five Republican Senators backed off because they feared that impeachment would set a bad precedent.

③ Congress can propose a constitutional amendment weakening the Supreme Court, and send it to the states for ratification. Since 1973 Americans have been divided over the abortion issue. Despite the controversy and about 30 million abortions, the Supreme Court has been reluctant to change its mind. Under the philosophy of *stare decisis* ("let the decision stand"), Americans courts are reluctant to overturn established precedents. Has the time arrived, however, to amend the Constitution and have life begin at conception?

Do some browsing and determine the current status of the abortion controversy.

Notes

1. "A Fatal 'Error of Judgment'," *Newsweek* (March 3, 1986), pp. 14-19.

2. James David Barber, *The Presidential Character: Predicting Performance in the White House*, 3d ed., (Englewood Cliffs, New Jersey: Prentice-Hall, Inc., 1985), pp. 460-499.

3. Shari Roan, "All the President's Men," Los Angeles *Times* (August 12, 1996), pp. E1, E6.

4. Barber, *The Presidential Character*, p. 121.

5. Robert A. Caro, *The Path to Power* (New York: Alfred A. Knopf, 1982), pp. 141-160.

6. Louis W. Koenig, *The Chief Executive* (New York: Harcourt, Brace & World, Inc., 1968), pp. 257-258.

7. Richard Ellis, "Square Pegs in the Oval Office?" *Time*) October 2, 1995), p. 66.

8. *Diary*, Sen. William Maclay (August 22, 1789).

9. Herbert Agar, *The Price of Union* (Boston: Houghton Mifflin Co., 1950), pp. 82-83.

10. Nancy Gibbs, "Perk City," *Time* (October 14, 1991), pp. 18-20.

11. Bob Woodward, *The Choice* (New York: Simon & Schuster, 1996), p. 23.

12. Lance Morrow, "Newt's World," *Time* (December 25, 1995/January 1, 1996), pp. 50-51.

13. Howard Dean, *Judicial Review and Democracy* (New York: Random House, 1966), p. 6.

Chapter 5

The Voice of the People

Was Perot's 1992 idea for a "teledemocracy" logical? If so, then why did he fail to capture a single vote in the Electoral College?

During the 1992 presidential election, Texas billionaire H. Ross Perot ran for President of the United States as an independent candidate. Tabbed the "Billionaire Boy Scout" by *Time* magazine, Perot promised Americans that he would, if elected, organize electronic town meetings from the White House. In Perot's futuristic **teledemocracy**, the President would appear before national television audiences and lay out problems like the national debt. During this televised town meeting, millions of voters would send the President their opinions by telephone, fax, computer, modem, video phone and two-way interactive cable TV. According to this Perot electronic democracy scenario, the President would have the opinions of American voters in computer printouts on his desk a few hours after the televised town meeting. He would then deliver the computerized opinions to Congress, which would be under considerable pressure to act according to the national mood. Eight years later Perot was no longer a viable presidential candidate. The two major party candidates George Bush and Al Gore were not using technology to get voter feed-back. Candidate Bush, for example, would spend $95 million for TV advertising and other traditional methods of voter manipulation. The closest any candidate got to a teledemocracy was the use of voter opinion polls similar to those used by Bill Clinton in 1996.

In the past, political party bosses searched for presidential candidates who were "available." A candidate is available if he or she can win. To win an American election, a candidate needs a good leadership record, political experience, popularity, charm and enough intelligence to run an effective campaign. This mind set dictated that only white men were "available." Now that the elections are more "democratic," the two major parties used their campaign funds to hire pollsters to survey voters and ask, "If the presidential election was held tomorrow, would you vote for George W. Bush or Al Gore?"

In 1996 the strategists for Bill Clinton showed how effective good pollsters can be. Remember these names: Mark Penn, Doug Schoen, Hank Sheinkopf, Marius Penczner, Tom Ochs, Bob Squier, and Dick Morris. They were the pollsters, strategists, consultants, and symbol manipulators who worked with Clinton to build "the most sensitive radar apparatus American politics has ever seen."[1]

During his first two years as President, Bill Clinton had pushed for a reform of national health insurance and gay rights in the military. Both issues, though commendable, were highly unpopular with powerful factions and with most voters. To reshape his image and win in '96, Clinton needed accurate information about the mood of voters. The Clinton team, through sophisticated public opinion survey techniques, gathered this "voters' mood." The most important contributor to the polling campaign was Mark Penn and his **Neuropersonality Benchmark Poll**, which they took at two secret polling places in Manhattan and Denver. It showed that Dole was ahead of Clinton with voters who were married and raising children. Penn's poll also showed that these key voters were most concerned about crime prevention, tobacco ads aimed at children, violence in the schools, and other **moral-value issues**.

The Clinton team also previewed proposed Clinton ads in special open booths set up at shopping malls to test voter reaction. Together, the **Neuro Poll** and **Mall Reaction Surveys** convinced the Clinton people that their candidate had to reshape his image and move to the "vital center" of the political spectrum. These surveys contributed substantially to the birth of a new Bill Clinton, one who would be tough on crime, work to strengthen the family, balance the budget, and even favor school uniforms for young students.

Curious about polls? To learn more, contact these Internet sources: The Roper Center or the Social Science Data Collection. [http://www.lib.uconn.edu/RoperCenter/] or [http://ssdc.ucsd.edu/ssdc/pubopin.html].

Clinton's new image clearly won over female voters. He proved that there is now a **Gender Gap** in American politics. This gender gap was apparent in 1994 when "angry white men" elected a Republican majority to Congress and helped put Newt Gingrich in control of the House of Representatives. This gap was also apparent in 1996 when most women cast their votes for Bill Clinton and—symbolically—showed their support for his much maligned wife Hillary.

According to political journalist Dick Polman, this difference in the way men and women voted was a significant political development in 1996: "It has validated Clinton's female-friendly campaign and exposed a fundamental flaw in the ill-fated Bob Dole operation. And it has the Republicans scared witless—particularly since women voters typically outnumber men."[2]

In 2000, however, the names on the presidential ballot were all male. So the ladies may have to wait until 2004 to see bumper stickers that say "Vote for Lizzie—She's Not Testy" or "Vote for Hilly—She's a Dilly." More likely, if a woman runs on a major party ticket for the presidency, we'll see bumper stickers that say, "Don't be Stupid, Stop the Sorceress," or "Don't Bewitched, Support Brother Bob."

Or we won't see any bumper stickers. They were one casualty of the Clinton-Dole campaign. The Dole campaign cost $40.5 million and only $476,000 was spent on bumper stickers. Clinton spent $30.4 million and only $173,717 for campaign trivia. So if you have a campaign button or bumper sticker for the '96 Presidential campaign, better save it.

In 1996 the voters reelected President Clinton with 49% of the popular vote (45,628,667). He carried 31 states and the District of Columbia for a winning total of 379 electoral votes. Republican Bob Dole, on the other hand, won 19 states, had 41% of the popular vote (37,869,435), and 159 electoral votes. With 7,874,283 popular votes, H. Ross Perot carried no states and therefore no electoral votes. The 7,874,283 voters who cast their ballots for Perot had no chance to elect him President, but they did deny both major parties a popular majority (50% plus 1). In a direct popular election based on a clear majority rule, no one would have been elected President on November 5, 1996.

They counted the 538 electoral votes on January 6, 1997 before a joint session of Congress. Bill Clinton was declared winner. Clinton won Nevada's four electoral votes by drawing 203,974 popular votes to 199,244 for Dole. Since the electoral vote is "winner-take-all" Dole's 199,244 popular votes gave him zero, null, nothing, naught, a big "goose egg." ☆ Did Bill Clinton get a clear majority of Nevada's popular vote, or merely a plurality? What additional information would we need to answer this question?

> On December 17, 1996, 379 electors went to their state capitols or other designated place and cast their votes for the Clinton-Gore ticket. At the same time, 159 electors voted for Dole-Kemp. H. Ross Perot, as expected, did not get a single electoral vote because he failed to carry any state and none of the 538 electors was "faithless." In Nevada, four long time Democratic party officials cast the state's four electoral votes for Bill Clinton and Al Gore. These electors were Doug Bache, Charles Waterman, and Marie Ripps, all of Las Vegas. Elector Virginia Cain of Reno cast the fourth vote. Nevada was entitled to four electoral votes because in 1996 it had two U.S. Senators and two Representatives in the House. None of Nevada's congressional delegation could be an elector, however.

As usual, the Electoral College came under fire for being archaic. In an editorial, the Sacramento (California) *Bee* pointed out that if Perot had received electoral votes he might have thrown the election into the House of Representatives, where the 435 members would have to vote by states, with each state having just one vote, "meaning that California would have no more voice in the outcome than Delaware or Wyoming or Alaska." This "unfair" possibility inspired the California newspaper to demand the abolition of this "clunky system" before it ends with "quirky outcomes, bizarre deals and even gridlock . . . " In Illinois, Representative Ray LaHood (R-Illinois) said he would introduce legislation to abolish the Electoral College. "It seems antiquated, arcane and just nonsense to continue the system," he said. In contrast, Alabama Governor Fob James said the Electoral College "is an underrated unifer" after an election, and students ought to study more about it in school."[3]

> Use your computer to bring up arguments for and against the Electoral College. Then answer this question: "Which argument makes the most sense to you, the clunky system criticism or the underrated unifier defense?" Why?

In 1996 about 93 million Americans voted out of a total of 197 million who were eligible. This was the lowest popular vote turnout since 1824. The highest percentage turnout came in 1876 when 82.4% of the eligible male voters went to the voting booths. The number of Americans who voted in 1996 was about the same as the number who sat for three hours and watched the Super Bowl. Critics claim the Electoral College is to blame for the low turnouts because it has created a system where people can complain and ask rhetorically, "Why should I vote when my vote doesn't count?" ☆ Is this a reasonable question?

Although President Clinton won easily in the Electoral College vote, he received only 49% of the popular vote while Dole had 41% and Perot 8%. Winning with only half the popular vote is not a clear mandate to rule, but winning 379 to 159 in electoral votes suggests—at least symbolically—that Clinton was the clear winner.

On the day before voters trudged to the polls in Las Vegas and waited in long lines for electronic machines to count the votes, a CCN-*USA Today* tracking survey revealed that Perot was the choice of 11% of the voters nationwide. In January 1995, Perot had appeared on the

Larry King TV talk show and was confident that his advocacy group, United We Stand America would someday be a viable political party. In 1992, Perot had 19% of the popular vote and did not carry a single state; which meant no electoral votes. Four years later, Perot's totals were 8% and another zero. By 2000 Perot was a trivia question, i.e., "who ran for President twice and failed to get a single electoral college vote?"

The 2000 Election

To understand the last election, you'll have to know a few basic facts about the Electoral College. For practice, try answering these questions:

- ❏ What is the formula for determining how many electoral college votes each state has?
- ❏ According to the Constitution, who is responsible for determining the method for selecting electors?
- ❏ Where does the electoral college meet?
- ❏ With respect to the electoral college, what is the winner-take-all rule?
- ❏ How many electoral votes are currently needed to win the presidency?
- ❏ For the 2000 elections, what were the results of the electoral vote for president?

On November 7, 2000, Nevada voters gave a plurality of their popular votes to Republican George Bush 301,575 to 279,978 votes for Al Gore. This meant that all four of Nevada's electoral votes would be cast for the Republican candidate. By state law, presidential electors in Nevada must vote for the person who has the most popular votes.

As a result of this law, on December 18, Nevada's four electors cast their votes for Republican candidate George W. Bush, giving him a total of 271 nationally and enough electoral votes to be President. The electors were Bill Raggio of Reno, Tom Wiesner and Jane Ham of Las Vegas, and Trudy Hushbeck of Carson City. They met in Carson City surrounded by applauding fellow Republicans. Because of the winner-take-all rule, there were no Democrats casting Nevada electoral votes on December 18. Nor were there any members of the state's five splinter parties, namely the Reform Party, the Natural Law Party, the Independent Americans, the Libertarians or the Green Party. Why not?

Nevada's four electoral votes were enough to give Bush a narrow electoral college majority but it didn't end the campaign. In Florida Democrats demanded recounts because of the closeness of the popular vote there and the possibility of gaining Florida's 25 electoral votes which would have given the decision to Al Gore. While Clark County residents were using over two thousand sophisticated electronic voting machines, voters in Florida's 67 counties were trying to figure out primitive punch card ballots. The fact that results in one or two states could prove decisive in a close election, we need to know what it is that makes the Electoral College so unique and controversial.

The Electoral College

James Buchanan showed why a weak and indecisive man should not be President. From 1857 to 1861, this timid and physically sick bachelor tried to govern the nation as it drifted toward a Civil War. By 1860, the "United" States were no longer united. The two party system was ready to collapse; a possibility shown by the fact that the country had four serious Presidential candidates running in the 1860 general election. The four were Republican Abraham Lincoln, Northern Democrat Stephen A. Douglas, Southern Democrat John C. Breckinridge, and Constitutional Unionist John Bell. The popular votes were cast in November 1860 this way:

Abraham Lincoln	**1,865,908**	**39.82%**
Stephen A. Douglas	**1,380,202**	**29.46%**
John C. Breckinridge	**848,019**	**18.09%**
John Bell	**590,901**	**12.61%**

Although no candidate had a majority of popular votes, the Electoral College votes were cast this way:

① Lincoln: 180.
② Breckinridge: 72.
③ Bell: 39.
④ Douglas: 12.

The fate of California's four electoral votes in 1860 provides a partial answer to this puzzle? In 1860 Lincoln had 38,733 of California's popular votes, Douglas 37,999, Breckinridge 33,969, and Bell 9,111. Lincoln, however, received all four of

> **How did Lincoln, with less than 40% of the popular vote, get more than half the electoral vote? And how did Lincoln win, since his combined opponents had nearly one million more popular votes?**

California's electoral votes because of a custom used since 1836 known as **Winner-Take-All**. This custom requires that the candidate who gets a **plurality** or the most popular votes gets *all* the state's electoral votes. Lincoln's 38,733 popular votes in California entitled him to all four of the state's electoral votes. With 37,999 popular votes, Douglas did not win a single electoral vote. Neither did Breckinridge with 33,969. This is why in 1996 H. Ross Perot with 8% of the popular vote nationally failed to win a single electoral vote; he didn't carry a popular vote plurality in any state.

This winner-take-all custom exaggerates the winner's margin of victory in Presidential elections and is very unfair to losers. On the positive side, it perpetuates the nation's two-party system and has helped elect leaders (like Bill Clinton in 1996) who can claim a mandate to rule if their electoral college victory is one-sided and their popular vote less than 50%.

> **In 1996 Bill Clinton had only 49% of the popular vote, but won by a substantial 379 electoral votes out of a total 538 possible. Did this fact make it any easier for him to run the country? Why or why not?**

The men who wrote the Constitution weren't sure how they wanted future

Presidents selected. During the Philadelphia convention, they considered four ways to select a President, namely:

❶ By direct popular election.

❷ by Congress.

❸ by state legislatures.

❹ by a special body of electors.

After considering the matter for less than a week, the Committee on Unfinished Business developed a plan which emerged as Article II. The original system gave each state a number of electors equal to its whole number of Senators and Representatives. Thus today Nevada has five electoral votes because it has two senators and three representatives. These electors were to be chosen in a manner decided by each state legislature. After their selection, the electors would meet in their respective states and vote by ballot for two persons. These ballots would be sent to the President of the Senate and opened before the members of both houses and counted. According to Article II, "The Person having the greatest Number of Votes shall be the President, if such Number be a Majority of the Whole Number of Electors appointed . . . " The Constitution originally provided that if more than one person obtained a majority and the vote was tied, the House would decide between the winners. And if no person had a majority, the House would choose from the five highest people on the list, with each state having only one vote.

Why did the Founding Fathers approve such a complicated system? The idea of electing the President by direct popular vote was considered, but the majority of delegates at the constitutional convention feared the masses were too "turbulent" to decide. These "elitists" agreed with George Mason's complaint that letting the people vote for their President would be like letting a blind man decide the color of clothes he would wear.

By giving each state a number of votes equal to its representation in Congress, the Founding Fathers had—in the opinion of writer James Michener—reached a "brilliant compromise." They designed the compromise to secure support for the Electoral College plan from state political leaders, and in that respect it worked.[4]

By letting special electors decide by ballot the President and Vice President, the

> Some critics of the Electoral College think it unfair that each state no matter what its population is entitled to 2 electoral votes for its 2 Senators. Thus Nevada gets 2 and California gets 2. Is this fair? What does it suggest about the nature of rules?

Founding Fathers hoped to have a system which would guarantee the election of the two best men in the nation. The vote for a separate Vice President was supposed to guarantee that another man equally qualified could take over for the President. These electors were to be the nation's most talented and popular men. They were also to be among the social, economic and intellectual elite. According to historian Herbert Agar, the Founding Fathers designed the Electoral College to keep the presidency beyond the control of the "turbulent mob."[5]

When George Washington was elected President, the Electoral College consisted of 69 men. Each cast two votes giving 69 to Washington and 35 to John Adams, who became Vice President. The original 69 electors were selected in a manner determined by each state legislature. By limiting the Presidential selection process to a small body of electors, the

Founding Fathers hoped to keep "politics" out of the Presidential selection process. In *Federalist 68*, Alexander Hamilton explained why the electors would rise above politics and not vote for inferior men:

> **Talents for low intrigue, and the little arts of popularity may alone suffice**
> **to elevate a man to the first honors in a single State; but it will require other**
> **talents, and a different kind of merit, to establish him in the esteem and**
> **confidence of the whole Union, or of so considerable a portion of it as would**
> **be necessary to make him a successful candidate for the distinguished**
> **Office of President of the United States.**

Did the Electoral College work as described here by Alexander Hamilton? What about the 1996 Presidential election? The incumbent President Bill Clinton had been Governor of Arkansas before running for President, had avoided Vietnam War duty, and was accused of sexual harassment. His opponent Bob Dole served in the United States Senate as Majority Leader and was seriously wounded in World War II. Neither was known for any "outstanding" qualities.

The Electoral College did not prevent "politics." Political parties today nominate candidates who are "available," meaning "who can win." And they nominate a Vice President to "balance the ticket," and not for any special personal attributes.

After they ratified the Constitution, Congress designated the first Wednesday in January 1789 as the day for choosing electors. The states selected 69 electors who each cast their two ballots. They sent these ballots to New York, where Congress was meeting, and counted. Of the 69, each elector gave one vote to George Washington. The second

> **Cultural literacy trivia time: What do we mean by "available" and by "balancing the ticket?"**

highest total went to John Adams, who received only 35 votes. Though both were Federalists, Adams trailed Washington by so many votes because Alexander Hamilton (who warned about "low intrigue" in *Federalist 68*) had told the electors not to vote for the second person they really wanted so Adams would not unintentionally tie Washington and send the election in the House of Representatives. Instead of advising only a few electors, Hamilton gave those instructions to several, causing Adams to get far fewer votes than he expected. His 35 votes so embarrassed Adams that he almost refused the vice presidency.

By 1796 the system devised by the Founding Fathers at Philadelphia was evolving. Instead of exercising their best judgment, the electors were committing themselves in advance to vote either Federalist or Republican. Moreover, the state legislatures were starting to let the voters decide who would be the electors through a popular vote.

Eleven years after the first election, the system began to self-destruct. In 1800, 73 electors committed to Republicans Thomas Jefferson and Aaron Burr, and cast their votes accordingly. Federalist John Adams received 65 electoral votes and his running mate Thomas Pinckney had 64. Something had gone wrong, however. Because the Constitution made no distinction, both Jefferson and Burr had the necessary votes to be elected President. Since Burr would not withdraw his candidacy, the election had to be decided by the House of Representatives. Of the 16 state delegations in the House, the Republicans controlled eight votes, the Federalists 6 and two were even. After 36 ballots, Jefferson was finally elected President.

In 1800 Federalist Alexander Hamilton used his influence with House of Representatives Federalists to give the presidency to Republican Thomas Jefferson. Though Hamilton feuded with Jefferson, he considered him a more stable person than the unpredictable Aaron Burr. Four years after Hamilton helped elect Jefferson, he opposed Burr's bid to become governor of New York state. Then Burr killed Hamilton in a duel. Hamilton then became a sort of martyr for the historians, who conveniently forgot he was an elitist who distrusted the common people. Hamilton and other Dead White European Males (DWEM's) have been disappearing from our history books to make way for common folk. Is this a good trend?

The eighteen hundred election convinced Congress to change the Electoral College. In the very important 12th Amendment, the President and Vice President were to be elected separately and to win would require a majority:

> The Electors shall meet in their respective states, and vote by ballot for President and
> Vice-President, one of whom, at least, shall not be an inhabitant of the same state
> with themselves; they shall name in their ballots the person voted for as President, and
> in distinct ballots the person voted for as Vice-President, and of the number of votes
> for each, which lists they shall sign and certify, and transmit sealed to the seat of the
> government of the United States, directed to the President of the Senate;—the president
> of the Senate shall, in the presence of the Senate and House of Representatives, open
> all the certificates and the votes shall then be counted;—the person having the greatest
> number of votes for President, shall be the President, if such number be a majority
> of the whole number of Electors appointed; and if no person have such majority,
> then from the persons having the highest numbers not exceeding three on the list of
> those voted for as President, the House of Representatives shall choose immediately,
> by ballot, the President.

These new rules, combined with new customs, have created a system which now works something like this:

❶ Would-be Presidential candidates enter the race by throwing their hats in state elections designed to give voters a chance to **nominate** them to run.

❷ Each major party holds a national convention and selects its candidates for President and Vice President.

❸ They nominate the most "available" candidates. The Vice President is now selected for qualities that enable him/her to **balance the ticket**.

❹ During the general elections in November, voters go to the polls and vote. These **popular votes** are counted. Under the **winner-take-all** custom whoever gets a plurality of a state's popular votes, gets **all** of that state's electoral votes.

❺ The 538 electors in the 50 states, and Washington, D.C. cast their electoral votes. These votes are sent to Congress, opened and counted. Whichever party ticket has 270 electoral votes or more wins the presidency and the vice presidency.

By 1836 new rules and customs had destroyed the unrealistic hopes that the turbulent mob and low intrigue could be kept out of the Presidential selection process. Instead of choosing the electors, state legislatures passed that responsibility to the voters in their states. This change opened the door to popular demagogues who could appeal over the heads of the presumably virtuous elites to the presumably turbulent

Key Fact: The 538 votes reflect the fact that the House of Representatives has 435 members, the Senate 100 and Washington D.C. gets 3 electoral votes. To win, a candidate needs a majority, or 270 plus electoral votes.

mob. Moreover, by 1836 the states were all following the custom of giving all of a state's electoral votes to the candidate with the most popular votes. This **winner-take-all** custom enhanced the power of urban political bosses by letting them deliver an entire state's electoral vote. This means, theoretically, that a candidate winning the state of California by a few thousand popular votes gets all of that state's 54 electoral votes; just as Lincoln did in 1860 when California's population entitled it to only four electoral votes.

Because a state's entire electoral vote can be lost through a word offensive to bloc voters, Presidential candidates have to be cautious. The power of voting blocs was underlined in 1992 when Democratic nominee Bill Clinton criticized words spoken by rap singer Sister Souljah, and risked offending African Americans. By 1996 Clinton was wiser, but was forced to risk offending someone when he vetoed the Partial-Birth Abortion Ban Act.

■ **Remember, it takes a clear majority or 270 plus electoral college votes to be elected President of the United States!**

Today there are 538 electors. This number reflects the fact that there are 100 Senators and 435 Representatives; and Washington, D.C. has three electoral votes. Over the years these electors have pledged themselves to candidates of their party, and voted "as instructed." This means that the electors are committed in advance to vote for their party candidates after they win all of a

state's electoral votes. Occasionally, however, an elector fails to rubberstamp the party choice; and this inevitably provokes the media to run scare stories about the mythical **faithless elector**. In reality, very few electors have ever been faithless and no faithless elector has ever changed the outcome of a Presidential election.

☆ They often say that the media operates on the principle that a dog biting a man is hardly important news, but when the man bites the dog—that is news! Does this truism also apply to the faithless elector phenomenon? How many actual electors have been "unfaithful" in the past? Was this information easy to find?

Under current rules and customs, this is how a typical Presidential election works. In November 1992, voters went to the polls and got ballots marked with the names of Republicans George Bush and Dan Quayle, Democrats Bill Clinton and Al Gore, and several splinter party candidates including H. Ross Perot and his running mate. In Nevada, the Clinton-Gore ticket received 188,169 popular votes to 174,775 for the incumbent Bush-Quayle ticket. Perot trailed with 131,013 popular votes, which was about 27% of the total cast. Because the Democrats had more popular votes than anyone else—but not a majority—they won all four Nevada electoral votes. So in mid-December, four loyal Democratic electors named Mike Sloan, Harvey Whittemore, Virginia Caine, and Sandy Miller went to the Secretary of State's office in Carson City and performed the perfunctory ritual of casting their four electoral votes for Bill Clinton and Al Gore. Nevada's four Democratic electoral ballots were then sent to Washington, where in January 1993, members of the House and Senate, in joint session, opened and counted the 538 electoral votes that came in from all 50 states, and Washington, D.C. The Clinton-Gore ticket received 370 electoral votes to 168 for incumbent's Bush-Quayle, and we had a new President.

Every time a new Congress meets, somebody proposes an amendment to abolish the Electoral College and replace it with a "fair" method of electing our President and Vice President. These "reformers" usually argue that the system needs to be more reliable, accurate and fair. To justify a change, the critics argue that the current system has severe defects, namely:

> **Despite getting a total of 19,228,530 popular votes in 1992 and 19% of the total vote from all of the states and Washington, D.C., H. Ross Perot failed to get a single electoral vote. Why? And is this fair?**

- ☹ <u>**Population determines the number of electors, not voter turnouts.**</u> **In 1960 this unfair rule meant that Richard Nixon with 562,474 popular votes in Kansas received only eight electoral votes, while John F. Kennedy, with only 198,121 popular votes in South Carolina received eight votes also. Since both states had about the same population in 1960, South Carolina was not penalized for its voter apathy. Nor was the state also penalized for depriving black adults of their right to vote.**
- ☹ <u>**The winner-take-all feature is unfair to the losers.**</u> **By custom, all electoral votes go to the candidate with the most popular votes. In 1960 Richard Nixon had 3,259,722 popular votes in California to John F. Kennedy's 3,224,099. Although the difference was only 35,623 popular votes, Nixon "won" all 32 California electoral votes. In effect, Kennedy's 3,224,099 popular votes were worthless.**
- ☹ <u>**The system turns losers into winners.**</u> **In 1824, 1876, and 1888 candidates with fewer popular votes than their opponents received more electoral votes and won. In 1888, for example, Benjamin Harrison had 5,443,892 popular votes to Grover Cleveland's 5,534,488, but still won in the Electoral College vote 233 to 168.**
- ☹ <u>**The winner-take-all system distorts the vote so that candidates with fewer than 50% of the popular vote can still get more than 50% of the electoral vote.**</u> **This has happened 15 times in our history. In 1860, for example, Lincoln had only 39.82% of the popular vote, yet he won with 180 electoral votes.**
- ☹ <u>**The winner-take-all system makes cheating pay off in a big way.**</u> **In 1960 Mayor Richard Daley's Chicago Democratic machine helped win the election for John F. Kennedy by getting out some unusual voters, including dead people, former presidents, and a woman's cat. After the election, Nixon was prepared to challenge the Illinois count, but changed his mind because Republicans had also cheated. As a result, Kennedy won all 27 of the Illinois electoral votes with only 8,858 more popular votes than Nixon.**
- ☹ <u>**Little mistakes make a big difference.**</u> **This was clearly the case in 1884 when Republican James G. Blaine lost the presidency by the margin of New York's 36 electoral votes. Cleveland carried New York State by exactly 1,047 popular votes. Blaine lost New York City because on October 29, 1884, he attended a banquet where Protestant Reverend S. D. Burchard said, "We are Republicans and don't propose to leave our party and identify with the party whose**

antecedents are Rum, Romanism, and Rebellion." Burchard's infamous "Rum, Romanism, and Rebellion" slogan was picked up by Democrats and circulated around New York City and blamed on Blaine. As a result, New York's Catholics voted for Cleveland—who was elected President by Burchard's ill-chosen words. Blaine had not heard the remark by Reverend Burchard and took no attempts to change the record. So by the time New York Catholics heard they were called drunks and traitors, it was too late for Blaine to issue any denials.

☹ **The Faithless Elector.** In 1984 a 19-year-old Republican elector from Utah told reporters he intended to give his vote to independent candidate Lyndon LaRouche instead of Ronald Reagan. The elector in this case was a college freshman who had learned in his government class that the Founding Fathers intended that Presidential electors use their independent judgment and not merely rubberstamp the popular vote choice.

❏ If it has so many flaws, why keep the Electoral College? Despite its weaknesses, the current system has three compelling virtues:

☺ The first virtue showed in 1860 when Lincoln, with less than 40% of the popular vote, captured the electoral majority. This allegedly unfair winner-take-all distribution of the electoral vote has one very powerful virtue—it settles elections by exaggerating the margin of victory, and thus keeps elections from being contested or going into the House of Representatives.

☺ The current system allows voting blocs and well-organized minorities to have more clout than their numbers justify. This means that African Americans, for example, can benefit from voting as a unified coalition for candidates who promise to improve their status through government programs and civil rights legislation.

☺ By giving all of a state's electoral votes to the popular vote winner, the Electoral College strengthens the appeal of a two party system. Why? Try getting 50% of any state's popular vote by running three or four strong candidates.

> **What happens when a third party enters a Presidential race with a strong popular candidate? This happened in 1912, and it's a lesson Republicans and Democrats will never forget.**

The 1912 story began in 1900 when Republican William McKinley defeated Democrat William Jennings Bryan in the popular vote 7,219,530 to 6,358,071 and in the Electoral College 292 to 155. Ten months later, McKinley was assassinated and Vice President Theodore Roosevelt became the President. After serving a full-term from 1904 to 1908, Roosevelt decided to step aside for William Howard Taft, who won the 1908 election 321 to 162 in the Electoral College, and had a popular vote margin of 7,219,530 to 6,358,071. Believing Taft was too conservative for his taste, Roosevelt reentered the Presidential race in 1912 as the candidate for a new third party, the Bull Moose Party. When the votes were counted, Democrat Wilson had 6,286,214 popular votes, Bull Moose Roosevelt 4,126,020 and Taft 3,483,922. In the Electoral College vote, Wilson was an easy winner with 435. Roosevelt had 88 and Taft, only 8.

Why are we so worried about protecting the two-party system? Consider this scenario: Suppose H. Ross Perot had won the 1996 election by some miracle. With a Republican or Democrat occupying all but one of the 535 seats in the House and Senate, how could Perot or any other single individual—no matter how rich and popular—run the national government without party support?

Try to imagine the real consequences of changing from a two-party system to a multi-party system. In *Federalist 10*, Madison warned that factions organized around religious beliefs could be dangerous. The New York Public Library *Desk Reference* lists 13 major world religions. Under Protestantism, the *Desk Reference* lists 15 major denominations. This could mean candidates running under party banners that include the Amish Mennonites, Baptists, Church of Christ, Church of England, Episcopal Church, Lutheran Church, Methodist Church, Pentacostal churches, Presbyterian Church, United Church of Christ, The Church of Jesus Christ of Latter-Day Saints, Jehovah's Witnesses, Religious Society of Friends (Quakers), and Unitarian Universalist Association. Besides all the religious groups, our multi-party system would have to find ways to accommodate ethnic groups ranging from African Americans to Zinbabwe Americans. Then throw in feminists, gays, militias, lesbians, liberals, conservatives, and Rush Limbaugh's ditto heads.

Congress is struggling now because some infantile members lack civility. Consider the chaos if we had several competing political parties instead of only two. ☆ Would Congress be more effective if it was made up of several political factions, all pursuing self-interest? Is this a loaded question?

Still worrying about the Electoral College? Think of a Presidential election as two separate votes to decide who will be the next President and Vice President. ① Vote one is cast when we go to the polls in Nevada and cast a popular vote. ② Vote two is cast when Nevada's four electors go to Carson City and vote for the candidate of their party. Finally, whoever gets 270 or more electoral (not popular) votes wins.

In the 1996 World Series the Atlanta Braves scored 26 runs and the New York Yankees scored 18. Yet, the Yankees won the series 4 games to 2. After the World Series, the Braves felt bad but nobody was gnashing their teeth and demanding that we change the system to make it "fair." Athletes play hard to win, but they respect the fundamental integrity of their sport. In politics, we need also to play to win but accept the outcome when we lose. If every World Series was followed by drastic rule changes, baseball would lose its appeal. In politics, we need also to play to win and accept defeat gracefully. ☆ Should we play the game of life as we would a World Series? Why or why not?

Now that we all understand the Electoral College, we need to add the **Plurality Factor** to our political literacy. The 800 or so elections that occur in this nation every year are not always settled by the majority. In fact, many of our elections are decided by a **Plurality Winner-Take-All** formula. According to *The American Political Dictionary*, it means "the winning of an election by a candidate who receives more votes than any other candidate but not necessarily a majority of the total vote." Winning by plurality means a candidate can carry a state with only

30 to 40 percent of the popular vote, depending on the number of candidates. In the 1996 Presidential election, for example, there were 21 candidates who received popular votes. These candidates had popular vote totals ranging from 580,627 for Green Party candidate Ralph Nader to 407 popular votes for Independent Steve Michael. Bill Clinton ended up with a 49% plurality of popular votes, but was an easy Electoral College winner.

Mathematicians have been studying the different electoral systems and decided that the plurality system used in most American elections is terribly flawed. They object because the plurality system hands victory to the candidate with the most votes, even if that candidate falls far short of a majority. According to the mathematicians, the current plurality system encourages extremism, rewards name-calling, alienates voters, and fails to mirror the feelings of the voters. Northwestern University's Donald Saari says this about the plurality system: "Of all the methods, it's the one where you can have most people preferring A over B, yet B is the winner."[6]

This apparently unfair situation occurred in 1860 when Abraham Lincoln, with only 39.82% of the popular vote was elected President. Despite his unpopularity, however, Lincoln proved to be an effective Civil War leader and is ranked among the top five Presidents in virtually every poll of historians.

This plurality winner-take-all system was defended in a 1992 column by George Will, a conservative newspaper columnist. According to Will, the Presidential election system is useful because it "promotes moderation by punishing parties that are ideologically, racially or geographically narrow."[7]

Although stability should be considered a compelling virtue, critics of the Electoral College want to change it and risk sailing on uncharted waters. Those who want to reform or eliminate the EC offer these alternatives:

> **Should Americans abandon the plurality, winner-take-all system of electing leaders and use a more "fair" approach? Why or why not?**

① **The Automatic Elector Plan.** Under this plan, electoral votes would be cast automatically thus eliminating the need for human electors.

② **District Plan.** Each congressional district would represent one elector vote, and each state would be worth two. This plan would divide up the electoral vote so that a candidate who carried 20 of California's 52 congressional districts and a majority of popular votes would get 22 electoral votes.

③ **Proportional Plan.** Under the proportional plan, the electoral vote would be retained, but the Electoral College would be abolished. Each state's electoral vote would be divided among candidates according to the proportion (or percentage) of popular votes received. This plan would eliminate the winner-take-all feature of the current system, but the winning candidate would need only 40% or more of the electoral vote to win, not a majority.

④ **Direct Popular Election.** This plan would abolish both the Electoral College and the electoral vote. The President would be elected by direct popular vote. To win, a candidate would need more votes than anyone else and at least 40% of the total. In case no candidate received at least 40%, a run-off election would be held. In 1960, for example, John F. Kennedy had 34,221,344 popular votes and Nixon had 34,106,671. So if direct popular election had been used in 1960, Kennedy would have been winner by a nose.

Why spend so much time on an archaic system like the Electoral College? Go back to Chapter 2 and review the characteristics of rules, namely "rules are never neutral," "whoever makes the rules controls the game," "know rule origins," etc. What does the current system of electing Presidents suggest about these rule dictums?

Factions and Elections

The Republican and Democratic parties seem so much alike that critics have called them "Tweedledum and Tweedledee" after the twins in Lewis Carroll's *Through the Looking Glass*. If the two major parties are so much alike, why have elections?

Want to know even more about the Electoral College? For current workings, use: [http://politicsusa.com/PoliticsUSA/news/electo 3.html.cgi]. For the Electoral College Calculator use: [http://www.bga.com/~jnhtx/ec/ec/html].

Elections are useful because they give voters the opportunity to judge the performance of elected officials who have held office and replace them if their job performance is unsatisfactory. Voting, moreover, is psychologically satisfying. It gives us the feeling of having participated in a useful process. In their book *The Irony of Democracy*, Thomas R. Dye and L. Harmon Zeigler argue that the most important function of democratic elections is to provide a "symbolic exercise to help tie the masses to the established order by giving them the feeling that they play a role." ☆ Is symbolic reassurance sufficient justification for holding elections?

What possible unintended consequences could occur if we abolished all elections and adopted a merit system for political office?

If Dye and Zeigler are right, then elections are merely a way for Americans to feel good about themselves and their freedoms. What if we abolished all elections and placed every government job under a "merit" system?

If every elected official from President George W. Bush down to Las Vegas Mayor Oscar Goodman was chosen on merit rather than political popularity, we could eliminate the tremendous influence which special interest groups have on political candidates. Why? Because our elected officials need money to win, and that money comes from various groups that represent corporations, foreign commerce, professional associations, unions, citizens' groups, civil rights groups, old people, young people, handicapped people, etc. Because they contribute to political campaigns, these factions are now a permanent fact of life for American elections.

James Madison had warned in *Federalist 10* that controlling the effects of factions was important, and he had assured New York readers in 1789 that the new Constitution would act as a buffer against religious and economic groups with radical agendas. ☆ Is the system working today to control the effects of factions, as Madison claimed in 1789?

One issue that some religious factions pushed in the 1996 election was Clinton's veto of the Partial-Birth Abortion Ban Act. Less than a month before Clinton was reelected, Martin Mawyer, President of the Christian Action Network, warned that many religious conservatives were planning to stay home rather than vote for Bob Dole. They had wanted Dole to campaign on issues of morality and values, but the Republican candidate seemed afraid to exploit Clinton's April 10th veto of the abortion ban. Instead, Dole promised a 15% tax cut, and complained that Clinton was dishonest.

Mawyer also criticized *Roe v. Wade*, and denounced Dole for ignoring how the Supreme Court in 1973 had twisted the Constitution to legalize abortion: "The high court has found, tucked in a secret drawer of the Constitution a right to kill unborn children. Dole has an anti-abortion voting record but he doesn't seem very proud of it since he never mentioned it in 90 minutes of debate with Bill Clinton, who is more supportive of abortion than any President in U.S. history."[8] Despite the criticism, Bob Dole refused to get drawn into an impassioned argument over abortion. ☆ Why did Dole ignore the abortion issue?

In *Federalist 10*, James Madison warned that one "durable source" of factionalism would be religion. And he was right. By 1800 religion was already a powerful force in American politics. That year Puritan Reverend Jedediah Morse called Thomas Jefferson an atheist who was part of a secret order known as the *Illuminati*. Morse accused Jefferson of being a leader of a conspiracy of skeptics, freethinkers and atheists who were trying to destroy traditional Christianity. Two hundred years later, the shoe is on the other foot. Instead of attacking skeptics, atheists and agnostics, Hollywood produces movies in which religious people are satirized as bigots. ☆ Check out the 1960 movie "Inherit the Wind" for an excellent example of how Hollywood treats religious fundamentalists.

While Hollywood satirizes religion, the media is busy making sure that no politician violates the First Amendment's guarantee that prohibits laws which respect an establishment of religion, or prohibits the free exercise thereof.

> **Skeptical about these so-called conspiracy theories? Get on your Internet and dial this number: [http://w3one.net/-conspira]**

During a 1984 televised debate, President Ronald Reagan said the world was close to "nuclear Armageddon." Armageddon is based on the way some religions interpret the *Bible's* account of the final days. As interpreted by some Protestants groups, the beginning of the end will start when all true Christians are taken to a place with Jesus in the sky. The end of the earth will come with a nuclear war and a final battle between Christ and Anti-Christ at the Battle of Armageddon, north of Jerusalem. When President Reagan uttered these words, the media had a feeding frenzy. ☆ Would it worry you if the President predicted that Armageddon was on schedule to occur in October 2004? What if this same President had a space craft capable of reaching Mars parked behind the White House?

Madison also warned that the unequal distribution of wealth and property would eventually become a durable source of factionalism. During the 19th century, companies, banks, labor unions, and other factions hired lobbyists to hang around Congress and bribe important legislators. Today, lobbyists are still around. They don't usually bribe legislators now. The more effective approach is to finance election campaigns. Since it costs millions to win election to Congress, a new style super lobbyist has evolved. There are over 20,000 lobbyists in

Washington. They work for diverse clients, who range from super patriots like the National Rifle Association to communist China.

> **Should Congress pass a law banning lobbyists from communist countries like China, Vietnam, and North Korea?**

> **We have never fought a nation that has a McDonald's. Should we deal with China by exporting our hamburger franchises, or get into a trade war?**

To secure "most favored nation" trade status, China already has lobbyists trying to influence Congress. Since Bill Clinton was elected in 1992, the trade deficit with China has tripled and is now $40 billion a year. The extent of our trade with China can be seen on the labels of your "U.S. Athletics" walking shoes and your "Sportcap." Now that China has a vested interest in U.S. trade, expect to read that a Political Action Committee funded by China is helping elect members of Congress. Political Action Committees (PAC's) are interest groups that collect money from their members. These funds are then used to help candidates win elections.

The number of PAC's grew from 722 in 1975 to 4,172 in 1990. Nearly half represented corporations, and the rest are spread among labor, trade, membership and health organizations, cooperatives and unaffiliated groups. In the 1990 elections, PAC's contributed $110 million to House candidates and about half that much to Senate candidates. Critics say PAC's are buying votes, but defenders think such special interest groups are inevitable in a democracy. ☆ What do you think about PAC's? Should political campaign spending be severely limited, and PAC's abolished? Why or why not?

In *Federalist 10*, Madison defined faction as "a number of citizens, whether amounting to a majority or minority of the whole, who are united and actuated by some common impulse of passion, or of interest, adverse to the rights of other citizens, or to the permanent and aggregate interests of the community." Today's common passions are aroused over issues like abortion, sexual harassment, crime, welfare, racism, child abuse, drugs, second-hand smoke, etc. In *Why*

> **In 1991 E. J. Dionne, Jr., wrote "by expecting politics to settle too many issues, we have diminished the possibilities of politics." What issues, in your opinion, are now being settled by government that should be settled by individuals working together?**

Americans Hate Politics (1991), E. J. Dionne, Jr. argued that moral-value issues now prevail. These types of issues, according to Dionne, are difficult to negotiate and compromise because they arouse too much passion. "If we are to end the cultural civil war that has so distorted our politics," concluded Dionne, "we need to begin to practice a certain charity and understanding. We need politics to deal with the things it is good at dealing with—the practical matters like schools and roads, education and jobs."

Rules exist to prevent disruptive behavior. However, every society defines "disruptive behavior" in its own way. In our classrooms, disruptive behavior means students who interrupt, disturb, agitate or cut in. To harass someone means to badger, torment, bother, annoy, irritate, pester, nag, pick on and even henpeck. Sexual harassment goes farther than the dictionary, however. The Equal Employment Opportunity Commission (EEOC) has ruled that making sexual activity a condition of employment or promotion is sexual harassment and violates the 1964 Civil Rights Act. The EEOC has also ruled that creating "an intimidating, hostile, or offensive working environment" also violates the law. Now, we have feminists who would destroy sexism. Since most of the Founding Fathers were chauvinists, they didn't worry about whether or not future factions would agitate to eliminate sexual aggression.

When James Madison wrote *Federalist 10* he worried about economic and religious factions. Though he later married young widow Dorothy Payne Todd, whom Washington Irving described as an attractive, "portly, buxom dame," Madison probably never envisioned a future where gentlemen would be sued by ladies.

In 1992 two Stanford University Medical School doctors were punished for sexual harassment and, as a consequence, the entire male medical faculty had to undergo special **sensitivity training** designed to teach them how to relate to female colleagues. In another famous case, the entire Scandinavian studies department (five men and one woman) at the University of Minnesota were charged with sexual harassment in 1989. In her book *Who Stole Feminism* (1994), Christina Hoff Sommers argues that in her research she discovered "no specific acts that could be remotely considered to describe sexual harassment." Instead, the five accused were guilty of such "crimes" as failure to interpret certain literature correctly, not having read a novel which one student accuser felt was important, and of "having greeted a student in less than a friendly manner."[9]

> Suppose in a political science class you write a paper discussing the difficulty of getting reliable polls, and wrote:
>
> "Let's say Dave [the] Stud is entertaining three beautiful ladies in his penthouse when the phone rings. A pollster on the other end wants to know if we should eliminate the capital gains tax. Now Dave is a knowledgeable businessperson who cares a lot about this issue. But since Dave is 'tied up' at the moment, he tells the pollster to 'bother' someone else."
>
> The female professor who reads your tasteless attempt at humor decides to charge you with sexual harassment. Is this charge justified? Why or why not?

In the past, customs like "good manners" were used to prevent aggressive males from bothering the ladies. In the past thirty years, Americans have waged unlimited social war to rid themselves of all customs that seem to bestow rank, race or gender roles. Now that we're all rude and crude, factions representing abused women have asked government to protect them from their significant others. Since women now vote, the two political parties have supported sexual harassment policies and given up on civility.

In Orwell's *1984* Anti-Sex League, women prowl the bureaucracy looking for Outer Party men and women whose facial expressions (facecrime) showed they were having lustful thoughts (thoughtcrime). Now we have factions that have made certain words a crime.

☆ Do you see any danger in using sexual harassment policies to stop men from using words that suggest lust? If so, which words would you consider the "top ten" most offensive?

On TV young Americans get a steady dose of sexual word games, yet they are expected to be asexual at work, play or in school. Eugen Bleuler, the medical director of the Burgholzli Hospital in Zurich, had a name for this condition: **Schizophrenia**.

Campaign Technology

Imagine a Presidential campaign in which the parties have nominated their most available candidate and election day is approaching. Instead of a long and expensive campaign—complete with questionable contributions from Chinese lobbyists—the final vote is determined by a single representative voter selected by a super computer.

> **Convinced that his conservative listeners believe feminism is too radical, radio talk show host Rush Limbaugh calls these extremists "Femi-Nazis." Is that an appropriate label?**

This is the scenario presented in Isaac Asimov's 1955 short story "Franchise." It is November 4, 2008 and the single voter who will determine the outcome of all local, state and national elections is Norman Muller, a clerk in a small department store in Bloomington, Indiana. Muller was chosen by Multivac to represent millions of voters. He will not actually vote, but his attitudes will be calculated by Multivac, which will decide who gets elected. Three days before the election, Muller will be surrounded by secret service agents and isolated so that his views are not influenced by anyone. After quizzing Muller and measuring his responses to certain questions, Multivac will decide the outcome of all elections in 2008.

Until Asimov's computer can pick a perfectly typical voter, we'll continue electing Presidents the old fashioned way. That means expensive and time-consuming campaigns in 50 separate states to nominate an available candidate, and a Vice President to **balance**

> **Is it possible for one voter to accurately represent an entire nation?**

the ticket. After the party conventions, the leading candidates will campaign for state popular votes and the 270 electoral votes needed to win. They will campaign hard and emphasize the negative side of their opponents. This negative advertising will flow through nearly ten thousand newspapers, over eleven thousand periodicals, nearly ten thousand radio stations, and nearly one thousand commercial TV stations. All the negative political advertising has a cumulative effect. According to political columnist Charles Krauthammer, a decade or two of negative advertising has finally made Americans mad: "We have really come to believe that politicians are as bad as their opponents have been telling us in a thousand 30-second spots."[10]

> Taken at face value, American political wars seem too negative. By giving aggression a socially approved form, however, our election campaigns are like regulated wars. In his book *Dark Nature: A Natural History of Evil* (1995), Lyall Watson argues that our species needs regulated ritual displays of aggression, otherwise we end up slaughtering our enemies for no logical reason. If Watson's premise is accurate, then ritualized warfare—like political campaigns—has a beneficial cultural purpose. What do you think?

In order to make our political campaigns as technologically aggressive as possible, Americans have developed the world's most sophisticated techniques of political warfare. We have mastered how to use newspapers, radio, television, direct mail, telephone marketing, public opinion polls, and the Internet with great skill. America, says writer Walter Shapiro, "leads the world in sophisticated techniques of manipulating voters in free elections."[11]

We sell candidates like we sell products. In 1985 *Newsweek* told the story of how our "Wizards of Marketing" use exotic techniques to sell their products. The Stanford Research Institute, for example, developed a values and lifestyle marketing system based on consumer attitudes about such things as new products, politics, work and education. From their surveys, the people at Stanford Research Institute classified buyers into distinct categories. Certain types such as the "Belongers" are not going to be attracted by the same advertisements that appeal to others, such as the "Achievers." Other marketing wizards have developed a system which uses voice pitch analysis (VOPAN) to measure consumer reaction to advertisements. This is done by asking consumers their reaction to a commercial, recording their replies and analyzing by computer the rate at which their vocal chords vibrate. The faster the vibrations, the more likely consumers are telling the truth.[12]

Behaviorscan is a market research system that combines the telescreens used in Oceania with the consumer brain washing described by Aldous Huxley in *Brave New World*. Behaviorscan is a market research system operated by Information Resources, Inc. It involves the close monitoring of the buying patterns and TV viewing habits of 30,000 households in twelve communities across the United States. Also, a microcomputer attached to the TV set keeps track of what the family watches. This information is used to correlate TV ads with their impacts on the buying habits of family members. And finally, the 30,000 households monitored are polled to find out their personal likes and dislikes.

☆ Is this monitoring of TV viewing habits and product preference an invasion of privacy?

Until 1987, A. C. Nielsen used only simple meters attached to TV sets and written diaries to determine our TV viewing habits. The meters were located in 1,700 typical households, and the diaries were filled out by another 1,600 households. Now Nielsen has a new approach, **The People Meter**.

> **Calvin Klein advertisements are notorious for their use of scantily clad young models. What type of buyers do the Klein ads target, in your opinion?**

Developed by London-based AGB Research Company, the People Meter is fairly easy to operate. When a member of the family decides to watch TV, he or she punches a button on a small key-pad connected to a meter on the top of the TV set. The meter monitors the channels being watched and periodically reminds viewers to record their presence. The system is linked by telephone lines to a central computer which correlates each viewer's number with demographic data about the person stored in its memory, including age, gender, ethnicity, and income. The system also calculates if a particular commercial has influenced a decision to purchase a product.

After a trip to the store, household members take a pencil-sized electronic wand attached to their meter and wave it above the universal product code that is stamped on all goods. The computer then matches the information with the family's recent TV viewing patterns and determines if the sponsor's commercials are effective.

To determine why buyers differ in their car tastes, the Opinion Survey Center in Toledo, Ohio has developed a system for identifying buyer types. After surveying ten thousand people, the Center identified seven personality types. The seven types are:

- ⊛ Car of My Dreams
- ⊛ Practical Price and Value
- ⊛ Engineering/I Know Cars
- ⊛ The Driver
- ⊛ King Size
- ⊛ First on the Block
- ⊛ A Car is a Car

Customers who belong to the "practical price and value" category tended to buy cars like the old Chevrolet Chevette, a sparse ugly car with no frills. The "king size" buyer, in contrast, wanted a big luxury car like the Chrysler New Yorker.[13]

> **Nielsen Media Research and the David Sarnoff Research Center have been working on a new ratings device that measures audiences by monitoring viewer faces. There will be no buttons to push and no diaries to keep. Just sit down, turn on the television set and let the machine do the rest. The new ratings device would contain a stored computer image of the face of each member of a Nielsen family. The device scans the room and compares the faces it sees with the image in its memory, and records who is watching TV. Would this new ratings device evolve into an Orwellian telescreen which could watch TV audiences and decide if members of the family were watching forbidden images? Could future TV devices be capable of reading our minds? What about TV commercials that feed us subliminal messages; are they now possible?**

Since Presidential candidates win electoral votes by states, wouldn't it make sense to market 50 difference personalities for a candidate—one for each state. Thus a candidate campaigning in Nevada could be shown in a casino wearing a cowboy hat, betting on the World Series and cheering for her team. When in Utah, the same candidate could be shown on the steps of an LDS church, drinking milk, shaking hands, and smiling.

These new buyer profiles are part of a new wave known as **psychographics**. In the past, advertisers sold expensive cars to rich people and economy cars to the rest of us. Modern cars, however, are not marketed for cost. Instead, they are advertised to appeal to subconscious feelings like lust, jealousy, and power.

Freud used the label "Id" for our unconscious primitive instincts. These instincts include our need for power. To get that power for a few days, visitors to Las Vegas will shell out over $500 a day to rent a Dodge Viper or Porsche 911 from Rent-A-Vette. Quite often these expensive rentals come back battered like an abused race horse. Why?

> **Fortunately, Americans separate their sexual fantasies and their politics. We would never elect a President for his or her sexual appeal.**

The computers that match buyer with car can sell political candidates using psychographics. In 1964 a New York advertising company knew from its research that Americans had a compelling fear that an accidental nuclear war might be started by a crazy general like General Jack Ripper, who starts World War III in the Stanley Kubrick movie *Dr. Strangelove*. So they developed for the Democrats the famous "Daisy Girl" commercial suggesting the election of hawkish Barry Goldwater would lead to the nuclear destruction of a little girl picking flowers.

Through the Internet, TV, fax machines and other modern technology, Americans can now achieve the electronic democracy envisioned by H. Ross Perot in 1992. We can enter a new era of "electronic democracy" by letting voters cast their judgment on all significant issues merely by dialing a phone, pushing a TV button, accessing the Internet, or faxing a message.

The Pollsters and Public Opinion

The nation now has more than a thousand polling organizations used by political candidates, TV networks, corporations, newspapers, news magazines, the Internet, government bureaucrats and anyone else who needs a poll. Nobody, it seems, wants to make a decision without the results of a poll.

> Would it be a good idea to let voters participate in making laws through their electronic helpers? If so, would we be abandoning the "republicanism" envisioned by the Founding Fathers? Could this type of electronic direct democracy result in any unintended consequences?

In 1982, Reynaldo Martinez, campaign manager for then Nevada First Congressional District candidate Harry Reid said, "To me, a campaign without a poll is like going out in the middle of the ocean without a compass."[14]

To get reliable information, pollsters need to ask good questions. When gathering public opinion on the abortion issue, pollsters may ask one of these three questions:

▸ **If a woman wants to have an abortion and her doctor agrees to it, should she be allowed to have an abortion, or not?**
▸ **The U.S. Supreme Court ruled in 1973 that a woman can have an abortion if she wants one at any time during the first three months of pregnancy. Do you favor or oppose that ruling?**
▸ **If a promiscuous teenager decides to have an abortion because she is unmarried, should your tax money be used to pay for it?**

Presidential candidates rely on professionals to conduct their polls. In 1980, for example, Ronald Reagan's political strategy was formulated on the basis of information supplied by Richard Wirthlin, a former college professor who specialized in polls for Republican candidates. While Reagan was campaigning in 1980, Wirthlin conducted polls and gathered other information. Wirthlin's polls showed Reagan 10 to 16 percentage points ahead of incumbent Jimmy Carter. As a result of these polls, Wirthlin advised Reagan to exploit dissatisfaction among southern white Protestants, blue collar city workers, urban ethnic groups and rural voters, especially in New York, Pennsylvania and Ohio. As with most Presidential elections, Wirthlin's advice included ways to win in the Electoral College. He advised Reagan to concentrate on California, Illinois, Texas, Ohio and Pennsylvania, whose 149 electoral votes were needed to win.

In 1980 incumbent Jimmy Carter got much of his political advice from pollster Patrick Caddell. Using polls and computers, Caddell decided that Carter had real problems. His data showed that the American people were soured by runaway inflation, high unemployment and the Iran hostage crisis. By and large, according to Theodore H. White, Caddell had concluded, "the American people

Earlier, we analyzed the role of Mark Penn and other pollsters who helped Bill Clinton win reelection in 1996. Use your sources, and see if you can locate the names of pollsters who are currently helping politicians win.

did not like Jimmy Carter." Caddell's polls showed Carter would only get 69 electoral votes, which was very close to his final 49.[15] ● How can pollsters so accurately predict the outcome of a Presidential election?

Polls are used to measure everything from Presidential candidates to our taste in automobiles. Many jobs now require workers who know how to conduct these types of surveys. To help you understand a standard process, we need to look at several factors:

① **The first step in polling is to decide the type of information you want to know.** In 1986, for example, the Hearst Corporation wanted to know what Americans knew about their Constitution, so the company hired Research & Forecasts to do a survey. After the poll results were released, the media reported the alarming fact that 45% of the American public thought the U.S. Constitution includes the words, "From each according to his ability, to each according to his need." This fact shocked some Americans, especially political scientists who knew that the phrase was certainly not in the United States Constitution.

② **After deciding your topic, you need to select an appropriate number of respondents.** The number of people interviewed varies from poll to poll, but the usual number for national surveys range from about 600 to 1,000. ☆ How can we

Where does the phrase "From each according to his ability, to each according to his need" first appear?

determine national attitudes on the basis of only one thousand respondents?

③ **While making these decisions, you should also be preparing the types of questions you plan to ask.** From experience, pollsters have developed five types of questions:

☎ Validation. **This type of question is used by pollsters to ensure the people they are interviewing are typical. Thus a poll to determine who is going to vote for Bill Clinton should ask, "are you a registered voter?" Otherwise, the poll data would be worthless.**

☎ Filter Questions. **These questions are designed to test the respondents knowledge of the subject. If you were doing a survey on the Food Stamp Program, you might ask, "Are you familiar with the Food Stamp Program?" "Can you tell me what you think about it?"**

☎ Closed End Questions. **These are used to force respondents to make a choice between two or more possibilities. A typical closed end question for the last Presidential election might be, "If you had to vote for a President today, would you prefer George W. Bush or Al Gore?"**

☎ Open Ended Questions. **These are used by pollsters to give people a chance to talk about issues that are important to them. Typically, you might ask, "What, in your opinion, are the most important issues facing the United States today?"**

☎ **Semantic Differential Questions.** Not really questions, these are value-laden statements designed to measure the respondent's intensity of feeling on a very controversial issue, like gun control. Thus you might have the respondent react to this statement: "Congress should enact a law requiring the registration of all hand gun owners."
Strongly Agree   Agree   Disagree   Strongly Disagree.

④ **While preparing questions for the survey, avoid using "loaded" ones that suggest a "correct" answer for the respondent.** On November 4, 1984, newspaper columnist Ann Landers asked

> Why is this Ann Landers' survey question loaded?

her readers to respond to the following question: "Would you be content to be held close and be treated tenderly and forget about 'the act'?" Landers received letters from about 90,000 readers, 72% of whom said "yes" to her question. Landers then wrote a subsequent column in which she concluded a "tremendous number of women out there are not enjoying sex . . . ."[16]

⑤ **Decide a reliable method for selecting a sample to be interviewed.** Since professional pollsters cannot interview 100 million registered voters to determine the winner of a Presidential contest, they have to rely on random or quota sampling techniques.

> On the basis of the information below, explain what is meant by a "random selection method"?

Currently, many pollsters use a technique known as "random-digit dialing." This means that a computer selects completely at random the phone numbers that the interviewers call. The key word is random. It means that numbers are dialed so that every American voter would presumably have an equal chance to be called and questioned. When a survey is not completely random, bad things happen. In 1936, for example, the editors of *The Literary Digest* thought they had a fool proof method for predicting the winners of Presidential elections. In the four previous elections, the *Digest* had mailed postcards to millions of voters and used their answers to predict the winners. For the election of 1936, the magazine received two million postcards back. On the basis of these postcards, the *Digest* editors predicted Alf Landon would win by a landslide. However, the actual winner by a landslide was Democrat Franklin Roosevelt, who had 27,747,636 popular votes to 16,679,543 for Landon, and won the Electoral College vote 523 to 8. What went wrong in 1936? The *Digest* postcard survey was wrong because the postcards were mailed to Americans who had registered automobiles and owned telephones. Since in 1936, these items were more likely to be possessed by Republicans than Democrats, the selection process had an unrecognized bias. Today, most of us own telephones so a phone survey is more likely to be truly "random."

⑥ **Not all polls are equal.** The most reliable are public opinion polls conducted by professionals, like the Gallup Organization. Polls conducted by colleges and universities for social research purposes are also usually reliable. Market research and candidate polls have to be reliable because important decisions are made on the basis of the input. The worst polls are those taken by factions to dupe voters. Thus you might get a late phone call and be asked, "Are you going to vote for the notorious child molesting Ted Bundy, or for our candidate, the saintly and kind Dudley Doright?" Sales efforts masquerading as polls are the most irritating. They call and ask, "Do you like healthy foods," and if you answer "yes" the phony pollster has her foot in your brain and then follows with the sales pitch.

⑦ **Watch out for SLOP.** This means a Self-Selected Listener Opinion Poll. In 1992 the Wellesley Center for Research on Women designed a questionnaire on sexual harassment and placed it in the September 1992 issue of *Seventeen*. The editors of *Seventeen* placed the questionnaire after an article that told the story of a Minnesota girl who was sexually harassed by her peers and eventually took legal action. The article was highlighted by large letters that said **It's Probably Happened to YOU! You Don't Have To Put Up With It—In Fact It's Probably Illegal. And Your School Is Responsible For Stopping It.** The questionnaire which followed the article contained 13 questions, one of which defined sexual harassment for magazine readers by asking:

> **Did anyone do any of the following to you when you *didn't* want them to in the last school year?**
> **(a) touch, pinch, or grab you**
> **(b) lean over you or corner you**
> **(c) give you sexual notes or pictures**
> **(d) make suggestive or sexual gestures, looks, comments, or jokes**
> **(e) pressure you to do something sexual**
> **(f) force you to do something sexual**
> **▲ If you've been sexually harassed at school, how did it make you feel?**

Of the magazine's 1.9 million subscribers, 4,200 returned the survey and nearly 90% said they had been sexually harassed. The data was then released to newspapers and a national scandal was exposed through headlines that said, typically, "Survey shows that girls harassed at school."

In her analysis of the Wellesley survey, Christina Hoff Sommers categorized it as SLOP on the basis of two premises, namely, "The study was confined to readers of *Seventeen*, whose readers were not necessarily representative of the population of adolescent girls; and readers who respond to such a survey tend to be those who feel most strongly about a problem."[17]

> **If a Self-Selected Listener Opinion Poll is unreliable, why do restaurants leave customer response surveys on the table? Can you think of any other abuses of surveys, questionnaires, or consumer feed-back policies?**

☆ If you need information about any poll topic, get on the Internet and dial this code: [http://allpolitics.com/polls/FAQ/polling.FAQ.shtml].

> **In the future, political party conventions may have to give way to nomination by public preference polls. The current parties are so unpopular with voters that they only need a small shove to lose their power to decide which Presidential candidates are most "available." Democracy is making way for a "pollocracy," which will mean the use of polls for most major decisions. Political parties are now a cultural lag, and at risk to become technologically obsolete. Future Presidential and other candidates will be nominated by polls, conduct their campaigns on TV, and respond to voters through their computers. Is this a plausible scenario?**

The Hawthorne Effect

Will all this research using public opinion polls and surveys have any long term unintended consequences? Humphrey Taylor, chief operating officer of Louis Harris and Associates, once claimed that polls are neutral and neither "inherently good or bad." They are just information, said Taylor, that can be put to good or bad use by the media, by political leaders, or by the voters. On the other hand, Larry Sabato, professor of government at the University of Virginia, believes that polls actually "manufacture" opinions. He argues that merely asking a question produces an opinion, whether or not the individual has even thought about the subject being examined. According to Sabato, "several studies have demonstrated that many respondents will forthrightly offer observations on non-existent acts of Congress."[18]

Suppose a pollsters called you on the telephone and asked "What do you think about the new law which makes it murder to have an abortion?" What would you say?

For about 60 years, social scientists have known about the **Hawthorne Effect.** This phenomenon was discovered back in the 1930's when Harvard University researchers interviewed and watched workers at the Hawthorne plant of Western Electric in Cicero, Illinois. During the research, experimenters from Harvard tried to discover a link between working conditions and worker output. After deciding an average for daily output, the researchers, with the help of management, changed conditions. At first, working conditions were improved by reducing the length of the work day and increasing the frequency and length of rest breaks. As working conditions improved, worker output increased as expected. The researchers were not surprised by this fact: **Conventional Wisdom** holds that happy workers are good workers.

Later, the Harvard group reversed the process by increasing the hours of work, reducing rest breaks, and worsening other work conditions. Surprisingly, worker productivity continued to climb. As a result of their findings, the researchers concluded that the workers deviated from normal behavior because they had realized that they were participants in an experiment.[19]

If the Hawthorne Effect is a reliable indicator of how people react when they are being studied by social scientists, then the possibility exists that poll results may be contaminated by the fact that respondents feel that they must give the answers that are expected of them.

This same phenomenon may explain why some Americans believe it is "cool" to bombard their Cro-Magnon ears with loud music, identify with celebrities who practice dangerous sex, or strive mightily to get on TV and reveal embarrassing family secrets like, "I slept with my girlfriend's mother." This type of talk may seem exciting, but in a primitive society it would be strictly taboo, and in Freudian terms, very dangerous psychologically and physically. So why is it happening so often? Has a sort of perverted Hawthorne Effect resulted, where otherwise normal, sane people imagine themselves as TV celebrities and would go to any lengths to achieve 15 minutes of stardom? Do teachers ask rhetorical questions?

Notes

1. Richard Stengel and Eric Pooley, "Masters of the Message," *Time* (November 18, 1996), pp. 76-96.

2. Dick Polman, "Clinton Proves to GOP That Huge Gender Gap Exists," Las Vegas *Review Journal/Sun* (November 10, 1996), p. 8A.

3. "Dismantle Clunky Electoral College," Las Vegas *Sun* (December 22, 1996), p. 2K.

4. James A. Michener, *Presidential Lottery* (New York: Random House, 1969), pp. 58-61.

5. Agar, *Price of Union*, p. 47.

6. K.C. Cole, "Experts Call For New Look at How America Elects Its Leaders," Las Vegas *Review Journal* (August 18, 1995), p. 12B.

7. George Will, "Presidential Winner-Take-All System Has Its Ups and Downs," Las Vegas *Sun* (June 21, 1992), p. 3D.

8. Martin Mawyer, "Activist Says Some Religious Conservatives Will Not Vote," Las Vegas *Review Journal* (October 14, 1996), p. 3A.

9. Christina Hoff Sommers, *Who Stolen Feminism: How Women Have Betrayed Women* (New York: Simon & Schuster, 1994), pp. 112-115.

10. Charles Krauthammer, "Why Americans Hate Politicians," *Time* (December 9, 1991), p. 92.

11. Walter Shapiro, "America's Dubious Export," *Time* (September 4, 1980), p. 72.

15. "Wizards of Marketing," *Newsweek* (July 22, 1985), pp. 42-44.

16. "Our Autos, Ourselves," *Consumer Reports* (June 1985), p. 375.

17. Mary Ann Mele, "Political Polling: It's Not Only an Art, It's Big Business, Too," Las Vegas *Sun* (June 14, 1982), p. 9.

18. Theodore H. White, *America in Search of Itself: The Making of the President 1956-1980* (New York: Harper & Row Publishers, 1982), pp. 377-381.

19. "Ann Landers and 'the Act'," *Newsweek* (January 28, 1985), pp. 76-77.

20. Sommers, *Who Stole Feminism*, pp. 181-185.

21. *USA Today* (November 6, 1984).

22. Betty H. Zisk, *Political Research: A Methodological Sampler* (Lexington, Mass.: D.C. Heath and Company, 1981), pp. 143-144.

Chapter 6

Equality

In the near future, Americans will be visiting a real Jurassic Park. Using computer images and virtual reality, we'll be able to travel back 75 million years and play with all those cute dinosaurs like in the movies. We'll sit at

How do we know that dinosaurs ever existed? What facts do we now know about those ancient beasts?

the top of a large tree and pet the small heads of an Apatosaurus, which measures 80 feet. And he'll purr, just like in "Jurassic Park." Those of us who like to fight can trade blows with the six foot Velociraptor and her predatory friends. Or wearing our $95 New Balance running shoes, we can engage in a foot race with the 42 foot Tyrannosaurus Rex and hope we're as fast as the human survivors of Michael Crichton's "Lost World." Some of us may wonder how Noah ever got such large beasts on the Arc.

Sedentary types, however, will avoid the dinosaurs. We'll go to "History World" and talk to humanoids created to resemble our Founding Fathers. We'll get to interrogate Thomas Jefferson. We'll ask him why he talked up a storm about equality and human rights, yet owned slaves. For $25 we'll get to spend 30 minutes talking to a computer that looks, talks, and thinks like the 33-year-old man who wrote the famous Declaration of Independence and gave us the July 4th holiday. We'll get an autograph from the man given credit for writing these words in 1776: "We hold these truths to be self-evident, that all men are created equal, that they are endowed by their Creator with certain unalienable Rights, that among these are Life, Liberty and the Pursuit of Happiness."

Then we'll go to a special section on World War II and listen to the angry speeches given by a coarse faced small man with a tooth brush mustache and clear blue eyes. We'll recognize Adolph Hitler as the world's greatest believer in inequality. We'll hear some of his favorite ideas given in a raspy, hoarse voice. He will tell us that, "Politics are the conduct and course of the historical struggle for life of peoples . . . . The aim of these struggles is the assertion of fittest." He will draw upon the arguments made by Social Darwinists to say that natural selection is nature's way of eliminating society's unfit. In Hitler's world people who have failed in life are unfit to survive. From this premise, Hitler will conclude that the world's Jewish and Slavic populations have proven themselves inferior and should be eliminated so that Hitler's mythical Aryan race can have more space to survive and bear children.

For Hitler then, there will be a display known as the "Face of Evil." It will contain a brief description of the propaganda techniques employed by Dr. Joseph Goebbels—Hitler's minister of propaganda. Viewers will hear radio broadcasts of Hitler's speeches, which were mandatory listening for Germans while Hitler ruled that nation from 1933 to 1945. They will also see posters that glorify Hitler's young SS and SA special soldiers. These posters will show young men who presumably belonged to the German Workers Socialist Party (Nazis). These

Nazi men are portrayed as members of the Aryan master race. Other posters will ridicule Jews and show them as a decadent race. To Hitler equality meant racial impurity. He and his followers imagined a future in which pure blood Aryan men would use young Aryan ladies to have their blond, blue eyed children.

To Hitler the greatest danger to society are those misfits who can't read, write, keep a job, and whose blood is Jewish.

As you listen to Hitler's ranting, you are reminded of Social Darwinism—the idea that through natural selection, nature favors the fittest competitors. You remember reading a 1927 statement by British writer Aldous Huxley: "That all men are equal is a proposition to which, at ordinary times, no sane individual has ever given his assent." You also recall that in Huxley's *Brave New World* children destined to perform menial jobs are sleep taught to have pride in their mediocrity. All this is compatible with modern advertising that glorifies young people who like sports and drink high energy drinks like Red Bull.

Hitler took society's misfits, called them Nazis and gave brown shirts to some and erotically impressive black uniforms and trench coats to his personal elite.

Under Hitler's tyranny from 1933 to 1945, the German people were bombarded with the idea that nature favors the strong and that only the most fit people should be allowed to live, work and bear children. In Hitler's words, as quoted by Ian Kershaw, *Hitler* (2000), "Politics are the conduct and course of the historical struggle for life of peoples . . . . The aim of these struggles is the assertion of existence."

This struggle led Hitler to believe that government had to actively weed out misfits. This was the theme of Hitler's favorite propaganda movie "Victims of the Past." This primitive black and white movie showed the wretched existence of mental patients. To Hitler the movie was proof that society should eliminate the mentally challenged; not try to improve their environment.

In the 2001 presidential election, punch card ballots used in Florida presumably denied equal voting rights to people who couldn't understand the instructions. Does our presidential election system deny equality?

As you listen to the raspy voice, you think back on your first constitutional law class where you studied the case of *Buck v. Bell* 274 U.S. 200 (1927). This case involved a Virginia state law under which persons "affected with hereditary insanity, idiocy, imbecility, feeblemindedness, or epilepsy could be subjected to compulsory sterilization." As you remember, the Supreme Court's opinion in this case favored the Social Darwinism that was being preached at universities after Charles Darwin's theory of evolution impacted the theories of sociologists, political scientists, and others.

Hitler's brand of Social Darwinism stressed the importance of being a "real man." To Hitler this didn't mean sexual conquests, although as dictator he was the target of women who wanted him to father their children. In his book *Mein Kampf,* Hitler wrote that the masses were like a woman "whose psychic state is determined less by abstract reason than by an emotional longing for a strong force which will complement her nature." The masses, he argued, "need something that will give them a sense of horror."

To soften this horror, the interview with Hitler ends with a showing of the 1940 movie *The Great Dictator.*

Do you agree with Hitler's argument that the masses are "like a woman."

One year before the Japanese attack on Pearl Harbor, American movie audiences were watching comic Charles Chaplin playing "The Great Dictator." In the movie, Chaplin plays a Jewish barber with amnesia who has a toothbrush mustache and is mistaken for the ruthless world leader "Adenoid Hynkel." American audiences in 1940 laughed when Hynkel clutched a balloon meant to resemble the world. In Germany, dictator Adolf Hitler was not amused by "The Great Dictator." As satire, the movie would have weakened Hitler's image so it was banned by the Ministry of Propaganda and never shown to German audiences.

Under Hitler, as with all dictators, there is no room for satire aimed at the regime. Nor would the Ministry of Propaganda approve any book which criticized Nazis. In the pre-Civil War South, slaves couldn't write movies that satirized slave owners. So they made up songs about blue-tailed flies which caused the Master's horse to throw him into a river.

> In the 1964 movie "Dr. Strangelove," a crazy U.S. Air Force General Jack Ripper decides to start World War III because the Communists have fluoridated his drinking water. Should movies that ridicule American generals be censored, or banned?

The End of Slavery

The Civil War was fought partly over the question, "Is slavery a violation of the Declaration of Independence or the Constitution?" To provoke that war, abolitionists cited Jefferson's words that "all men are created equal." They also pointed out that the Constitution counted blacks as only three-fifths of a person for the purpose of determining a state's representation in Congress. This three-fifths clause was often used by the abolitionists as evidence that the Constitution was a covenant with the devil. After the Civil War, the Thirteenth Amendment abolished slavery. Still, the Republicans who controlled Congress wanted to protect the former slaves from discriminatory state laws. So they proposed the Fourteenth and Fifteenth Amendments, which were ratified by three fourths of the states in 1868 and 1870, respectively.

Ratified in 1870, the Fifteenth Amendment was designed to let former slaves have the vote so they could defend themselves. The Fifteenth Amendment says, "The right of citizens of the United States to vote shall not be denied or abridged by the United States or by any State on account of race, color, or previous condition of servitude."

From 1865 to 1877, the South was "reconstructed" by an alliance between Republicans, former slaves, and poor whites. During this era of Reconstruction, blacks for the first time were able to participate in southern politics. They helped elect Ulysses Grant to be President. During Reconstruction, several former slaves were elected to Congress. In Louisiana, Pinckney Benton Stewart Pinchback became the first black governor in U.S. history. According to African American historian Kennell Jackson, black elected officials during and after Reconstruction "were actually pivotal in restoring democracy to the South. For the most part, they were sober, responsible lawmakers who wanted to make the South into a new society, where both races could progress."[1]

Though former slaves were responsible leaders, their power was secure only while union soldiers were occupying the South. When the soldiers were pulled after the disputed election of 1876, the Ku Klux Klan and other white racists set out to restore the former slaves to their "rightful place" in society.

The Fifteenth Amendment had banned voting discrimination on the basis of race, color, or previous condition of servitude. Republicans who proposed the amendment believed it would enable the former slaves to seek their own destiny. Some, however, felt the words were indecisive. During debates over the proposed amendment, Indiana Republican Senator Oliver P. Morton warned that it would allow states to use literacy tests and other devices to legally deprive blacks of the right to vote.

Explain why the Fifteenth Amendment did not stop states from using literacy tests to keep black Americans from voting.

The Reconstruction Act of 1867 made the South accept black voting as a condition of getting back into the Union. For ten years after, blacks in the South participated in government and helped make the rules. After federal troops were withdrawn in 1877, the white majority threw its political support to racist candidates who promised to redeem the South and restore white power. Thus, an era of "redemption" followed. Using violence and intimidation, whites threw their political support to the men who promised to bring back a new form of slavery.

To keep blacks from voting or holding political office, the southern states passed a series of laws now known as the "Mississippi Plan." In 1890, Mississippi adopted a state constitution which contained a bewildering array of legal ways to deny the vote to blacks. The Mississippi Plan included good character qualifications, a poll tax, literacy tests, and a requirement to interpret sections of the Federal or State Constitutions. The good character test allowed registrars to disqualify voting applicants who had been convicted of bribery, burglary, theft, arson, perjury, forgery, embezzlement or bigamy. Before they could register and vote, applicants had to produce a receipt showing they had paid the $2 poll tax. Since the poll tax was accumulative, prospective voters usually had to pay more than $2. Mississippi's 1890 constitution also required that potential voters be able to read, understand and give a reasonable interpretation of the state constitution. Since some portions were in Latin, white registrars usually had an easy time finding clauses that could be used to deny the vote to people who failed to convince the registrar they were able to read.

The Mississippi Plan had one fatal flaw, however. All the rules devised to keep blacks from voting also disenfranchised whites. To compensate for this irony, southern political leaders produced a loophole known as the *Grandfather Clause.* As it appeared in the 1898 Louisiana Constitution, the grandfather clause said:

No male person who was on January 1, 1867, or any date prior thereto, entitled to vote under the Constitution or statutes of any State of the United States, wherein he then resided, and no son or grandson of any such person not less than twenty-one years of age at the adoption of this Constitution, and no male person of foreign birth, who was naturalized prior to the first day of January, 1898, shall be denied the right to register and vote in this State by reason of his failure to possess the educational or property qualifications prescribed by this Constitution . . . .

If you plan to work in any job requiring interpretation and communication skills, you must be able to comprehend legal language. Read this grandfather clause carefully, and then decide what it means. Then decide which of the following statements is True or False:

① The Grandfather Clause was designed to help immigrants vote in Louisiana.
② The Grandfather Clause disenfranchised blacks who had not voted before 1867.
③ The Grandfather Clause reinfranchised whites who had failed literacy tests.
④ The Grandfather Clause disenfranchised blacks who had voted since 1867.

Although the Supreme Court declared the Grandfather Clause unconstitutional in 1915, other strategies were adopted to keep blacks from voting. In 1923, Texas adopted the *White Primary*. This election law stipulated that "in no event shall a Negro be eligible to participate in a Democratic party primary election held in the State of Texas." Primaries are elections where party candidates are nominated for the general elections. By the time the Texas law was passed, the South was virtually a one party area. Winners of the Democratic primary almost always won the general election. By keeping African Americans from voting in primaries, Texas and other states excluded them from the actual selection process.

In some states, black Americans were gerrymandered out of districts where important elections were held. The **Gerrymander** is an old American custom of drawing voting districts to the advantage of the group in power. In 1957, for example, whites in the Alabama legislature took the square shaped voting district for the city of Tuskegee and transformed it into a 28-sided gerrymander, which removed nearly all of the city's four hundred black voters and deposited them where they couldn't vote for Tuskegee city officials.

Eventually African Americans took their grievances to the one place where they expected impartial justice. But in 1898, the U.S. Supreme Court upheld most of the Mississippi Plan.[2] Then in 1937 the Court said the poll tax did not violate either the Fifteenth Amendment nor the equal protection clause of the Fourteenth Amendment.[3] After several attempts, black lawyers were able to get the Supreme Court to rule in 1944 that the white primary was unconstitutional.[4] Sixteen years later, the racial gerrymander fell when the Court ruled unanimously that the Alabama law which removed black voters from Tuskegee was unconstitutional.[5]

Because the Supreme Court was reluctant to abolish poll taxes, Congress in 1962 proposed the 24th Amendment which was ratified two years later. This Amendment reads: "The right of citizens of the United States to vote in any primary or other election for President or Vice President, for electors for President or Vice President, or for Senator or Representative in Congress, shall not be denied or abridged by the United States or any State by reason of failure to pay any poll tax or other tax."

One year after the 24th Amendment was ratified, Congress passed a sweeping Voting Rights Act. This important law authorized federal officials to go into election districts and insure that blacks could register, vote and have their ballots counted honestly. Ninety-five years too late the Fifteenth Amendment was finally being enforced.

> Does this amendment prevent a poll tax from being levied during local or state elections?

> In June 1997 the Supreme Court by a five to four vote ruled that Georgia could only gerrymander one congressional district to favor African Americans. This decision was made to limit the practice of concentrating African Americans in districts where they would have enough votes to control the election. In its decision, the Court majority reasoned that one gerrymandered district was O.K., but more were unconstitutional. Is this a reasonable decision?

Jim Crow

Frederick Douglass was a famous man in the 19th century. The son of a black slave and white father, Douglass escaped to freedom from Baltimore in 1838. Later, he became a leader in the abolitionist movement. He was a strong writer, and one of the best orators of his time. Often attacked by mobs, Douglass was a man of good manners, tremendous courage, and justified anger.

In the 1840's Douglass boarded a train bound from Boston to Lynn, Massachusetts. Douglass had purchased a first-class ticket, so he got on a car for first class travelers. The conductor, however, ordered him to the "Jim Crow" car, which Douglass considered dirty and uncomfortable. When Douglass refused to budge, the conductor and six other men tried to move him. In the struggle, two or three seats were ripped out. Eventually, railroad superintendent Stephen A. Chase tried to stop Douglass from traveling on his Eastern Railroad by having all passenger trains pass through Lynn without stopping. When Douglass and other abolitionists approached Chase on the matter, he defended segregated trains by pointing out that even churches in the North had separate pews for Negroes.

Douglass refused to board the Jim Crow car because he did not feel inferior to any white man. **Jim Crow** goes back to a minstrel show song first introduced in Louisville by Thomas D. Rice (Daddy Rice) in 1828. Rice was a white man who got paid to put on black face makeup and sing. His act was patterned after a black man named Jim Crow, whom Rice had seen singing and dancing in Kentucky. Later, the label Jim Crow was used as a symbol for laws, rules and customs that prohibited black people from sharing accommodations with whites.

> **This account of Frederick Douglass' problems with the Eastern Railroad was gleaned from his autobiography *Life and Times of Frederick Douglass*. Events described by witnesses who were there, or participated, are known as primary sources. Writers should always try to get this type of information from eyewitnesses, and not rely too much on "secondary" sources. What is a secondary source?**

Before the Civil War most of the Northern states practiced Jim Crow. Most whites in the North considered blacks to be an inferior race, so they provided them with separate public accommodations, such as restaurants, railroads, and cemeteries.

The Thirteenth Amendment freed slaves, but it did not give them equality. The Fourteenth Amendment gave citizenship and equal protection to blacks, but did not give them the vote. The Fifteenth Amendment provided that blacks in the North and South *should* be able to vote. In the minds of the Republicans who controlled Congress during Reconstruction, the Fifteenth Amendment settled the issue. It supposedly gave black people the power to participate in democracy, and reap its benefits.

To head off future state Jim Crow laws, Congress, in 1875, passed a Civil Rights Act designed to end segregation in public accommodations. The Supreme Court, however, ruled in 1883 that the Civil Rights Act was unconstitutional. Moreover, the Court also limited the Fourteenth Amendment's "equal protection" clause by saying that it only applied to government discrimination, not the acts of private individuals.[6]

What if a state discriminates by passing a segregation law? The Supreme Court had to face this issue in the now famous case known as *Plessy v. Ferguson* (1896).

What do we mean by the "equal protection" clause?

If you plan to be a paralegal or lawyer, you will have to "brief" cases. A brief usually contains a concise description of the facts. To brief *Plessy v. Ferguson*, you would need to have these facts: In 1890 the Louisiana legislature passed a law, euphemistically called, "An Act to Promote the Comfort of Passengers." In reality, the law provided separate railway accommodations for black and white people. Testing the law's constitutionality, a Citizens' Committee arranged for Homer Plessy to ride the East Louisiana Railroad from New Orleans to Covington. The Citizens' Committee warned the railroad that having Plessy aboard was meant to challenge the Louisiana law. Though he looked white, Plessy was one-eighth "African blood" and therefore defined by Louisiana law to be legally colored. After he boarded the "Whites only" coach at New Orleans, Plessy was ordered to the "Colored Only" coach by the conductor. When Plessy refused to move, he was arrested and charged with violating state law. After his arrest, Plessy asked the Louisiana Supreme Court to rule that the law had violated his rights under the Thirteenth and Fourteenth Amendments.

Why did Homer Plessy and his lawyers argue that the Louisiana law violated the Thirteenth and Fourteenth Amendments?

"Does segregation by race violate the Constitution?" This was the question raised in *Plessy v. Ferguson*, 163 U.S. 537 (1896). Now that you've learned a few research skills, locate the decision in this case and prepare a lawyer's brief complete with the essential facts, the constitutional issue, and the Court's decision.

By 1950 Jim Crow had become absurd. The battle to secure civil rights for black Americans was eased somewhat by the silly extremes to which segregationists had gone. A typical nonsense idea had been developed by the State of Oklahoma, which had grudgingly passed a law that allowed blacks to do graduate work at the state university if they remained segregated on campus. Predictably, the Oklahoma law was challenged in court.

In order to earn a doctorate in education, a black college teacher named G.W. McLaurin had to attend the University of Oklahoma as a "special student." McLaurin was forced to sit apart from the other students either in a special colored section of the classroom or at a designated desk in a hallway where he could see and hear the instructor, but was not too close to other students. In the library, McLaurin was assigned a special desk. He was required to eat in a segregated portion of the cafeteria.

McLaurin challenged the state law as a violation of his constitutional right to equal protection. The U.S. Supreme Court agreed, holding that the segregated conditions would "impair and inhibit his ability to study, to engage in discussions and to exchange views with other students."[7]

An Oakland school board stirred up a hornet's nest in 1997 by proposing that a new language called "Ebonics" be taught to African American students there. Why was this idea so controversial?

As late as the 1960's, hotels, theaters, and Las Vegas strip casinos were segregated. Before World War II, blacks had flocked to Nevada, looking for jobs on Hoover Dam and later, at the Basic Magnesium Corporation. According to Earnest Bracey, the segregation and other "racist" practices were the result of white prejudices and the "separate but equal" doctrine which the Supreme Court had sanctified in *Plessy v. Ferguson.* [8]

Four years after the Supreme Court rejected Oklahoma's segregating of graduate students, the Supreme Court ruled in *Brown v. Board of Education*, 347 U.S. 483 (1954) that segregated public schools at any level were inherently unequal and in violation of the Fourteenth Amendment's equal protection clause.

Brown, however, did not immediately make things better for African Americans. Many southern school districts resisted the decision, and were slow to integrate. In the North, schools remained segregated because neighborhoods were segregated. It took one heroic woman and several court decisions to finally achieve the equality that had been promised by Congress during Reconstruction.

One year after the *Brown* decision, Rosa Parks refused to give up her seat on a Montgomery, Alabama bus to a white man and became a heroine. Her symbolic gesture triggered a boycott of the South's Jim Crow laws. Nine years after Rosa Parks staged her one woman protest, Congress passed the sweeping Civil Rights Act of 1964. This law was designed to stop racial discrimination in public accommodations, education, housing and employment. Title II of the Civil Rights Act was aimed at public accommodations, and prohibits segregation or racial discrimination in motels, restaurants, theaters, or sports arenas.

One important civil rights case involved Ollie's Barbecue, a family-owned restaurant in Birmingham, Alabama. The restaurant had accommodations for about 220 persons in its dining room. Although it employed 24 blacks, Ollie's Barbecue since 1927 had refused to serve black customers inside. Charged with violating the Civil Rights Act of 1964, the owner of Ollie's Barbecue argued that his restaurant did not come under federal jurisdiction and the "interstate commerce clause." His lawyers argued that since few customers were traveling from outside Alabama, that Ollie's Barbecue did not fall under Article I, Section 9, which grants Congress the power to "regulate Commerce with foreign Nations, and among the several States, and with the Indian Tribes." The key question in this case, known as *Katzenbach v. McClung*, 379 U.S. 294 (1964) was "whether Title II, as applied to a restaurant annually receiving about $70,000 of food which was moved in commerce, is a valid exercise of the power of Congress?" How did the Supreme Court rule in this case?

With the end of Jim Crow, and the right to vote, secure black Americans were ready by 1965 to take their place in American society as educated, productive and active citizens. However, as much as we would like to consider ourselves a color-blind society, this lofty ideal does not exist today. The facts speak for themselves: "One in three Black men are ensnared in the criminal justice system. More than half of Black children live in poverty, and drugs are infused into the community to spread death by AIDS or violence. Moreover, Jim Crow Jr. still works to confine opportunity for African Americans."[9]

When it comes to giving out punishment for drug violations, for example, African Americans are still being treated unfairly. Investigative journalist Malaika Horne supports this premise with these arguments:

There are increased penalties for possession and trafficking of crack cocaine, the drug of choice for many low-income African Americans. While users and small time dealers of smokable cocaine are facing the heavier hand of the law, more lenient sentences are imposed on those convicted of trafficking in as opposed to possessing similar amounts of powder cocaine. The disparate sentencing for crack cocaine versus powder cocaine, many say, has an obvious class imprint. The low income crack user does the jail time while the more affluent powder cocaine user is allowed to remain on the streets . . . more African Americans than ever are being arrested, convicted and jailed. While African Americans make up 12 percent of the nation's population and constitute 13 percent of all monthly drug users, they represent 35 percent of arrests for drug possession. They comprise 55 percent of all convictions and 74 percent of all prison sentences. African Americans are approximately 38 percent of crack users but comprise a staggering 90 percent of crack defendants in federal court. By contrast, white Americans are 46 percent of crack users, but account for a mere 3.5 percent of convictions for federal crack offenses. This disparity has resulted in African Americans serving sentences that are 41 percent longer than whites.[10]

If African Americans make up 12 percent of the population and 38 percent of crack users, why do they comprise 90 percent of defendants in federal courts? If white Americans are 46 percent of crack users, why do they only account for 3.5 percent of convictions for federal crack offenses? Are blacks and whites being treated differently for the same crimes? Is this "justice?" Is this "fair?"

African Americans make up 12% of the population, but 41% of death row inmates. Source: "States of Execution," *Time* (June 16, 1997), pp. 34-35.

Affirmative Action

The 1964 Civil Rights Act was supported by Americans who wanted to end Jim Crow forever. But President Lyndon Johnson wanted to go further. He wanted "Affirmative Action," which means that government ought to remedy the *effects* of past discrimination. To justify affirmative action, President Johnson used a metaphor which he called the "Shackled Runner."

Imagine a hundred-yard dash in which one of the two runners has his legs shackled together. He has progressed ten yards while the unshackled runner has gone fifty yards. At that point, the judges decide the race is unfair. How do they rectify the situation? Do they merely remove the shackles and allow the race to proceed? Then they could say that 'equal opportunity' now prevailed. But one of the runners would still be forty yards ahead of the other. Would it not be the better part of justice to allow the other runner to make up the forty-yard gap; or to start the race all over again? That would be affirmative action toward equality.

Judging from these words and his actions, President Johnson seemed to be making the following arguments:
- ❍ In the race of life, shackled runners fall behind.
- ❍ In order to help previously shackled runners achieve, they need more than equality.
- ❍ Therefore, affirmative action should be taken to help these runners make up the gap.

Is this an accurate interpretation of President Johnson's logic. If so, is his argument reasonable? Why or why not?

The Civil Rights Act had clearly implied that no person is to be subjected to discrimination under programs receiving federal funds. Under instructions from President Johnson, the Department of Health, Education and Welfare went further, defining the law to require affirmative action programs to achieve racial balance, especially in education. This led to favored treatment of minorities who applied to be admitted to graduate programs such as medicine, which were traditionally dominated by whites.

In *Regents of the University of California v. Bakke*, 438 U.S. 265 (1978), the Supreme Court had to decide if a university setting aside 16 of its 100 places in the medical school for minority applicants had violated Title VI of the Civil Rights Act, which reads: "No person in the United States shall, on the grounds of race, color, or national origin, be excluded from participation in, be denied the benefits of, or be subjected to discrimination under any program or activity receiving Federal financial assistance." What are the key facts in this case, and what did the Supreme Court majority decide?

Despite all the laws and court decisions designed to eliminate racism, it still exists in the minds of white men who wear bomber jackets, steel toed boots, shave their heads, and have Nazi flags in their homes. The biggest threat to African Americans, however, is the belief that Affirmative Action has outlived its purpose. This belief in California led to passage of initiative 209, which bans race and gender-based discrimination or preferences in public hiring, promotion and university admissions.

Although the debate goes on about white males being victims of reverse discrimination, a 1995 Labor Department Report "found little evidence of widespread reverse discrimination." The Report stated, for example, that "Of 3,000 federal and appellate court decisions issued in discrimination cases between 1900 and 1994 that the Labor Department studied, only 100 involved reverse discrimination claims. And of these cases, there were only six in which white or male employees were found to have been discriminated against in favor of minorities or women." Source: Larry Reynolds, "As Affirmative Action Debate Heats Up," Public Support is Split," *HR Focus* (June, 1995), p. 8.

Although California's Proposition 209 is still tied up in the courts, African Americans fear that Affirmative Action may be on its way out. So now some are proposing compensation for those years that their ancestors labored as slaves. To understand this "Reparations" issue, we need to know some facts about the era after the Civil War, known as "Reconstruction."

During Reconstruction, Congress passed a bill to provide a homestead for each Negro family. This bill aroused hopes among the former slaves that by Christmas 1865 they would be settled on small farms with "Forty Acres and a Mule." These hopes were dashed, however, when President Andrew Johnson vetoed the proposed law. Without land, the former slaves were turned loose with few resources, except the right to vote. This fact has encouraged some African Americans to seek the kind of reparations given to Japanese Americans wrongly imprisoned during World War II. According to Kennell Jackson, "More than twenty thousand blacks, most of them from California, filed claims with the Internal Revenue Service based on post-Civil War legislation to provide former slaves with forty acres. Each claim was for $43,309. Two theories exist about the origin of this figure: one says that it is today's value of forty acres and a mule, and a second that it is the difference between the Median income of white and black households. The IRS denied the claims."[11]

Until the IRS softens up, African Americans will have to settle for a Presidential apology. On June 12, 1997, the apology proposal was introduced in the House Judiciary Committee with eleven white co-sponsors. The resolution stated: "Congress apologizes to African Americans whose ancestors suffered as slaves under the Constitution and laws of the United States until 1865." After reading the proposal, President Clinton said he would consider it. The apology, however, aroused the usual storm of words. The Rev. Jesse Jackson said the proposal lacked "substance." House Speaker Newt Gingrich dismissed it as "emotional symbolism."

> Since Japanese Americans have been compensated for being wrongly detained in camps during World War II, should the national government pay African Americans compensation in the amount of $43,309?

> In his criticism of the slavery apology, Professor Sowell says it would promote further polarization. What name have we learned to classify this type of prediction?

With his usual honesty, Stanford University scholar Thomas Sowell, an African American, tried to keep the apology in perspective. Citing all the places in the world where slavery has existed, Professor Sowell asked, "Why then is slavery being spoken of as if it were a national problem peculiar to the United States?" Noting that all races have either been enslaved, or had slaves, Sowell asked, "Are those people who want the United States to apologize for slavery also demanding that Africans, Asians, and Western Hemisphere Indians likewise apology for the same thing?" After asking several similarly tough questions, Sowell defines the apology as similar to "The idea of inherited racial guilt—a Nazi conception—behind the proposed apology would do nothing to heal the racial divisions in this country today. Instead, it would promote further polarization." To end his argument, Sowell asks rhetorically, "Is a heightened sense of grievance an asset or a liability in the job market? In education? In human relations across racial lines? Is looking backward the way to prepare for the future?"[12]

The best way for any minority to get ahead in this country is through a good education. Through Affirmative Action, many African Americans and other minorities have studied law. Thanks to Proposition 209, minority law school enrollments at the University of California in Berkeley and UCLA have dropped 80%.[13]

Critics, however, dislike Affirmative Action because they believe it is "social engineering" based on race. They argue that only "race-blind" admissions procedures are fair. What do you think? How about your grade in this class? Should the

> What factors should teachers consider when deciding grades?

instructor take into account your race, gender, age, physical disabilities, emotional problems, or personality before awarding a grade? What other factors should be considered in determining your grade? Should the teacher grade you on test performance only, or take into account such subjective features as your manners, habits, looks, values, perceived ambition, skin color, gender?

Equal Protection of the Laws

In 1976 the Supreme Court had to decide at what age young men and women could legally drink beer. Under Oklahoma law selling 3.2% alcohol beer to males under 21 and females under 18 was illegal. A young Oklahoma man had challenged the law on the grounds that it unreasonably deprived males of the equal protection of the law. His lawyers used the Fourteenth Amendment to argue their case, citing Section One which says no State shall deny to "any person within its jurisdiction the equal protection of the law." This

California and Texas voters have ended the use of race as a criteria for admission to law schools in those states. As a result, the minority enrollments at law schools in those two states have plummeted to 1963 levels. This has led to complaints that minorities have difficulty with law school tests because public schools fail to prepare minorities for "cognitive" thinking. What does this mean, and how can we improve the education of racial minorities?

phrase was orbitally meant to protect the former slaves. Now it was being used to uphold the rights of young men who, like the ladies, wanted to drink beer at 18.

The legal question before the Court, however, was "Does a state law which discriminates on the basis of gender violate the Fourteenth Amendment?" To justify the law, attorneys for the state introduced statistical evidence showing that males 18 to 20 were more likely than females in the same age group to be arrested for driving under the influence of alcohol. These lawyers argued that the DUI statistics provided a **Rational Basis** to have a beer drinking law that let women drink at 18, but made men wait three more years.

Despite the inherent logic of this argument, the Supreme Court held that Oklahoma's facts failed to prove a rational basis for its beer-age drinking law. Instead, said the Court majority, Oklahoma had failed to prove that its law was "substantially" related to government objectives important enough to justify gender classification. On the basis of this reasoning, the Supreme Court struck down the Oklahoma beer law holding that it "invidiously discriminates against males 18 to 20 years of age." In dissent, Justice William Rehnquist accused the majority of inventing "out of thin air" confusing standards by which to measure state compliance with the equal protection clause of the Fourteenth Amendment.

Under the **Rational Basis Test**, Oklahoma's lawyers had to show that the state law was free from "invidious discrimination." They also had to show that the "facts" justified age discrimination based on gender.

The statistics used, however, only showed that young males had a 2% higher percentage of DUI arrests than young females. This slight difference was rejected by the Court's majority in 1976 as "unduly tenuous." Oklahoma, concluded the majority, had failed to prove that its law was "substantially" related to government objectives important enough to justify gender classification.[14]

The "Rational Basis Test" is used whenever state laws are challenged as a violation of the equal protection clause of the Fourteenth Amendment. As a rule of thumb, the test holds that government may classify and discriminate if the basis for the law is rational, reasonable, or justifiable. Is there a rational basis for a state law which defines rape differently for males and females? The California legislature thought so in 1859 and passed a statutory rape law which imposed a jail term for up to three years for any male convicted of having sex with a female under 18—whether she consented or not—but did not impose any penalty on a female who had sex with an underage male. In 1978 a 17-year-old Rohnert Park, California male was charged with statutory rape under the 1859 law. On June 3, Michael M. and two male friends approached 16-year-old Sharon and her sister at a bus stop. After talking and flirting, Michael and Sharon moved away from the others and ended up on a bench in the park. When Michael made advances, Sharon tried to shove him away. After he struck her in the face two or three times, Sharon submitted. Afterwards, in July 1978, a complaint of statutory rape against Michael M. was filed by Sharon's parents. Because the California law only applied to males accused of rape, not females, Michael's lawyers argued that it violated his constitutional rights.[15]

Suppose Nevada had a law which banned driving by red-haired women over 50, and tried to justify it by arguing that "everyone knows red-heads are temperamental." Would such a law satisfy the rational basis test? Five years ago in Utah a single male age 20 was paying $959 for auto insurance sold by the Allstate Insurance Company. A married male or female aged 37 only paid $255. Was this fair?

> What do you think about the case of Michael M.? Was he treated fairly? Does a state law which punishes a male for having sex with an underage female—but does not apply the same standard to women—violate the equal protection clause? Does it satisfy the rational basis test?

Without civil rights laws and the Fourteenth Amendment, there would be few lawsuits by minorities. To understand American politics today, we have to understand the history behind the Fourteenth Amendment.

Soon after the Civil War ended in 1865, Abraham Lincoln was shot to death, and former Tennessee Democrat Andrew Johnson became President. While the Republican majority which controlled Congress watched uneasily, Johnson pursued Lincoln's "lenient" policy of letting the ex-rebels reorganize their state governments after taking an oath of allegiance to the Union. Under the Johnson reconstruction plan, the white men in each southern state met in convention and drafted new state constitutions and laws. Each state abolished slavery, repudiated the confederate war debt, and repealed the acts of secession. While the Johnson Plan went forward, Northern Republicans realized they had three serious problems:

① The South would be restored to the Union able to count its entire slave population for the purpose of representation in the House. Under Article I, Section 2 the South before slavery ended could only count three-fifths of its slave population. When the South seceded in 1861, Republicans were outnumbered 37 to 29 in the Senate, and 129 to 108 in the House. Letting the Southern Democrats back in the Union without certain "guarantees" was unthinkable to Northern Republicans.

② The Northern Republicans were also enraged when Southern white leaders under the Johnson Reconstruction Plan failed to show proper regard for the rights of the former slaves. When the new state conventions met during the summer of 1865, they passed a series of laws which seemed designed to keep Southern blacks from ever becoming equal citizens. Known as the "Black Codes," these laws denied voting rights to Negroes, barred them from serving on juries, and imposed harsh limits on their other civil rights. To Northern Republicans, the Black

162

Codes smelled like resurrected slavery, and they were furious. "We tell the white men of Mississippi," said the Chicago *Tribune*, "that the men of the North will convert the state of Mississippi into a frog pond before they will allow any such laws to disgrace one foot of soil in which the bones of our soldiers sleep and over which the flag of freedom lives."

③ To offset the increased representation and to protect the former slaves from state repression, the Republican Radicals in 1865 whipped up support for "Negro Suffrage." The enthusiasm for the vote, however, created another dilemma for the Republican Party. To force the Negro vote on the South in 1865 was pure hypocrisy. At the time, only six Northern states let black people vote. Even more damaging was the fact that most Negroes living in the North were treated as second class citizens. In Indiana, for example, Blacks were barred from public schools, could not vote or serve on juries.

In the 1960's Affirmative Action was often used to benefit white women rather than minorities. Since Affirmative Action was originally designed to offset the effects of slavery, should it be used to help white women get ahead?

By 1865 the Republicans knew their party was in grave danger. They had to do something about the representation problem, the Black Code problem, Negro Suffrage, and a Negrophobe President.

By 1865 the Republicans in Congress knew their party was in grave danger. They had to do something about the representation dilemma, the Black Codes, Negro Suffrage and President Johnson. Though popular in the South, Johnson's "lenient" reconstruction policies threatened the future of the party which had nominated him—a Union Democrat—to be their Vice President. When Congress reassembled in December 1865, the Republicans had two-thirds majorities in both the House and the Senate, so they went around Johnson's veto power by proposing a constitutional amendment. This amendment was ratified by 1868 and became the famous Fourteenth Amendment. This amendment was originally designed to protect the former slaves, punish the South, and resolve the representation dilemma.

For our purposes, however, the words in Section One are the most important in the Fourteenth Amendment. Section One was clearly designed to protect the former slaves from legislation passed by vindictive whites. It says, "**No state shall make or enforce any law which shall abridge the privileges or immunities of citizens of the United States; nor shall any State deprive any person of life, liberty, or property, without due process of law; nor deny to any person within its jurisdiction the equal protection of the law.**" Then men who helped write these words into the Constitution were convinced that the spirit of Christianity motivated them. What do you think?

While the Fourteenth Amendment was being debated in the House of Representatives, Ohio Republican John A. Bingham urged passage saying that Section One was a simple, strong and plain declaration "that equal laws and equal and exact justice shall hereafter be secured within every State of this union by the combined power of all the people of every State."[16]

Though designed to prevent future Black Codes, Section One has been used to prohibit states from passing discriminatory beer drinking laws. It has been used to legalize abortion on a national level. It has been used to protect citizens from state infringement of speech and other First Amendment Rights. Using the Fourteenth Amendment, the Supreme Court has made states use "due process" in law enforcement. By stretching the intent and meaning of the Fourteenth Amendment, the Supreme Court has clearly demonstrated the dictum that "whoever interprets the rules controls the game."

In the final analysis, Affirmative Action was controversial and polarizing. But why is it under attack today? The timing of the current voter assault on minority set-asides, special programs in college admissions, and race-or-gender-based hiring is puzzling. Why now? Is there some ominous and hidden scheme. Perhaps a conspiracy? Are powerful people determined to turn back the clock on racism? Is the history of Reconstruction being ignored because Americans won't study their history, or is there a plot to dump history books down a "memory hole?" Was George Orwell predicting our future when he wrote, "those who control the present, control the past. Those who control the past, control the future."

The Politics of Gender

In 1981 writer Michael Korda asked *Playboy* readers, "What do you do if the boss is wearing a neat skirt slit up to the thighs, a silk blouse with the top three buttons unfastened and a fetching pair of high-heeled sandals?" Korda asked this question in an article about "Sexual Office Politics."[17] He was, of course, using the type of stereotype that appeals to *Playboy* readers. In the real world, women with power would never use their sexual attributes to manipulate men, and achieve power—would they?

Korda stereotyped female bosses to tickle male lust. That's the big problem for American women. Most men believe conventional wisdom, which says a woman who dresses seductively is looking for "it." Some men believe women who wear short skirts are inviting rape. They tell jokes like, "How does a prostitute know she's been raped? When the check bounces!"

These stereotypes were around in 1988 when young Brenda Taylor, an assistant state attorney in Broward County, Florida was wearing short skirts, designer blouses, and spiked heels to work. One day her male boss called Ms. Taylor aside and insisted that she quit dressing like a "bimbo." Taylor then filed a complaint with the federal Equal Employment Opportunity Commission; and was fired. So she sued.

What do you think? Does a woman who wears short skirts, designer blouses, and spiked heels look like a "bimbo?"

By itself, the word *Bimbo* hardly applies to a successful lawyer. According to Hugh Rawson, *Wicked Words* (1989), Bimbo means a young, dumb, promiscuous woman. At one time, however, it also meant a dumb, tough guy. Should dumb men be called Bimbos?

On the other side of the fashion coin was Ann Hopkins, a highly successful executive who wore plain clothes to work and was not sexy. Hopkins worked at the Washington Office of

164

Price Waterhouse, and had made large profits for the company. But she was denied an important promotion because her evaluators thought she was not feminine enough. She was advised by one high ranking Price Waterhouse male to "walk more femininely, talk more femininely, wear makeup, have her hair styled and wear jewelry." Ann Hopkins quit and filed a lawsuit under Title VII of the Civil Rights Act of 1964, which forbids employment discrimination because of a person's sex."[18]

In May 1989 by a six to three vote, the U.S. Supreme Court held that Price Waterhouse had been guilty of unlawful sexual stereotyping. In his opinion for the majority, Justice William Brennan wrote, "An employer who objects to aggressiveness in women but whose positions require this trait places women in an intolerable and impermissible Catch 22: out of a job if they behave aggressively and out of a job if they don't"[19]

After flying combat missions as a World War II bombardier, Joseph Heller wrote his famous novel *Catch-22*. In the novel, American pilots are required to fly too many combat missions. The only way for the pilots to be excused from their dangerous duty is to be certified as "insane" by the base doctor. Under Catch 22, however, a pilot who refused to fly was by definition "sane" because he was thinking clearly. In other words, there was no way out. When we use the phrase "Catch-22" it means an impossible dilemma.

Congress had tried to protect women from unfair job practices through Title VII, which was designed to insure equal employment opportunity irrespective of race, color, religion, sex, or national origin. Affirmative Action was also designed to improve job opportunities for women.

Many women wanted more than jobs, however. They wanted complete equality, and so they burned their bras, wore earth shoes, read *Ms.* magazine, sang Helen Reddy's "I Am Woman," and booed Paul Anka for his song "Having My Baby." These "Feminists" also wanted a constitutional amendment.

In every session of Congress since 1923 someone has introduced an Equal Rights Amendment. By 1972 this proposed amendment said:

> **Section 1, Equality of rights under the law shall not be denied by the United States or by any state on account of sex.**
> **Section 2, The Congress shall have the power to enforce, by appropriate legislation, the provisions of this article.**
> **Section 3, This amendment shall take effect two years after the date of ratification.**

With the support of many men, the ERA sailed through Congress in 1972, and was sent to the state legislatures for ratification. The deadline for ratification, established by Congress, was March 22, 1979. By 1977, 35 states had ratified and only three

Should the Constitution be amended to make it easier to amend?

more were needed. The opposition, however, had hardened by 1977. When the original deadline passed, Congress moved the date for ratification forward to June 30, 1982. Despite this boost from the men in Congress, the ERA died unratified. Later, a spokesperson for the National Organization for Women singled out 12 powerful state politicians who killed the ERA. Male politicians should not get all the blame, however. Blame the Founding Fathers who made it difficult to amend the Constitution.

In *Wicked Words,* Hugh Rawson describes "nag"
as a word meaning to scold or a horse. Should
feminists be described as militant nags?

While the ERA was being debated, conservatives were predicting that it would start the
nation down a slippery slope toward the
ultimate horrors of unisex toilets, homosexual
marriages, and pregnant soldiers. Meanwhile,
feminists were being portrayed in the media
as militant "nags" whose favorite posture was
a uplifted fist and perpetual scowl. To many Americans, the raised fist and scowls symbolized
the extremism of the "gender" feminists. They wanted all manifestations of sexism erased from
school books. They wanted lesbians honored for carrying a "double burden of oppression."
They wanted Jesus called "Child of God," not "Son of God." Some even wanted unisex toilets.

There is an old photograph showing former President Theodore Roosevelt as a young
college wrestler. Roosevelt is sitting with arms crossed, and his face darkened by a scowl which
historian Richard Hofstader called "paranoid." Some athletes use the paranoid scowl in an
attempt to intimidate their opponents. While the ERA was being debated, feminists were
photographed raising clenched fists and scowling. This body language, which is traditionally
associated with aggressive males, seemed out of place on the fairer sex. Psychologists say body
language often reveals power needs. In the case of feminists, the up-raised fist meant, "we want
power."

Many of the women who pursued careers in the 1970's have discovered that their
biological clock has run out. This means they have grown too old to have children safely.
Nature limits the child bearing ages. When she interviewed career women in 1989, *Time* writer
Claudia Wallis discovered that older women who had fought for feminist goals now consider
themselves the "human sacrifice generation." According to Wallis, many of these women now
bitterly complain that they sacrificed by having put their careers over children. Noting how male
executives did not have to make the same sacrifices, Wallis asked this rhetorical question: "Is it
fair that 90% of male executives 40 and under are fathers but only 35% of their female
counterparts have children?"[20]

Militant feminists still wear a T-shirt that says, "A woman needs a man like a fish needs a
bicycle." Eventually, however, the backlash came and it was brutal. The movie "Fatal
Attraction," for example, featured Glenn Close as a crazed career woman who tries to kill her
adulterous boy friend who has, as the old cliche goes, "loved her and left her."

In her book *Backlash: The Undeclared War Against American Women* (1992), Susan
Faludi argues that the mass media has sent a collective message to women that says feminism is
your worst enemy, and all this freedom is making you miserable, unmarriageable, infertile, and
unstable. Faludi argues that the backlash was triggered by movies, TV dramas and
advertisements that featured blissful mothers and frazzled career women. These stereotypes,
argues Faludi, were designed to sow doubts in women's minds about their real goals.

Feminist ideology is based on the
premise that environmental factors are more
important in shaping our lives than genetic
ones. Feminists argue, for example, that girls
play with dolls because of what they are
taught, not what they are. UCLA behavioral

How are contemporary women being
portrayed in movies, TV dramas, and
commercial advertising?

scientist Melissa Hines, however, has done research which seems to challenge that conventional wisdom. For two years, Professor Hines studied the play habits of very young boys and girls. In her lab at UCLA, little boys and girls get to play with a toy box filled with toys like police cars, Lincoln Logs, and Barbie Dolls. Although both sexes play with all the toys, the boys have their favorites and the girls have theirs. According to Hines, the videotaped play sessions show clearly that as a group, boys have their favorites and girls have theirs. The boys favor sports cars, fire trucks and Lincoln Logs. The girls, on the other hand, prefer dolls and kitchen toys.

Why would little boys be drawn to trucks, and little girls to dolls? In the past, conventional wisdom attributed most differences in male-female behavior to the sex hormone testosterone which is secreted from the male sex organs. During the 1970's, however, it was politically incorrect to argue that men differ from women because they had more of this hormone. To admit a biological reason for gender differences weakened the feminist argument that all male-female differences were merely cosmetic and social.

In her studies, however, Melissa Hines discovered a link between testosterone and child's play. There is at the UCLA lab, one batch of girls who have a rare genetic abnormality that caused them to produce elevated levels of testosterone during their embryonic development. When they play with the UCLA toy box, these girls are more likely to play with the trucks and Lincoln logs than with the dolls. Why? In her analysis of the UCLA experiments, *Time* writer Christine Gorman asks these pertinent questions regarding the high testosterone girls: "Could it be that the high levels of testosterone in their bodies before birth have left a permanent imprint on their brains, affecting their later behavior? Or did their parents, knowing of their disorder, somehow subtly influence their choices?"[21]

In primitive societies men who wanted a bride had to play "Love Chase." As described by James George Frazer in *The Golden Bough* (1922), the Kirghiz play love chase this way. Armed with a formidable ship, the bride mounts a fleet horse and is pursued by all the young men with any pretensions to her hand. "She will be given as a prize to the one who catches her," wrote Frazer, "but she has the right besides urging her horse to the utmost, to use the whip, often with no mean force, to keep off those lovers who are unwelcome to her, and she will probably favor the one whom she has already chosen in her heart."

Today, American women have the equivalent of the Kirghiz whip. It is called "sexual harassment." When an unwelcome lover makes advances, American women can now file a lawsuit and let the courts whip the culprit.

Several years ago, Teresa Harris worked as a manager for Forklift Systems, an equipment rental company. For approximately two years, Harris and other female employees had to suffer the sexist behavior of their boss Charles Hardy. He had them on occasion retrieve coins from his front pants pocket. Hardy also asked Harris and other female employees to retrieve objects that he had thrown on the ground, and made sexual innuendos. In front of witnesses, Hardy suggested to Harris that if she wanted a promotion they could go to the Holiday Inn.

These hurtful words forced Harris to resign her job and sue Forklift Systems for sexual harassment, claiming that Hardy's conduct toward her had created an abusive work environment for her because of her gender. In *Harris v. Forklift Systems, Inc.,* 114 S. Ct. 367 (1993), the Supreme Court held that "an objectively hostile work environment is created when a "reasonable person" would find it hostile or abusive, and the victim subjectively perceives it as such. Sexual harassment in the workplace has become a serious political issue. As a result of several lawsuits, sexual harassment has become a minefield of definitions. In general, it now means "unwelcome sexual advances,

In the case above, the Supreme Court used a "reasonable person" standard to decide what is meant by a "hostile environment?" What does the Court mean by a "reasonable person?"

requests for sexual favors, and other verbal or physical conduct of a sexual nature." To qualify as sexual harassment, one or more of the following has to happen:

- ☒ A person feels that submission to the conduct is necessary to keep the job.
- ☒ A person feels that a pay raise, promotion or demotion depends on submission to the request.
- ☒ The conduct interferes with a person's work performance or creates an intimidating, hostile, or offensive working environment.

The two most common types of sexual harassment are *quid pro quo* and hostile work environment. *Quid pro quo* is Latin for "something for something." An employee asked for sex in exchange for a job promotion, by this definition, has been sexually harassed. When harassment makes the job intolerable, then it has created a hostile work environment.

To avoid a sexual harassment charge, don't do any of the following:
- ☐ Place sexual pinups over your desk.
- ☐ Ask a co-worker for a date.
- ☐ Be rude to a female employee.
- ☐ Make sexual jokes.
- ☐ Touch anyone intentionally.

The American Psychological Association has described five types of sexual harassment, and labeled them as follows:
① Gender Harassment.
② Seductive Behavior.
③ Sexual Bribery.
④ Sexual Coercion.
⑤ Sexual Imposition.

What Can You Do If You Are Harassed? To get the answer to this important question, use your computer and dial this code on the Internet: [http://www.apa.org/pubinfo/harass.html].

To make sexual harassment seem fair, advocates claim men have the same rights as women to file charges. This may be true, but do women hang nude male photos over their desks, ask co-workers for dates, act rude, make sexual jokes, grab ye old arse?

Using the Internet [http://www.vix.com/pub/men/harass/dershowitz.html], Harvard Law School Professor Alan Dershowitz tells a story that should frighten any teacher who tries to discuss taboo topics. According to Dershowitz, "A group of feminists in my criminal-law class threatened hostile-environment charges against me because of the way in which I teach the law of rape. They found the atmosphere of my classroom hostile because I spent two days discussing false reports of rape and because I made arguments in favor of disclosing the names of complaining witnesses in rape cases. Despite the fact that the vast majority of students wanted to hear all sides of the important issues surrounding the law of rape, a small minority tried to use the law of sexual harassment as a tool of censorship."

Newspaper headlines keep reminding us that sexual harassment rules are borderline ludicrous. In October 1996, six-year-old Johnathan Prevette planted a kiss on the cheek of a female classmate at their Lexington, North Carolina school. The teacher saw crime, the victim complained, and Johnathan was barred from class for one day, therefore missing coloring, playtime, and an ice-cream party. Defending the punishment, school officials said the kiss was "unwelcome." ✪ Was Johnathan denied his rights, or is it reasonable to add "unwelcome kiss" to the growing list of sexual harassment definitions?

Although Americans accept sexual harassment rules as a necessary protection for workers, the penalties being handed down seem excessive. In 1994, for example, a temporary employee for a law firm was awarded $7 million by a jury for conduct which she said actually caused her "very little distress."

Predictably, humor has been used to soften sexual harassment's harsh logic. On an episode of "Saturday Night Live," the comedians satirized a "Date Rape" game which ridiculed Antioch College's dating code. This code requires verbal agreement before either the man or the woman can initiate a kiss, touch a buttock, or negotiate sexual intercourse.

While comedians satirized date rape, Army drill sergeant Delmar Simpson was on trial for allegedly raping female recruits under his authority at the Aberdeen Proving Ground, Maryland. In this case, a military judge ruled that drill sergeants have so much power over trainees that they don't need to use a weapon or threaten force to be found guilty of rape.

Is there any rational basis for a military rule defining rape as a drill sergeant who has sexual intercourse with a female recruit, even if she cooperates? What would a reasonable person say about such a rule?

Now that women's rights is a high priority, the media is having a field day reporting all the gender crimes being committed by insensitive men. Read the following list, and decide which are serious infractions of a woman's rights, and which are merely silly.

- ♀ Amateur bodybuilder Debra DiCenso was arrested in Boston for illegally lifting 65 pound weights in the men's weight room at a city-owned gym. The powerfully built DiCenso invaded the men's weight room because the facilities for women weight-lifters were inferior.
- ♀ Women earn 72 cents on the male dollar, usually because they lose seniority while raising children.
- ♀ Firefighter tests require picking up a 170 pound dummy and dragging it 100 feet. Lacking the same body strength as men, most women flunk this part of the test.
- ♀ Women are now attending military schools like the Virginia Military Institute. In order to graduate from VMI cadets have to do 60 sit-ups in two minutes and run a mile and a half in 12 minutes. When informed of these requirements, a spokesperson for the National Organization for Women (NOW) referred to VMI as a "phallocracy."
- ♀ In September 1996, VMI was blasted again by NOW; this time for shaving bald the scalps of female fresh persons. According to the NOW spokesperson, the scalping was done to humiliate women, and it merely proved that VMI's leaders were "poor losers."

The idea of women performing military combat roles is still controversial. Those who oppose women in combat say they aren't physically strong enough. They argue that women captured in combat would be raped and abused, and that the idea of women being tortured is offensive to Americans. Opponents also argue that women will fall behind in training because of pregnancies or other specifically "female problems." They argue that combat units require a "team spirit" that would be weakened by women.

Four Chicago men sued a few years ago claiming the right to serve beer alongside breast enhanced waitresses working for the infamous Hooters. Seeing an opportunity to correct a mental and physical injustice against men, let's call it "Hooter Envy," the Equal Employment Opportunity Commission demanded a $22 million fine from the 170-restaurant chain. In addition to the fine, the EEOP told Hooters to hire male waiters, compensation for any men it had turned down for jobs, and set up a scholarship fund to enhance employment opportunities for men. In the face of media sarcasm, the EEOP backed off.

> In the 1970's American soldiers trained by marching and chanting "two, four, six, eight, rape, kill, mutilate!" As the military has become more politically correct, such words have disappeared. Are tough words necessary for a tough military?

Sex and Politics

When it comes to politics, are men and women different? Are men more capable of sizing up political issues than the ladies? Now that female voters were largely responsible for putting Bill Clinton in the White House, have they changed the face of American politics? Did Al Gore also get the majority of female votes?

What happens now in mixed company when women talk politics? Will they prove to be more sophisticated about politics than the men? Is there a new "gender gap" in politics? Has the Democratic Party become the party of choice for the ladies? Has the Republican Party become the party of angry white men? What did we learn from the 2000 election of George W. Bush?

Will President Bush be the Republican hero who brings female voters into the party ranks in big numbers. Is it unusual for voters to switch parties? Political scientist Ann Delaney says it is not unusual for voters to change parties:

> **Party identification doesn't necessarily stay constant. It can evolve over time. Women and African Americans used to associate themselves more with the Republican Party. From the Civil War to Franklin Roosevelt's second term, African Americans voted Republican. From the time women received the vote nationally in 1920 until the 1980's, women were more likely to vote Republican. These days, both groups are more likely to identify with the Democratic Party.[22]**

This voting shift is described by some political activists as a "gender realignment." In the future, you can expect gender issues to take center stage during the political season. This could lead eventually to passage of the Equal Rights Amendment. If so, expect women to be filing lawsuits to achieve equality in employment, pay, promotion, and opportunity at all levels.

Remember what we said earlier about the "rule of unintended consequences." The ERA was meant to unite women. However, when the amendment was winding its way through the fifty state legislatures twenty years ago, its most creative opponents were often women. At the time, women opposed to the amendment filled the air with propaganda. In Utah, for example, groups like "Humanitarians Opposed To Degrading Our Girls" were organized. Speaking for HOTDOG, Mrs. Reba Lazenby said:

> **Each mother who loves her children, her husband and her home and who wants the respect and honor a mother should have should oppose ratification. I want people awakened to the hidden aspects of the amendment. Its passage means more regimentation. Women have certain standards. I don't think making her equal to a man will help. A woman's standards involve the special privilege of being a mother. This amendment tears down the family and the home and this is the purpose for which it is intended.**

Today, the most vocal opponents of equality for women are those men who write syndicated columns for the newspapers. In 1996 columnist Samuel Francis wrote these scathing words when the Supreme Court ordered Virginia Military Institute to admit female cadets: "VMI is now famous . . . because of the feminist-sponsored lawsuit that has succeeded in forcing it to accept female cadets. After years of pestering VMI all the way to the Supreme Court, after winning a judgment last summer from Justice Ruth Bader Ginsburg that ordered the 157-year-old military school to accept women . . . the feminists and their friends have pretty much won what they wanted."

> **Have women "won" by finally being admitted to VMI and the Citadel? Is the equality achieved by Supreme Court dictate likely to be "real" equality?**

In the Near Future

The most extreme feminists believe all men are potential rapists. This conventional wisdom is logical from a biological perspective. To curb biological impulses, men used to be reminded that "16 will get you 20." Although this statutory rape warning was not always heeded, it helped contain the predatory imperatives of most men.

> **Is a female serial rapist a future possibility? If so, what type of punishment or treatment should society use to discourage this type of behavior by women?**

Now that women have power, are they developing predatory impulses similar to men? In her 1992 book *Women on Top: How Real Life Has Changed Women's Sexual Fantasies,* Nancy Friday says modern women now have sexual fantasies in which they visualize themselves in control. According to Friday, women know there is a world of sexual experience out there and, "They are flexing their erotic muscles . . . testing their power."[23] Suppose our first female president is accused of sexual harassment by a man named Paul Jones. Jones says the President, while governor of California, had him brought to her hotel room where she tried to kiss him and asked him to perform "a type of sex." Should our President be impeached for this type of behavior? Should men be protected from such predatory behavior?

The rational basis test requires that there be reliable facts to substantiate any preference shown on the basis of race, gender or other factors. Are there facts to support statutory rape laws aimed at controlling men? Yes. In 1995 the United Nations issued a 137-page report showing that women in the United States run a much higher risk of being raped than women in Europe. The U.S. rape statistics, according to the U.N. report are extremely high, even allowing for differences in reporting rates. The United States reported 118 rapes per 100,000 women aged 15 to 59 between 1987-89 (the latest period available). The 118 number was nearly three times higher than Sweden, which was second with 43 rapes per 100,000 women.

It is a fact that 60% of the babies born to unwed teenage mothers in the U.S. are fathered by adult males. California pays out annually between $5 billion and $7 billion in state and federal aid to families begun by teens. To stop the money flow, California Governor Pete Wilson in the summer of 1995 allocated $2.4 million to a pilot program for 16 counties to begin prosecuting men who engage in sex with underage girls, and in January 1996 Wilson pledged $6 million more for a statewide crackdown.

Despite AIDS, rape, "children born out of wedlock," we're now advising women to dress for power and indulge in their sexual fantasies. In the words of the cigarette advertisers, "We've Come a Long Way Baby!"

Not to worry, however. The feminists were right. Women now need men about as much as they need a bicycle. According to the tabloid *Examiner* (April 8, 1997), p. 25, "Tomorrow's Gals Won't Need Guys."

THE phenomenon of "virgin births" among animals is paving the way to a world without en! Researchers in Japan have succeeded in removing unfertilized eggs from female cows and bathing them in a series of chemicals that spark the development of embryos. And that means it won't be long before gals won't need guys to become moms! "The methods are absolutely identical to the techniques you would use on human cell lines," says Matt Kaufman, an anatomy professor at Edinburgh University in Scotland. "Anyone putting their mind to it would be able to reproduce any mammal this way."

While scientists work on virgin births, some women are coming out in favor of a new lifestyle. In March, 1997 the big TV story was Ellen DeGeneres admitting through humor that she was Lesbian. This "coming out" combined with Disney studios extending employee benefits to same sex couples to outrage Southern Baptist, and other fundamentalists.

To prepare Americans for the eventual virgin births, and the inevitable same sex marriages, Leslea Newman's controversial book "Heather Has Two Mommies" may end up required reading in school. The user friendly book tells the brief story of a little girl who has two mamas: Jane, a carpenter, and Kate, a doctor. They build things and go on picnics together. The book portrays a loving family. In 1992 it was chosen to be a part of the Rainbow Curriculum in New York City public schools, but had to be dropped because it was too controversial. What do you think? Has the time arrived for our elementary school children to be reading "Heather Has Two Mommies"? If so, what about Michael Willhoite's book "Daddy's Roommate," about a young boy and his two fathers?

172

Future Shock and Cultural Lag

While office Cro-Magnon's risk sexual harassment penalties for seeking sexual favors from subordinates, scientists are busy creating a huge cultural lag. The gap between science and the rest of our culture can be seen daily in newspaper stories that appeared below in the first six months of 2001:

① By July 2001 President Bush's major priority was developing federal rules for funding research on human embryos. This research can be used to preserve the lives of people with Parkinson's Disease and other ailments. The research, however, begs this question: "Is it moral to kill a just begun human life in order to improve the lives of older humans?"

② Should the U.S. Constitution be amended to declare that marriage can only be between a man and a woman? What about marriage of two gay men who want to have test tube babies and raise them?

③ In *Brave New World*, Aldous Huxley predicted a future world in which all children were "decanted" and born as part of 96 identical twins. These children would be taught by chemicals and conditioning to be satisfied with the role assigned them by society. Current studies show that test tube babies mature to be emotionally healthy. Is Huxley's world a reality? Is it a good idea?

④ Cloned mice have developed abnormalities in the way their DNA creates proteins. Should Congress ban all human cloning?

⑤ Evaluate the logic of this argument:
   Premise 1: No African American has ever been elected President.
   Conclusion: Therefore, Colin Powell will never be President.

Notes

1. Kennell Jackson, *America is Me* (New York: Harper-Collins Publishers, Inc., 1996), p. 182.

2. *Williams v. Mississippi*, 170 U.S. 213 (1898).

3. *Breedlove v. Settles*, 302 U.S. 277 (1937).

4. *Smith v. Allwright*, 321 U.S. 649 (1944).

5. *Gomillion v. Lightfoot*, 364 U.S. 399 (1960).

6. *Civil Rights Cases*, 109 U.S. 3 (1883).

7. *McLaurin v. Oklahoma State Regents,* 339 U.S. 637 (1950).

8. Earnest N. Bracey, "The Moulin Rouge Mystique: Blacks and Equal Rights in Nevada," *Nevada Historical Quarterly* (Winter, 1996), pp. 272-288.

9. Mary Frances Berry, "'Plessy v. Ferguson': Separate Has Never Been Equal," *Emerge* (May, 1996), p. 56.

10. Malaika Horne, "Racc and the Criminal Justice System," *The Crisis* (January, 1996), pp. 10-11.

11. Kennell Jackson, *America Is Me* (New York: Harper-Collins Publishers, Inc., 1996), p. 183.

12. Thomas Sowell, "Slave Apology is Just Grandstanding," Las Vegas *Review Journal* (June 22, 1997), p. 2D.

13. S. C. Gwynne, "Back to the Future," *Time* (June 2, 1997), p. 48.

14. *Craig v. Boren*, 429 U.S. 190 (1976).

15. *Michael M. v. Superior Court of Sonoma County, California,* 450 U.S. 464 (1981).

16. Joseph B. James, *The Framing of the Fourteenth Amendment* (Urbana: University of Illinois Press, 1956), p. 160.

17. Michael Korda, "Sexual Office Politics: A Guide for the Eighties," *Playboy* (January, 1981), pp. 156-282.

18. "A Hard Nose and a Short Skirt," *Time* (November 14, 1988), p. 98.

19. "A Slap at Sex Stereotypes," *Time* (May 15, 1989), p. 66.

20. Claudia Wallis, "Onward, Women!" *Time* (December 4, 1989), pp. 80-89.

21. Christine Gorman, "Sizing Up The Sexes," *Time* (January 20, 1992), pp. 42-51.

22. Ann Delaney, *Politics for Dummies* (Foster City, California: IDG Books Worldwide, Inc., 1995), p. 111.

23. Janis Johnson, "Real Life Experiences Produce Sexual Fantasies in 'Women on Top'," Las Vegas *Review Journal/Sun* (January 5, 1992), p. 5D.

Chapter 7

Freedom

What is freedom? That is the kind of question that got Socrates in trouble. He might have defined it as being able to ask tough questions, or paint landscapes with green skies. Freedom means saying the Emperor is parading nude. It means being able to peaceably protest abortion clinics. Freedom means we can go to the college library or computer lab and look up different theories about the Pearl Harbor attack. We are free if we can say that politicians are unscrupulous liars, and not be shot. If we live in Nevada, freedom means legal gambling, legal prostitution, buying booze on Sunday, owning a registered gun, or going to church. We are free to believe that all people are equally entitled to life, liberty and property. Freedom means a political process that includes the secret ballot, direct primaries, frequent elections, the referendum, initiative and recall. These are ways that enable citizens to take a more direct role in creating laws. Some scholars believe direct participation in making laws is a critical dimension of our political freedom. What do you think?

Freedom means a fair trial if we drive drunk and kill someone. It also includes all the blessings of modern technology, including birth control pills, BMW's, television, personal computers, cloning, and Prozac. We are free to be indifferent to politics. Like Dennis Rodman, we can wear multicolored hair, excessive tatoos, nose rings, and cross dress.

There is freedom in the United States because we have no Thoughtpolice looking for *facecrime*, *thoughtcrime*, or *ownlife*. We are not followed around by Anti-Sex League bigots, nor imprisoned on the testimony of our own children. The TV doesn't watch us. There are no hate rallies, no Victory Gin, and no Newspeak. We may engage in collective stupidity on occasion, but we don't have to love Big Brother. Most of our technology is used to make our jobs easier, improve our education, entertain us, and make our lives easier. Unlike Orwell's *1984*, our scientists are not developing methods of torture. Instead, they spend most of their time creating commercial products, improving computers, and looking for a cure for AIDS.

Throughout history, we've had pessimistic scholars who have questioned the premise that "freedom is good." Thomas Hobbes was a typical doubter. In his famous 1651 book *Leviathan,* Hobbes argued that freedom is dangerous because humans have savage instincts that need to be controlled. Siding with the English King, Hobbes argued that the chaotic masses needed strong rulers. "The condition of man," wrote Hobbes, "is a condition of war of everyone against everyone." To control this perpetual war, Hobbes advocated strong government and few freedoms. In other words, "law and order." In a society where there is no order, argued Hobbes,

> In his book *Freedom in the Making of Western Culture*, Harvard Sociologist Orlando Patterson argues that "freedom was generated from the experience of slavery." What do you think about this paradox? Can freedom emerge from a society where slavery exists?

there are no arts, no books, and no society. Instead there is "continual fear and danger of violent death; and the life of man, solitary, poor, nasty, brutish, and short."

These words reveal the *Hobbesian* belief that strong government is always preferable to anarchy. When critics accused Hobbes of being against freedom, he asked them to consider what life was like in 1651. Hobbes then described how English gentlemen had to carry guns, lock their doors, and fear for their lives.

The type of fear that plagued Hobbes was still around in 1992. After rioters torched Los Angeles, Californians went out and in one week purchased more than fifty thousand more guns to go along with the millions they already had. Thus by Hobbesian standards, the United States in 1992 seemed to be a place where life was becoming nasty, brutish and short.

> **Do contemporary Americans need strong leaders to protect our arts, books, and society? Why or why not?**

A few Founding Fathers were Hobbesian. The most famous was Alexander Hamilton, who helped write the *Federalist Papers*. During the 1787 Philadelphia Convention, Hamilton gave a five hour speech in which he advocated having a king-like leader who had enough power to control the passions of the masses, whom he considered turbulent, demagogue-ridden, and incapable of ever being logical. In his opinion, the majority was a great beast that had to be controlled. Typically Hobbesian, Hamilton saw nothing wrong with English laws that applied the death penalty to more than three hundred crimes, including such terrible deeds as apple stealing, tree cutting, or setting fire to hay stacks.

In 1997 *USA Weekend* in its May 2-4 edition announced the results of its annual teen survey of 218,350 ages 13-19. According to the survey results, many teenagers would place new restrictions on freedom, namely:

- 58% believe school officials should have the right to search a student's locker for drugs or weapons without permission.
- 75% think schools should ban clothing with gang symbols.
- 50% support nighttime community curfews for teens.
- 35% think it's OK for parents to block violent or offensive content on TV.
- 30% want restrictions on teens' internet access.
- 43% say public schools should be allowed to lead students in prayer.
- 69% say students should be required to stand for the national anthem.

Nearly forty years after Hobbes argued for an absolute dictator, John Locke was advocating a parliamentary republic. In his famous *Two Treatises on Government* (1690), Locke wrote that men were reasonable enough to

> **Are these teenage attitudes Hobbesian? Why or why not?**

govern themselves by majority rule. In Locke's world men would restrain themselves from doing harm to others because they believed in a natural law that "no one ought to harm another in his life, health, liberty or possessions." This belief in the rights to life, liberty and property lets Americans dream of someday being equal to others. Is being equal a form of freedom?

During the 1776 Revolution, most of the colonists favored a Lockean interpretation of human nature. To justify that bloody revolution, Thomas Jefferson borrowed from Locke. In the famous Declaration of Independence, Jefferson wrote that all men were created equal and endowed with the unalienable rights to life, liberty and the pursuit of happiness. Locke had argued for life, liberty and property. In 1776, however, the idea of asking poor farmers to fight for the property rights of merchants, bankers, lawyers and slave owners was controversial.

After using guns to force England to recognize their freedom, the former colonies created a weak central government known as the Articles of Confederation. This weak government survived to 1786. When the Shays' Rebellion showed that a few thousand angry farmers could bring a state government to its knees, the new nation's political elites decided it was time to hold a convention and write new rules.

The 39 men who signed the Constitution in September 1787, hoped the new government would be capable of living up to the promises in the Preamble, which says: "WE THE PEOPLE OF THE UNITED STATES, in order to form a

> What did the Constitution have to say about slaves? Were they going to secure the blessings of liberty?

more perfect Union, establish justice, insure domestic Tranquility, provide for the common defense, promote the general Welfare, and secure the Blessings of Liberty to ourselves and our Posterity, DO ordain and establish the Constitution of the United States of America." For over two hundred years American leaders have been guided by this dictum, though not always willing to abide by its promise.

Other than the Preamble, the Constitution said little about freedom. The Founding Fathers were mostly upset that England taxed them without representation in Parliament, and conducted general searches of their ships. Thus the Founders put words in the Constitution that prohibited *writs of assistance*, *bills of attainder*, and *ex post facto laws*. These three limitations on Congress, and the vague phrase "Blessings of Liberty" are about the only direct references to freedom among the 4,004 words in the document created in Philadelphia.

So where did our freedoms come from? Give credit to those Americans who were not at Philadelphia, but made their voices heard during the ratification process. Under the label, Anti-Federalists, they campaigned to get a Bill of Rights added to the Constitution as soon as Congress held its first session. When it comes to such freedoms as speech, press, religion, assembly, and guns, give credit where it belongs—to the first 10 amendments, otherwise known as the **Bill of Rights**. These amendments also require the national government to protect citizens from unreasonable police procedures, guarantee a fair trial, and prohibit cruel and unusual punishment. In *The Story of American Freedom* (1998), Eric Foner claims that the freedoms in the Bill of Rights are central to the existence of freedom. What do you think? Is a "fair trial" all that important?

Over the years, the 10 sentences in the Bill of Rights have been explored, analyzed and expanded by the Supreme Court. Today, it takes a constitutional scholar to figure out what our rights are. However, most of us loudly proclaim our right to "do what we want if it doesn't hurt others" without understanding the limits. Television and movies often trivialize the meaning of freedom by suggesting that freedom means we can drink beer, carry guns, and blow up those who are trying to take away our freedom. Too often TV and Hollywood suggest that freedom is something you take, not earn. Remember Hitler. He argued that life is always a struggle between the winners and losers. In the Third Reich members of the ruling Nazi Party had power, but they were always afraid of being singled out whenever Hitler decided to purge the party members who had failed to follow out his orders.

> In Hitler's Darwinian world, life, liberty and the pursuit of happiness had to be "earned," they were not rights bestowed by a benevolent government. Critics would say that nature never intended us to all be equal. Who's right? Locke or Hobbes?

> **Words like "democracy" and "freedom" are value-laden because they suggest something good to Americans. Sometimes we call these "emotive words" because they make us feel good. In North Korea there is now a government known as the "Democratic People's Republic of Korea." Do the people of North Korea have a freedom-loving democracy? What about an HIV-infected man who uses his freedom of speech to sweet-talk over one hundred young women to have sex with him, and infects 30. Should this man be allowed to continue pursuing his freedom and right to happiness?**

Freedom of Speech

Freedom of speech is all about words. Popular singer Eminem has used these words in the past: "My words are like a dagger with a jagged edge/that'll stab you in the head whether you're a fag or lez/or the homosex, hermaph or a trans-a vest/pants or dress-hate fags? The answer's 'yes'"

> Should these lyrics be banned, or is Eminem merely exercising his freedom of speech?
> Source: Cathy Renna, "Group Simply Exercising Its Rights By Highlighting Eminem's Lyrics," *Las Vegas Review Journal*

During the 1980's rap music emerged as the latest rage for young Americans. Consisting of lyrics repeated in a monotonous tone set to thumping background rhythm, rap music is especially popular with inner-city youth. By 1992 it was big time and was being used, in the words of one writer, to sell "soda pop, shoes and defiance of social norms."[1]

The most defiant rap music was being chanted by groups known as "Public Enemy," "2 Live Crew" and "Ice Cube." In the lyrics of *By the Time I Get to Arizona*, "Public Enemy" was advocating the killing of politicians who opposed a holiday honoring Martin Luther King. In *As Nasty As They Wanna Be*, "2 Live Crew" was peddling enough questionable lyrics to be tried and later acquitted of violating a Florida obscenity law.

The most shocking lyrics, however, were being rapped by "Ice Cube." In *Death Certificate*, "Ice Cube" warned Korean store owners to "pay some respects to the black fist, or we'll burn your store right down to a crisp."

To stem the flow of rap music videos, Washington state in March 1992, passed a law which outlawed selling "obscene" music to minors. Under the law, record store retailers and their employees were criminally liable for selling some rap music to anyone under 18. After the Washington state law was adopted, ACLU representative Jerry Sheehan said the "symbolism will have a chilling effect on artists."[2]

Is the Washington law a violation of First Amendment rights? **To answer that question, we need to examine these words:** **"Congress shall make no law respecting an establishment of religion, or prohibiting the free exercise thereof; or abridging the freedom of speech, or of the press, or the right of the people peaceably to assemble, and to petition the Government for a redress of grievances."**

When the first Congress was preparing the Bill of Rights, House member James Madison introduced a proposed amendment which stated that, "No state shall infringe the right of trial by jury in criminal cases, nor the right of conscience, nor the freedom of speech or press." But Madison's proposal to limit state governments was killed in the Senate, largely because the Senators were then being appointed by state legislatures. So the question of whether states could infringe on freedom of speech was left unsettled.

If you plan a career in law, you need practice briefing cases like *Barron v. Baltimore*. If not, take our word. In this famous 1833 case the Supreme Court said, in effect, that none of the protections in the Bill of Rights apply to states.

In 1833, the Supreme Court closed the door on this issue in *Barron v. Baltimore*, 7 Peters 243 (1833). This case involved the question, "Does the Bill of Rights limit the power of state governments?" The Supreme Court declared "no," holding that the Bill of Rights was intended solely as a limitation of the power of the United States, "and is not applicable to the legislation of the states." After the *Barron* decision, the states proceeded on an uneven course, some granting rights beyond those in the Constitution and others granting fewer rights.

In order to protect former slaves from Black Codes, Congress pushed through the very important Fourteenth Amendment, which was ratified in 1868. For our purposes, we need to remember these words: **"No state shall make or enforce any law which shall abridge the privileges and immunities of citizens of the United States; nor shall any state deprive any person of life, liberty, or property, without due process of law; nor deny to any person within its jurisdiction the equal protection of the laws."** Designed to protect the rights of African Americans, the Fourteenth Amendment opened the door to a momentous Supreme Court opinion in 1925.

The 1925 case involved Benjamin Gitlow, a Marxist who had given speeches and circulated a pamphlet calling for a socialist revolution. Gitlow was indicted by the Supreme Court of New York for criminal anarchy. As defined in the 1902 New York Criminal Anarchy Law, *anarchy* is "the doctrine that organized government should be overthrown by force or violence . . . ." Gitlow had clearly violated the law by urging in a pamphlet "The Left Wing Manifesto" the necessity of accomplishing the Communist Revolution through revolt, industrial strikes and revolutionary mass action. Though no violence was triggered by Gitlow's words, the Supreme Court upheld his New York conviction on the grounds that the Anarchy Law was constitutional, and therefore justified. (Source: *Gitlow v. New York*, 268 U.S. 652.)

While deliberating the case, Justice Edward T. Sanford argued in a now famous *obiter dictum* (opinion not necessary to the conclusion on the merits of the case) that: **"For present purposes we may and do assume that freedom of speech and of the press—which are now protected by the First Amendment from abridgement by Congress—are among the fundamental**

personal rights and 'liberties' protected by the due process clause of the Fourteenth Amendment from impairment by the States . . . ."

These words warned state legislators that in the future the Supreme Court would use the Fourteenth Amendment to strike down unreasonable state restrictions on freedom of speech. This case reversed *Barron* and opened the door to using the Fourteenth Amendment to expand the meaning of freedom.

Nationalization of the Bill of Rights

Since *Gitlow v. New York*, (1925), the Supreme Court has "nationalized" most of the Bill of Rights. This means today that states cannot infringe on these rights without risking a review by the federal courts. This process, also known as "selective incorporation," has placed the First, Fourth, and Sixth Amendments under the umbrella protection of the Fourteenth Amendment. Parts of the Fifth and Eighth Amendments have also been incorporated. So far, the Second, Third, and Seventh Amendments have not been nationalized.

In 1942, the Supreme Court had to decide a case involving a Jehovah's Witness named Chaplinsky. He had stood outside the City Hall in Rochester, New Hampshire distributing pamphlets and denouncing other religions as a "racket." After local citizens complained, the City Marshal and a traffic officer tried to remove Chaplinsky from the scene. Angry, Chaplinsky cursed the Marshal and said, "You are a God damned racketeer . . . a damned Fascist and the whole government of Rochester are Fascists or agents of Fascists." Later at his trial in Rochester municipal court, Chaplinsky admitted cursing, but denied using God's name. He was convicted, however, of violating a state law which stated, "No person shall address any offensive, derisive or annoying word to any person who is lawfully in any street or other public place, nor call him by any offensive or derisive word . . . ." The trial court excluded Chaplinsky's claim that he was preaching the true facts of the *Bible*, that the crowd was unruly, and that the Marshal and traffic officer had neglected their duties. Later, the Supreme Court rejected Chaplinsky's claim that his rights had been violated, and upheld the state law.[3]

What is significant about this case? Chaplinsky challenged the constitutionality of the New Hampshire law on the grounds that it violated his right of free speech protected from being abridged by the state, not the Congress. In order to argue his case, Chaplinsky's lawyers had to use the Fourteenth Amendment's due process clause *and* the First Amendment. To understand why, go back to *Gitlow v. New York* and carefully read Justice Sanford's *obiter dictum*.

Someday you'll run into one of those people who likes to quote the Constitution. He'll probably say, "I've got freedom of speech because the First Amendment says so!" Will you agree, or challenge his premise? Why?

Academic Freedom of Speech

In 1970 the American Association of University Professors (AAUP) adopted a statement on *Freedom and Responsibility*. The statement said, "Membership in the academic community imposes on students, faculty members, administrators, and trustees an obligation to respect the dignity of others, to acknowledge their right to express differing opinions, and to foster and defend intellectual honesty, freedom of inquiry and instruction, and free expression on and off campus . . . ." This means that the AAUP is committed to freedom of speech for all people, not just those whose opinions are popular.

Einstein defined academic freedom as "the right to search for the truth and to publish and teach what one holds to be true." This definition leaves much room for interpretation, however. Does it mean teachers are free to discuss such controversial issues as racism, sexism, and homophobia. Einstein's definition seems to imply that teachers should be able to have opinions on controversial issues. What do you think? Should a male teacher of political science be allowed to question the value of sexual harassment rules? Should a female political scientist be allowed to defend sexual harassment rules?

Since 1985, a conservative group called Accuracy in Academia has been secretly monitoring college and university classrooms. The privately funded organization looks for teachers who fail to meet its standards of objectivity. For the most part, the AIA leaders worry about the estimated ten thousand "Marxist Professors" among the

> Those who defend academic freedom of speech argue that individuals must be allowed to challenge the dogma of religious groups and other factions. What do you think?

about 850,000 college teachers in this country. Student volunteers are used to monitor classes in political science, history, economics, and sociology. A typical case occurred at Arizona State University where one professor was cited by the AIA for devoting too much classroom time complaining about nuclear war. Now that the Cold War seems over, college professors are worrying about a new attack on academic freedom. Instead of coming from conservatives, the new attack has been launched by groups typically associated with liberal causes.

Under pressure from factions on the left, college professors are now expected to be sensitive to the feelings of minorities, women, gays, lesbians, and the disabled. This is known as being *politically correct*. To be politically correct means to have proper attitudes about those Americans who have been "victimized" by the dominant culture.

The PC issue was dramatized in 1991 by the fate of Linda Chavez, a politically incorrect Mexican American who had served in the Reagan administration. Chavez had been invited to speak at several universities about her new book *Out of the Barrio*, on Hispanic-American politics and assimilation. The invitation to speak at Arizona State University was withdrawn, however, when the director of the university lecture series discovered that Chavez was controversial among Hispanic students because of her stand on the issue of bilingualism. Later, the University of Northern Colorado, Rutgers University, and State University of New York all withdrew invitations to speak.

When he discovered Chavez' fate, Washington *Post* columnist George Will was outraged. In a strongly worded column, Will attacked PC, which he called

> Late one night at the University of Pennsylvania, a white student is awakened by noisy sorority sisters outside his dorm. The student yells "Will you water buffaloes get out of here!" The noisy students are African American, and the irritated white student is slapped with a racial harassment charge, and disciplined. Was this fair?

182

"the enforced orthodoxy of leftism." To make his point that PC was a new brand of political oppression, Will cited several cases of college professors who were oppressed for seemingly harmless behavior. One case involved six University of Minnesota professors charged with sexual harassment. Their offensives included, wrote Will, "Not greeting a student in a friendly enough manner . . . Not teaching in a sensitive-enough way. . . Not having read a certain novel." Although the charges against the six professors were eventually dropped, they suffered substantial expenses and pain, according to Will.[4]

Judging by some accounts, PC is having a "chilling effect" in the classroom. This is especially true at multi cultural campuses such as the University of California (Berkeley), San Francisco State University, and Stanford University. During interviews conducted in 1991, students at these campuses admitted they were afraid to give their honest opinions in class for fear of being called racist, sexist, or homophobic. Deanna Cunningham, a black reporter on the staff of the student newspaper at San Francisco State, interviewed several students and discovered one unifying theme: "Students talked about being afraid to talk about concerns or ideas that could not remotely be regarded as blatantly racist or sexist," she noted. "Rather, they are afraid to say anything about a controversial topic that they feel could be misconstrued."[5]

In most cases, PC norms are enforced by students, faculty and administrators. So far, there are no government Thoughtpolice hiding in every classroom listening for unorthodox opinions. In effect, this weakens the First Amendment freedoms by leaving the door open for hecklers. This was the case in 1985 when forums at New England colleges on South Africa, the Middle East, U.S. defense policy were hampered or halted by demonstrators who blocked the airing of opposing views. Jeanne Kirkpatrick, former U.S. ambassador to the United Nations, was shouted down by hecklers at several university campuses. These hecklers were apparently upset because Kirkpatrick had incorrect views on apartheid, abortion and Israel. **The Heckler's Veto** is an effective way to discourage dissent on a college campus, or during a revolutionary assembly. In 1918 the various Russian factions which had overthrown Czar Nicholas tried to set up a democratic government. But the Russian attempt at democracy was defeated by a minority of Bolsheviks led by Lenin. During speeches by opponents, the Bolsheviks howled, jeered, and made catcalls. Lenin distracted the crowd by either lolling on the steps leading to the platform or pretending to sleep. Bolshevik armed guards pointed their rifles at the deputies. After meeting one day, the Constituent Assembly was dissolved and Russia lost its chance to have democracy.

Speech and Technology

There is a scene in the movie "Star Trek IV: The Voyage Home" (1986) in which Captain James Kirk and Mr. Spock are in a San Francisco bus. Since they have crossed the time barrier to the twentieth century, Kirk and Spock are suffering from reverse culture shock. As the two space travelers try to calm their nerves, they are bemused by loud noises blasting from a full volume "boom box" held by a punk rocker attired in weird

In 1991 black students in an economics class at Berkeley walked out of the room because a foreign student kept using the term "black" instead of "African American." According to one witness, the black students and the professor had objected, but the foreign student did not respond. So the black students left. Was the exodus by African American students justified? Why or why not?

Source: Nat Hentoff, "Look at it as 'Increased Freedom to be Sensitive'," Las Vegas *Review Journal* (January 6, 1992), p. 7B.

clothes and a matching hair style. Ignoring requests by Kirk and Spock, the rocker keeps his boom box at full volume until Spock discreetly applies a Vulcan pinch and sends the punk into unconsciousness. Movie audiences cheered this scene, for good reason.

Loud music is possible because we have solid electrified guitars and amplifiers. In the early days of our republic, however, the loudest noises came from children playing with drums and adults playing with guns. By the time radio music came along, Americans had developed enough civility to deal with the noise. If the radio was too loud, Mom came to the bedroom door and said "Christina, would you please turn your radio down." During the 1960's, however, manners began to erode, and music got louder and louder. This, of course, led to demands for more laws, regulations, and policies aimed at lowering sound levels. After years of complaint from people at the beaches, authorities in Long Beach and New York City banned certain radios. People who wanted to play their boom boxes on beaches had to do so in designated areas, or through their earphones. Violators risked having their radios confiscated until they paid fines up to $200. When promoters arrange a rock concert, they have to worry about strict liability laws that hold them accountable for damaged ears.

Television is another technological miracle influencing the morality of American children. To protect these children from violent programs, President Clinton in 1996 signed a sweeping telecommunications bill passed by Congress. This law officially launched the era of the "V" chip. This is a little device that will be required equipment on most new TV sets. It allows parents to automatically block out programs labeled as high in violence, sex, or other objectionable material.

Then came computers and the Internet. Now children can type in "toy" on the popular AltaVista site-search engine and end up watching the "Nice 'N Naughty's Adult Toy" store. In 1996, Congress passed the Communications Decency Act. This law was supposed to keep pornography off the Internet. In June 1997, however, the Supreme Court ruled 7 to 2 that the law violated the First Amendment. This was the Court's first free-speech ruling for the computer age.

Worried parents, however, can purchase software designed to protect their children from objectionable websites. This software includes CyberPatrol, Cybersitter, Cyber Snoop, Net Nanny, Rated-PG, Surfwatch, and X-Stop. Most cost between $20 and $50. These "Cybercops" are relatively easy to install. But they've already produced one serious unintended consequence. Counties like Essex, Middlesex, and Sussex are being censored for the S - X word. Moreover, anything that looks like F - - K or TR - - K gets the AX.

In *Brave New World*, citizens are sleep taught to enjoy playing sexual games like "Find the Zipper" and "Orgy Porgy." Are Americans now being bombarded with subliminal messages that encourage us to be preoccupied by sex?

Earlier, we learned that subliminal messages can be flashed on the movie screen too fast for the naked eye to see. Thus the words "Hungry? Eat popcorn, Drink Coke" were flashed on the screen at a drive-in theater during the 1950's and caused a run on the snack bar. Parents now can worry if little Chad CyberKid decides to play the Time Warner video game "Endorfun."

According to Los Angeles *Times* reporter Amy Harmon, Endorfun is a puzzle game with subliminal messages. According to Harmon, the goal of Endorfun "is to match the colored sides of a moving cube to the corresponding squares on a series of grids." While the players are working the puzzle, their teenage subconscious minds are fed uplifting subliminal messages like "I am powerful," "I am at peace," "I am in harmony," "I love being alive." These "positive affirmations" are defended by Time Warner executives, but psychologists and media experts are worried about the potential for mind control.[6]

In his study of the effects of technology on our thinking, Neil Postman says the United States has become a technological technocracy where traditional attitudes about free expression are being pushed aside by a new world of **Technopoly**. In this brave new world, technology has eliminated all alternatives to itself in precisely the same way as in Huxley's *Brave New World*.

When it comes to traditional ideas, the new technopoly does not make them unpopular, immoral, or illegal. Instead, "It makes them invisible and therefore irrelevant." It does so, says Postman, by redefining religion, art, family, politics, history, truth, privacy, intelligence.[7]

Freedom of the Press

> How is technology redefining religion, art, family, politics, history, truth, privacy and intelligence?

During the 19th century, writers described ordinary sex with the words "took," or "gave pleasure." If the sex was really wild, like in most R rated movies, the Victorian Era writers used shocking words like "frenzied, almost convulsive delights."

Euphemisms are words designed to disguise or soften the impact of language. They are often substitutes for forbidden or "indecent" words. What does it mean to be **Indecent**? Indecent can mean distasteful, immodest, indecorous, indelicate, coarse, outrageous, rude, gross, filthy, lewd or licentious.

The First Amendment was designed to protect the rights of citizens who might use indecent words to criticize government officials. At first, the protected words appeared in speeches, letters, broadsides, tracts, and newspapers. Since 1925, however, the Supreme Court has stretched the meaning of the Constitution. Now, freedom of the press acts as a barrier to government censorship of newspapers, magazines, books, radio, television, and the Internet.

Freedom of the press is rarely absolute. Every society tries to restrain the media through various types of censorship or punishment for excessive words. In this country, freedom of the press is generally limited two ways, by *prior restraint* and *ex post facto punishment*.

Prior Restraint occurs when government censors in advance what can be printed or broadcast. This technique was practiced on a grand scale in Orwell's *1984* when Winston Smith pushed facts down a "memory hole" and rewrote history to conform to Big Brother's predictions. Prior restraint is practiced when TV networks use a "vice president of broadcasting standards" to decide what to censor when showing a movie that has violence, adult language, or strong sexual context. In 1974, Mel Brooks' popular movie "Blazing Saddles" made audiences laugh by showing cowboys around a campfire eating beans and releasing explosive stomach gas. When "Blazing Saddles" is shown on television, however, the sound effects have disappeared.

> Should "Blazing Saddles" be shown on prime time TV with the flatulent sound effects intact? Why, or why not?

Huxley satirized prior restraint by showing it as a form of aversion therapy. In

Brave New World, babies are placed on electric floors near books and flowers. When the babies crawl toward these objects, they are shocked and frightened by loud noises. When they grow up these children will hate books and flowers. They're perfect candidates to work in coal mines.

Ex Post Facto Punishment, on the other hand, occurs when the media has the freedom to publish questionable facts, but then can be sued for libel. Government regulates the media through laws against libel, slander, obscenity, sedition, contempt of court, or incitement of crime.

Is Huxley's "aversion therapy" approach being used to make American's hate books and flowers? Or do the bright colors of the computer make drab print irrelevant?

For decades, the Supreme Court has tried to protect words that are "wide-open and robust." The Court has even protected words that are "offensive and disagreeable." No longer. In a Massachusetts' case decided in 1995, the Court moved away from this tradition. The Massachusetts' case began in 1987 when 66-year-old Sylvia Bowman ran for the presidency of a state public employees union. A co-worker named David Heller—who supported Bowman's opponent—cut out her photograph from a flier and pasted it on the photo of a nude model and made five copies. When the photo was passed around, Bowman saw a copy and sued for "intentional infliction of emotional distress" and sexual harassment. Despite defense arguments that Bowman was a public figure, the Massachusetts' Supreme Court upheld her lawsuit five to two. In December 1995, the U.S. Supreme Court upheld Bowman and ordered Heller to pay the $35,000 awarded by lower courts.

In this case, the Supreme Court said the First Amendment does not shield a public employee who crudely ridicules a co-worker by putting her face on a photo of a lewdly posed nude model.[8]

Suppose a student as a joke places the photo head of one of your authors on the body of Madonna in a typically lewd pose. Would this justify a lawsuit, and monetary settlement? Why or why not?

In an advertisement for the "Naked Gun" movie, the head of actor Leslie Neilsen is super-imposed on a nude, pregnant body. The ad is an obvious parody of a magazine cover of actress Demi Moore, who posed in the nude when she was pregnant. Should there be a law banning such silliness?

Mark Twain's famous novel *The Adventures of Huckleberry Finn* was published over one hundred years ago. Once considered the best novel ever written by an American, Twain's satirical look at the foibles of white men is still being censored because it uses the "N" word about two hundred times. Chicago educator John H. Wallace was traumatized when as a high school student he was required to read *Huckleberry Finn* as part of a class assignment. According to Wallace, the book is offensive. To protect other African Americans from his painful experience, Wallace published a politically correct version which eliminates the "N" words and substitutes less offensive words "slave," "black man" and "Jim." Judith Krug, Director of the American Library Association's Office for Intellectual Freedom, criticized Wallace's version for stripping the novel of "its irony, it humanness and its values."[9]

Words, words, words. These are the symbols that make us human, and also vulnerable to propaganda.

On September 22, 1995 President Clinton was discussing his reasons for opposing a plan to raise the debt ceiling and said, "we don't welsh on our debts and we're not about to start doing it now." After the remark Rees Lloyd, lawyer for Glendale-based Twm Sion Cati-Welsh-American Legal Defense Education and Development Fund, said that his phones hadn't stopped ringing over Clinton's offensive remarks. In a press release, Lloyd said, "It's outrageous that the President of the United States would use this slur in a statement he knows would be reported and would be legitimized throughout the country." Later, White House spokeswoman Ginny Terzano apologized on behalf of the President to the estimated three million of Welsh descent in the United States.[10]

> In 1995, *Huckleberry Finn* led the American Library Association's list of most challenged book. Anyone who has read the novel knows that the character "Nigger" Jim is, next to Huck Finn, the most appealing and heroic character in the novel. In their journey down the Mississippi River, Huck and Jim encountered white con men, white lynch mobs, white thieves, and stupid whites. In fact, there are good reasons why white people should feel offended by the book. But the focus on the "N" word has made it impossible to judge the novel on its merits as a moving portrayal of the friendship between a runaway boy and an escaped slave.

Whether the words are spoken or printed, the threat of PC hangs over the heads of public figures like the sword of Damocles—ready to fall on every mistake or Freudian slip of the tongue. In the past, businessmen were generally the targets of most PC lawsuits. Now they're ready to defend themselves by pointing out that most TV shows are unfair to the white men who run our corporations. From 1995 to early 1997, 863 network sitcoms, dramas and TV movies were studied over a 26-month period for the Media Research Center, a conservative watchdog group. They found that of the 514 criminal characters found during the survey period, nearly 30 percent were business owners or corporate executives. In other words, corporate executives have become TV's favorite villains. The symbol of these evil white men is Montgomery Burns, the evil Springfield nuclear power plant owner featured in the Fox animated series, "The Simpsons."

> In your opinion, is TV unfair to business owners and corporate executives? Can you cite an example of this bias from your own TV viewing?

Should the networks have a vice president who censors TV shows that stereotype businessmen as evil men who are using their power against the common people?

Obscenity

Obscenity is almost always a definition issue. In Huxley's *Brave New World*, for example, the word "mother" is obscene. Why? Because in his fictional world all babies are born in decanters, and all women are merely sex objects. Thus the word "mother" is considered subversive of the social order, and therefore "obscene."

When did we decide to argue over the meaning of obscenity? Judging by the art work on European caves, our Cro-Magnon ancestors didn't seem preoccupied with smut. They drew wonderfully realistic figures of oxen, bison and horses. But when it came to the human figure, the prehistoric artists drew stick figures.

By the fifth century B.C., however, the people of Athens were embroiled in a debate over obscenity and censorship. This controversy centered around the famous philosopher Socrates. Despite his love for "truth," the bare foot philosopher had to swallow hard when he attended "The Clouds," a satirical play written by Aristophanes. In this play, Socrates was portrayed leading a class discussion at his "School of Very Hard Thinkers" while suspended in a basket from the ceiling of his academy. On the ground, Socrates' students had their noses in the dirt and their rear ends up in the air. When asked "why" by a skeptical citizen, the students said their noses were searching for deep secrets and their rear ends studying astronomy.

> **What is the truth about Socrates' attitude toward censorship? Where would you find an answer to this question?**

In his book *The Trial of Socrates*, I.F. Stone claims Socrates wanted "The Clouds" censored. Will Durant, on the other hand, claims in *The Life of Greece* that Socrates was a friend of Aristophanes, often attended performances of "The Clouds," and even stood up so his enemies could laugh and jeer.[11]

Pornography, which is Greek for "writing of harlots," was a privilege limited to citizens who could afford classy art or tickets for an Aristophanes' play. The masses, however, were often denied erotic luxuries and had to rely on their imaginations. With the invention of the printing press, however, smut and political propaganda was available to the masses. To control the flow of information, governments defined as "obscene" anything that might be "disruptive."

Since the First Amendment does not protect obscenity, we need to look at how the courts have defined the word "obscenity."

Defining Obscenity Through the Eyes of a Twelve Year Old

In 1868 a British court gave us one of history's first attempts to render a precise definition of obscenity. The court had to decide the fate of Benjamin Hicklin, who was accused of breaking an obscenity law passed by Parliament in 1857. Hicklin had gone to London and purchased from the Protestant Electoral Union copies of a pamphlet which purported to show the depravity of Catholic confessions. The pamphlet was entitled, "The Confessional Unmasked; showing the depravity of the Romish priesthood, the iniquity of the Confessional, and the questions put to females in confession." Hicklin took a few thousand pamphlets back to his town of Wolverhampton and sold them to other Protestants. But a complaint was made, and Hicklin was arrested, and the pamphlets destroyed. At Hicklin's trial, Chief Justice Lord Cockburn gave a definition of obscenity that provided the common law basis in British and American courts for nearly one hundred years after. Noting that the pamphlet violated the 1857 Obscene Publications Act which said, "You shall not publish an obscene work," Cockburn next defined obscenity in this fashion: "The test of obscenity is this, whether the tendency of the matter charged as obscenity is to deprave and corrupt those whose minds are open to such immoral influences, and into whose hands a publication of this sort may fall."[12]

Suppose you discovered your 12-year-old sister watching a Madonna video. Like Madonna, your sister is dressed in leather and singing about bizarre sex. Would you judge the video obscene?

Defenders of the **Hicklin Standard** thought it a good way to keep pornography out of the hands of children. Critics, however, believe it let censors ban such classics as Aristophanes' *Lysistrata*, Sinclair Lewis' *Elmer Gantry*, and James T. Farrell's *Studs Lonigan* because children could not understand the irony presented in these books, and the censors could not appreciate it.

Whether justified or not, the Hicklin Standard was typical of the Victorian Age. This was the era when England's Queen Victorian reigned, from 1839 to 1901. The age was characterized by self-appointed guardians of public morality. Anthony Comstock was easily the most famous. According to historian Page Smith, Comstock was, "The self-appointed guardian of the morals of Americans . . . a one-man vice squad of formidable and unsleeping vigilance." At the tender age of 29, Comstock formed the Society for the Suppression of Vice. As its secretary from 1873 to his death in 1915, Comstock waged a relentless war against all forms of pornography, especially sexual lust.

Backed by money supplied by tycoons J. P. Morgan and Samuel Colgate (of toothpaste fame), Comstock got his backers to pressure a compliant Congress into passing the Comstock Act of 1873. This law prohibited sending any obscene material through U.S. mail. Armed with this law and the state and local ordinances suppressing all forms of vice, Comstock was able to destroy more than 50 tons of books, 28,425 pounds of printing plates, and nearly four million obscene pictures. Comstock's crusaders used the Hicklin Standard to justify their hunt for obscenity, taking isolated passages from books and arguing that they would corrupt the mind of a 12-year-old girl.[13]

The Hicklin Standard was finally abandoned in 1933 by Federal District Judge Woolsey. Asked to authorize customs officials to seize copies of James Joyce's novel *Ulysses* for being "obscene," Judge

Why did Comstock and other censors use a 12-year-old girl standard to prove obscenity?

Woolsey made the would-be censors wait while he read the entire book. *Ulysses* is not an easy book to read. It portrays the stream of consciousness taking place in the minds of people living in Dublin, Ireland on one particular day in June. Since these Irish characters are lower class and Celtic, Joyce puts four-letter words and lust in their thoughts. After reading the novel, Woolsey concluded that it truly deserved the literary praise that had been heaped on it since 1921. Thus, in his conclusion, Woolsey wrote: "in spite of its unusual frankness, I do not detect anywhere the leer of the sensualist." In Woolsey's judicial opinion, *Ulysses* was neither pornographic nor obscene.[14]

Woolsey rejected the Hicklin Standard by dealing with the entire book, not isolated passages. He decided the merits of the book from the perspective of an adult, not a 12-year-old.

After abandoning the Hicklin Standard, American courts tried to develop a definition of obscenity better suited to an era of movies and television. The first major attempt came in *Roth v. United States*, 354 U.S. 476 (1957). In this case, Roth was charged with violating federal law

189

by mailing obscene materials through the U.S. mails. After his conviction by a federal district court in New York City, Roth appealed to the Supreme Court claiming his freedoms of speech and press under the First Amendment had been violated. Affirming the lower court ruling, the Supreme Court defined obscenity this way: ". . . whether to the average person, applying community standards, the dominant theme of the material taken as a whole appeals to prurient interests." This definition was modified in 1973 when the Supreme Court ruled in *Miller v. California*, 413 U.S. 15 (1971) that states could adopt obscenity codes consistent with three criteria, namely:

① The average person, applying contemporary community standards, must find that the work as a whole appeals to lust.
② The state law must specifically define what sexual conduct is obscene.
③ The work as a whole must lack serious literary, artistic, political or scientific value.

If the work charged as obscene survives any one of these definitions, it is not legally obscene. Because the definition includes "community standards," obscenity differs from state to state. In 1975, for example, a Montgomery, Virginia review panel decided the book *Animals Everywhere* was not appropriate for first and second graders because it stereotyped owls as wise, wolves as cruel and showed a little boy petting a tiger. At about the same time, school administrators from thirty elementary schools in Peoria, Illinois banned Judy Blume's books *Blubber, Dennie* and *Then Again, Maybe I Won't* because they dealt too candidly with feelings about menstruation and other biological changes.

The community standards criteria has not stopped the censors who want "national" standards based on their objections. As mentioned before, African Americans want to censor *The Adventures of Huckleberry Finn* for using the "N" word. Ironically, some African Americans want to restore the word "Nigga" as a friendly one when used by friends. Have you read any news about the "new" N word?

Religious fundamentalists object to the comic book, "Heather Has Two Mommies" because it describes a little girl with Lesbian parents. Some Feminists favor a Senate Bill numbered 1521, which is known as the Pornography Victims' Compensation Act. Under this proposed law, victims of sexual crimes would be able to bring suit for unlimited money damages against publishers, exhibitors, distributors and retailers of any book or movie that the victims can convince a jury is obscene and triggered violence against them.[15]

To understand why Patrick Buchanan criticized the NEH in 1992, we need more facts. To get those facts, we need to read William A. Henry III, "A Cheap and Easy Target," *Time* (March 9, 1992), pp. 72-73.

Conservative Republican candidate Patrick Buchanan in 1992 ran an ad criticizing the National Endowment for the Humanities because it supplied $5,000 for a PBS documentary by a gay African American who presumably glorified homosexuality and perverted the image of Christ.

In the past, Americans worried about obscene pamphlets, books, paintings, radio, movies, and television. By 1996, however, the debate had shifted to the Internet. Critics like the Family Research Council used the Internet [http://www.townhall/FRC/infocus/if954k4pn.html] to warn viewers that:

The entire spectrum of pornographic material is available on computer networks including images of soft-core nudity, hard-core sex acts, anal sex, bestiality, bondage & dominion, sado-masochism (including actual torture and mutilation, usually of women, for sexual pleasure), scatological acts (defecating and urinating, usually on women, for sexual pleasure), fetishes, and child pornography. Additionally, there is textual pornography including detailed text stories of the rape, mutilation, and torture of women, sexual abuse of children, graphic incest, etc.

All this was available to any child able to push the right Internet buttons. To curb the Internet pornography, Congress passed the Communications Decency Act, which was signed into law in 1996 by President Clinton. Under the CDA it would be a federal crime to put online, where children could see it, not just the obscene or the pornographic but any "indecent" word or image.

Challenged by the American Civil Liberties Union and the American Library Association, the CDA ended up being debated before the U.S. Supreme Court in February 1997. Defending the law, Deputy Solicitor General Seth P. Waxman called the Net "a free pass into the equivalent of every adult bookstore and video store in the country." Opposing the law, Bruce Ennis stated his case with these words: "For 40 years," he said, "this court has repeatedly and unanimously ruled that government cannot constitutionally reduce the adult population to reading and viewing only what is appropriate for children. That is what this law does."[16]

The CDA raised an important issue for the new age of CyberSpace, namely: "To what extent can the operators of interactive media be held responsible for the material that moves through their systems?"

Was the CDA an attempt by Congress to restore the 1868 Hicklin Standard to modern interpretations of obscenity? Why, or why not?

This question was argued in Florida courts after a 14-year-old boy was sexually assaulted by Richard Lee Russell in 1994, after the two met by exchanging messages in an AOL "chat room." The lawsuit had sought $8 million in damages. In June 1997, however, a state circuit court judge ruled that America Online was not liable for customers who use the service to peddle pornography in cyberspace. Why didn't the Hicklin Standard apply in this case?

While headlines spoke of "porno via E-mail," "Cyberporn battles," and "Internet is highway to indecency for minors," the federal government's Office of Adolescent Pregnancy Programs was trying to figure out why adolescent girls were confused. Teenagers, according to OAPP evaluation director Robin Robinson, are confused. As reported in the Los Angeles *Times*, Robinson said: "They are worried about AIDS and other sexually transmitted diseases. Meanwhile, adults keep bombarding them with sexual messages—in the form of movies, advertising, music, television. Calvin Klein uses nymphs to sell underwear. Ross and Rachel sleep together on "Friends." All the while, parents and teachers hammer home the virtues of abstinence. Don't have sex; you could wind up pregnant. Don't have sex; you could wind up dead."[17]

Despite the sexual angst suffered by modern teenagers, the Supreme Court during its October 1996 to June 1997 term ruled that Congress had violated First Amendment free speech rights when it passed the Communications Decency Act. The Court did, however, rule that states could keep sexual predators locked up after they serve their prison sentences if they are considered still dangerous.

Meanwhile, U.S. Senator Orrin Hatch (R-Utah) has introduced a law that makes it illegal to film adults pretending to be minors depicting sexual intimacy on film. The Child Pornography Prevention Act provides penalties of 10 years to life in prison for people who possess such material. In other words, a 27-year-old who portrays a 17-year-old having sex will go to prison. Is this a reasonable law? Why or why not?

Freedom of Religion

Until 1992, New York state public school children started their day by saying aloud the following little prayer:

> **Almighty God, we acknowledge our dependence upon Thee, and we beg
> Thy blessings upon us, our parents, our teachers and our country.**

Although simple, voluntary and apparently nonsectarian, this prayer was offensive to the parents of ten children at Union Free School District No. 9, New Hyde Park, New York. They brought action in that state court, insisting that this prayer, composed by the New York Board of Regent, had violated their constitutional rights. After their claims were rejected in state courts, the parents asked the United States Supreme Court to review their case. Eventually, the Supreme Court granted *certiorari* to review the case and decide if the twenty-two word prayer violated the First and Fourteenth Amendments. By a six to one vote, the Supreme Court decided that the prayer was unconstitutional.

In his majority opinion, Justice Hugo Black proclaimed that the First Amendment prohibition against laws respecting an establishment of religion, "must at least mean in this country it is no part of the business of government to compose daily prayers for any group of the American people to recite as a part of the religious program carried on by our government." In dissent, Justice Potter Stewart disagreed and wrote, "With all respect, I think the Court has misapplied a great constitutional principle. I cannot see how an 'official religion' is established by letting those who want to say a prayer say it. On the contrary, I think that to deny the wish of these school children to join in reciting this prayer is to deny them the opportunity to share in the spiritual heritage of our Nation."[18]

> The First Amendment says, "Congress shall make no law respecting an establishment of religion, or prohibiting the free exercise thereof . . . ." Read the comments by Justice Hugo Black and Justice Potter Stewart, and decide which is more consistent with the intent of the First Amendment.

The school prayer was not buried by the New York case, however. In virtually every session of Congress since 1963, someone has introduced a proposal to amend the Constitution so that prayers can be said in public schools. In 1984, President Ronald Reagan supported this prayer amendment:

> Nothing in this Constitution shall be construed to prohibit individual or group prayer
> in public schools or other public institutions. No person shall be required by the United
> States or by a state to participate in prayer. Neither the United States nor any state
> shall compose the words of any prayer to be said in the public schools.

The Senate in March 1984 approved the amendment 56 to 44. But it did not pass because the Constitution requires that a constitutional amendment be proposed by at least two-thirds majorities in both houses, and then ratified by at least three-fourths of the states. Before a proposed amendment can be sent to the states, it needs 67 of 100 Senate votes and 290 of 435 in the House. Despite a clear majority of votes in the Senate, and public opinion polls showing over sixty percent popular support, no school prayer amendment has passed, yet.

> Those who oppose school prayer ask, "Is there a way for Catholics, Protestants, Jews, Mormons, Buddhists, Moslems, and others to pray together happily?" Those who favor school prayer ask, "How can children learn morality if religion is banned from their schools?"

Since 1962 some states have tried to circumvent the establishment clause through laws permitting a moment of silence at the beginning of each school day. By 1985, 26 states allowed a moment of silence. Nevada law, for example, called for every school district in the state to set aside a time at the beginning of each school day "during which all persons must be silent for voluntary individual meditation, prayer or reflection by pupils." In 1985, the Supreme Court had to decide if an Alabama law violated the establishment clause. The law stipulated that at the beginning of class every day the teacher "may announce that a period of silence not to exceed one minute in duration shall be observed for meditation or voluntary prayer, and during any such period no other activities shall be engaged in." The wording, however, bothered the Justices and on June 4, 1985 a majority struck down the Alabama law. ☻ If you were judging the Alabama law, which words would you consider to be in violation of the establishment clause?

Critics believe that religion now is directly involved in politics because local, state, and federal agencies have been unable to keep religion from a direct involvement in the mechanics of our political process. What do you think?

Does Congress violate the First Amendment when it gives tax-exempt status to religious schools? In 1909 Congress exempted church-related schools and colleges from paying taxes. Schools that practice racial discrimination, however, have lost the tax exemption. For years, Bob Jones University in Greenville, South Carolina banned African Americans. In 1970, however, the IRS changed its rules so that institutions that practiced racial discrimination lost their tax exempt status. After 1975, Bob Jones University allowed African Americans to enroll, but continued to ban interracial dating. As a result, the IRS eliminated the school's tax exempt status.

> In 1986 Abortion Rights Mobilization Inc., filed a federal suit contending the IRS should revoke the tax-exempt status of Catholic organizations on grounds they violate the IRS code by supporting political candidates who oppose abortion. Should the tax exempt status of Catholic organizations be revoked for this reason? Would other religions be adversely affected by such a decision?

How much government assistance is too much? In 1971, the Supreme Court had to decide this question in *Lemon v. Kurtzman*, 403 U.S. 602 (1971). In this case, the Court struck down Pennsylvania and Rhode Island laws that set subsidies for the salaries of parochial school teachers. After declaring the subsidies unconstitutional, the Court proposed a threefold **Lemon Test** to determine when government aid was improper:

① State action must have a secular or nonreligious purpose.
② The primary effect of the state action must neither advance nor inhibit religion.
③ There should be no "excessive entanglement" between church and state.

As a consequence of the establishment controversy, public school textbooks are watched closely by concerned factions. Fundamentalists want books that emphasize "creation science" rather than evolution. On the other side, secularists have managed to keep virtually all references to religion out of the textbooks. If school kids want to know the role of religion in our history, they'll need to ask questions like, "Why does the Declaration of Independence refer to "Nature's God," "their Creator," and "Divine Providence?"

The First Amendment also says Congress shall make no law prohibiting the free exercise of religion. What does "free exercise" mean? In 1982 Royston Potter, a 30-year-old Murray, Utah police officer, was fired by the city because he had three wives. Potter defended himself by saying that polygamy was part of his religious beliefs. Does free exercise mean being able to practice polygamy? Should neighbors opposed to polygamists next door have any rights over their property?

In 1882 Congress passed the Edmunds Act which defined polygamous marriage as a felony and polygamous living as a misdemeanor. Anyone found guilty of either was fined and disenfranchised. The Edmunds Act was aimed at Mormons who were practicing polygamy in Utah. The law was upheld by the Supreme Court, but Mormons continued to practice polygamy until 1890 when church president Wilford Woodruff issued a manifesto ending the practice.

Should the Free Exercise Clause protect the right of Royston Potter to have three wives? What about Americans who want to smoke marijuana as part of a religious ritual? What about the religious freedom of churches that preach racial supremacy? Should Jehovah's Witnesses be required to say the Pledge of Allegiance to the flag? What about the Nellis AFB airman who in 1983 refused to salute the flag, obey commands or salute female officers because of his religious beliefs? What about Alfred Smith and Galen Black, two members of the Native American Church, who chewed peyote as part of their church's religious rituals and were fired from the jobs as drug counselors and denied unemployment benefits?[19]

The free exercise clause is no guarantee of absolute freedom of worship. It acts mostly as a speed limit sign to keep Congress and state legislatures from going too far. Above all, it helps to make sure that no single religious faction will ever use the power of government to force its will on the nation's nearly two thousand religions.

Government then may not mess with our religious "beliefs," but it can regulate our religious "actions." Thus the Supreme Court in *Employment Division v. Smith* (1990) outlawed the use of peyote in Native American religious ceremonies on the ground that it is an illegal hallucinogen.

In this case, the Justices declared that laws that otherwise were neutral toward

Remember how freedom of speech and press were "nationalized" in 1925 through the Fourteenth Amendment? In 1940 the Supreme Court incorporated the free exercise clause, and seven years later used the Fourteenth Amendment to also incorporate the establishment clause.

194

religion could be valid even if they infringed on some religious beliefs. Reacting to this controversial premise, Congress passed the Religious Freedom Restoration Act. Signed by President Clinton in 1993, this law required that any federal, state or local law imposing a "substantial burden" on someone's religious beliefs must serve a "compelling" government interest in the least intrusive way.

Four years later, however, the Supreme Court declared the law unconstitutional on the grounds that Congress had unlawfully usurped power from federal courts and the states. This decision angered some religious minorities. Marc Stern of the American Jewish Congress said that the Court's 1997 ruling "means that there's no realistic federal protection for religious believers anymore. States and local governments can intrude, as long as they don't single out any faith."[20]

Has Stern's prediction come true?

The Evolution Debate

For many Americans it is wrong to ban school prayer, and yet still keep teaching evolution in public schools. To them, this paradox is symbolic proof that public schools are godless. They don't want their children taught a "theory" that suggests life on earth is the product of natural selection, not divine creation.

The theory of evolution was popularized by the work of British naturalist Charles Darwin. After five years observing South American wildlife as a naturalist aboard HMS Beagle, Darwin wondered why he kept seeing different birds, seals and tortoises on islands that were physically identical. Why, he asked, did species with the same origin apparently change in different ways in different places? After he returned to England, Darwin theorized that these differences could be explained if species had not been created by a divine force but had evolved gradually over millions of years from a few common ancestors.

Many years after the Beagle voyage, Darwin's faith shattering book *On The Origin of Species By Means of Natural Selection* (1859) appeared. Because it proposed a world millions of years old, Darwin's theory was immediately controversial. He had directly challenged the biblical account of creation, and the theories of religious leaders. In 1654, for example, Irish Protestant Bishop James Ussher determined that the earth was created October 24, 4004 B.C. While many people did not accept Bishop Ussher's precise date, they did agree that the earth was just a few thousand years old. The idea that the earth had evolved over millions of years simply did not fit their idea of creation. And they were outraged by the possibility that man's ancestors might be distant cousins of the apes.

The debate over evolution began in June 1860 at Oxford University where Oxford Bishop Samuel Wilberforce and Thomas Huxley clashed. Attended by shouting students, *Bible*-waving ministers and grim professors, the evolution debate almost collapsed in chaos after Wilberforce asked Huxley if it was by his grandfather or grandmother that he claimed descent from an ape.

By 1925 evolution was being accepted by liberal ministers who saw no serious gap between the biblical account of creation and Darwin's theory. This accommodation outraged most fundamentalists, however. Evangelist William A. "Billy" Sunday with typical flourish told

195

a reporter, "If a minister believes and teaches evolution, he is a stinking skunk, a hypocrite, and a liar."[21]

To stop the spread of Darwinism, states passed laws banning the teaching of evolution. Typical was a law passed March 21, 1925 by Tennessee which forbad any public school "to teach any theory that denies the story of the Divine creation of man as taught in the *Bible*."

Soon after this law was passed, a Dayton, Tennessee high school biology teacher named John T. Scopes taught evolution. He was tried in July 1925 as a nationwide audience watched by newspaper, radio and movie newsreel. Scopes was declared guilty by a local court, and fined. Evolution survived the "Scopes Trial" and is taught today in most public schools.

During the Scopes Trial, fundamentalist and three time presidential candidate William Jennings Bryan served as prosecutor. On the other side, famous criminal lawyer and agnostic Clarence Darrow defended Scopes. The confrontation was dramatized in the 1960 movie *Inherit the Wind*, which showed evolutionist Darrow clearly winning the debate.

Most Americans have reconciled Darwinism with their religious beliefs. This accommodation, however, has not ended the debate. In December 1981, Scopes II began in Little Rock, Arkansas. Only this time a state law, the "Balanced Treatment for Creation-Science and Evolution-Science Act" was on trial. The act required public schools to give equal treatment to both evolution and

> To get an idea of how the 1981 Arkansas Act 590 defined Creation-science, use this computer address:
> [http://cns-web.bu.edu/pub/dorman/mva.html] and get a copy of *McClean v. Arkansas Board of Education*.

creationism. "Creationism" is the theory that life on earth began suddenly about ten thousand years ago and did not evolve over millions of years, as suggested by Darwin and most of the scientific community today. Creationists clashed in Arkansas with Evolutionists after the American Civil Liberties Union brought suit May 27, 1981 in U.S. District Court for 23 clients who claimed the Balanced Treatment Act unconstitutionally infringed on academic freedom. Although the law provided no punishments for teachers who refused to teach creationism, the ACLU was afraid teachers who rejected creation-science as "hogwash" could be fired.

> Do we need another monkey trial, only this time a debate between Creation-science and Evolution? Why, or why not?

Opposition to evolution has made school boards, teachers and textbook publishers nervous. In 1985, a California state textbook review committee discovered that biology books used by seventh and eighth graders in that state were too vague about evolution. By 1997 schools in Macon County, Georgia were pasting disclaimers calling evolution a "controversial theory" in the district's biology books. In addition to Georgia, the teaching of evolution has been challenged in California, Washington, Pennsylvania, Tennessee, Michigan, Indiana, Ohio, New Hampshire and other states.

Freedom of Association

During World War I, Congress passed laws aimed at preventing speech or behavior which might hinder the war effort. These laws made it possible for government agents to arrest socialist Eugene Debs and send him to prison for advising young American men to avoid military service, and not be cannon fodder for capitalism.

To control communism, Congress in 1940 passed the Smith Act. This controversial law made it unlawful for any person to "knowingly or willfully advocate, advise, or teach the duty, necessity, desirability, or propriety of overthrowing or destroying any government of the United States by force or violence."

The federal government, however, does not always wait for either revolutionary words or bombs when it acts. This was the case in 1942 when 120,000 Japanese-Americans living in California, Oregon, Washington and Arizona were rounded up by U.S. soldiers and taken to internment camps. This relocation of Japanese Americans was accomplished through Executive Order 9066, which was signed by President Franklin Roosevelt. Americans were afraid that Japanese Americans would commit sabotage to help Japan win the war. Some justified the Order by saying it was designed to protect Japanese Americans from retaliation for the December 7, 1941 attack on Pearl Harbor. Whether the relocation was justified is questionable. Japanese Americans, however, suffered humiliation and considerable loss of property. In 1980 the Federal Commission on Wartime Relocation ruled that there was no military reason for the relocation, since no Japanese Americans were ever convicted of collaboration with the enemy. In fact, during World War II, the most highly decorated unit in the U.S. Army was the 442d Regimental Combat Team, comprised entirely of Japanese American volunteers, who fought valiantly in Europe. In the 1951 movie "Go for Broke," Hollywood made amends by portraying the bravery of the Nisei soldiers. Then in 1986 the U.S. government admitted its relocation policy was wrong and compensated Japanese Americans with a formal apology, and $20,000 for each of the sixty thousand or so survivors.

What about groups that claim to be patriotic, but break the law? What should be done about anti-abortion groups that torch abortion clinics? Should people opposed to stem cell research be allowed to protest at research centers where scientists are using stem cells to cure Parkinson's Disease? What

> Was it a good idea to apologize to Japanese Americans? Was it a good idea to pay $20,000 reparations to the survivors? What about African Americans who claim that slavery was a much greater evil than the internment camps?

about militia groups that practice the revolution that they predict is coming someday? Should racist groups be banned? Hitler used hatred against Jews in Germany to rise to power in the 1920's. Should groups that preach religious hatred be banned, censored, or imprisoned?

In June 1997, Timothy McVeigh was sentenced to die for blowing up the Oklahoma federal building and killing 168 people. During his trial, McVeigh's lawyers argued that the former Gulf War soldier was corrupted by reading *The Turner Diaries*.

> Should the FBI arrest all members of The Order now so they can't bomb federal buildings in the future? Why, or why not?

Members of "The Order" believe white people are God's chosen, and Jews are the children of Satan. The First Amendment protects the right of people to assemble together and organize protests, if they are peaceful. Bombing a federal building or an abortion clinic are not protected by the First Amendment, however. Because Timothy McVeigh was inspired by *The Turner Diaries*, should the book be banned? Should it be against the law to belong to any group which advocates violent overthrow of the government? Why or why not?

The Right to Keep and Bear Arms

The British are proud of their civility and self-control. To maintain this civility, England has some of the world's toughest gun laws. In a population of 58.4 million, fewer than one million people are certified to own firearms, and most of these are farmers who keep shotguns to control foxes, rabbits and other pests. Another 57,510 Britons are certified to own handguns, and they are nearly all members of target-shooting gun clubs. Although there are between 200,000 and one million illegally held firearms in Britain, the number of offenses in which handguns are used averages fewer than three thousand a year. In comparison, U.S. dealers sell about 7.5 million guns a year, including 3.5 million handguns. There are about 67 million handguns owned by private U.S. citizens, and some of these are used to commit about 640,000 violent crimes every year. Despite England's success with tough gun laws, Americans continue to insist that the Second Amendment protects their right to keep and bear arms.

Despite England's success at keeping down crime by regulating guns, Americans seem reluctant to even attempt strong gun controls. When police officers run into well-armed criminals, they are outgunned. Is this a cultural lag?

Conventional wisdom holds that learning can only take place in schools where teachers control the students, and nobody carries guns or knives. Sometimes conventional wisdom is correct. In 1990, Congress decided there were too many guns being brought to public schools and passed the Gun-free School Zones Act which set up a gun-free zone of one thousand feet around the schools. In the past, the Supreme Court has upheld such laws as a legitimate exercise of congressional power to regulate interstate commerce. In 1995, however, the Court decided in *U.S. v. Lopez* that the Gun-Free School Zones Act was unconstitutional. So now schools have to rely on student searches and security guards for protection. To hide their weapons, gang members wear baggy clothes. To look tough, law-abiding teens wear baggy clothes.

"A well regulated Militia, being necessary to the security of a free State, the right of the people to keep and bear Arms, shall not be infringed." What do these Second Amendment words means? Did the framers of the Bill of Rights intend that Congress pass no law infringing on the right of the American people to keep and bear arms?

During his 1996 campaign, President Clinton suggested that public school children wear uniforms. Uniforms symbolize uniformity and patriotism, and could be a useful way to reduce violence and encourage learning. Moreover, uniforms would make it more difficult for teenagers to hide weapons on their persons. Are school uniforms an idea whose time has come?

Despite the popular idea that guns are a symbol of our freedom, the right to keep and bear arms does not have the same constitutional protection as the rest of the Bill of Rights. In *United States v. Cruikshank*, 92 U.S. 542 (1876), the Supreme Court held that the Second Amendment does not guarantee to individuals the right to bear arms, it only protects the right of the states to maintain and equip a militia. Then in *United States v. Miller*, 307 U.S. 174 (1939), the Court ruled that defendants who violate federal gun laws cannot expect Second Amendment protection unless they belong to a state militia. As a result of these and similar rulings, Congress and state legislatures can pass gun registration laws, ban mail order sale of guns, and prohibit the sale of automatic weapons such as the AK-47.

However, Congress in 1986 passed the Firearms Owners' Rights Act. This law allows interstate sale of rifles and shotguns, makes it easier to carry weapons across state lines, and reduces penalties for record-keeping violations. Moreover, police from 21 states had to lobby hard to keep out a provision allowing interstate sale of handguns. The 1986 law was devised to ease restrictions on legitimate gun owners, and it did nothing to curb the widespread sale of semiautomatic weapons like the AK-47 assault rifle.

On January 17, 1989, 26-year-old Patrick Edward Purdy used an AK-47 assault rifle to kill five children and wound 29 more in an elementary school yard in Stockton, California. Purdy used an AK-47 imported from China, which he purchased in Oregon. He could have purchased the rifle in California at the time by just showing his driver's license, marking a few "no" answers on a form, and paying $400. Under California law at the time, handguns were harder to buy than assault rifles because they could be "concealed."

After Purdy slaughtered the Stockton children, the California legislature passed a law which banned the sale of imported semiautomatic rifles like the AK-47. After the California law passed, an editorial writer for the Las Vegas *Review Journal* objected because now Californians could no longer obtain automatic weapons as self-protection from an oppressive government. The constitutional right to keep and bear arms, said the editorial, was not designed to protect hunters or sportsmen:

> **It was designed to allow an armed citizenry to effectively resist the rise of an oppressive government . . . . Couldn't happen here you say? America is not China, you say? History has shown that anything can happen. If China and the Soviet Union can move toward democracy, surely the United States can move in the opposite direction.**[22]

Despite this argument, the 9th U.S. Circuit Court upheld the 1989 California gun law by a 3-0 vote on May 22, 1992. The federal appeals court rejected arguments made by NRA spokespersons and ruled that the Constitution does not prevent states from keeping certain types of guns out of private hands. After the ruling, Robert Vanderet, lawyer for the Center to Prevent Handgun Violence, said, "I hope this puts to rest the lie that the NRA has been spreading about what the Second Amendment means. States are free under the Bill of Rights to regulate firearm possession as they see fit."[23]

> **Is the United States moving toward the type of society described in science fiction books like *1984* and *Brave New World*? Could this be prevented by an armed citizenry?**

The most powerful faction opposing gun control is the National Rifle Association. According to NRA's conventional wisdom, "guns don't kill people, people kill people." Is this premise logical? Why, or why not?

If still alive, Thomas Hobbes would be shocked by the NRA's association of gun ownership with freedom. In his *Leviathan* (1651), Hobbes argued that without strong government to control their impulses, men would make perpetual war against their fellow citizens. In a society where government is too weak, Hobbes argued, "there is perpetual war of every man against his neighbor; no inheritance to transmit to the son, nor to expect from the father; no propriety of goods or lands; no security; but a full and absolute liberty in every particular man . . . ." In Hobbesian terms, **nasty, brutish and short**.

Privacy

What preserves liberty? Guns, laws, police, courts, self-control, compromise, tolerance, politically correct words, strong government, weak government, lots of Soma?

Don't worry about guns, worry about your right of privacy. Guns will someday be a survival of our violent past. Guns will end up in George Orwell's "memory hole," along with baggy jeans. Baggy jeans and guns will end up in the same place as accordion music, ashtrays, bell bottoms, day-glo colors, elevator shoes, heavy metal, mood rings, spam, tupperware, and zoot suits.

Guns will someday disappear into the cultural lag bin. They'll be recycled by a sensor made by Trilon Technology that now detects the location of gun shots. Fire a gun in Las Vegas and the Trilon sensor will immediately detect the location. The Firearms Police will arrive in a few minutes and march the shooter off to jail. The only barrier to the Trilon sensor is the Fourth and Fourteenth Amendments, which ban unreasonable searches and seizures.

Is a gunfire detection system equipped with microphone monitors and computers a violation of the Bill of Rights?

Now that concealed weapons are legal in some states, the Justice Department has funded a $2.15 million project for the National Institute of Justice to develop prototypes for concealed weapons detectors. Using the techniques developed for airport metal detectors, the federal researchers are confident they'll be able to use a wave-imagining system to reveal handguns concealed under a suspect's clothing. Only one problem: The Fourth Amendment prohibits frisking someone for illegal weapons without a reasonable suspicion that he or she is armed and dangerous.

Should concealed weapons detectors be used, despite possible Fourth and Fourteenth Amendment objections?

In a poll taken by the Los Angeles *Times* in August 1996, 58% surveyed said they would give up some civil liberties in exchange for protection from terrorists. At the same time, Millimetrix was testing its "Passive Millimeter Wave Imager." This is a device that police can aim from 90 feet away into a crowd to "see" through people's clothing for weapons, plastic explosives, or drugs. Supporters of the Imager believe it to be an effective new weapon in the continuing fight against terrorists.

As technology gets more and more sophisticated, the word "Orwellian" is used more and more. There was no right of privacy in the nightmare world created by

Is the "Imager" a violation of any constitutional rights?

George Owell. Winston Smith had to hide in a corner of his apartment to escape the telescreen, read a forbidden book, or write the words "I Hate Big Brother" in his diary. When Julia and Winston made love, they had to worry about hidden microphones. At work, both were surrounded by telescreens that watched them. Whenever Winston left his drab apartment he had to worry about being followed by Youth League Boys and Anti-Sex League Girls. Always, he had to worry about being accused of *Thoughtcrime*, *Facecrime*, or *Ownlife*. In other words, Smith could not enjoy such simple pleasures as walking alone, or being too much his own man.

In the United States we don't arrest people for "ownlife," but "the controllers" often intrude on our privacy through surveillance, lie detector tests, sobriety tests, blood tests, personality tests, and rules that regulate everything from drug use to sexual harassment.

Each of the following is a possible example of an Orwellian form of control. "Orwellian" means any practice by government that deprives people of their basic humanity. It can range from censorship to torture. Read the list below, and decide which of these described practices is truly Orwellian:

▼ Computers at the Drug Enforcement Administration, FBI and U.S. Marshal's sites have buttons that make it easy for friends and family of accused felons to expose them. In the words of one observer, "With just a click of the mouse, Web surfers can tip off the feds to drug traffickers and deadbeat dads."

▼ The military's "don't ask, don't tell" policy toward gays was called Orwellian in 1995 by U.S. District Judge Eugene Nickerson because it equates sexual orientation with misconduct.

▼ Users of the Internet can hide behind screen names and criticize others without fear of reprisal.

▼ In June 1959, the Supreme Court, six to three, upheld a drug-testing program for school athletes in a small Oregon logging town. In its majority opinion, the Court ruled that the Fourth and Fourteenth Amendment protections did not apply to high school students.

▼ In Illinois there is a state law that permits bosses to eavesdrop on employees' work phones. Under the law, which passed December 13, 1995, the boss can listen to your phone conversation if the surveillance serves "educational, training or research purposes."

▼ While Illinois was passing its telephone listening law, the Clinton Administration was circulating a proposal to require all computer hardware and software manufacturers to produce encryption products that contain a key to unlock encoded information to government officials.

201

▼ The federal government is setting up a national computer registry to keep track of the nation's approximately 250,000 sex offenders. The purpose of the registry is to prevent rapists and child molesters from crossing state lines where, according to President Clinton, they would terrorize unsuspecting communities.

▼ To get a job you may be required now to agree to the following stipulation: "My doctor, hospital or testing laboratory has my consent to conduct medical or drug tests on me, and I hereby give my consent to physical searches of myself and my tool box, lunch box, car, locker or any packages or purse I have while on the employer's premises, whether or not I have a lock on such items."

▼ While losing your money at a local casino, you have a mysterious feeling of well-being, which comes from pleasant odors being pumped into the playing area. The pleasant odor is the product of research conducted at the Las Vegas Hilton casino in 1993 by Alan Hirsch, who runs the Smell and Taste Treatment and Research Foundation, which treats people with smell disorders and researches how odor affects behavior.

▼ In October 1996, President Clinton signed a bill outlawing Rohypnol and other "date rape" drugs used to incapacitate victims. Supporters of the bill argue that dropping a pill into a victim's throat is like putting a knife to her throat.

▼ At Riverwood Middle School in Houston, officials suspended Brooke Olson for a day after a dog sniffed a bottle of Advil in her backpack while she was in gym class. Defenders of drug searches believe schools have to be tough.

▼ During commentary on a CBS golf telecast, British commentator Ben Wright said that "boobs" hamper the female golf swing. On another occasion, ABC sportscaster Howard Cosell got into trouble for saying on Monday Night Football that a black running back scampered like "a little monkey." In June 1995, African American Democrat Willie Brown celebrated a political victory by declaring about his Republican opponents: "Those white boys got taken, fair and square." It has been suggested that people who make these types of remarks undergo special sensitivity sessions.

▼ Because "hackers" pose a threat to companies that rely heavily on computers, IBM has an advertisement aimed at alerting the public to the threat. The Ads asks, "Will a 14-year-old SOCIOPATH bring my company to its knees?" The Ad also says, "It can keep you up at night, the thought of some wily hacker, or worse, a paid professional creeping through your company's most valuable informa-tion." To discourage hackers, IBM has some of its "smartest people" working on the problem of *Information Security*: One group consists of 'ethical hackers' who try to break into your system and reveal the cracks in your armor."

▼ Under the 1996 Communications Decency Act, using "indecent" or "patently offensive" words and pictures posted online where children might see them can be punished by up to two years in prison and a $250,000 fine.

Orwellian means a totalitarian government that tries to control all thought and behavior. Since 1948 the word has been expanded to mean any attempt to control people through their language, thoughts and sexual behavior.

Although Orwell's words are being resurrected to describe technology that threatens privacy, some writers are skeptical. Michael Kinsley, for example, claims that "Orwell got it wrong." Kinsley is convinced that technology didn't give us Big Brother. Instead, home computers, fax machines, VCRs and the Internet have "*expanded* human freedom. Kinsley, who works for Microsoft, makes a persuasive argument for the "technology has made us free" disciples by arguing that the advantages outweigh the disadvantages. "On the more profound political level," he asks, "is there anyone who thinks the world would be a freer place if computers, fax machines and the Internet didn't exist?"[24] ☺ Is this a good question?

The Social Control Complex

Some Americans make their living designing technology that can be used to identify employees who might lie, steal, cheat, or get sick. This "social control" technology includes lie detectors, personality tests, handwriting analysis, brain wave scans, facial expression analysis, voice pitch monitors, videotapes, and computer data banks.

To understand Orwell, we need to know the words he used to describe his nightmare society, namely: Big Brother, ThoughtPolice, Newspeak, Crimethink, Doublethink, Prolefeed, and Unperson. Orwell is also famous for these words from *Animal Farm*: "All animals are equal but some animals are more equal than others."

How are your research skills? Use your computer, telephone book, local media, and national magazines to locate articles dealing with the current use of lie detectors, brain wave scans, facial expression analysis, voice pitch monitors, videotapes, computer data banks or any other technology designed to control how we behave. Prepare a 5 x 8 card describing <u>one</u> example of the social control complex, and footnote your source on the same card.

During a May 1992 news conference in Washington D.C., Senator Dennis DeConcini (D-Ariz.) was telling reporters that a balanced budget constitutional amendment was needed to get the national debt under control. His exact words, however, were, "we're finally going to rassle to the ground this gigantic orgasm [sic] that is just out of control."[25]

In psychoanalytic theory, the *Freudian Slip* refers to a momentary breakdown in our consciousness so that a word slips out in an unintended fashion and reveals subconscious thoughts. No doubt Senator DeConcini meant to say this "gigantic organism" when he spoke. According to Freud, these verbal slips often reflect repressed thoughts and feelings. Thus a student who has just received a low test grade might try to say, "I don't care about the grade, I still love this class" but end up saying, "I still loathe this class."

Verbal slips were studied at the University of California (Davis). There, male student volunteers were asked to silently read pairs of words on a computer screen and, if a buzzer sounded, to read the words aloud. One group of students was tested by a very sexy researcher, and their verbal slips were revealing. Instead of saying "past fashion"

when the word pair appeared and the buzzer sounded, male students often said "fast passion." In these and other cases, the researchers discovered that verbal slips could be triggered by merely changing the external environment.[26]

Americans want big government off their backs. They aren't too happy that more than 125,000 federal employees are working on about five thousand regulations that cost taxpayers about $500 billion. Americans don't want government telling them to get yearly smog checks of nearly new cars. They don't like being told to wear seat belts, and pay for air bags. Some don't like being told where and when to smoke cigarettes.

Americans don't like Big Brother government. Big Brother, however, has a sibling. For the sake of gender equity, we'll call the sibling "Big Sister." Big Sister is busy everywhere keeping an eye on people who work for corporations—what we used to call the "free enterprise system." Judging by *Time* magazine's June 2, 1997 "Notebook," nearly two-thirds of companies spy on their employees. Big Sister is keeping records of employee phone calls, videotapes employees, stores and reviews electronic mail, stores and reviews computer mail, tapes phone conversations, and tapes and reviews voice mail.

Big Sister Is Reading Your Mail!

Notes

1. Laura Ofobike, "Blaming and Hating Koreans in Rap Music Doesn't Advance Black Merchant Class," Salt Lake *Tribune* (January 11, 1992), p. A10.

2. Timothy Egan, "Washington Governor Signs Measure on Obscene Music," *New York Times* (March 21, 1992), p. 6y.

3. *Chaplinsky v. New Hampshire*, 315 U.S. 568 (1942).

4. George Will, "Politicking Turns Tyrannical on Campus," Las Vegas *Sun* (October 20, 1991), p. 2D.

5. Nat Hentoff, "Look at it as 'Increased Freedom to be Sensitive'," Las Vegas *Review Journal* (January 6, 1992), p. 7B.

6. Amy Harmon, "Subliminals Creeping into High-Tech World," Las Vegas *Review Journal/Sun* (October 1, 1995), p. 1A-2A.

7. Neil Postman, *Technopoly: The Surrender of Culture to Technology* (New York: Alfred A. Knopf, 1992), p. 48.

8. "High Court Rules on Free Speech," Las Vegas *Review Journal* (December 12, 1995), p. 6A.

9. *USA Today* (February 19, 1985).

10. "President Criticized for Remarks Deemed a Slur," Las Vegas *Review Journal/Sun* (September 23, 1995), p. 8B.

11. Will Durant, *The Life of Greece* (New York: Simon and Schuster, 1939), p. 426. Fred S. Holley, "I.F. Stone Takes on Socrates," Las Vegas *Review Journal* (March 20, 1988), p. 10AA.

12. *Queen v. Hicklin*, L.R. 3 Q.B. 350 (1868).

13. Page Smith, *The Rise of Industrial America: A People's History of the Post-Reconstruction Era*, VI (New York: McGraw-Hill Book Company, 1984), pp. 277-278.

14. Stanley N. Worton, *Freedom of Speech and Press* (Rochelle Park, New Jersey: Hayden Book Company, Inc., 1975), pp. 44-46.

15. Marcia Pally, "Pornography Didn't Make Him Do It," Las Vegas *Review Journal* (March 12, 1992), p. 11B.

16. Joshua Quittner, "The Supreme Court," *Time* (March 31, 1997), p. 74.

17. "Sexy World Confuses Teenagers," Las Vegas *Review Journal* (December 5, 1996), p. 18B.

18.*Engel v. Vitale*, 370 U.S. 421 (1962).

19.George W. Cornell, "Religious Rights Cases Shake Precedents," Las Vegas *Review Journal/Sun* (January 4, 1992), p. 5B.

20. "Supreme Court Ruling Upsets Congress, Religious Groups," Las Vegas *Review Journal* (June 26, 1997), p. 5A.

21.Nat Shapiro (ed.), *Whatever It Is, I'm Against It* (New York: Simon and Schuster, 1984), p. 84.

23. "California Trashes Second Amendment," Las Vegas *Review Journal* (May 26, 1989), p. 14B.

24. "Semiautomatic Weapon Sale Ban Upheld by Court," Reno *Gazette-Journal* (May 23, 1992), p. 4A.

24.Michael Kinsley, "Orwell Got It Wrong," *Reader's Digest* (June 1997), pp. 131-134.

26."DeConcini Calls Budget an 'Orgasm'," Las Vegas *Sun* (May 14, 1992), p. 8E.

27."Studying Verbal Slips," *Newsweek* (October 21, 1985), p. 73.

Chapter 8

Justice

On December 6, 1985, 47-year-old Carroll Edward Cole was the first person to die by lethal injection in a Nevada prison. In October 1984, Cole was convicted of murdering by strangulation 51-year-old Marie Cushman, whose body was found in a room at the Casbah Hotel in Las Vegas. A catheter was slipped into a vein in Cole's arm, and he was injected with a lethal dose of three poisonous chemicals. After about twenty minutes he was pronounced dead. Later, Las Vegas surgeon Lonnie L. Hammargren, psychologist Janice M. Bruner, and pathologist John Peacock removed Cole's brain, and examined it for abnormalities. No abnormalities or lesions were found in the rage center of Cole's brain.

Cole died because he had committed murder, which is a felony. Felonies include murder, manslaughter, rape, larceny, robbery, burglary and arson. Cole confessed to 13 murders. They convicted and executed him despite extenuating circumstances. Carroll Edward Cole was an abused child, forced to watch his mother have sex with various men she had picked up in bars. Still, he was also a cold-blooded killer who as an adult strangled his victims after having sex with them. He may have killed as many as 35 people.

Did Cole receive justice? Since he confessed, Cole was guilty under the law. However, was cruel and unusual punishment imposed on this former abused child? The Eighth Amendment says, "Excessive bail shall not be required, nor excessive fines imposed, nor cruel and unusual punishments inflicted." The Supreme Court applied this provision to the states in 1962 through the Fourteenth Amendment's due process clause, so Cole's lawyers could have argued that the death penalty had violated his constitutional rights.

What is cruel and unusual punishment? Legally, it means any lingering torture, wanton infliction of pain, mutilation, or degrading treatment or any sentence too severe for the offense committed. In the fifteenth century, England had a particularly barbaric penalty for treason and other high crimes. They hanged the traitor until nearly dead, then cut his stomach open. After they "burnt the bowels before his face," the criminal was beheaded and his body torn into four parts—sometimes by horses. This cruel punishment was the fate of William Wallace, who led the Scots against England's King Edward I. In the 1995 movie "Braveheart," Mel Gibson plays Wallace, and is hanged, drawn and quartered. With a typically Hollywood perspective, Gibson suffers heroically, stoically, and bravely, just like in the movies.

Despite the lofty ideals in our Declaration of Independence and the Constitution, Americans have imposed legal death penalties through drowning, fire, hanging, the guillotine, firing squads, the electric chair, the gas chamber, and now lethal injection.

> Since torturing prisoners conflicts with American values, should we let the censors ban movies like "Braveheart?" Why or why not?

Every culture has its own idea of justice. In general our culture has defined it as fair play, due process, impartiality, authority in the maintenance of rights, etc. The symbol of our justice system is a blind-folded woman holding a scale. Justice is blind because its decisions are supposedly weighed without regard for person, rank, skin color, race or gender. The scales are a traditional symbol for a judicial system that weighs the facts and renders justice. In the Dutch City Oudewafer, there used to be a witches scale that was used to determine whether an accused person had been levitated by the devil or had the normal weight of an ordinary mortal. In the Middle Ages they threw witches into a river to determine if the accused would float or not. Would this be a plausible way to identify a witch?

The Puritans who settled Massachusetts Bay Colony were believers in witches and justice. So in 1692, when residents of Salem Village had a witch hunt, they took great care to insure that the 20 or so women, one man, and dog accused of witchery were given a fair trial, then hanged. By the early 1950's when Wisconsin Senator Joseph McCarthy conducted a witch hunt for communists alleged to be state department traitors, Americans insisted that the accused get due process. In the case of persons accused of being communist, what does due process mean?

The Founding Fathers went to Philadelphia in 1787 to correct the weaknesses of the government under the Articles of Confederation. The delegates from Massachusetts had lived through violent riots now called Shays' Rebellion when men angry over taxes and mortgage foreclosures shut down the government of Massachusetts in 1786. One of the delegates, John Adams, would argue in defense of the new Constitution that its "checks and balances" would guarantee justice by weakening the power of ambitious demagogues who held government offices. In your opinion, how would checks and balances provide "justice?"

The French Revolution that began in 1789 was a product of factions running amuck. These factions included the Jacobin Club, the Paris Commune, the Committee for the Surveillance of the Commune, etc.

Fair play is another component of justice. This can be seen especially in sports where a head-hunting pitcher gets thrown out

Anatole France in 1894 said, "The law in its majestic equality, forbids the rich as well as the poor to sleep under bridges, to beg in the streets, and to steal bread." What is his point?

of the game by an alert umpire; or in the media's hostile reaction to a heavyweight boxer who decides to bite off a chunk of his winning opponent's ear. The notion of fair play was behind the electoral college's recount crisis after the November 2000 presidential election. For the first time since 1888, American voters were stunned to discover that under our "winner-take-all" custom, a candidate trailing in the popular vote can still achieve a winning majority of the electoral vote. Would the system be more "just" if only the popular votes were counted?

Revenge and justice sometimes overlap. This happened in 2001 when audiences were crowded into theaters with stadium seats at the Sun Coast casino to see the popular movie, "Pearl Harbor." The movie features two U.S. Army pilots and a nurse engaged in a love triangle that is played against the backdrop of the December 7, 1941 attack on Pearl Harbor by Japanese bombers. During the attack the two pilots get airborne and shoot down six Japanese planes. Four months later the same two pilots have volunteered to fly as crew members on the 16 B-25 bombers under command of Lt. Col. James Doolittle. On April 18, 1942, the U.S. bombers took off from the deck of the aircraft carrier "Hornet" to bomb targets in Tokyo, Yokohama, Kobe, and Nagoya. This risky raid bolstered morale in the United States but the impact of the bombs was merely psychological. The two atomic bombs dropped on Japan ended the Pacific War in 1945, not the symbolic bombs dropped by Colonel Doolittle, who was awarded the Medal of Honor for his brave attack. So far as we know, the two Army pilots featured in the "Pearl Harbor" movie were not in the B-25's launched from the unsteady deck of the Hornet.

Adolf Hitler, ruler of Nazi Germany from 1933 to 1945, did not view justice as fairness, impartiality, proper procedures, or the use of authority to uphold righteousness. The charismatic speaker was driven by a mania to punish all Jews for Germany's humiliating defeat in World War I. Unlike blind justice which is impartial, Hitler was driven by anger directed toward innocent people. Like many fascists, Hitler was a believer in a forged Russian document known as, "The Protocols of the Elders of Zion." This 1905 forgery outlined a presumed Jewish plot to control the world. In his autobiography *Mein Kampf*, Hitler argued that the world was like nature, a place where the fittest survive and the losers don't.

> In 1941 the Japanese considered their Emperor to be a direct descendant of the sun god. After War World II ended Americans occupied Japan. Seven Japanese leaders were executed, but the Emperor was allowed to keep his title. Was that justice? Did Doolittle's bombers have the Emperor's name on their list of targets?

By July 1944, Hitler's Germany was clearly losing World War II. Hoping to negotiate a cease fire with western powers, a group of German army officers tried to kill Hitler with a bomb left in a brief case where Hitler was making war plans. Hitler survived to set up a People's Court under a hanging judge to provide justice for about 5,000 suspects, rounded up and shot, or lynched and hung up on meat hooks. On Hitler's orders the accused were harangued, humiliated, and movies were made of their agony.

Hitler committed suicide before he could be captured by the British, the Americans, or the Russians. If the dictator had lived, he would have been tried at Nuremberg for war crimes; along with other leading Nazis.

> Who should have tried Hitler, the allies or the nation of Israel?

The two young men who killed their classmates at Columbine High School were fans of Adolf Hitler and all the symbolism associated with the Third Reich. Were they inspired to kill by web sites that celebrated the virtues of Hitler's swastika, trench coat, and master race?

In Huxley's *Brave New World*, the drug Soma is used to keep adults out of trouble. To control young people, the government in *BNW* uses sleep teaching and sex in the form of "find the zipper," "orgy porgy," and other erotic games.

In 1720 England had six thousand gin shops. To keep young people out of trouble, they were fed gin. Instead of gin, moderns are fed methylphenidate—otherwise known as Ritalin. This is a drug that stimulates the central nervous system and is used to treat attention deficit disorder. What, in your opinion, is more effective—erotic games or Ritalin?

Since pedophilia has become a serious justice issue, it may be time to consider various ways to punish the offenders. What

> What type of justice comes in a bottle labeled Ritalin or Soma?

should we do about a 34-year-old man who gets on the Internet and propositions a 13-year-old girl; who turns out to be an agent working for the FBI's Sexual Assault Felony Enforcement Team? Would the death penalty be a reasonable way to deter potential pedophiles?

The Death Penalty

Nevada pioneered the gas chamber, which was once considered the most humane way to execute convicts. On October 12, 1979, Joseph Zentner watched the gas chamber execution of Jesse Bishop in Nevada. Zenter, professor of political science at the University of Southwestern Louisiana, did not come away thinking the gas chamber was "humane." He wrote:

> **The condemned man wrinkled his nose at the first fumes. Then came deep, desperate gulps for the air. His face turned up to the ceiling of the gas chamber. He convulsed, saliva ran from his mouth, his face turned red. His eyes then closed and his chin fell to his chest. Bishop's gasps and spasms took six minutes. He twitched for two more.[1]**

In 1995 movie audiences watched the movie "Dead Man Walking," which featured Sean Penn as death row inmate Matthew Poncelot. While awaiting his execution for murder, Poncelot is given counsel by Sister Helen Prejean, played by Susan Sarandon. This true story has Poncelot confess to Sister Helen that he participated in the vicious murder of two teenagers. Reviewing "Dead Man Walking," Carrie Rickey said it had an ambiguous message, namely, "On the one hand *Dead Man Walking* eloquently argues that capital punishment is political theater; on the other it poetically suggests that in this case, the death penalty leads to repentance and redemption."[2] Typically Hollywood, the movie has Sean Penn make a heart-rending speech as he is being lifted crucifixion style.

Dead Man Walking reminds us that there is no easy way to legally kill a man. For years Americans debated whether the death penalty was cruel and unusual punishment. In 1972, by a five to four vote, the Supreme Court decided to prohibit states from applying the death penalty. This decision in *Furman v. Georgia*, 408 U.S. 238, fueled a national debate. In 1974, movie audiences cheered Charles Bronson who, in his role as architect Paul Kersey, kills thugs vigilante-style on the back streets of New York City. "Death Wish" was a highly popular movie because it showed would-be killers getting justice swift and sure.

> What do you think? Should Hollywood produce movies that suggest the death penalty leads to repentance and redemption? Would Sean Penn in the role of Matthew Poncelot and Susan Sarandon as Helen Prejean influence the opinions of movie audiences?

When the Supreme Court ruled against state death penalty statutes in 1972, it left the door open to resume the grisly practice if states would be more fair in applying death penalties. By 1976, the Court was satisfied that states were making an honest effort to impose death penalty laws more objectively, and upheld the 35 states that executed murderers.

So two years after *Death Wish* popularized a lone cowboy vigilante, the Supreme Court was upholding the ultimate punishment for murderers. Did the movie change popular attitudes enough to influence the Court's attitude toward the death penalty? Doubtful? Possible?

On January 24, 1989, serial killer Ted Bundy was executed in Florida. He was a sentimental guy, whose last words were, "Give my love to my family and friends." Bundy was also a cold-blooded killer who murdered about fifty people, most of them young women. If there had been no eighth amendment, the families of his victims would have gladly had him hanged, drawn and quartered.

By September 11, 1995, there were 75 men and one woman under the death penalty in Nevada. Since the state legislature in 1977 restored the death penalty, there have been five executions, and all five were inmates who waived their right to appeal and went to their deaths voluntarily.

Typically, more than 98% of executed criminals are men and less than 2% are female. Why this gender difference? Are modern men still behaving according to their Cro-Magnons' genes, as William Fielding Ogburn observed when explaining his theory of cultural lag?

The ancient Greeks viewed the death penalty as the symbol of society's punishment for people who committed high crimes. When the Athenians carried out a sentence of death, they executed the convicted murderer in the presence of the relatives of the victim. We reimposed the death penalty in 1976 because most Americans, like Athenians, want justice.

> Though handsome and a law student, Bundy was a deranged killer. He raped, sodomized, and bit his victims. Those who oppose the death penalty argue that as a child Ted Bundy was psychologically abused, and therefore not responsible for his actions. This view is not shared, however, by John Douglas, an FBI agent who specializes in serial killers. In his book *Journey into Darkness* (1997), Douglas describes Bundy as a handsome monster who deserved to be executed. Are you for or against the death penalty?

Most philosophers define justice as fairness, equality and impartial treatment. The symbol of justice most familiar to Americans is a blindfolded woman holding scales. In terms of impartial justice, what does the blindfold symbolize? Why the scales?

If the death penalty is so popular with most Americans, why do we have protests at the prisons when someone is executed? In the first place, killing anyone through electrocution, firing squad, gas chamber, hanging or lethal injection is still shocking. There is always the possibility of making a mistake. Professors Hugo Adam Bedau of Tufts University and Michael L. Radelet of the University of Florida in 1985, reported that of the more than seven thousand executions for capital offenses in this country between 1900 and 1985, there were 343 instances in which convicted defendants were later proven innocent. Of the 343 mistakes, 26 were not caught in time. Henry Schwarzschild, Director of the American Civil Liberties Union (ACLU) Capital Punishment Project, released the study and argued that the death penalty teaches that the "killing of human beings is a socially acceptable answer to our problems."[3] Disagreeing with the ACLU position, FBI agent John Douglas in his book *Journey into Darkness* suggested that a civilized society cannot forgive certain crimes:

> Does a civilized and enlightened society believe in redemption? As opposed to rehabilitation, which is a more practical notion, I see redemption as belonging in the spiritual realm and so is a different kind of idea. But here I would argue . . . that until we take seriously the most serious of crimes, we have no right to call ourselves civilized or enlightened. There are certain crimes that are simply too cruel, too sadistic, too hideous to be forgiven.

Should Timothy McVeigh be forgiven?

The Founding Fathers hoped that divisive issues like the death penalty would be handled at the state level. Federalism, as we noted in Chapter 2, was supposed to keep contentious issues limited to the states. They were not supposed to divide the entire nation. So why do our federal courts persist in handing down rulings that elevate issues like abortion and the death penalty beyond state politics and into the realm of national controversies?

Since the Supreme Court restored the death penalty, 35 states have capital punishment and 15 do not. This modern application of states rights and federalism seems to have quieted the capital punishment issue, for now. Would it make sense now for the Supreme Court to reverse itself on abortion and return that issue to the states for resolution? Why or why not?

> African Americans believe the death penalty is wrong. Killers of white people are about eight times more likely to receive a death penalty than killers of blacks. Is this still true?

Besides being shocking, mistake-prone, possibly racist and applied almost entirely to male criminals, the death penalty has other flaws. The Sixth Amendment guarantees trial by an impartial jury. In many states they exclude prospective jurors opposed to the death penalty from serving. Critics argue that this exclusion stacks the average jury with pro-death penalty advocates. This is unfair, they say, because jurors willing to impose capital punishment often don't believe as strongly in a presumption of innocence as opponents. ☆ What do you think? Is there any fair way to choose jurors?

In the future, courts will decide a bewildering array of issues which come under the Eighth Amendment. [These issues will range from police use of weapons like the Taser stun gun to state laws which chemically castrate pedophiles.]

With palm-sized video cameras, every citizen can capture images of police brutality. Officers using force during an arrest are at risk of Rodney King lawsuits. With real life TV programs, every American runs the risk of being shamed or sued. Suppose, for the sake of speculation, that Paula Jones had carried a video camera when they allowed her allegedly the privilege of seeing Bill Clinton's *gladius*.

What about assault with a deadly weapon "under color of authority?" That was the charge brought against four Los Angeles Police Department officers because they stunned, clubbed and kicked Rodney King, who appeared defenseless on a video made while they were arresting him in March 1991. After a Simi Valley jury declared the officers "not guilty," all hell broke loose in Los Angeles. In a special column for the Los Angeles *Times*, writers Eric W. Rose and Steven S. Lucas asked, "Was this decision by a jury without a single black juror in Simi Valley, Calif., simply another sign of deep-seated racial animosity, a darkening of the cloud that has hung over the city for more than a year? Or is there a reason to commend the judicial process?"[4]

> In October 1995, 12 jurors acquitted football great O.J. Simpson of first-degree-murder charges. What did we learn about the nature of justice from the trials of Rodney King and O.J. Simpson?

Is cruel and unusual punishment ever justified? Suppose a terrorist has hidden a nuclear bomb in the top floor of a Las Vegas hotel? The bomb is set to explode on July 4th, at noon unless $100 million is paid to the terrorist. Suppose the terrorist is captured at 10 a.m. on that day, and the police only have two hours to find the location. Should Metro give the terrorist a quarter and permission to call his lawyer? Or should they torture him until he confesses the nuclear bomb's location?

In Old England, for mild punishment they branded people on the face with a hot iron, gouged out their eyes and cut off the hands, feet, ears and nose. When they wanted to get nasty, the English cut off the criminal's testicles as a warning to others. Should captured terrorists be tortured as a warning to others? Or should we take away their television sets?

Is it cruel to isolate prisoners in cells without television? At the maximum-security prison in Alden, New York, inmates in 1986 surrendered by unanimous vote the right to receive packages from outside in exchange for the option to buy their own TV sets. The program is designed to stop drugs from getting into the prison, but has had other benefits. Prisoners preferred to stay in their cells and watch programs on their $55 twelve inch black-and-white TV sets, and all they ever complain about is "more channels."

Taxpayers, however, are angry. They resent the approximately $20 billion that it costs every year to house the nation's convicts. According to a September 4, 1995 *Time* article, "the hottest development in criminal justice is a fast-spreading impulse to eliminate anything that might make it easier to endure a sentence behind bars." In state after state they are denying the nation's 1.5 million prison inmates such former luxuries as bodybuilding equipment, televisions, record players, radios and computers. Taxpayers now vote for people like Maricopa County, Arizona Sheriff Joe Arpaio. He put stripes on his prisoners, organized 5,900 of them into chain gangs, housed them in tents, and made baloney a staple of their diet.

Some Americans, however, are not ready to jump on the "let's get tough" bandwagon. Advocates for prisoner right's point out that prison under any circumstances is a miserable place. They point out that prisoners usually pay for luxuries like their TV sets. According to the Bureau of Justice statistics, 91% of prisoners in the federal system and 70% in state prisons already work. Many prison wardens argue that the get-tough policy neglects the fact that prisoners need recreation to curb their rage and prevent uprisings.

> **Get tough, or rehabilitate prisoners by letting them watch TV, lift weights, and play baseball? Is there a third possibility?**

Jail inmates at the Orleans Parish Jail in New Orleans filed a complaint September 19, 1988 because they were segregated in cramped quarters, denied regular exercise, and had inadequate medical care. Some inmates complained also that they had to wear pink uniforms because they had tested positive for the HIV virus. These prisoners claimed in a lawsuit that the pink outfits stigmatized them, which is cruel and unusual punishment. Sheriff Charles Fori defended the uniforms saying the color coding designated the fact that they assigned inmates to the jail's infectious disease unit.[5]

> **Is it wrong to make HIV positive prisoners wear pink uniforms? Why or why not?**

In 1994, 72% of California voters approved the "three strikes" ballot initiative. Under its provisions any criminal with a serious or violent prior felony automatically has his sentence doubled for a second conviction. The third conviction would require a sentence of 25 years to life. By July 1996, however, the rule of unintended consequences had emerged. California courts were clogged with nonviolent criminals who had struck out. According to *Time*, one man got 25 years to life for shoplifting two packs of cigarettes, another for stealing a slice of pizza. Under the new law, California faces an annual prison cost increase of $5.5 billion.[6] ☆ Should Nevada's legislature adopt a three-strike law?

Thanks to psychologists and lawyers, every criminal has a legal excuse and a mental problem. In his book *The Abuse Excuse* (1994), Harvard Law Professor Alan M. Dershowitz examines 53 excuses given by accused criminals for their behavior. The excuses described by Dershowitz range from "Antisocial Personality Disorder" to "Vietnam Syndrome." Perhaps the most bizarre excuse was used during the late 1970's by Dan White who successfully excused his killing of San Francisco Mayor George Moscone and Supervisor Harvey Milk by claiming the "Twinkie Defense." White, a former police officer, was found guilty of involuntary manslaughter, not first degree murder, because the jury accepted his claim "that he had become mentally incapacitated at the time of the killings in part because of his consumption of junk foods . . . ."

When lawyers argue the insanity plea, they try to convince the jury that the defendant's mental illness is so severe that he lacked a substantial capacity to appreciate the wrongfulness of his acts and could no longer control his own conduct. The "insanity plea" is based on the belief that a civilized society should not punish a person who is mentally incapable of controlling his own conduct. The plea grew out of the religious belief that since a madman could not make his peace with God, executing him would be a sentence to eternal hell.

The modern idea of legal insanity was devised in 1843 by a British jury which acquitted Daniel M'Naughten of killing the Prime Minister's private secretary. This M'Naughten Rule requires that a defendant must not have understood right from wrong when the act was committed. Since they adopted the rule, most U.S. courts have used it to decide responsibility. State courts also apply another rule known as "irresistible impulse" as a second reason for absolving a defendant from criminal responsibility.

Should our courts continue to allow defendants to use insanity to escape responsibility for their actions? What about the excuses described in Professor Dershowitz? Do you recognize any of these excuses, abused child syndrome, black rage, battered woman syndrome, posttraumatic stress disorder, rape trauma, urban survival syndrome, repressed memory, crimes of passion, Super Bowl Sunday syndrome?

Hate Crimes

In December 1991, white hooligans in New York City sprayed some black kids with white paint. Though no one was killed, raped, robbed, or seriously hurt, this "hate crime" shocked New York City's political establishment. Mayor David Dinkins held special meetings, and vowed to eliminate all hatred. The city's Human Resources Commissioner launched a special effort to stop "those who would spread hate." The Police Department's special *Bias Incident Investigation Squad* went on special alert for hate-spreaders wielding spray guns. "Hate Crimes" are those acts committed against people because of their race, ethnic background, religion, gender, age, sexual preference, or disability. In July 2001, newspapers reported that "People in northeastern Congo have killed more than 800 suspected witches they blame for diseases in the remote, heavily forested

Is a "Bias Incident Investigation Squad" typical for big city police departments?

area." Would the Congo killings of suspected witches qualify today as a hate crime? What about an angry driver who throws a small dog into traffic on a freeway. Would that qualify as a hate crime?

After New York City mobilized its resources to capture a few spray paint wielding whites, Washington *Times* columnist Samuel Francis criticized hate crime laws as:

> **The special political and legal privileges of racial and religious minorities, and they are weapons by which white people can be bullied, bludgeoned, beaten, prosecuted and persecuted into shutting up about race and the cultural institutions that attend it. Hate crimes don't protect minorities. Minorities, like everyone else in the United States are already protected by laws that impose the same penalties for everyone. If you are raped, robbed, assaulted or killed, the law punishes your assailants for rape, robbery, assault or murder, regardless of your or their race or religion or why they did whatever it was they did.**

According to Francis, the legal tradition in this nation usually ignores the motivation for committing a crime like murder, and makes the act not the feelings illegal. Under hate crime laws, he argues, we are acclimating Americans to believe that it is the idea or feeling that is the real crime "and the motivation that ought to be punished." Hate crimes have a double standard. Francis argued that we prosecute white racists for inciting murder but no one "even considers prosecuting hatemongering rap groups like Public Enemy for belching in support of burning out Korean store owners and assassinating the governor of Arizona."[7]

In the fictional world created by George Orwell, citizens are programmed to practice a form of self-deception called "doublethink." This occurs when people have enough mental flexibility to hold and accept simultaneously two entirely conflicting views or beliefs. Thus the citizens of Orwell's Oceania can shout slogans like "War is Peace," "Freedom is Slavery," and "Ignorance is Strength" without worrying about the inconsistency of their words.

> In the O.J. Simpson murder trial, the key question was, "Did O.J. Simpson kill Nicole Brown Simpson and Ronald Goldman?" During the proceedings lawyers for the prosecution did not try to exploit the fact that the two victims were white. Defense lawyers, however, emphasized that detective Mark Fuhrman, who found the bloody glove at Simpson's estate, had used the "N" word. After the murder jury acquitted Simpson, the Brown and Goldman families brought a wrongful-death lawsuit and won. In your opinion, did O. J. Simpson commit a hate crime?

> When street mobs riot and shout "No Justice, No Peace" are they being consistent, or are they practicing doublethink?

Treason

In his history of England, former Prime Minister Winston Churchill tells the story of Thomas Wentworth. Wentworth was a central figure in the 1625 to 1640 era of continuous conflict between King Charles I and Parliament. For most of this time Charles governed without Parliament, had his enemies imprisoned in the Tower of London, and fought off the threat of internal armies raised to fight the cause of Parliament. Wentworth, also known as the Earl of Strafford, was a loyal minister to King Charles. So, Charles appointed him Lord Lieutenant of

Ireland. Though loyal to his King, Strafford was a harsh ruler over Ireland. By 1640 Parliament had the upper hand, and Charles I was in trouble. The "Long Parliament," which met from November 3, 1640 to March 16, 1660, impeached Strafford a week after it convened and sent him to the Tower of London. At Strafford's trial the following March, the impeachment was dropped because Parliament could not prove its charges. However, in April 1641, both the House of Commons and the House of Lords passed a bill of attainder charging Strafford with treason.

A "bill of attainder" is a legislative act that declares an individual guilty of a crime. The act also provides a penalty for the crime. In other words, the legislature not only defines a crime but then arbitrarily decides the punishment. Thus Parliament is both judge and jury.

In this case, Strafford was declared guilty of treason and sentenced to die. He was beheaded May 12, and went to his death—according to Churchill—with dignity and fortitude.[8]

What is significant about the beheading of the Earl of Strafford? It demonstrates how easily a legislative body containing a majority who hated Thomas Wentworth to declare him guilty of treason and have him executed. This type of justice was very much on the minds of the Founding Fathers. Many of them had been guilty of treason several years earlier when they fought against British rule. They didn't like the idea of a legislature empowered to condemn people to death by a special law, nor did any of them want to be hanged, drawn and quartered.

Because they were familiar with how Parliament could be as arbitrary as any monarch, the Founding Fathers included in their Constitution Article I, Sections 9 and 10. These forbade both Congress and the states from passing any bill of attainder. Moreover, the Founding Fathers wanted to make it very difficult to condemn anyone of treason. Consequently, they wrote a definition of treason that was very specific and very limited:

> **Treason against the United States, shall consist only in levying war against them, or in adhering to their Enemies, giving them Aid and Comfort. No person shall be convicted of Treason, unless on the Testimony of Two Witnesses to the same overt Act, or on Confession in open Court.**

This definition and other parts of the Constitution have made it virtually impossible to get a treason conviction. Still, there is room for interpretation. What does it mean, for example, to give aid and comfort to the enemies of the United States?

During the Vietnam War, actress Jane Fonda made a controversial trip to North Vietnam. Many American veterans' organizations complained that Fonda's trip was giving aid and comfort to the enemy, but she was never officially charged with treason by the government. ☆ What information would we need before accusing Jane Fonda of treason during the Vietnam War?

In June 1953, Julius and Ethel Rosenberg went to the electric chair for giving atomic bomb secrets to the Soviet Union. The information that convicted the Rosenbergs came from David Greenglas, who had given them secrets while he worked as a machinist at the Manhattan Project in Los Alamos, New Mexico from 1944 to 1945. Since they gave the secrets to Soviet agents at a time when the United States and Soviet Union were wartime allies, the Rosenbergs were convicted for espionage, not treason.

The Rosenbergs were executed because they helped the Soviet Union develop an atomic bomb. When they wrote the treason clause into the Constitution, the threat of atomic war did not hover over the United States like the sword of Damocles.

By giving atomic bomb secrets away, the Rosenbergs helped make the Soviet Union a deadly force and a threat to world peace after World War II. Should we amend the Constitution to make it easier to bring treason charges against Americans who help other nations obtain secret information about

> Cultural literacy search. Use these search engines, and see what you can find out about treason, Rosenbergs, or Sword of Damocles: Alta Vista, Excite, Hotbox, Infoseek, Lycos, Magellan, Open Text, Webcrawler, or Yahoo.

our defense and weapons systems? What about those American corporations which sold weapons to the Saddam Hussein before the Persian Gulf War?

What about protesters who may be giving aid and comfort to the enemy? On January 27, 1987, more than 70 protesters were arrested for demonstrating against a planned nuclear test at the Nevada Test Site. One of those arrested was actor Martin Sheen. Sheen

> Is the current treason clause a dangerous cultural lag in an era of nuclear bombs and highly sophisticated electronic weapons?

was taken to the Beatty jail and booked on charges of threatening to commit a crime. Nye County deputies had arrested Sheen before the demonstration because he had said during an interview on *Good Morning America* that he "intended to return to the test site and commit civil disobedience . . . ."[9]

To protect protesters like Martin Sheen, the first Congress added the First Amendment to the Constitution. It reads: "Congress shall make no law respecting an establishment of religion, or prohibiting the free exercise thereof; or abridging the freedom of speech, or of the press, or the right of the people peaceably to assemble, and to petition the Government for a redress of grievances." ☆ Do these words, in your opinion, provide constitutional protection for those Americans who showed up to protest nuclear explosions at the Nevada Test Site?

> Since TV coverage encourages "copy-cat behavior," is it a good idea to show celebrities like Jane Fonda and Martin Sheen demonstrating against the United States government? Why or why not?

Exclusionary Rule

In this country, justice has meant using power or authority to uphold what is right, just, or lawful. In the case of the Earl of Strafford, Parliament used its power to issue a bill of attainder to declare him guilty of treason. Strafford had been loyal to his king, but in 1641, the House of Commons was ruling England, not King Charles I. Charles met his fate in January 1649, when a Rump Parliament consisting of only 60 members was ruling England. Justice is like that. It is often a matter of who has the power to decide right and wrong, whether it be a tribal witch doctor, chief, king, dictator, parliament, or Charles Bronson carrying a .32 caliber revolver.

The Founding Fathers devised a political system in which the executive, legislative and judicial branches would check and balance power. They thought, however, that the greatest threat to fair play and justice would be the abuse of power by ambitious members of the executive and legislative branches. So they created an independent judiciary to act as a final barrier when either the President or Congress got carried away and tried to oppress the people. In *Federalist 78*, Alexander Hamilton explained how this independent judiciary was designed as a future barrier to oppression:

> **The standard of good behavior for the continuance in office of the Judicial magistracy is certainly one of the most valuable of the modern improvements in the practice of government. In a monarchy it is an excellent barrier to the despotism of the prince; in a republic it is a no less excellent barrier to the encroachments and oppression of the representative body. And it is the best expedient which can be devised in any government to secure a steady, upright, and impartial administration of the laws.**

Have the federal courts secured a steady, upright, and impartial administration of justice? This question haunts most judges today because they have to decide questions of guilt or innocence on the basis of vague words like "probable cause."

In April 1995, four men who dumped two duffel bags containing cocaine worth $4 million into the trunk of a car at 5 a.m. were caught red-handed by New York City cops.

> **"Read between the lines." This advice is often given to students by their teachers. In the past when messages were sent, invisible ink was used to write secret information between the lines. Now the phrase means "look for the hidden meaning." Is there any hidden meaning to Hamilton's argument that giving judges lifetime tenure is a good way to head off tyranny?**

The four men ran away, but were captured later. Under interrogation, the driver confessed and admitted that she was a professional drug courier making her 20th trip. Despite the evidence, Federal Judge Harold Baer ruled that the cops lacked "probable cause" to search the bags and had the four men released after they had served nine months. In his opinion, Judge Baer justified the four men seeking to escape by saying that in a neighborhood where police are known for being "corrupt, abusive and violent" it made sense for the four men to run away.

Since Judge Baer had been appointed in 1994 by Democratic President Bill Clinton, Republicans were outraged by his decision. When the decision to release the men was made it was January 1996 and Bob Dole was gearing up for a run at the presidency. Predictably, he criticized Judge Baer. By April 1, Judge Baer had a change of heart and reversed himself.

Some of the most controversial judicial opinions were made during the turbulent 1960's. Until 1961 state and local police could use a variety of exotic ways to get evidence against suspected criminals. These questionable police tactics ranged from telephone bugs to stomach pumps. Many of these police tactics were possible violations of the Fourth Amendment, which prohibits unreasonable search and seizures. Since

> **Ever been cornered by someone who likes to ask questions, and isn't afraid to appear stupid. Like your average six year old? Or a college professor? Try these on for size: "What is red-handed? Why were the men dumping duffel bags into the trunk of a double-parked red Chevrolet Caprice? Why did the cops need probable cause to arrest these guys?"**

1914 federal courts have not allowed evidence gathered illegally to be used in federal trials. But this restriction, known as the **Exclusionary Rule** was not applied to state and local police until the famous Mapp case.

On May 23, 1957, three Cleveland police officers arrived at the home of Dollree Mapp on a tip that there was a person hiding there who was wanted for questioning in connection with a recent bombing. The police were also investigating a tip that there were lottery tickets hidden in the Mapp home. After they arrived, the three officers knocked on the door and demanded entry. Instead of opening the door, Mapp called her lawyer and was advised not to let the police enter until they produced a search warrant. After a three hour wait, the officers forced their way into Mapp's home. When she demanded to see a search warrant, one of the officer's held up a sheet of paper and said he held a legal warrant. Mapp then apparently grabbed the sheet of paper and plunged it into her bosom. After a struggle, the police recovered the paper, handcuffed Mapp, and conducted a search of her home. During the search, police discovered pornographic books and photographs which violated a state law against possession of lewd and lascivious materials. Mapp was arrested, tried, and convicted. At her trial, no search warrant was produced by the prosecution, nor was it ever found. Mapp appealed, but the Ohio Supreme Court upheld her conviction on the grounds that the evidence had not been obtained through brutal or offensive physical force.

> In a law class you would need to analyze the Mapp case by first writing a brief. This means a concise statement describing the important facts. After stating the facts, a good lawyer gets to the constitutional issue being decided. In *Mapp v. Ohio* (1961) what was the constitutional issue?

But in *Mapp v. Ohio* (1961), the United States Supreme Court reversed the conviction, ruling that hereafter evidence illegally seized by state or local police would be considered in violation of the Fourth and the Fourteenth Amendments. The Mapp decision thus incorporated the exclusionary rule, which means states cannot use illegally seized evidence to prosecute suspects without risking a review by federal courts.

By putting limits on state and local police investigations, the Supreme Court unleashed a storm of criticism. Typically, Hollywood exploited public anger with movies like *Dirty Harry* (1971). Popular actor Clint Eastwood plays Harry Callahan, a San Francisco police detective who gets all the dirty jobs. Eastwood is assigned to catch a sadistic killer named Scorpio, who wears love beads and brutally murders young girls. After a hazardous investigation, Eastwood gets a verbal confession and has the murder weapon. Since he broke a few rules, however, Dirty Harry is forced to let Scorpio go. So Callahan gets mad, throws out the rule book, and becomes a vigilante hunter, not a police detective. Eventually the killer is brought to a bloody and brutal end by the vengeful Callahan. Audiences loved this movie in 1971, and it stills shows on cable TV. The idea of a tough, lonely vigilante cop who deals out on the spot punishment still appeals to an audience tired of crime, lenient judges, and wimpish politicians.

This feeling was exploited by Ronald Reagan in 1980 when he campaigned for the presidency. During his speeches, Reagan told audiences the story of police in Colton, California who searched the homes of two suspected drug users. The police, according to candidate Reagan, eventually found a packet of heroin hidden in the diaper worn by the nine month old daughter of one of the suspects. When the case reached municipal court, it was thrown out by a judge who ruled the baby had not been named in the search warrant, and so her diaper had been illegally searched. Reagan promised, if elected, he would appoint conservative judges who would not let drug dealers use the exclusionary rule to escape justice. Eventually, public opinion and Reagan appointees have led to some easing of the rule. In 1984, for example, the Supreme Court ruled that police could make "good faith" mistakes and not lose their suspects.

The good faith case involved police in Burbank, California who were investigating drug dealers. After an extensive investigation, Burbank police got a local judge to issue a warrant so they could search an automobile belonging to the suspects. The search produced more than five pounds of cocaine, more than 1,110 Quaalude tablets and large amounts of money. As a result of the search, four persons were indicted on drug charges. A federal judge, however, ruled the warrant invalid because it was based in part on information provided by an informant whose reliability and credibility had not been fully established. Later, a federal appeals court in San Francisco affirmed the decision to suppress the evidence because it was obtained in violation of the exclusionary rule. Overturning the appeals court, the Supreme Court allowed the evidence to be used and ruled that Burbank police had acted in good faith and thought the warrant was valid.

The "good faith exemption" is now part of the rules of justice in this nation. President Reagan was happy with the decision. Critics, however, feared that police

> **Should police who act in "good faith" be allowed to make arrests without a valid search warrant?**

would shop for lenient judges willing to sign any request for a search warrant. In his dissent, Justice William J. Brennan, Jr., warned that it was dangerous to weaken the Fourth Amendment because "once lost, such rights are difficult to recover."[10]

In February 1989, undercover District of Columbia police bought $50 worth of "crack" cocaine from Keith McCrory. After field testing the cocaine evidence, the police returned to McCrory's apartment and arrested him. While they were in the apartment, the officers seized more drugs and several guns. Later, the additional evidence was entered into consideration when McCrory was being sentenced. As a result, he was given twenty years and one day in prison. Three years later, the Supreme Court had to decide if the evidence used against McCrory had been seized in violation of the Fourth Amendment. The Court left intact the verdict and, in effect, ruled that police might enter homes without a search warrant and find evidence which can be used later to make the sentences harsher.

In a January 14, 1992 editorial the Las Vegas *Review Journal* used the McCrory case to predict that freedom was being eroded by such decisions. In the opinion of the editorial writer, these expanded police powers could someday be used against people who possess pornographic novels in their homes, belong to radical parties, or participate in peaceful protest marches.

> **What could be the unintended consequences of courts letting police introduce evidence not accounted for in the search warrant, but found in the house incidental to the search for evidence?**

Five years after this editorial, the Supreme Court had to decide if police officers looking for illegal drugs need to knock and announce themselves before breaking down doors. In the war against drugs, American courts have allowed police officers to conduct no-knock raids if announcing themselves before entry would lead to destruction of evidence, a suspect's escape or imminent danger to human life. To prevent drug users or dealers from destroying evidence while the police are announcing their presence, six states in 1997 allowed police to search the suspect's home without knocking, if they have a search warrant. The practice was challenged by Steiney Richards, who was arrested after police in Milwaukee burst into his hotel room on New Year's Eve in 1991. The Milwaukee police had a search warrant, but did not knock before entering. The officers found the cocaine, and Richards was convicted and sentenced to 13 years in prison. After the Wisconsin Supreme Court upheld the conviction, Richards appealed to the United States Supreme Court. On April 28, 1997 the U.S. Supreme Court in a unanimous decision ruled that police officers with search warrants sometimes may not barge unannounced into homes to search for narcotics. Writing for the majority, Justice John Paul Stevens said giving a blanket exception to police would violate the Fourth and Fourteenth Amendment's protection against unreasonable searches and seizures.

In the 1925 case of *Gitlow v. New York* the Supreme Court began the process of nationalizing the Bill of Rights to limit state power. Over a span of 47 years, the Court has said that state governments cannot impair the citizens' civil liberties without risking a review by the highest court in the land. These civil liberties include speech, press, religion, assembly, counsel, public trial, searches and seizure, association, exclusionary rule, cruel and unusual punishment, self-incrimination, confront witnesses, privacy, impartial jury, speedy trial, and double jeopardy. The effect of this well-intentioned nationalization of civil liberties has been to make the U.S. Supreme Court the final say on the meaning of freedom. When they wrote the Bill of Rights the members of Congress added the Tenth Amendment which says, "The powers not delegated to the United States by the Constitution, nor prohibited by it to the States, are reserved to the States respectively, or to the people." For the sake of argument, let's assume that Las Vegas is in the midst of a brutal crime wave because gangs selling drugs are at war. Would the state legislature be justified in empowering police without search warrants to conduct fishing expeditions through bad neighborhoods looking for drugs, weapons and gang members?

Let us emphasize: The **Exclusionary Rule** only applies when federal, state or local police illegally seize evidence to use against suspects. Workers not protected by union contract or other company rules can expect to have their lockers searched, be required to take urine tests, have dogs sniff out any drugs they may have in their lunch pails, expect a modern version of the wiretap when they talk to customers, be watched by video-tapes, and someday have their genetic code inspected for in-born traits like compulsive behavior.

Meanwhile, state and federal police will continue to use whatever legal weapons they have in the war against crime. During the Simpson trial, former Los Angeles detective Mark Fuhrman boasted how he had beaten suspects until they confessed. Despite the exclusionary rule, self-incrimination protection, and the Miranda Warning, police are still able to extract confessions. Bashing suspects is illegal, but police can use several "unfair" tactics to trap their prisoners. These tactics, as described by Los Angeles *Times* reporter Stephanie Simon include:

- Telling lies, forging documents, using deception to get a confession.
- Wrongfully tell suspect his fingerprints were found at the crime scene.
- Tell suspects the police have tracked down witnesses to the crime—even when they haven't.
- Police will show the suspect a phony confession from a conspirator.[11]

Police interrogation is still bound by rules. They cannot, for example, use the slap-them-on-the-face approach shown in TV's "NYPD Blue." But under current interpretations of the Fourth Amendment, you might be pulled over for speeding and end up in jail for drug possession because you had a small amount of marijuana in your car.

Self-Incrimination

The Fifth Amendment provides that no one "shall be compelled in any criminal case to be a witness against himself." This provision of the Bill of Rights is generally used for two purposes. It prevents defendants from being required to testify in a criminal case and it also discourages police from forcing confessions from suspects.

> The Fifth Amendment uses a word that would today be considered sexist. Identify that word, and prove you understand the meaning of politically correct.

The significance of this amendment can be demonstrated by the case of Arthur Culombe. Culombe was an illiterate adult with the mental age of a nine year old. By 1956 he had been in both a mental hospital and a prison. Though married and the father of two children, Culombe in 1957 was a prime suspect in a series of gas station robberies and execution-like killings in the area around Hartford, Connecticut. In 1957 he was taken into custody by New Britain police and interrogated for several days. By the fifth day Culombe had confessed at least three times and had implicated his friend Joseph Taborsky, who also was being interrogated. During the questioning, Culombe was not told he had the right to remain silent, and his request to see a lawyer was denied. When told Culombe had confessed, Taborsky admitted his guilt.

Two months later Culombe and Taborsky were tried for the double murders of a gas station attendant and his customer in New Britain in December 1956. Both were convicted of first-degree murder and sentenced to death. After their appeals were rejected by the state supreme court in February 1960, Taborsky decided not to appeal further and died in the electric chair five months later. But Culombe's lawyer persisted, claiming his client's will had been broken by the prolonged interrogation and the three confessions should not have been admitted as evidence. In July 1961, the Supreme Court agreed and overturned Culombe's conviction and death sentence.[12]

> Since Arthur Culombe had confessed, why didn't the Supreme Court merely ignore the appeal and let him be executed? In this case, the Court weighed the evidence of executing a confessed murderer against the justice of letting arresting officers take advantage of a retarded subject, and decided an injustice was done to Culombe. What do you think? In the case of Arthur Culombe, was justice served?

If you plan to be a legal aide or a lawyer, you will need to buy law books and use the Internet. Currently, the World Wide Web can provide information about law-related issues. REFLAW is a good reference source for law-related issues from the Washburn University of Law Library in Topeka, Kansas. To link up to this source use the following code: http://lawlib.wuacc.edu/washlaw/reflaw/reflaw.html.

The Miranda Warning

The Culombe case was one of a series in which the Supreme Court took the self-incrimination clause of the Fifth Amendment, the right-to-counsel clause of the Sixth Amendment and the due process clause of the Fifth and Fourteenth Amendments and established a comprehensive limit on police interrogation procedures. Today, the **Miranda Warning** has come to symbolize judicial decisions that put limits on the police.

Ernesto Miranda was a Phoenix drifter arrested in 1963 for the kidnaping and rape of a teenage girl. His car matched a description given Phoenix police officers by the girl, but she could not conclusively identify Miranda in a police line up. The officers, however, told Miranda that she had made the identification and began to question him about the rape. After about two hours, Miranda confessed. On the basis of the confession, he was convicted in 1964.

After Miranda's lawyer appealed, the Supreme Court in June 1966 overturned the conviction on grounds that Miranda was not warned of his constitutional rights, so the confession was tainted evidence. In his opinion for the 5 to 4 majority, Chief Justice Earl Warren wrote: "Prior to any questioning, the person must be warned that he has a right to remain silent, that any statement he does make may be used as evidence against him, and that he has a right to the presence of an attorney, either retained or appointed." The majority also ruled that the defendant could voluntarily "waive the effectuation of those rights," but that if he did not want to talk the police could not question him.

Since the majority opinion in *Miranda v. Arizona*, 384 U.S. 436 (1966), police officers have to "Mirandize" suspects by readings these five statements:

① You have the right to remain silent and refuse to answer questions.

② Anything you say may be used against you in a court of law.

③ You have the right to consult an attorney before speaking to the police and to have an attorney during any questioning now and in the future.

④ If you do not have an attorney available, you have the right to remain silent until you have had an opportunity to consult with one.

⑤ Now that I have advised you of your rights, are you willing to answer questions without an attorney present?

Critics say the Miranda warning goes too far in the direction of protecting suspects in custody. Defenders say, however, that the warning has made law enforcement more professional. What do you think?

Since the original ruling in 1966, the Supreme Court has issued other opinions clarifying, refining, and defining appropriate police conduct for questioning suspects. In the late 1970's, for example, the Supreme Court narrowed the Miranda guidelines by ruling that a suspect not yet under arrest can be questioned without being read his rights. In 1981 the Court widened the sweep of Miranda by ruling that murder defendants must be warned about their rights prior to psychiatric testing. Ten years later, the Court held that a coerced confession may be "harmless error" that does not fall under self-incrimination.

Despite the easing of Miranda by the Supreme Court in recent years, many police officers consider the warning a frustrating nuisance. Since 1966, however, police procedures have grown more sophisticated

To research this last "coerced confession" case, you need a legal citation. Here is a clue: The case title is *Arizona v. Fulminate* (1991). Use your resources and obtain the complete citation, which includes volume, source, and page numbers. If you locate the case in its entirety, prepare a brief containing the facts, the constitutional issue, and the rule of law. Good luck.

223

and the Miranda Warning seems a small price to pay for justice. In the minds of the mass public the Miranda Warning remains a symbol of wimpish courts and impotent cops.

Typically, Hollywood has exploited public frustration with the justice system. Sylvester Stallone made the Miranda Warning an object of scorn in his 1986 movie *Cobra*. In that wretched movie, Stallone plays the role of a police detective from the so-called Zombie Squad, which deals with psychotic killers. After catching the sadistic leader of a gang of brutal killers, Stallone douses him with gasoline, lights a match and hisses, "You have the right to remain silent . . ."

What happened to Ernesto Miranda? Because he admitted the 1963 rape to his wife, Miranda was retried and convicted by his wife's testimony. After leaving prison in 1972, Miranda drifted around selling autographed "Miranda Warning" cards for $2. In 1976 he was stabbed to death in a Phoenix skid row bar. The man suspected of killing Miranda was picked up by police officers and read his rights. He chose to remain silent, and was released. Though later evidence proving the suspect had stabbed Miranda was found, he had taken advantage of his right to remain silent and disappeared while the police were searching for more evidence.

Earl Warren presided as Chief Justice when the Miranda Warning was interpreted into the U.S. justice system. Warren always defended the Miranda Warning on the basis of his belief that "hardened underworld types" already knew their right to remain silent, and this same knowledge must be supplied to the "unwary" criminals. ☆ What do you think? Should criminals be warned before the interrogation, or should the justice system be based on the Darwinian premise that only the informed criminals deserve to survive?

> Before the 1960's, the police could have lied to Miranda's killer and got him to confess. The Miranda Warning, however, delayed the investigation and allowed the suspect to leave town. In this case was justice served?

Warren's belief that police procedures should be "fair" provoked a column by Thomas Sowell, a senior fellow at Stanford's Hoover Institute. In April 1992 the Las Vegas *Review Journal* printed Sowell's column. Our criminal justice system, wrote Sowell, has become preoccupied with fairness and created too many loopholes. When applied to criminal justice, the concept of fairness has created a wonderland of endless delays and appeals, with plea bargains being an inevitable consequence of the soaring costs and uncertainties of convicting anybody of anything." In the matter of justice, wrote Sowell, "Guilt and innocence have become almost irrelevant." "Crime is not a sporting contest between rivals who have agreed to meet on a certain field to play under certain rules," concluded Sowell. "It is a threat to those who want no part of it."

> Reminder. To verify the facts in Sowell's column, we need this footnote: Thomas Sowell, "Beware of the Phony 'Fairness' Issue," Las Vegas *Review Journal* (April 19, 1992), p. 2D.

To listen to some Americans these days, you would get the impression that every rule, custom, law or policy had to be "fair." In Chapter Two we learned that rules are never neutral, i.e., someone benefits, others don't. Why would any society have rules to benefit suspected criminals?

A Fair Trial

The O.J. Simpson case exposed the weaknesses in the way justice has evolved. First, there was the search for truth. On June 17, 1994, while police slowly chased driver Al Cowlings and Simpson along several Southern California freeways, TV viewers were hearing a letter read by Simpson's attorney Robert Kardashian. The letter ended with these possibly incriminating words: "Don't feel sorry for me. I've had a great life, great friends. Please think of the real O.J. and not this lost person. Thanks for making my life special. I hope I helped yours. Addressed to his friends, the letter began, "First, everyone understand I have nothing to do with Nicole's murder. I loved her, always have and always will. If we had a problem, it's because I loved her so much." To some, the O.J. "Suicide Letter" sounded like the last words of a man who had gone temporarily crazy and committed a heinous act. To others, O.J.'s note was evidence that he was innocent, but under a terrible burden. In this search for truth, Los Angeles police found DNA, a glove, bloody footprints, and hair fibers. So they brought charges and went to trial.

During the murder trial, both sides used words carefully selected to manipulate the jury. The prosecution portrayed the accused as an abusive husband, who killed his estranged wife in a rage and was driven by the single impulse, "If I can't have her, nobody will." On the other side, the defense lawyers hammered home the theme that Los Angeles police were either incompetent or part of a racist scheme to frame a famous African American sports hero. Using Martin Luther King Jr.'s words, "Injustice anywhere is a threat to justice everywhere," the defense successfully portrayed Simpson as a martyr to the cause of racial justice.

After 16 months on TV, the Simpson murder trial ended in October 1995, when all 12 jurors voted to acquit him of first degree murder charges.

The Simpson spectacle cast doubt on the use of TV cameras to demonstrate American justice at work. In the words of *Time* reporter Jill Smolowe, there is a growing backlash to the use of TV in the courtroom, and it owes "little to concerns about the First Amendment's guarantee of a free press vs. the Sixth Amendment's promise of a fair trial . . ." Instead, the legal community is upset about the fallout from the Simpson trial. According to Smolowe, this fallout includes media stalking of witnesses, the glut of pop books, the glamorization of commentators, and the impact of TV on the lawyers. Those observers inside the courtroom, wrote Smolowe, observed how "lawyers have learned to turn their back to the camera when exchanging jokes and smirks." Home viewers noticed how prosecutor Marcia Clark had a "Di-like make over, with hair that's gone from shaggy mane to Madison Avenue sleek and a once frumpy wardrobe that now rivals Grace Van Owen's on *L.A. Law*."[13]

How much did justice suffer in the Simpson case? Were important facts, like a possible suicide note, ignored? Were the jurors baffled by the big words used to describe the DNA evidence? Did Marcia Clark's televised fashion show distract the

> **What do you think? Can American justice survive smirking lawyers and female prosecutors whose clothes make the headlines?**

jurors? Did O.J. Simpson buy his freedom by spending about $6 million on consultants and lawyers? How many defendants can afford a dream team comprised of skilled lawyers like Robert Blasier, Barry Sheck, Johnnie Cochran Jr., and Robert Shapiro? Is justice now a matter of money?

In *Dead Man Walking*, Sean Penn's character is on death row because he could not afford a good lawyer. The older man who helped murder the two teenagers received a life sentence because he could. Is this justice?

Nearly two years after the Simpson trial, prosecutor Christopher Darden—a black man—told Barbara Walters on ABC's "20/20" that he knew the verdict would be "not guilty" when he saw a mostly black jury. "From the very moment I saw that jury, I didn't believe we had a snowball's chance in hell. I saw anger in that jury . . . I sensed it's payback."

Every TV viewer knows what happens at criminal trials. The prosecuting attorney and defense lawyer stage an exciting debate, complete with eyewitnesses, psychologists, evidence, and legal trickery. As the twelve jurors watch and listen with solemn faces, the defense lawyer unleashes a brilliant strategy and saves the beautiful woman who is on trial. The trial audience breaks into a loud cheer, and tears of joy are shed. Meanwhile, the TV viewers are turning their remotes from old Perry Mason reruns hoping to find an old "Law and Order" episode, and a more realistic view of justice in America.

The exciting adversarial approach is based on the assumption that by following certain procedures we assure justice. Trial procedures are specified in the Sixth Amendment, which requires that trials are public before an impartial jury with each side entitled to competent counsel and the right to confront and challenge witnesses.

> The Supreme Court ruled in 1932 that states had to provide adequate counsel or be in violation of the Sixth and Fourteenth Amendment. This case, which had racial overtones, is one of the most famous in American history. Jump on your Internet and see if you can locate the facts in *Powell v. Alabama*, 287 U.S. 45 (1932).

Our ancestors had more primitive notions of adversarial justice. They settled their lawsuits through **Trial by Ordeal**. Persons of high rank, for example, suffered the ordeal of fire. The accused had to carry a red-hot iron or walk barefoot and blindfolded over red-hot plough shares. If the accused showed no wound after three days, he was declared innocent. To prove their innocence, witches were bound and tossed into a river or lake. If the accused floated, she was declared guilty and either left to drown or hauled out and executed properly. Witches who sank were declared innocent and hauled out of the water, usually. A third ordeal was battle. The accused was obliged to fight his accuser. By the Middle Ages, Lords were having serfs fight for them, while women and priests were allowed to have hired warriors known as their champions.

> When a witness makes a solemn oath to tell the court his truth, he is giving his "testimony." The word "testify" is a survival from ancient times when a man made a solemn oath by placing one hand over his testicles, thus signifying he would become impotent if he lied. *Ms. Magazine* once published a letter protesting the use of the word "testimony" when referring to a woman's statement. What, in your opinion, would be a politically correct female version of giving testimony?

Lawyers are the modern equivalent of the champions who fought for the nobles during the Middle Ages. The need for lawyers, however, goes back to ancient Greece where private citizens first argued their own cases, but discovered by experience that juries could be swayed by eloquence. Eventually, a class known as the rhetorical specialists hired their speaking talents to defendants who didn't have the ability to speak for themselves. Today, these rhetorical specialists are hired because they know the law and its mysterious language. They also know how to use the techniques of manipulation to sway juries. Going to trial today is an ordeal. Instead of fire, water or combat, however, the participants in modern justice go through the ordeal of words.

Words are crucial in criminal trials. Chicago lawyer Lori B. Andrews says the modern trial "is a labyrinth of language, with the words of the judge, lawyers and witnesses creating numerous obstacles that prevent juries from making accurate decisions." She notes that in rape cases prosecutors use words that suggest force and aggression, whereas defense lawyers use words that suggest romance and consent by the victim. According to Andrews, the situation is complicated by the fact that jurors are not allowed to ask for clarification of words or for more precise definitions. They can only sit and listen while the lawyers talk.[14]

To assure a fair trial, lawyers question prospective jurors and weed out those who might be prejudiced. In the past, lawyers used a common sense, rule of thumb approach to jury selection. The great Clarence Darrow, for example, always preferred older men as jurors because they were more charitable and kindly disposed than younger men. Today, however, instinct and common sense have been replaced by surveys, computers and the shadow jury. Lawyers representing wealthy clients can hire behavioral scientists to do a demographic survey of the areas from which the jury is drawn. Later, these experts pick a shadow jury which is supposed to contain people with characteristics and attitudes similar to the actual members of the jury. The shadow jury is then planted in the courtroom to hear witnesses and testimony. Later the same day, the lawyers will ask members of the shadow jury for their reactions to what was said. Based on the shadow jury's feedback, the lawyers will plan their strategy.

Eskimos used to butt heads and the winner was declared innocent. Modern justice is meted out by juries confused by legal language manipulated by lawyers who hire psychologists to create shadow juries.

> **Was O.J. Simpson acquitted because the jury wanted to send a message against racism and police misconduct?**

These words and ploys may help win cases, but do they ensure impartial justice? In the O.J. Simpson murder trial the prosecution lawyers saw eight women on the jury and decided to portray Simpson as an abusive male who finally killed his spouse to keep her from leaving him. They put words in Simpson's mind like, "If I can't have her, nobody will." On the other side, defense lawyers portrayed the Los Angeles police as white racists who were trying to deny a black man of his rights, thus turning Simpson into a martyr.

> **Should lawyers be prohibited from using mass psychology, manipulation techniques, and moral-value language during a trial? Why or why not?**

Victim's Rights

In the 1988 movie *The Accused*, Jodie Foster plays the role of a woman gang raped in a bar. The movie shows the woman, Sarah, enter the bar wearing a low-cut T shirt. After downing a few drinks and smoking a joint, Sarah does a sensual dance. She is subsequently spread-eagled on a Slam Dunk pinball machine and assaulted by three men. While Sarah is being raped, other men in the bar watch and cheer. As portrayed by Foster, Sarah is vulgar, sexy and drives a car with SXY SADI license plates. The movie, however, makes the point that no woman should be raped, whether she is seductively dressed or not. Conventional wisdom holds that no woman in her right mind wears a low-cut T shirt and flirts with men in a seedy bar. Many Americans, as a result, feel some rape victims are at least partially responsible for what happens.

In the movie, the audience is expected to sympathize with Sexy Sarah. Many Americans, however, have difficulty deciding whether the victim is the person raped or the people who go to jail for committing a rape.

In a nutshell, we're mixed up on the matter of defining victimhood. Jonathan Kaplan, who directed *The Accused* said there is a "blame the victim" mentality in America. "We blame the poor for poverty. We blame the homeless for being in the streets."[15] But when a crime is committed by young men who live in poverty, we want to blame the system not the culprits.

Blaming the victim is as American as apple pie and Chevrolet. We like winners who get on top and stay there. But we also feel sorry for unfortunate people who are waiting on death row to be executed for a heinous crime.

> **Unless random violence is controlled better, we may someday be seeing executions on TV as a deterrent. Would this be a good idea?**

When Jeffrey Dahmer was tried for killing and eating young men, forty seats were reserved in the Milwaukee courtroom for members of the families of Dahmer's victims. This practice goes back to ancient Greece where killers were publicly executed so the victims' family could watch and go home satisfied that justice was done.

Some lawbreakers become martyrs. Take the case of Paula R. Cooper. In 1985 Cooper and her three friends killed a woman during a robbery in Indiana. She was sentenced to the electric chair, even though she was only 15 at the time. While Cooper appealed her death penalty, Roman Catholics and European leftist groups adopted her as the symbol of their campaign against the death penalty. In 1987 Pope John Paul II wrote Indiana's Governor Robert D. Orr to ask for clemency for Cooper. The Italian organization "Thou Shalt Not Kill" presented a clemency petition with one million signatures to the United Nations. All the publicity helped. In July 1989, the Indiana state supreme court ruled that Cooper could not be executed but instead should serve a 60-year prison sentence. According to the Associated Press, Cooper "jumped up and down" with joy when she heard how the Indiana court had ruled.[16]

While the killer was jumping for joy, the family of the victim, 78-year-old Bible teacher Ruth E. Pelke stabbed 33 times during the robbery, were wondering when they would get "justice."

In the current scenario, victims are women who get raped and young girls who stab old ladies. Why celebrate clemency given to a young girl who is capable of driving a knife into a harmless old woman? By some twisted logic, the rationalizers in our society have managed to make martyrs of people who kill for money or pleasure.

After a gang of black New York teenagers out for a night of "wilding" brutally assaulted and raped a 28-year-old jogger, the rationalizers tried to blame the attack on society, parents, poverty, racism and public schools. Most ignored the savage norms of youth gangs. After a Harvard psychiatrist blamed the attack on "free-floating anger and rage," columnist Charles Krauthammer lashed out scornfully: "What distinguishes these boys is not their anger, but their lack of any moral faculty. Acts of rage are usually followed by reflection and shame."[17] By all accounts, the New York teenagers showed no remorse or shame. They thought the assault and rape was fun, a good way to relieve boredom.

Many Americans are angry enough to try vigilante justice. They want justice, whether it comes from a jury or a .38. On the afternoon of December 22, 1984, shy, introverted electronics engineer Bernard Goetz was approached on the New York subway by four black teenagers who asked him for $5. Goetz then pulled out a silver .38 revolver and said, "I have $5 for each of you" and fired four times into the bodies of the teenagers. Before leaving the scene, Goetz put a second bullet into 19-year-old Darrel Cabey after saying, "You don't look too bad, here's another." The 38-year-old Goetz became a media celebrity and was portrayed as a vigilante, similar to the Paul Kersey character played in *Death Wish* by Charles Bronson. Between February 28 and March 1, 1985, the Gallup Organization polled Americans and discovered that 57% of their respondents approved of what Goetz had done.

Do we need a **Victim's Bill of Rights**? Should the right to bail be revoked so that criminals would be kept in jail while awaiting their trial? Should illegally seized evidence be admissible in court? Should prosecutors be able to inform juries about the prior criminal records of defendants? Should felons have to pay restitution to their victims? Should "victim-impact" statements be included in evidence weighed during the sentencing phase of criminal trials? Should the most heinous criminals be publicly hanged, drawn and quartered over TV as a deterrent to others? Should the insanity plea be disallowed except when the criminal is obviously crazy?

A Victim's Bill of Rights would require changing the Constitution to allow excessive bail, illegal evidence, and cruel punishment. Many Americans are ready to go that far. They agree with one cynic who called the Las Vegas KDWN radio show "Talk of the West" on September 19, 1986 and said, "The Constitution gives criminals the right to rob and kill us . . . it guarantees their pursuit of happiness."

> In 1991 Arkansas Governor Bill Clinton allegedly propositioned Paula Jones and exposed his genital area to her in a Little Rock hotel suite. In 1994 Jones came forward about the alleged incident. When Clinton called Jones a liar, she decided to sue him for sexual harassment and defamation of character. By now, the Jones v. Clinton case should be settled. If so, was justice served?

Final Solutions

Wouldn't it be easier to prevent crime at its source rather than wait for a murder and then mete out punishment then? Aldous Huxley had one answer to that question. In his fictional *Brave New World* (1932), he described a perfectly safe society where sleep teaching, casual sex, and Soma kept the people pacified and peaceful. In Huxley's world, justice meant being processed in a test tube environment to be perfectly happy, sexually gratified, and productive at work. Moreover, the citizens had no elections, no politics, no responsibilities outside work, and no guilt.

In Huxley's world citizens learn about sex when they are very young (by playing "find the zipper") and grow up playing electronic games and watching "Feelie" erotic movies. Would you give up your civil liberties and right to vote to live in a brave new world? Why? Why not?

George Orwell began with a different premise in his novel *1984*, published in 1948. Through torture and brainwashing, the citizens of Orwell's fictional country Oceania are simply incapable of having rebellious thoughts. The end result of the fear and word manipulation is "Crimestop." This form of collective stupidity makes it impossible for Oceania's people to even consider breaking the rules. Moreover, they are convinced by the propaganda that Big Brother is omnipotent and will catch anyone who breaks the law.

In his novel *Clockwork Orange* (1962), Anthony Burgess suggested that society now has the technology to make would-be young criminals virtually "sick" of violence. The central character of the novel is Alex, leader of a London gang which terrorizes older people. Eventually, Alex goes too far and murders a woman. In prison, he volunteers to participate in a special government experiment to cure criminals. The cure requires that Alex be strapped in front of a huge screen and shown scenes of bloody fights, brutal rapes and Nazi atrocities. Because he has been injected with a special experimental drug, Alex is seized with a terrible feeling of paralysis and death. The "cure" proceeds until Alex is programmed through aversion to associate feelings of death whenever he feels the need to be violent. When the experiment is over, Alex is released from prison apparently cured of his criminal tendencies.

Now, however, Alex is completely helpless to defend himself against his former victims and the members of his gang, who are now police officers. In Stanley Kubrick's 1971 movie version of "Clockwork Orange," a clergyman objects to Alex's cure because it has deprived him of free will. Instead of free will and a conscience, Alex seems to be merely an aversion avoiding robot with no sense of honor, shame or guilt.

In the Kubrick movie, Alex describes his feelings as being like drowning or dying. This feeling was also used over two thousand years ago to punish heretics who questioned the authority of the Catholic Church. A favorite tactic used by Inquisition courts was to shove rags and water down victims' throats to create the sensation of drowning.

Happily, we moderns don't have to resort to the water torture, or having criminals hanged, drawn and quartered. We have technology!

○ We have drugs that alter brain chemistry and could be used to reduce crime. Instead of Soma, we can provide drugs like Prozac and Xanax to help people deal with problems that could lead to violence. We'll have to be careful, however. In 1991, a modern languages instructor at the University of San Francisco stopped taking her Prozac, went berserk, and tried to bite her 87-year-old mother to death. [Alan Dershowitz describes this incident under his description of the "Prozac Defense" in *The Abuse Excuse.*]

○ Richard Allen Davis shocked the nation by kidnaping and murdering Polly Klaas. When Davis walked into the Santa Clara County Superior Court during his trial he wore a belt that could shoot 50,000 volts of electricity through his body, causing Davis to lose all muscle control for 30 seconds.

○ The "Electronic Tether" is a ankle bracelet now attached to about 80,000 convicts who get to serve their jail time at home. About the size of a package of cigarettes, the bracelet gives out an electronic signal to a monitoring station if the wearer strays outside her limits.

✪ Compulsory genetic screening will show those citizens whose brain chemistry will lead to criminal behavior in the future. Scientists are convinced that criminal behavior is linked to genetic factors. In the future, we can identify through DNA testing people carrying dangerous genes and require them to undergo sterilization.

✪ Lawyers and judges now have access to Internet sources. Hopefully, computers will finally start to eliminate paperwork and help us to achieve the goal of quick trials and impartial justice.

Although technology may someday solve our crime problems, certain primitive instincts go beyond any current technology. On April 25, 1997, the Las Vegas *Review Journal* carried on page 8A a news story about a St. Louis man recently murdered who had sex with about 100 women and infected 30 with the AIDS virus. According to the story, Darnel McGee, 28, was able to obtain sex from young women by making them feel important with flattery and gifts. McGee practiced unsafe sex despite being diagnosed in 1992 as HIV infected. What kind of technology do we need to keep HIV infected men off the streets? How do we convince men and women not to have sex with strangers, no matter how charming they appear to be? If we can't develop a vaccine for AIDS, why not a drug that lowers the biological sex drives of unmarried young people and television shows that stress the virtues of chastity?

On July 18, 2001 the Las Vegas *Review Journal* carried an opinion column by Kathleen Parker under the headline "Court Threatens Right to Bear Children." The article deals with the fact that the Wisconsin Supreme Court by a 4 to 3 vote prohibited a "deadbeat dad" from having any more children while he's on probation. Parker indicated her opinion with the following rhetorical questions: "How do you stop a man from having sex?" "Do we really want the state deciding who can have children and under what conditions?" What do you think?

On the same day as the Parker article, the *RJ* carried a story entitled "Disproportionate Share of Blacks Imprisoned." This article pointed out that in Nevada, 27% of the jail and prison population is black, while the state's population is 6.5% black. The 2000 census showed that more than 12% of the country's 281 million were black, but 29% of arrests were black. Is this a case of racial profiling? Or a case of the fact that minorities tend to have higher rates of poverty and to live in cities?

What if you read also that deadbeat dad David Oakley has nine children by four women and owes $25,000 in child support? Would this change your opinion?

In her book *The Chrysanthemum and the Sword* (1946) anthropologist Ruth Benedict divided cultures into two main types, the shame culture and the guilt culture. In studying Japanese character as a Japan specialist for the Bureau of Overseas Intelligence (1943-46), Benedict thought it would be a mistake to execute the Japanese Emperor after World War II ended. Most Americans, however, told a Gallup Poll in 1945 that justice required the Emperor Hirohito be tried for war crimes for the Pearl Harbor attack.

So what do we mean when we talk about justice? A blind lady holding scales? Witches being drowned? Checks and balances of power? Popular vote election of the President? Bombing the Emperor's Palace? War crimes? Denying children and marriage to a deadbeat dad?

Notes

1. "No Nice Way to Die," Las Vegas *Sun* (April 23, 1992), p. 1B.

2. Carrie Rickey, "Sarandon, Penn Give Strong Performances in 'Dead Man Walking'," Las Vegas *Review Journal* (January 19, 1996), p. 7K.

3. Las Vegas *Review Journal* (December 3, 1985).

4. Eric W. Rose and Steven S. Lucas, "Seeing Past Hysteria, Media Hype," Las Vegas *Review Journal* (May 3, 1992), p. 1C.

5. "Inmates Sue Over Pink Uniforms," Las Vegas *Review Journal* (September 21, 1988), p. 3A.

6. "Three Strikes Are Out," *Time* (July 1, 1996), p. 54.

7. Samuel Francis, "Thought Crimes," Las Vegas *Review Journal* (February 9, 1992), p. 1D.

8. Winston S. Churchill, *The New World* (New York: Dodd, Mead & Company, 1956), pp. 216-222.

9. Las Vegas *Review Journal* (January 28, 1987).

10. *United States v. Leon*, 82 L.ED.2d 677 (1984).

11. Stephanie Simon, "Police Can Use Deception to Gain Confessions During Interrogations," Las Vegas *Review Journal* (September 22, 1995), p. 12B.

12. *Columbe v. Connecticut*, 367 U.S. 568 (1961).

13. Jill Smolowe, "TV Cameras on Trial," *Time* (July 24, 1995), p. 38.

14. Lori B. Andrews, "Exhibit A: Language," *Psychology Today* (February 1984), pp. 38-39.

15. "'Bad' Women and Brutal Men," *Time* (November 21, 1988), p. 127.

16. "Indiana Rules Teen Can't Be Executed," Las Vegas *Review Journal* (July 14, 1989), p. 5A.

17. Charles Krauthammer, "Crime and Responsibility," *Time* (May 8, 1989), p. 104.

Chapter 9

Nevada Politics

Rebel fans used to watch UNLV basketball at the 7,200 seat Convention Center. Then they built the Thomas & Mack Center, which needs over 18,000 spectators for a full-house. Now if current Mayor Oscar Goodman and others are successful, Las Vegas will have a huge multi-sport complex on land west of the downtown area. The complex will probably end up being the home base for major league baseball and the National Basketball Association. Now all we need are mascots and team labels that won't offend anyone. So we'll keep the name 51's for the baseball franchise. As for pro basketball, a good start may be the "Tarks."

Does Nevada have enough population to support professional big league teams? The 2000 census says the state population is currently nearing the two million mark. This alone is not enough people to fill a major league ball park so the state's power brokers are looking at building a high speed train that will transport thousands of Californians here in 90 minutes or less. Skeptics think Las Vegas is a bad bet for big time sports because the "sporting" population in southern Nevada would rather watch televised games and make bets. What do you think?

In 1990 Nevada's population was 1,201,833. After the 2,000 census this number leaped to 1,998,257 and the state legislature scrambled to create a third congressional district. The population

> **How do we know that Nevada's Electoral College vote is now five instead of four?**

spurt meant that Nevada now will have three seats in the House of Representatives. Combined with the usual two Senators, Nevada's count in the Electoral College will be five in the next presidential election. This would be cause for great jubilation except that California's electoral vote will be 54 and Nevada's puny influence on presidential candidates will stay puny. Major league sports, however, will give Las Vegas an aura of power and in the long run power and gambling are profitable symbols for a male fantasy world like Las Vegas.

To understand Las Vegas and Nevada, go to the Riviera and watch the Crazy Girls bounce their butts. Or spend some time with Senator Harry Reid (D-Nev.) Senator Reid is a cautious man and he looks faintly like movie mogul Woody Allen. In the Senate, however, Reid holds jobs that make him a powerful figure in state and national politics. Currently, he is the Senate Whip which is the second most powerful job in the Senate. Senator Reid also serves on important committees, namely Aging; Appropriations; Environment and Public Works; Indian Affairs; and Select Ethics.

Nevada's other national figures, Rep. Shelley Berkley (D-Nev.), Rep. Jim Gibbons (R-Nev.), and Senator John Ensign (R-Nev.) all have their own spheres of influence that they can call upon whenever Congress gets crazy and decides to ban betting on college sports, or plant 77,000 tons of nuclear waste 95 miles outside Las Vegas.

How come California gets more votes in the Electoral College than Nevada and the other 48 states? Not sure? What question do you need to ask, or research?

In the past 10 years, Las Vegas has emerged as the world's foremost tourist destination and the country's fastest growing state population. As a consequence, our city streets are jammed with road rage clients who proudly display their middle fingers while driving to pick up their physician approved marijuana.

Las Vegas is now able to house the very largest conventions in the United States. This could someday include the Republican or Democratic national conventions. Huge conventions attracting more than one hundred thousand visitors already coming to Las Vegas are Comdex, Electronic, and Homebuilders. Each December, Las Vegas hosts the National Rodeo Finals. Now there is a push to let casinos feature the type of nudity you'll find at places like "Little Darlins." If you can, imagine 500,000 tourists on Las Vegas roads exploding with road rage after buying watered champagne to impress a little darling; then losing at the craps table.

To keep pace with the prodigious growth, the Las Vegas metropolitan area needs schools. Building these schools has necessitated multi-million dollar bond issues and the hiring of about 500 new teachers each year. Currently built or under planning are over 100 schools for grades K-12, making Clark County the tenth largest school district in the nation. Growth also has brought forth concern about future water resources for Nevada's desert. However, the Southern Nevada Water Authority presently has an excess of some 50,000 acre-feet annually from its Colorado River allocation of 300,000 acre feet. While this excess in past years has been pilfered by over-populated California, Secretary of the Interior Bruce Babbitt reported early in 1997 that California has agreed to "carefully conserve its usage of the Colorado River" and live within its allocation.

Other than California, six states use Colorado River water. These states are Colorado, Wyoming, Utah, New Mexico, Arizona and Nevada. Should California fail to conserve its usage, Babbitt added, "the six other states using Colorado River water may file a lawsuit asking the federal government to take jurisdiction of the river, and oversee that each state receives its fair share." The six other states have 12 U.S. Senators to California's two. So when push comes to shove, it is likely that Congress might act before any lawsuits are settled.

Nevada has entered into an agreement with Arizona for storage of fifty thousand acre-feet of water annually. Arizona has soil geologically suited to carry out this task. The terrain of Nevada, however, is not suitable for long term storage of water. So Nevada will pay a storage fee to Arizona, and withdraw such stored water as needed.

> **Geological literacy quiz: Why is Arizona's soil better for water storage than Nevada's?**

Western states, unlike most of the other states, have an unusual relationship with the federal government. The national government owns much of the land in such states as Nevada, California, and throughout the West. About 83% of Nevada is owned by this benevolent Big Brother, and managed by the Federal Bureau of Land Management. Some of this federally-owned land is leased by ranchers in the cattle-raising or sheep-raising businesses for grazing at relatively low fees. This benefits people in those industries. Federal land, however, cannot be taxed by the state so the burden of paying for schools falls heavily on home owners.

234

In that property taxes carry most of the costs for education, there is constant agitation applied by taxpayers to have the federal government give this land to the state. There have been some land trades between the federal and local governments in recent years, with some of the traded fed lands being sold to private entrepreneurs for development. This brings such property onto county tax rolls.

Nevada, as the most arid of the fifty states, is also the most mountainous. On the other hand, it is blessed with two of the largest recreational lakes in the Western United States. Lake Tahoe in the Sierra Nevada Mountains is one of the most picturesque Alpine lakes in the world. Its circumference is about one hundred miles, surrounded by forested mountains. Boating in summer, skiing in winter, makes the area attractive to tourists throughout the year. Lake Mead receives the Colorado River. Between Bunkerville and Boulder City it is a national recreation area of some 500 miles. Visitors pour forth to boat and fish during spring, summer and autumn.

Politics, skillfully applied, has turned a harsh desert into a mecca for pleasure seekers. That is the story of Nevada, least diversified of the American states in terms of its natural resources. Many people contend that it has but one industry, tourism based upon gambling, which has as its lure the attraction of sex wrapped in sparkling theatrical extravaganzas. Food, lodging and wine add to the entertainment as commodities sold to happy tourists.

> **Would Nevada's tourist and recreational comfort be disturbed greatly if the Department of Energy built a Yucca Mountain nuclear repository able to store 77,000 metric tons of high level nuclear waste for 10,000 years?**

Nevada's gambling culture, its primitive view of women and sex, has made Las Vegas the "New All-American City," according a *Time* magazine cover January 10, 1994. The cover story argues that despite competition from other cities, Las Vegas "remains the epicenter of the American id, still desperate to overpay schmaltzy superstars like Barbra Streisand, still focused on the darker stirrings of chance and liquor and sex."

Despite gambling, booze, and babes, Nevada's political system is fairly traditional. To understand our state government we need always to remember that most people in Nevada earn their living through gambling, liquor, sex, and entertainment.

> **What does *Time* mean by the words "epicenter of the American id?"**

> **In 1962 former President Harry Truman opposed a proposal to legalize gambling in Idaho, and during a speech called Nevada "the one black spot in the United States government." Many of Truman's fellow politicians felt the same way. Today, however, Nevada is celebrated for its good wages, and high employment. Has public opinion toward gambling changed since 1962?**

Politics Defined

Political scientist Harold Lasswell defined politics as people interacting to determine who gets what, when and how. By this definition, politics is the struggle for power to determine how goods and services will be allocated. If the word "politics" can be exchanged for the governing process, it is obvious that politics pervades all aspects of society. Those who govern us have the power to tax and to use legitimate force, such as the military and the police. Politics, however, also involves the use of "non-force," such as persuasion through diplomacy and more subtle means. In *The Prince* (1517) Machiavelli explained all the devious ways to get and keep power. When an ambitious woman wears perfume and smiles at passing men is she being friendly, or Machiavellian? Is perfume a form of power? It certainly is not force, yet it has the power to turn a man's head. Power is often defined as getting people to do what you want. If a woman wearing perfume, or scanty clothing, gets men to turn and look at her, is that power? Government is part power and part perfume. It gets our attention by using the stick and carrot approach.

> A perfumed woman gets a man to turn his head, and perhaps make a fool of himself. Would the same spell work in reverse, i.e., a man wears perfume to get a woman to notice?

Government exists for two reasons. The first is to provide services for people living together who cannot provide their own national defense, police and fire protection, unemployment insurance, or old age benefits. Government also regulates the various elements of society to keep people with different interests from tearing one another apart. This regulation enables people to live together more or less peacefully rather than being in a constant state of turmoil and civil war.

It can be seen, then, that politics must exist in some kind of place. Politics are different in Nevada than in such states as California, Arizona, Utah, New York, Hawaii, or anywhere else. That politics are different in Nevada can be seen through our economy. Gaming and its related commercial enterprises are the results of people using politics creatively for their advantage. Such enterprises came about through a need of finding means by which to survive.

Physical Characteristics

> Cultural literacy quiz: This English philosopher wrote in 1651 that without strong government, life would be "nasty, brutish and short."

To understand Nevada politics, we need to know its physical characteristics. First of all, we know it to be the most arid of the 50 states. This is largely due to its location on the leeward side of the Sierra Nevada Mountains. With prevailing winds blowing in from the west and southwest, much of the moisture is removed from the clouds before they reach Nevada. This leads to desert conditions where rainfall varies from a mere three inches to twelve inches a year. Most of Nevada is a plateau ranging between four thousand and six thousand feet elevation, except for the southernmost part of the state. There are mountain peaks jutting out of the plateau. The highest ones are Boundary Peak of the White Mountains in Esmeralda County, 13,145 feet high, and Wheeler Peak of the Snake Range in White Pine County, rising to 13,063 feet. Almost all of the state is above two thousand feet. The lowest elevation is 470 feet, where the Colorado River leaves Nevada just south of Laughlin.

With the exception of its northeast and southeast corners, Nevada lies entirely within the Great Basin. The Sierra Nevada Range forms the western edge of the Great Basin, which its lone national park is named after. The Great Basin is a tableland lying between four thousand and five thousand feet elevation, except for its lofty spur, the Washoe Mountains.

Geography and natural resources explain how Nevadans earn their living. In the past, Nevada was merely a stopping-off place for people traveling to California. The discovery of gold in California, however, made Nevada the scene of boom towns. Later, silver was mined and Nevada became the "silver state." Predictably, Nevada was dominated by mining companies.

In contrast to mining and farming revenues, income from gaming soared after Bugsy Siegel opened his famous Flamingo hotel on property later known as "the strip." More hotel-casinos followed. So did the mob. In 1966, however, Las Vegas began the

> **Conventional wisdom holds that Las Vegas was much safer when the "mob" ran the city. Is that true?**

transition to a "legitimate" resort city when billionaire Howard Hughes arrived. He and his entourage, which included his wife actress Jean Peters, rented rooms in the Desert Inn Hotel. Because the group did not gamble, they were asked to leave by Christmas to make room for gamblers during the busy week between Christmas and New Year's. Hughes instead bought the Desert Inn for $13 million.

Loaded with fresh money from the sale of Trans-World Airlines, Howard Hughes began buying up other hotel-casinos. He bought the Sands Hotel, the Castaways, the Frontier, and the Silver Slipper. Hughes tried to buy the Stardust, but this was denied him by state regulators, who felt that such an acquisition would place too much of the gaming industry under the control of one man. He next bought the Landmark, which ended his string of gaming property purchases.

Billionaire Kirk Kerkorian jumped on the buyers' bandwagon with Hughes. He purchased the Flamingo, and built the Las Vegas International Hotel which then became one of the largest hotel properties in the world. Kerkorian sold the Flamingo and International to the Hilton Hotel Corporation, and then built the MGM Grand.

Enterprising men like Hughes, Kerkorian and Steve Wynn have made Las Vegas a popular place for tourists, and provided jobs for all of us. To spark interest in men like Hughes, Kerkorian and Wynn, American historians like to ask rhetorically, "Robber Barons or Industrial Statesmen?" ☆ What should we call them?

Big Brother

On Monday morning, June 29, 1992, at 3:14 a.m. a moderate 5.6 earthquake rumbled through the southern Nevada desert. The quake did little property damage, and nobody was hurt. But it was a psychological blow to the Department of Energy.

The earthquake shook up DOE because it was centered 20 miles southeast of Yucca Mountain. This 4,800 foot flattop ridge located about 95 miles northwest of Las Vegas was the DOE's prime choice to be a 10,000 year repository for 77,000 metric tons of high level nuclear waste from the nation's 95 nuclear reactors.

Yucca Mountain was chosen for three reasons. First, it offers an extremely dry location. According to DOE sources, most of the six-inch-per-year rainfall runs off or evaporates without penetrating the surface. This dryness would keep contaminated water at a minimum. Secondly, Yucca Mountain's ground water is 1,700 feet below the desert surface. Since the nuclear waste casks containing spent fuel rods will only go 1,200 feet deep, this would isolate the stored containers from water sources. Finally, Yucca Mountain is comprised of a rock formed 12 million years ago by volcanic ash. According to DOE, this *tuff* "may combine with today's topography and climate to provide a suitable setting for isolating, permanently, commercial high-level radioactive waste from man's environment."[1]

While these cautious words were appropriate for a government agency, they were hardly reassuring to those Nevadans who wanted positive assurance that the repository would not explode, spew radiation and ruin Nevada's image as an adult Disneyland. These Nevadans are convinced that DOE words are mostly Newspeak designed by Big Brother to dupe them into accepting the presence of an explosive nuclear dump.

After the 1992 earthquake, Senator Richard Bryan (D-Nev.) said in a Washington, D.C. speech: "This weekend Mother Nature delivered a wake-up call to America's policy-makers. . . . Placing 70,000 metric tons of the most dangerous substance known to man, high-level radioactive waste, in an active earthquake zone defies common sense. But that is exactly what the Department of Energy intends to do at Yucca Mountain."[2]

> If the Yucca Mountain repository is built, there will be jobs provided for thousands of Nevadans. Through the "multiplier effect" the employed workers will spread their paychecks throughout Southern Nevada. Given these economic benefits, should Nevada accept the Yucca Mountain repository? Why or why not?

Socialization in Nevada

Since Congress singled out Yucca Mountain for nuclear waste, the Department of Energy has tried to convince the kids that a repository would be good for their future. The DOE, according to critic Ann Peirce of the State of Nevada Commission on Nuclear Projects, "has developed course materials for use in the public schools, from grade school through high school, which are being made available to schools and teachers as science information about nuclear energy and related subjects." According to Peirce, the DOE materials are designed to change public attitudes toward the "nuclear waste dump and create a public atmosphere that is more accepting of the project." In her opinion, this socialization of school children is part of an intensive campaign by DOE to "convince Nevadans that the dump is inevitable and, as a result, the state should stop fighting the project and make a deal now for purported benefits, and that nuclear waste is high tech and good for the state."[3]

In his book *Propaganda: The Formation of Men's Attitudes* (1965), Jacques Ellul argued that industrial democracies use "sociological" propaganda to get their citizens to accept technology, and ignore technology's dangers. This propaganda, according to Ellul, is used to "solve problems created by technology . . . and to integrate the individual into a technological world." Ellul, a French political philosopher, would probably argue today that high-level waste created by nuclear reactors have created a problem that cannot be permanently resolved. So we bury the waste for 10,000 years hoping future generations will have improved their technology enough to get rid of the waste permanently and safely. Ellul would also argue that Nevadans are being propagandized to accept this high tech waste as a necessary price to pay for progress.

In July 1996, Nevada's two U.S. Senators—Harry Reid and Richard Bryan—staged a filibuster to block a bill that could have forced the state to accept high-level nuclear waste for 100 years. The filibuster delayed once again the decision

If the nuclear repository is built at Yucca Mountain, how will it be sold to curious tourists? What slogan would you use to attract tourists to view the Yucca site?

over a waste site. During the presidential campaign, Bob Dole came to Las Vegas and refused to answer the question, "Will you veto a Yucca Mountain waste site bill if elected President?" Dole's reluctance to side with Nevada's Senators on this controversial issue probably cost him the state's four electoral votes, since he lost by a total of 4,730 popular votes.

How did "winner-take-all" hurt Bob Dole's Nevada chances in 1996?

Nevada's Unique Culture

Geography and natural resources determine how people earn their living. In the past, Nevada was merely a stopping-off place for people traveling from the east to California. The discovery of gold and silver made Nevada a paradise for miners, and the barren territory was suddenly populated with boom towns and miners. Soon Nevada was dominated by mining giants like Kennecott Copper and Anaconda Copper. Silver was such a dominate factor in mining that Nevada became known as the "Silver State," and adopted the colors silver and blue.

On October 31, 1864, President Lincoln proclaimed Nevada's admission to the Union as the 36th state. Lincoln hastened this action so that Nevada's three electoral votes could be cast for him a few weeks later.

Since becoming a state, Nevada has adopted all the symbols that any self-respecting state requires. These symbols include the Desert Bighorn (state animal), Lahotan Cutthroat Trout (state fish), Mountain Bluebird (state bird), Sagebrush (state flower), Desert Tortoise (state reptile), Indian Ricegrass (state grass), Sandstone (state rock), and Nevada Turquoise (state semiprecious gemstone). Nevada even has a state artifact known as the Tule Duck, which was created almost two thousand years ago by inhabitants and discovered in 1924 by archeologists during an excavation of the Lovelock Cave. As described by the current *Guide to the Nevada State Legislature*, "the 11 decoys are each formed of a bundle of bullrush (tule) stems, bound together and shaped to resemble a canvasback duck."

Nevada is "hard" country, with its harsh winters in the north, and its scorching sun blistering across the deserts in summer. Predictably, the state was settled by men who were equally hard. Jedediah Smith is believed to be the first white man to visit

Many Americans consider history "boring." Is there any reason why college students should learn about the history of their state, and all its symbols?

Nevada. He and about a dozen trappers crossed Southern Nevada in 1826 on their trek from Utah to California. Others followed, including John C. Fremont, who made the first careful exploration of the area. Using crude maps and information gleaned from hunters and trappers, Fremont surveyed central and northern Nevada. Two years later Peter Skene Ogden led a group of the Hudson Bay Company into Nevada.[4]

Several events brought migrants to Nevada. These events included the migration of Mormons, the Mexican War, gold discovered in California, the Comstock Lode, and the Civil War. The men who came to Nevada for wealth and fame set a pattern that exists even today. Nevada's current "vices" are the product of a frontier mentality created by the lonely men who lived in the isolated mining towns. These original settlers had fierce eyes and unbridled ambition. In 1861, Mark Twain noted these characteristics when he worked as a Virginia City newspaper reporter. According to Twain, these fierce eyed men had money-getting schemes seething in their brains. They also kept busy organizing military companies, fire companies, brass bands, political powwows, and civic processions. When they weren't organizing, Nevada's settlers were building banks, hotels, and theaters. When they relaxed they went to "wide-open gambling palaces," and "hurdy-gurdy houses," and there was a "whisky mill every fifteen steps." In their spare time, according to Twain, these frantic men were engaged in street fights, murders, inquests and riots.

Why would a territory filled with rowdy men qualify for statehood? Some historians have mistakenly suggested that Nevada became a state because of the need during the Civil War for the gold and silver being produced by the Comstock Lode and other mines. Such is not true. The Civil War had been in progress for three years when statehood was granted. Nevada was admitted for its three electoral votes and so that it could help ratify the Thirteenth Amendment, which abolished slavery. Abraham Lincoln, who proclaimed Nevada a state, gets all the credit. Anyone visiting the State Assembly in Carson City will see a portrait of Lincoln on the wall behind the Speaker's podium. When Mike O'Callaghan served as governor in the early 1970's he placed a small bust of Lincoln on his desk. Reporters who came to interview Governor O'Callaghan were asked to place the pennies in their pockets on the bust of Lincoln. Since Lincoln's profile appears on the penny, this act was a symbolic tribute to the great man. From time to time, Governor O'Callaghan would donate the pennies collected to his favorite charities.

Nevada was "Battle Born," as inscribed on its state flag. And Nevada could have properly changed the state name to "Lincoln" after he was assassinated in the Ford Theater, only six weeks after his second inauguration.

After Nevada and its three electoral votes were admitted to the Union in 1864, the state's political leaders tried to clean up its image by outlawing gambling. By 1931, however, it was clear to lawmakers that legalized gambling would be easier to license, tax and regulate. So they took advantage of federalism and legalized gambling statewide. This same frontier spirit eventually led to legalized prostitution. Under current state law, voters in each county get to decide if they want prostitution. Over the years, voters in most of the state's 17 counties have said "yes" and at latest count there were over 30 brothels operating throughout the state.

In brothels, prostitutes undergo regular checks for AIDS. Clark County, however, has not legalized prostitution. So men who visit Las Vegas for sex usually rely on streetwalkers. As a result, police estimate that about 200 streetwalkers have AIDS. Has the time arrived to legalize prostitution in Clark County, or to crack down on hookers and their customers? Is there a third alternative?

When it comes to crime, Nevada is not unique. Random violence by gangs now plagues Las Vegas. By 1995 the city had 146 youth gangs with 4,263 members who between 1994 and 1995 had committed 527 drive-by shootings and caused 18 deaths. Now in 2001, has the number of shootings continued to climb, or has it gone down?

In their *Encyclopedia of Bad Taste* (1990), Jane and Michael Stern describe Las Vegas as "the most equal-opportunity place on earth: Any slob, however low his social standing, however ugly his clothes, and no matter how uncouthly he may behave, gets treated like royalty if he has money to spend." In our politically correct world a stupid man has to be called "cerebrally challenged." Las Vegans, however, are more realistic. We measure people by their wallets, not their brains.

On Thursday, June 14, 2001, pollsters waited outside the Riviera Mardi Gras Plaza and asked exiting customers their opinion about a topless show called "Crazy Girls." The poll revealed that the audience especially liked the "butt routines." Only in Las Vegas.

Technology and Cultural Lag

As Las Vegas grows from gambling city to "resort destination," we place more emphasis on technology. Despite a ban by the Federal Communications Commission, Nevada TV stations have aired casino ads since 1993. This became possible when U.S. District Judge Philip Pro of Las Vegas ruled the FCC ban unconstitutional. Pro's decision was appealed to the 9th U.S. Circuit Court of Appeals in San Francisco. In the meantime, the 5th U.S. Circuit Court of Appeals in New Orleans voted 2 to 1 to uphold the FCC ban on casino advertising on television and radio as constitutional. This means that the gaming advertising issue may someday end up in the U.S. Supreme Court for a final ruling. Has a final decision on gaming advertising been made yet?

> What do you think? Should the gaming industry be able to advertise on television and radio? Why or why not?

These casino ads remind us that Las Vegas is no longer a frontier watering hole between the East and California. This gaming mecca has gone high tech in a colorful way. Casino ads show common folk winning big jackpots, and promising to build their parents a new home. Viewers also see glamorous showgirls in scanty clothing, and statues of Crazy Girls who are decidedly not buttock impaired.

Once inside, customers are kept occupied dropping coins into hypnotic machines bathed in primary colors red, yellow and blue. Using the behavioral principle known as intermittent reinforcement, these machines pay off unpredictably but the customers are being programmed like Pavlov's famous drooling dog. Now they are experimenting with smells that make people feel good, and may someday be pumping these odors into casinos.

Huxley's *Brave New World* showed how sexual gratification could be used to

> Ivan Petrovich Pavlov (1849-1936) would ring a bell, and then feed his dog. Each time the dog was fed it would salivate. Later, the bell is rung but no food is provided. Yet, the dog still salivates. What does Pavlov's dog suggest, if anything, about the appeal of gambling?

control young people. By 2001, Las Vegas had to face the fact that violent young men were engaged in drug wars on the streets of some neighborhoods. Now that marijuana can be prescribed by doctors perhaps the time has arrived to give free drugs to thugs.

In Huxley's world "Soma" is the drug of choice for law-abiding citizens. Should we create similar "drugs for thugs?"

Unlike Huxley's passive citizens, modern society is cursed with super predators who prowl the streets in their cars armed with high tech weapons. Like animals, the predators are ready to kill if they feel threatened by your looks or words. Above all, don't "dis" them.

> In this increasingly high tech, gender-equal society have young male predators become survivals of an era when being tough was a useful trait?

Cultural lag happens. It can be seen on the famous Las Vegas strip where the technologically sophisticated $1 billion MGM Grand, largest hotel on earth, features scantily clad showgirls and waitresses to lure testosterone laden troglodytes to tables where they play frontier games like Blackjack and Roulette.

In the "good old days," Las Vegas was a profit-making location for organized crime. Many old-timers still romanticize the old days and grumble about how the corporations moved in to "Disneyfy and democratize gambling." According to this conventional wisdom, Las Vegas then was a much safer city because the mob used selective violence to control random violence. Would Las Vegas be safer today if organized crime was running the city?

While old-timers talk about the happy days when gangsters ran the casinos, Nevadans now worry that the abortion controversy could dampen the tourist trade. Outside Reno there is a $1 million West End Women's Medical Group clinic completed in November 1995, and fortified like a military fortress. This abortion clinic has solid steel doors, magnetic locks, bullet-resistant windows, infrared detectors, panic buttons, and is surrounded by thorn trees.

Unlike other states, Nevada has no income tax or inheritance taxes. This fact has caused people to relocate to Nevada, but has caused problems. The state now relies substantially on gaming and sales taxes for its revenues. Both taxes are *inelastic*; that is, when there is an economic downturn state revenues decline, even though the demand for

> Is an abortion clinic built like a medieval fortress symbolic of a Nevada cultural lag? When a modern clinic is built to ward off people with old-fashioned ideas about abortion, is this a cultural lag?

public services remain at least constant. In addition, sales taxes are considered *regressive* because the poor are affected disproportionately more than the rich. Despite their opposition to more taxes, Nevadans still want better roads, more schools, and improved health care. Since an income tax is prohibited by an amendment to the Nevada Constitution, how will Nevada legislators continue to finance all the public services demanded by a growing population?

On Sunday June 17, 2001, the Las Vegas *Review Journal* published a list of taxes that may be considered when the state legislators meet in 2003. The list included 11 new taxes, including a gross receipts tax, filing fee on out-of-state corporations, service tax, gaming tax increase, business profits tax, business activity tax, Internet sales tax, Internet gaming, state lottery, split property tax rolls, and state property taxes. Of these taxes, which in your opinion would be least fair? Most fair? If you're not sure, get on your computer. If taxes are raised, Nevada drivers will have one more excuse for road rage. Some people express rage with hostile slogans on T-shirts. Think up a road rage slogan, and make lots of money: How about, "To err is human, to give the Bird is divine."

"New Taxes to be Debated in 2003," Las Vegas *Review Journal* (June 17, 2001), p. 3B

Florida voters went to the polls during the November, 2000 presidential vote and got obsolete punch card ballots. These votes caused controversy, lawsuits, and delays that forced the United States Supreme Court to get involved.

That's what happens when officials try to get by with cheap, obsolete ballots. To avoid a similar Nevada poll disaster in 2002, our Clark County officials have been looking at $5,000 ATM-like electronic voting machines that can give you a ballot in English or Spanish.

Can you think of any unintended consequences of multi-language ATM-like voting machines in Nevada?

Nevada's Constitution

From 1859 to 1879, Virginia City was Nevada's most famous spot. During this period $500 million in silver and gold were taken from the famous Comstock Lode. This wealth attracted ambitious men from California and other states. Although Mark Twain portrayed them as ambitious schemers who spent their time gambling, drinking, brawling, and organizing parades, Nevada's founding fathers managed somehow to organize a territory, apply for statehood, and write two constitutions.

The combination of activities after the discovery of the Comstock Lode led to a number of events. Among them was the demand for better government in order to maintain law and order. There were all kinds of seamy people floating through Northern Nevada. To provide stability, President Buchanan signed on March 2, 1860 an enabling act to create the Nevada territory. When Congress organized the territory in 1861, power and authority were vested in a governor and a legislative assembly consisting of a Council and a House of Representatives. Both houses established rules in order to conduct their business.

When the governor and legislative assembly failed to provide a satisfactory way to tax the profits being made in gold and silver mines, Nevada's first constitution was rejected by the national government. In 1864, however, a satisfactory constitution was submitted and Nevada became the 36th state on Halloween. Before this

Read the speech below given by a Mr. Sterns, and decide his argument and his basic premise (reason).

final step, however, the state's founders argued over the name "Nevada." It was one of the first orders of business at the 1863 constitutional convention, and arguments raged for the selection of Washoe, Humboldt and Esmeralda to replace Nevada. The record shows that a Mr. Sterns, the delegate from Esmeralda County, had this to say: "Nevada is proposed by some. I had the honor of putting the first article in print advocating that proposition in this Territory; but I have repented, and abandoned my first love for that more endearing one which is named in my report Nevada anglicized is 'Snow'—the Snow State. This would impart to the foreign and eastern mind an abundance of snow—an uninhabitable, desolate region that would congeal the first impulse and make frigid the every maiden effort to migrate here. Nevada is euphonious, but how much more so is Esmeralda. Besides, the latter occupies the very center of the new state. . . ." And so it went. He concluded his argument saying that Esmeralda would be the first state to begin its name with the letter E, as he urged all to name the state Esmeralda. When Sterns finished speaking, a motion was made to continue the name of Nevada, which then carried, 32 votes to 4.

To sum up, in March 1861, Nevada was given territorial status through a federal law. Less than two years later, the occupants voted for statehood. To prove their determination, the founders held a constitutional convention at Carson City. This first constitution was rejected by Nevada voters because it contained a controversial tax on the state's profitable mines.

Nevada's entry into the Union was rushed because the Republican majority in Congress wanted the three electoral votes that would accompany the new state. After a brief debate, Congress pushed through the enabling act for Nevada, which President Lincoln signed. Because Nevada achieved statehood during the Civil War, its flag carries the proud motto "Battle Born."

On July 4, 1864, battle-born Nevada delegates gathered in Carson City to write their second constitution. The 35 delegates who met were typical of the type of people who worry about stability. Like the original Founding Fathers, Nevada's constitution writers were wealthy, influential men with good vocabularies. Their ranks included lawyers, miners, merchants, editors, mechanics, millers, bankers, physicians, and a surveyor. Their task was eased because many were former Californians who had helped write a state constitution there. The former Californians included J. Neely Johnson, a former governor of California chosen by Nevadans in 1864 to be president of their convention. Although the convention was held more than one hundred years ago, it had a decidedly modern flavor. Most of the delegates kept arguing for a constitution which lacked the excessive taxes and regimentation of California.

> Since the only "battle" was over Nevada's three electoral votes and ratification of controversial Civil War amendments, we might consider changing the state motto to "The Glorious Three" or "Ratification Forever."

> In its editorials, the Las Vegas *Review Journal* often disparages our western neighbor as the "People's Republic of California." What is meant by a people's republic?

For the most part, Nevada's 1864 constitution reflects the anti-tax philosophy of the settlers. Article X, for example, uses very detailed language so that future legislatures cannot easily impose burdensome or even fair taxes on the mining industry. After a lengthy debate, delegates imposed a small tax on Nevada's powerful mining interests. The only other major tax controversy at the convention was provoked by a poll tax levied on male voters between the ages of 21 and 60. After a convention marked by the usual political arguments, Nevada voters approved their new constitution by a 10,375 to 1,284 margin.[5]

244

The U.S. Constitution was drafted when Americans feared a too strong national government would deprive them of fundamental rights. This concern is reflected in the First Amendment which says, "Congress shall make no law respecting an establishment of religion, or prohibiting the free exercise thereof; or abridging the freedom of speech, or of the press; or the right of the people peaceably to assemble, and to petition the government for a redress of grievances." To match these 45 words (and one sentence), the Nevada Constitution says:

> **Section 1. Inalienable rights. -** All men are by Nature free and equal and have certain inalienable rights among which are those of enjoying and defending life and liberty; Acquiring, Possessing and Protecting property and pursuing and obtaining safety and happiness.

> **Section 4. Liberty of conscience. -** The free exercise and enjoyment of religious profession and worship without discrimination or preference shall forever be allowed in this State, and no person shall be rendered incompetent to be a witness on account of his opinions on matters of his religious belief, but the liberty of conscience hereby secured, shall not be so construed, as to excuse acts of licentiousness or justify practices inconsistent with the peace, or safety of this State.

> **Section 9. Liberty of speech and the press. -** Every citizen may speak, write and publish his sentiments on all subjects being responsible for the abuse of that right; and no law shall be passed to restrain or abridge the liberty of speech or of the press. In all criminal prosecutions and civil actions for libels, the truth may be given in evidence to the Jury; and if it shall appear to the Jury that the matter charged as libelous is true and was published with good motives and for justifiable ends, the party shall be acquitted or exonerated.

> **Section 10. Right to assemble and to petition. -** The people shall have the right freely to assemble together to consult for the common good, to instruct their representatives and to petition the Legislature for redress of Grievances.

> **Section 20. Rights retained by people. -** This enumeration of rights shall not be construed to impair or deny others retained by the people.

To understand both the U.S. and Nevada constitutions, you need to compare the similarities and differences with these questions:

① Why are state constitutions almost always longer than the U.S. Constitution?

② The U.S. Constitution says Congress shall make no law prohibiting the free exercise of religion, whereas the Nevada Constitution says "The free exercise and enjoyment of religious profession and worship without discrimination or preference shall forever be allowed in this State. . . ." Why the difference?

③ Nevada's 1864 document says "All men are by Nature free and equal and have certain inalienable rights; the original U.S. Constitution, however, said nothing about any natural right to be free or equal. Why the difference?

④ Critics often claim that the 13th, 14th, and 15th Amendments added to the U.S. Constitution after the Civil War were inconsistent with the intentions of the Founding Fathers. What do you think?

Several other differences exist between the Nevada Constitution and the U.S. Constitution. The document ratified in 1789 had about four thousand words before the Bill of Rights was added in 1791. Counting the first 10 amendments, the U.S. Constitution has been amended 27 times. In comparison, Nevada's original 1864 document had over 15,000 words when adopted and has been amended nearly 100 times. To get an idea of the sheer volume of this document, ask your computer to show you a few pages. But don't push that print button, unless you have plenty of spare time and extra sheets of paper.

For sheer wordiness, however, no state has ever surpassed Louisiana's 1974 constitution which had 256,000 words and has been amended nearly 800 times.

When Nevada entered the Union, it had a population of 21,406. Now the state assembly has 42 members, and a population nearing two million. Now that Nevada is the world's leading resort destination has the time arrived for Nevadans to hold a new convention and bring the state constitution up-to-date?

> **Which type of Constitution is best? One which uses few words, but requires interpretation by courts or a document of many words?**

In 1864 Nevadans ratified a constitution that states, "no idiot or insane person" can vote in Nevada. In 2001 Assemblywoman Chris Giunchigliani won committee approval to introduce an amendment to banish these words and instead have a phrase stating people can vote "unless adjudicated as mentally incapacitated." To change the state constitution to include these words would require legislative approval in 2001 and 2003.

Actually, the Nevada Constitution established a governmental system more democratic than the one created at Philadelphia in 1787. To make it easier to understand, we've simplified the differences and listed them below:

☻ The Constitution originally provided that U.S. Senators would be chosen from each state by its legislature. Direct popular vote did not come until ratification of the Seventeenth Amendment in 1913. Nevada's state senators, in contrast, have always been directly elected by the voters. Moreover, Nevada senators serve four year terms, not six.

☻ Nevada's "bill of rights" contains more specific guarantees than the largely negative prohibitions placed in the U.S. Bill of Rights.

☻ The U.S. Constitution has no provision for the passage of laws initiated by voters and referred to the Congress. Nevada, on the other hand, has the initiative and referendum.

Whereas the framers of the U.S. Constitution seemed unwilling to place power in the hands of the masses, Nevada's founders created a document that provides three ways for citizens to make the rules.

① **Using the initiative to propose amendments:** Nevada citizens may propose state constitutional amendments through an initiative petition which if judged legal places the proposed amendment on the ballot in the next general election. If approved, it is then placed on the ballot of the next (two years later) general election. If the voters endorse the proposed amendment again, it becomes part of Nevada's Constitution. In the past, Nevada voters have used this process to eliminate the poll tax, limit the governor to two terms, create judicial commissions, and exempt household goods from property taxes.

② **Using the Initiative to propose laws:** Nevadans may also propose new laws through the use of the initiative. Like a proposed amendment, the initiative petition must be proposed (signed) by at least ten percent of the number of voters who voted in the previous election in seventy-five percent of the 17 counties.

By requiring signatures from voters in at least 13 counties, the initiative petition process prevents voters in one or two of the more populous counties from "railroading" through some change that may not have the blessings of a wide base of support.

③ **Using the Referendum to refer a law back to the people:** If some citizens are unhappy with a law passed by the Nevada legislature, they can obtain the necessary signatures and have it put to a vote at the next general election. If a majority of voters reject the legislative enactment, it is void.

Unlike Congress where each house determines whether or not to expel its members, the voters in Nevada can recall elected officials. The specifics for this process are set forth in Article II, Section 9. Basically, angry citizens collect signatures of registered voters equal to 25 percent of the number of voters who participated in the election of the villain. Then within 25 days a special election is held and whoever gets the most votes—the villain or the contender— takes office for the remainder of that term.

During your college career you will encounter "comparison" essay test questions. These usually ask the student to "Compare and contrast the United States and Nevada Constitutions." Like death and taxes, essay questions are certain. Your best weapon against the inevitable essay questions is a list of points to cover, and so read on:

① Congress is currently comprised of 535 members, 100 Senators and 435 Representatives. The Nevada Legislature has 63 members, 42 in the Assembly and 21 in the Senate.

② The Nevada Legislature meets every two years (biennially) while Congress meets yearly (annually).

③ The Nevada Constitution prohibits lotteries, while the U.S. Constitution is silent on the matter.

④ Nevada's 21 Senators serve four year terms. The U.S. Senators serve six years.

⑤ The Nevada Constitution sets a specific limit for the amount of public debt, while the U.S. Constitution is silent on this matter.

⑥ Nevada judges are elected, but the U.S. Constitution provides that the President shall nominate all federal judges for Senate approval. Once confirmed, federal judges serve for life or good behavior.

⑦ The governor of Nevada has full authority to appoint the heads of departments and agencies, while the President may only nominate individuals to the Senate; unless Congress expands his power.

In our evaluation of Congress, we emphasized that the single-member district system used to elect members to the House of Representatives every two years favors a two-party system. In electing the 42 Assembly members Nevada also uses single-member districts. Eleven of Nevada's 21 State Senators are also elected from single-member districts. The other 10 Senators are elected from two member districts.

> Critics of the elected Regents want Nevada to adopt a system whereby Regents are appointed by the Governor. Should Nevada adopt this approach? Why or why not?

The Nevada Constitution states that higher education shall be controlled by an elected Board of Regents. There are now 13 board members, who recommend a biennial budget for the state's universities and community colleges. Since these Regents are elected from single-member districts, they are politicians in the same sense as other elected officials.

Nevada lawmakers include lawyers, physicians, small business persons, corporate managers and even a few professors. Of the 63 members of the Nevada Legislature, 41 are men.

In September 1992, it appeared that Nevada voters would decide if they wanted to put term limits on future U.S. Senators and Representatives. Under Question 7, a proposal to amend the Nevada Constitution, members of the House of Representatives would be limited to six years of service in any 12-year period. U.S. Senators would be limited to 12 years in any 24-year period.

At the time, Nevada's incumbents in Congress criticized Question 7. Representative James Bilbray said, "In a small state like Nevada, if the two Representatives were limited to six years, they'd never even have a subcommittee chairman from Nevada . . . . We'd be devastated. What has made us strong was keeping people in for a long time."

The importance of seniority was emphasized in late July 1992, when Harry Reid, who served on the Senate Appropriations Committee, released a list of 13 Nevada projects worth nearly $20 million that might be lost if the state's Representatives and Senators had no seniority.

Why would voters in Nevada want to limit the terms of office for their Representatives and Senators in Congress?

Power in Nevada

Who are the chief wielders of political power in Nevada? It is an old adage of politics that those who pay the piper have the power to determine what music will be played. Most powerful are the entrepreneurs of hotel-casinos; they function both as individuals and collectively through the Nevada Resort Association.

Candidates for political office need money for their increasingly expensive political campaigns. Biggest contributors are the people who run the hotel-casinos as individuals and as collectivists through the Nevada Resort Association.

Through state gaming taxes, these hotel-casinos provided 37.9% of the 1995-1997 General Fund budget. There is also an entertainment tax that differs from county to county, but accounted for 2.9% of the revenue collected by the state.

The Gaming industry is regulated by the Nevada Gaming Commission, which oversees the Gaming Control Board. This board is responsible for overseeing, auditing and investigating candidates seeking to be licensed.

Since money is the "mother's milk of politics," the gaming industry has considerable influence in Nevada. But as Madison warned in 1789, liberty provides the air that nourishes the fiery ambitions of factions. These factions can be seen in the credentials of the over 500 lobbyists who are registered so that they can legally try to influence the 63 members of the Nevada Legislature. These lobbyists represent such traditional American factions as business, labor, state workers, tax payers, poor people, rich people, black people, God-fearing people, and gun owners. Among the most powerful are the Nevada Resort Association, Southern Nevada Home Builders Association, Nevada State Education Association, and the Nevada Bankers Association. There is even a Nevada Brothel Association.

Nevada's Governor has the type of power that goes with the job. Governor Kenny Guinn, for example, appoints directors and boards to supervise over 40 state agencies. The Governor's most visible appointments are to the Department of Motor Vehicles and Public Safety, the Gaming Commission, and the Nevada Equal Rights Commission.

> The Las Vegas *Review Journal* opposes the election of college faculty to serve as state legislators. The RJ bases its opposition on Article III, Section 1 of the Nevada Constitution which prohibits executive branch employees from serving in legislative or judicial branch positions. Is this a valid argument? Why or why not?

The Governor, however, has little power to control the Board of Regents for the University and Community College System of Nevada. The 13 regents are to be elected from single-member districts. In effect, that makes them politicians. To do their job, the Regents make sure that faculty and staff in higher education act in accordance with sexual harassment policies that have been criticized as too complicated and over-reaching. Get a copy of the Regents policy and decide for yourself if it goes too far.

> Does a description of sexual harassment taboos belong with a discussion of power in Nevada? Why or why not?

If a state employee is fired for sexual harassment, he or she may end up in the state courts. Nevada has a fairly simple judicial system. It begins at the grass roots where Justices of the Peace and municipal court judges are elected to decide matters like minor traffic violations and to hold pre-trial hearings. At level two, Nevada justice consists of about 25 district judges who preside over the courts in nine judicial districts. These district courts are responsible for holding major trials like murder cases, and civil matters which involve more than $1,500. These district judges are also elected, but for longer terms than JP's and municipal judges. At the top are Nevada's five supreme court justices, who are elected for six year terms on nonpartisan ballots. These justices hear cases appealed to them from lower courts, or which involve substantial constitutional or federal issues.

Though the Founding Fathers wanted independent judges who would vote their conscience, Nevadans prefer to have elected judges. At every level, Nevada judges are elected and they can be removed through recall, impeachment, legislative action, and a special Commission on Judicial Discipline.

> Under Article I, Section 1, the Nevada Constitution stipulates that, "All men are by Nature free and equal and have certain inalienable rights among which are those of . . . pursuing . . . happiness." Could these words be used to strike down as unconstitutional current state sexual harassment policies? Why or why not?

Despite unique features like the initiative and referendum, Nevada plays politics just like the other 49 states. And politics is played in this country by Democrats and Republicans.

In other words, Nevada is mostly a two-party state. Governor Kenny Guinn is a Republican. Senate majority leader is Bill Raggio (R-Reno). In the General Assembly, the speaker is Richard Perkins (D-Henderson). Other important jobs like Assembly Majority Leader and Senate Minority Leader are held by Democrats.

In Washington, D.C., Nevada is represented by Senator Harry Reid (D-Nev.), Senator John Ensign (R-Nev.), Representative Shelley Berkley (D-Nev.) and Representative Jim Gibbons (R-Nev.). As of February 2001, the Nevada Senate had 12 Republicans and 9 Democrats. In the Assembly there were 27 Democrats and 15 Republicans. Thus the total number of state legislators is currently 63.

The legislators are paid $7,800 for each 120 day session in Carson City. For this modest sum the state legislators from February 5, 2001 to June 4, 2001 met as the 71st session of the Nevada legislature and considered such issues as air quality, traffic, court services, emergency vehicles, graffiti removal and health care. By the time you read this, the state's political leadership will have to decide if Nevada wants to build a super speed train that will cost passengers $42.50 to ride from California to Las Vegas in 86 minutes.

During the 71st session, Senate Majority leader Bill Raggio (R-Reno) and Assembly Majority leader Richard Perkins (D-Henderson) had to broker a new congressional seat and also had to deal with the question, "Should the Nevada legislature add more districts or maintain the current maximum of 63?"

Nevada's frontier independence has fostered splinter parties like the Libertarians, who oppose most of the restraints placed on our freedoms by government. Libertarians want the income tax abolished and the

> Is medical marijuana an idea whose time has come?

Internal Revenue Service dismantled. They also argue for fewer government regulations, less military spending, education vouchers for parents, more freedom for women seeking abortions, and the decriminalization of drugs such as marijuana and cocaine. Though anti-government, Libertarians attract only a few thousand votes. But sometimes their ideas catch on. This happened during the 2000 election when 65% of voters in Nevada supported an initiative to let victims of AIDS, cancer and other illnesses to be able to use marijuana to relieve their symptoms. Now the state legislature has to decide the fate of "medical marijuana."

> **Nevada may need "juice" in Congress. In 1997 Congress formed a federal gambling commission to investigate gaming throughout the U.S. This nine-member commission is headed by Kay Coles James, an outspoken opponent of gambling. By now, we should know if the commission has done any harm to Nevada's major industry.**

In July 1996, Nevada Democratic Senators Harry Reid and Richard Bryan staged a filibuster to block a bill that could have forced Nevada to accept high-level nuclear waste for a minimum of 100 years.

Four years later, Senator Bryan decided to retire from politics. As a consequence, Republican John Ensign was elected to be Nevada's "other" Senator. This begs the question, "Will Republican Ensign and Democrat Reid work together if Congress decides to force nuclear waste on Nevada?"

There is also the danger that Congress will ban legal gambling on college sports? If this happens Reid and Ensign will have to work together, or face the probability of deep cuts in the gaming taxes and other sources of state revenues.

Now that a nine-member federal commission is studying the effects of compulsive gambling, we may hear more arguments over the question, "should casino ads be banned from TV?" Despite a ban by the Federal Communications Commission, Nevada TV stations since

1993 have aired casino ads. This became possible when U.S. District Judge Philip Pro of Las Vegas ruled the FCC ban unconstitutional. Pro's decision was appealed to the 9th U.S. Circuit Court of Appeals in San Francisco. In the meantime, the 5th U.S. Circuit Court of Appeals in New Orleans voted 2 to 1 to uphold the FCC ban on casino advertising on television and radio as constitutional. This means that the gaming advertising issue may someday go to the U.S. Supreme Court for a final ruling.

In 1992 Nevadans for Term Limits gathered 32,596 signatures to put Question 7 on the ballot. If approved by a majority of voters, Question 7 would have amended the Nevada Constitution to limit the years served by the state's members of Congress. Under its provisions, the two members of the House of Representatives would be restricted to six years of service in any 12-year period. U.S. Senators would be limited to 12 years in any 24-year period.

Proponents of term limits argued that it was designed to turn government back over to the people. In the words of one advocate, "the people are unhappy with a professional political class. They want to return to a citizen politician, rather than the professional politicians."

Opponents challenged the term limits on constitutional grounds. Two faculty members at Western Nevada Community College and a former law school dean challenged the constitutionality of the referendum, asserting that it violated Article I, Sections 2 and 3 of the U.S. Constitution. They also contended that insufficient signatures were gathered in one of the Nevada counties. The Nevada Supreme Court surprised the advocates by voting 3 to 2 to keep the term limits off the ballot in November 1992.

By having seniority, Nevada's congressional delegation should be more effective in the fight to protect the state's highly important gaming industry. Currently, the people who protect our interests are named Reid, Ensign, Gibbons and Berkley. With the addition of a third House seat, we'll be considering a fifth name after the 2002 election.

Was Question 7 a bad idea? Should state courts get involved when citizens try to change the rules through an initiative petition? Why or why not?

Would it be wise for Nevadans to limit the terms of their members of Congress if the other 49 states play by the old rules?

In May 1997, the partial-birth abortion issue surfaced again when the Senate 64 to 36 approved another ban on the controversial procedure and sent it forward to be vetoed by President Clinton. Like most issues in the culture wars, the ban on partial-birth abortions aroused conflicting emotions. In a typically emotive editorial, the Las Vegas *Review Journal* on May 21, 1997, thrashed Richard Bryan for opposing the ban, and congratulated Harry Reid for being in favor of the ban.

A matter of morality ■ Sen. Bryan votes to preserve a cruel procedure.

Few Nevadans acquainted with Sen. Richard Bryan's mostly moderate record would consider him likely to vote with the radical fringe on any issue. But when the issue of brain-suction abortion came before the Senate on Tuesday, Sen. Bryan did just that, giving his blessing Tuesday to the continued use of this gruesome form of virtual infanticide.

In voting against the partial birth abortion ban, Sen. Bryan joined some of the most far-left members of the Senate.

251

To his ever-lasting credit, Nevada's other senator, Harry Reid, joined 12 of his Democratic colleagues and 51 Republicans in voting to outlaw the hideous "procedure." (In an earlier House vote, Nevada's two Republicans John Ensign and Jim Gibbons, also favored the ban.)

The Senate vote was lopsided, 64-36 in favor of the ban, but President Clinton will veto this bill. And without the help of Sen. Bryan, proponents of the ban won't muster the requisite 67 votes to override that veto. If Sen. Bryan and just two of his colleagues reexamined the morality of their position and switched their votes, each year hundreds of fully formed, healthy babies on the very verge of entering the world would be spared the horrendous fate of having their skulls split open and their brains vacuumed out

❒ What is the most important point being made by this editorial?

❒ Identify five value-laden words.

❒ Did Senator Bryan's vote hurt his political career?

❒ Did Senator Reid's vote help his political career?

Freedom in Nevada

Unlike the federal government, which had to add a Bill of Rights to the original Constitution in 1791, Nevada's founders integrated protected civil liberties under Article I inside the main document. Nevada's fundamental law guarantees every citizen certain rights such as trial by jury, freedom of worship, *habeas corpus*, freedom from cruel and unusual punishment, double jeopardy, due

> Nevada's unique culture creates unique freedom issues. On the famous Las Vegas strip handbills advertising adult entertainment are handed to walkers. These handbills are the subject of lawsuits to keep the strip clear of paper waste and visual rot. Should all such advertising be banned?

process, freedom of speech and press, right of assembly and petition, security against unreasonable search and seizure, the "right to keep and bear arms for security and defense, for lawful hunting and recreational use and for other lawful purposes."

The Nevada Constitution also contains a clause borrowed from the 1776 Declaration of Independence. Under the title **Inalienable rights**, Article I, Section 1 reads: "All men are, by Nature, free and equal, and have certain inalienable rights, among which are those of enjoying and defending life and liberty; Acquiring, Possessing and Protecting property, and pursuing and obtaining safety and happiness."

These lofty words were borrowed from men justifying a revolution over two hundred years ago. Are they appropriate for the men and women who live in Nevada today?

In July 1992, Las Vegas Metro vice officers were looking for 37-year-old Vanessa Wolfe, a convicted AIDS carrying prostitute who had mistakenly been released from jail. Under Nevada law, Wolfe could be sentenced to a maximum 20 year prison sentence for prostituting herself despite knowing she carried the deadly virus.

Should Vanessa Wolfe be sent to prison? Would it help to know she had been previously arrested 130 times for prostitution?

In 1992 Las Vegas had about thirty out-call dance businesses. Under a new county ordinance, the Metropolitan Police Department's vice section planned to crack down on the adult dancers. The county ordinance was challenged, however, by out-call promoters who argued that it violated the First and Fourteenth Amendments by limiting freedom of expression. Five years later, the Sprint telephone had over 100 entertainment pages advertising out-call services, which Metro claims is a front for prostitution.

Topless dancers in Nevada usually have to follow rules which include not touching the customer. Lap dancing, however, is apparently protected by the state and national constitutions. This was the judgment made November 10, 1996 by District Judge Myron Leavitt. He granted an injunction preventing Clark County from enforcing regulations on how much contact is permissible between topless dancers and adult nightclub customers. Judge Leavitt made his decision after the Club Paradise and two of its dancers challenged as unconstitutional the rules which put restrictions on touching or mingling with patrons, placing of tips in the entertainer's G-string and specifically prohibited lap dancing or couch dancing. In his decision, Judge Leavitt ruled that topless dancing is protected as "expressive conduct" under the First and Fourteenth Amendments.

Should topless lap dancing be a right protected from county ordinances? Where does it say that lap dancing is a legitimate form of expression, and therefore protected by constitutional law?

During its 1995 session, the Nevada Assembly passed a law which said those who "sexually portray" children in advertisements, performances, tapes or photographs that "appeal to the prurient interests" are subject to one to six years in prison. The law also stipulates that people who possess child pornography also may be punished with a felony offense. Two years later the Senate passed a bill to chemically castrate pedophiles, but the bill failed in the Assembly.

Carrying child pornography in Nevada can send you to prison. Carrying a concealed weapon, however, is perfectly legal. Since 1995 it has been legal in Nevada to carry a concealed weapon, if you

Is there any constitutional right to carry a concealed weapon?

have a permit. From October 1995 to July 1996, Clark County issued a total of 4,422 permits to carry concealed weapons. Under the law, a concealed firearm can be a loaded or unloaded pistol, revolver or other firearm that is carried on a person in a way that it would not be discernible by ordinary observation. In other words, "hidden." The law bans permits for criminals, mental cases, and people under 21.

While Nevada's frontier mentality survives as lap dancing and guns, members of the Elks Lodge are supposed to be letting the ladies join. In September 1995, however, the "male-only" Las Vegas Elks Lodge 1468 voted unanimously to retain their constitution, which limits membership to males. Explaining the vote to keep women out, the lodge's exalted ruler said the Elks had been a fraternity for over one hundred years, and they wanted to keep it that way.

In May 1995, the Nevada Senate by 20 to 1 approved a law which would establish procedures to chemically castrate pedophiles considered dangerous. Under Senate Bill 102, district attorneys would be able to petition judges for an order to give certain drugs to pedophiles once they are released from prison. One of the drugs is Depo-Provera, which is a woman's birth control drug. This drug shrinks testicles and lowers testosterone levels in men. So far the drug has been used to control pedophiles released from prison in California and Texas. Opposing Senate Bill 102, Senator Joe Neal (D-North Las Vegas) compared it to Hitler's use of castration to punish his opponents. According to *Review Journal* reporter Ed Vogel, Senator Neal also compared chemical castration to tests performed on black Tuskegee, Alabama sharecroppers with syphilis between 1932 and 1972. In your opinion, is Senator Neal's argument logical? Why or why not?

Nevada law allows employers to perform pre-employment drug tests on applicants for jobs. The law also established a "rational basis" criteria for requiring drug tests of about 12,000 current employees. For existing employees, testing can be required when a supervisor has a reasonable belief—based on evidence—that a worker is under the influence of drugs or alcohol. Under the regulations, the employee who tests positive is referred to the state's Employee Assistance Program for treatment. Two offenses inside five years could cost the employee his or her job.

In the very near future, Nevadans can expect more and more intrusions on their privacy. These intrusions will include, but not be limited to, the following:

- ☹ The Tropicana Hotel in Atlantic City, N. J. is now testing an infrared detection system that alerts employers whenever workers leave the rest room without washing their hands. The device is being used to control infectious diseases caused by workers who do not wash their hands after using the toilet. Is the detection device Orwellian, or merely a necessary precaution?
- ☹ High school students who use the Internet to research "breast cancer" may be denied information by a filter banning use of data containing the sexually emotive word "breast." Would filtering sexual words off the Internet be Orwellian, or a reasonable precaution?
- ☹ When you walk into a Wells Fargo Bank to cash a check, they'll require your driver's license, bank card, and fingerprint. Would requiring a fingerprint to cash checks be Orwellian, or a legitimate policy?
- ☹ Employers are starting to videotape employees to monitor job performance, store and review e-mail, and tape phone conversations. Is this Orwellian?

Whether in the shape of employer or government, Big Brother is making Nevadans nervous. This fear has provoked some citizens to arm themselves and prepare for an eventual war against the forces of evil. As of July 1996, about eight thousand Clark County residents had qualified for concealed weapons permits. Does this fact make you feel more secure, or less secure?

Fifty years ago sexual behavior was considered a private matter between persons, usually of different genders. Now, sexual harassment policies and media publicity have turned sex into headlines and lawsuits. This fact of modern life was splashed on the May 27, 1997 cover of the tabloid *Globe*. The keyhole newspaper showed former football star and Monday Night Football commentator Frank Gifford cheating on wife Kathie Lee. The evidence published by the *Globe* was described as "10 sizzling photos expose his sex romps with blonde

254

in hotel love nest." ☆ Frank and Kathie Lee Gifford were considered a perfect couple. Now their ideal marriage is besmirched by fuzzy photos. Should Nevada ban tabloids like the *Globe*?

Celebrity role models like Kathie Lee and Frank Gifford help socialize young Americans. Many lawmakers today, however, feel that young Americans have bad role models, and are ignored by their parents. Badly socialized youth sometimes get into trouble. To curb bad behavior by juveniles, the Nevada legislature in 1995 passed these laws:

> Since adolescent sex is a national scandal, why not require young ladies to wear chastity belts?

* Teen-age delinquents could be ordered by courts to help remove graffiti from buildings and streets. Delinquents can also have their driving privileges suspended for six months.
* Those who "sexually portray" children in advertisements, performances, tapes or photographs that appeal to "prurient interests" are subject to one to six years in prison.
* Juveniles under 18 convicted of drunken driving or using illegal drugs will have their driving licenses revoked for 90 days, and be evaluated medically to determine if they are addicted to drugs or alcohol. If addicted, the juveniles may be ordered to undergo treatment and perform community service.

> **Do any of the 1995 laws aimed at juveniles violate any provisions of either the Nevada State Constitution or the U.S. Constitution?**

Nevada Justice

Nevada justice is handed down through a state court system that includes justice courts, municipal courts, district courts and a state supreme court. At the bottom end, justice and municipal courts hear cases involving small scale disputes, misdemeanor trials, and traffic violations. The district courts are Nevada's major trial courts. They have *original jurisdiction* in cases involving civil matters over $1,500 and criminal offenses defined by state law as felonies. The district courts also hear appeals from the justice and municipal courts. Appeals from the state's nine district courts go directly to the Nevada Supreme Court, where five justices decide the outcome.

Like federal courts, Nevada state courts have the power of judicial interpretation and judicial review. This means the district courts and the Nevada Supreme Court may someday have to decide if state police roadblocks are constitutional.

When Nevada police officers pull over a DUI suspect, they look for used beer cans, the smell of alcohol, glazed eyes, and slurred speech. If the driver acts suspicious, the police use field sobriety tests and blood tests. Under Nevada law, it is a crime to drive with a blood-alcohol level of 0.10 percent or more. State law stipulates that blood-alcohol levels recorded after an arrest are presumed to be the same as when the person was driving. This last stipulation was challenged by the 9th U.S. Circuit Court of Appeals in San Francisco which ruled in May 1992 that an "after-the-fact test" like the one in Nevada may give a reading higher than when the suspect was actually driving the car. In his opinion for the circuit court, Judge Robert Boochever argued that the U.S. Constitution, which requires proof of guilt beyond a reasonable doubt, is violated when a blood test that is subject to change over time is used as conclusive evidence of guilt.[6]

If a DUI driver kills a child, the victim's parents have to wait for the felony case to proceed through Nevada's justice system. If you are a victim of age discrimination at work, however, the system works much faster. If you suspect age discrimination, you can make a phone call to the Equal Rights Commission and start the paperwork. The alleged victim has 180 days to begin proceedings. The ERC requires the victim to complete a series of forms containing the names of possible witnesses. After the complaint forms are returned to the ERC, agency personnel file a formal signed complaint. Then the case proceeds through a typical bureaucratic maze and could eventually end up in federal court. Though time consuming, the ERC process provides a uniquely modern approach to justice. Rather than killing an enemy in a blood feud or watching him hanged, the modern victim gets to recover economic losses from the villain or the offending government agency.

In 1992 the State of Nevada paid $184,000 to Kathleen Leander because she was sexually harassed while she worked as a female correctional officer at the Ely State Prison. ☆ Every day somewhere in the United States a victim of injustice is collecting money from government, spouse, or lover for sexual harassment, sexual assault, broken promises, children born out of wedlock, or adultery. Are all these lawsuits good for our national welfare? Why or why not?

> In the murder trial of O.J. Simpson, the trial jury judged him not guilty. Later, in a civil trial, another jury judged him guilty of depriving Nicole Brown Simpson and Ronald Goldman of their civil rights. In your opinion, which jury rendered the more "exact" justice? Explain.

In the Las Vegas-based 1995 movie *Casino,* Robert De Niro plays stylish gambler Sam Rothstein. Rothstein is an intelligent man with two weaknesses. The first is his tolerance for a crazy friend named Nicky Santoro (Joe Pesci). Rothstein's other weakness is his obsession with Ginger McKenna (Sharon Stone). As described by *Time* reviewer Richard Schickel, Ginger is "a hustler whose excessive interest in furs and jewels would ward off a more worldly man."[7]

Nevada's infamous *Black Book* is a list of people deemed "notorious" or "unsavory" by the Nevada Gaming Commission. These people are excluded from the premises of Nevada casinos. In a number of cases, the U.S. Supreme Court

> In the opinion of writer Lyall Watson, men compete violently because the stakes are high. He says "Men have a lot to gain and lose in such competition. The winners get women, the losers don't."
> Judging by this premise, sexual harassment would merely be the normal biological activity of men hoping to be evolutionary winners.
> Source: *Dark Nature* (1995), p. 196.
> Watson also argues that women are biologically attracted to aggressive men. Is this logical?

has held that punishment based on status or reputation violates the U.S. Constitution. Article I, Section 10 prohibits states from passing a *bill of attainder*. This is a legislative act that declares the guilt of an individual and metes out punishment without a judicial trial. Critics of the *Black Book* argue that it unconstitutionally punishes individuals merely because they are known to be unsavory or notorious. Yet both the U.S. and Nevada courts have upheld the book as a legitimate use of government power. ☆ Suppose, for the sake of argument, our courts allowed states to publish lists of citizens suspected of crimes but were never indicted and found guilty. Would this be the same as a black book? Suppose Nevada had a law requiring publication of the home address of convicted pedophiles now out of prison. Would such a law be a violation of either the U.S. or Nevada Constitutions?

> **How many men are listed in the *Black Book*? How many women? Should the book be revised to list as many women as men? Why not?**

Equality in Nevada

In 1992 Nevada casinos had to consider ways to remodel and make "reasonable accommodations" for the disabled. This was required under a law passed by Congress one year earlier known as The Americans With Disabilities Act. Under this law, all U.S. businesses with more than 25 employees had to provide the reasonable accommodations. The law, which went into effect, January 26, 1992, would require Nevada hotels and resorts to make several expensive changes. In his column, Las Vegas *Review Journal* entertainment writer Mike Weatherford predicted the following accommodations for disabled customers and employees would be needed to satisfy the law:

① **All swimming pools and hot tubs must be equipped with lifts to accommodate the disabled.**
② **Showrooms must be reconfigured to allow the disabled access to all types of seating.**
③ **Showrooms and lounges must include listening equipment for the hearing impaired.**
④ **All casino games must be available to the disabled.**

In a scathing editorial, the *Review Journal* used the disabilities act as proof that Big Brother was mushrooming under former President George Bush and the Democrats who controlled Congress. The law, noted the *RJ*, is so imprecise that most companies had no idea what was expected of them. This would leave these companies at the mercy of lawyers and judges since "ignorance of the law is no defense."

Calling the disabilities act a "classic case of misplaced good intentions," the *RJ* editorialist compared the law to a Robin Hood mugger and asked several provocative rhetorical questions:

> **The logic used to justify such government raids on economic and property rights is not unlike the thinking of a mugger who hopes to warm the heart of a needy child with the gift of a lovely wristwatch and so steals one at gunpoint. It's for a good cause isn't it?**

Where will this crazy drive toward forced egalitarianism end? Does society have to try to provide every American with the means to enjoy the sensations and experiences of every other, even though physical and mental differences render it impossible? Will a small Alaskan mountain climbing outfit be forced to provide air service to the 20,320-foot south peak of Mount McKinley so disabled customers needn't be left out of expeditions? Or would even that not be adequate? Shall government make them install an escalator, with no regard for cost? Will a construction company face a court fight if it refuses to hire a proper quota of paralyzed iron workers to walk the high beams?

This editorial sounds like the arguments made by Yale Professor William Graham Sumner about one hundred years ago. According to Sumner, it was always unwise for government to use its power to make men equal. The only true equality, according to Sumner, was the freedom to succeed or fail on your own merit, and without government assistance. Professor Sumner always believed that no man was entitled to have happiness, only the chance to pursue it. To Sumner there were few people truly poor and weak. Rather, those who failed in life were more likely to be "negligent, shiftless, inefficient, silly, and imprudent." He resisted all attempts by government to help those who failed in life by taxing those citizens who had worked hard, saved their money and invested wisely. For Sumner, any man who could be forced to divert his wealth to aid others was not a free man. In 1883 he wrote: "We shall find that all the schemes for producing equality and obliterating the organization of society produce a new differentiation based on the worst possible distinction—the right to claim and the duty to give one man's efforts for another man's satisfaction."[8]

> In 1991 New York City officials considered placing six portable toilets on the sidewalks in different parts of the city. "Then came the glitch," wrote Philip K. Howard, "Wheelchairs couldn't fit inside them." Because New York law made it illegal to deny access by disabled persons to public accommodation, the City put two toilets at three locations, one for the general public and another, with a full-time attendant, for wheelchair users. In his book *The Death of Common Sense* (1994), Howard used the wheelchair-portable toilet controversy as evidence that American laws lack common sense. Do you agree or disagree?

> William Graham Sumner's survival of the fittest philosophy was perfectly suited to the late 19th century when this nation led the world in production, and didn't mind having children work in sweat shops. Would his philosophy be suitable to modern day Nevadans? Why or why not?

In 1996 Las Vegas had new road projects everywhere in the city limits. One project was to resurface several roadway segments at a cost of $1.7 million. The project also included median modifications at several locations to accommodate Americans with Disabilities standards. Drive around your neighborhood and see if you can spot any of these improvements. By 1997 movie theaters in Las Vegas had reserved spaces front and back for handicapped persons in wheelchairs. At this college we have prime parking spaces for handicapped drivers. Building doors operate electronically off push buttons. All these improvements are added to help people who may be handicapped or disabled, but sometimes insist on being called "differently abled," "physically inconvenienced," or even "handi-capable."

On Friday, July 24, 1992, former White House aide Oliver North gave a speech to the Non-Commissioned Officers Association convention at the Nugget hotel casino in Sparks, Nevada. During the speech, former Marine Colonel North expressed his opposition to women in combat with these ill-chosen words: "Real men don't need to send their mothers, wives and daughters to fight for them." Although the men and women in the audience cheered North's words, women's rights activists later said his comments were sexist and insensitive. Sarah Chvilicek, co-chairperson of the Nevada Women's Lobby, said, "If women are actively choosing to support their country and serve their country, they should not be discriminated against." North also managed to offend gay rights groups by saying homosexuals should not be allowed in the military at all. Holly Wilson of Parents and Friends of Lesbians and Gays called North's comments "outrageous" and told a reporter, "Sexual orientation should have nothing to do with a person's ability to serve their country, their intelligence or anything else. People need to know and be educated. I'm getting real tired of people being put down for an orientation that's not a choice."[9]

> **What do you think of North's words? Do you agree with his argument that women and gays should not serve in the U.S. military? Is being gay a biological fact that is determined by our genes, or is it a learned lifestyle? Does it really matter whether or not being gay or lesbian is biologically or environmentally decided?**

When cocktail waitresses in skimpy outfits are sexually harassed by drunken men, are they the innocent victims of biological forces which men cannot control? In Atlantic City, some cocktail waitresses filed suit in 1992 because they had to wear high heels and skimpy outfits. ☆ What do you think? Should the uniforms worn by cocktail waitresses be more conservative and proper? Why or why not?

Someday a sexual harassment lawsuit will reach the Nevada Supreme Court where it will most likely be heard by five justices elected on nonpartisan ballots for six-year terms of office. Most likely, a majority of the justices will be men. Under a 1910 Nevada law, Supreme Court justices must be licensed attorneys admitted to practice law in the state. In the minds of Marilyn O'Connor of Fallon and Reno's Eleanor Waugh, the law is unfair. Speaking to reporters outside the Supreme Court building in Carson City, Waugh argued five years ago that a justice need only common sense, not a license to practice law. Earlier in 1992, the Nevada Supreme Court had ruled that O'Connor could not run for justice because she was not an attorney. In its decision, the court reasoned that the lawyer requirement to be a Nevada Supreme Court justice was reasonable.

> **Should state law be changed to allow non-lawyers to qualify to be elected to the Nevada Supreme Court?**

As interpreted, the Holy Bible seems to imply that Sodom and Gomorrah were destroyed because the inhabitants of these sinful cities practiced sodomy. Until repealed in 1993, Nevada had a law which defined sodomy as "the infamous crime against nature." Under this 88-year-old law, sodomy was a felony which could be punished with up to six years in prison. The law was repealed by the Nevada legislature largely because gay activists claimed it violated their privacy. Throughout history, Christians have considered sodomy to be a mortal sin. Pope

Gregory III, for example, called sodomy a "vice so abominable in the sight of God that the cities in which its practitioners dwelt were appointed for destruction by fire and brimstone."

By repealing the sodomy law, Nevada showed that most people in the state have joined a national trend toward greater tolerance of alternative lifestyles.

Genesis 19, 4-11 is usually cited as the source for God's punishment against homosexuals. Read this source and determine, for yourself, if the words used there suggest that Sodom and Gomorrah were destroyed because the citizens practiced sodomy.

When it comes to sex, Nevada is probably the most broad-minded state. But we sometimes go too far. This was the case in 1997 when the Riviera recognized its famous "Crazy Girls" with statues that obscured their faces but showed nearly nude, shapely butts. The buttock statues were offensive to the National Organization for Women which objected to the seven naked women's bodies being displayed where men could rub, pat, fondle and grope them for "luck."

What do you think? Has Nevada's pampering to male sexual fantasies finally gone too far?

The People's Voice

In 1986 Nevada Senator Paul Laxalt seemed to have most of the qualifications to be an *available* presidential candidate. Throughout Ronald Reagan's tenure the media had identified Senator Laxalt as the President's close friend and confidante. Moreover, in 1986 Laxalt became a media celebrity by persuading Ferdinand Marcos to step aside as president of the Philippines. Laxalt, in the words of one admirer, was a "charming, graceful, honorable and decent man, a classy guy with intelligence, moxie and a gift for making friends."[10] Despite these qualities, Senator Laxalt had two strikes against him in 1986; Nevada had only four electoral votes in the Electoral College, and the state is populated by gamblers.

By the end of May 2000, Nevada had 900,575 active voters. Of this number, 41.6% were Democrats, 41.3% Republican and the rest belonged to third parties.

Despite having only 43.9% of Nevada's popular vote, Bill Clinton won all four of the state's electoral votes. Why?

On November 5, 1996, 553,324 of these registered voters stopped gambling long enough to stand in slow moving lines and push the electronic squares that would cast and count their votes. With 203,388 popular votes, Democrat Bill Clinton won all four of the state's electoral votes. Bob Dole placed second in the presidential race with 198,775 popular votes. H. Ross Perot was third with 43,855. "None of These" picked up 5,575 votes. Another 11,431 popular votes went to candidates representing political factions with no chance to win.

Thus Bill Clinton was reelected to his second four year term, and would continue to be paid his annual $200,000 salary. Because President Clinton and Vice President Al Gore had a "plurality" of Nevada's popular votes, the two Democrats were awarded all four of the state's electoral votes. Oddly, Nevada's Republican Party in 1996 held a 291,320 to 287,306 voter advantage over Democrats; yet Clinton and Gore carried the state. Why?

In the First District race for the U.S. House of Representatives, Republican John Ensign had 84,958 popular votes and 50.1% to win over Democrat Bob Coffin. District Two was easily won by Republican Jim Gibbons, who had 161,633 popular votes to 97,241 for Democrat Thomas Wilson. As a result of these congressional races, Nevada until 1998 will have two Democratic Senators and two Republican Representatives. If Nevada's voting habits were followed by the rest of the nation, Americans would now be governed by a Democratic President, a Democratic Senate, and a Republican House. In practice, this would give Republicans control of the purse strings while the President and Senate ran the country. Is this what the Founding Fathers had in mind?

Nevada's voters also had to vote for their favorite candidates for the legislature, judges, local officials and 20 ballot issues. These issues included referendums, constitutional amendments, and bonds. Two were especially controversial. Question 17 would have limited congressional terms to 12 years in the Senate and six years in the House if a federal constitutional amendment was approved. In its advice to voters, the Las Vegas *Sun* said, "This is a phony issue that can be resolved by voting unqualified officials out of office during regular elections. Calling for a convention of states also risks serious tinkering with the Constitution, a terrifying idea." Question 11 would require a two-thirds vote of the Legislature or local governments to impose new or increased taxes. On this issue, the *Sun* argued, "The so-called 'super majority' raises concerns about how a two-thirds vote would affect Nevada politics. Northern Nevada politicians could hold the growing South hostage, if Las Vegas needed additional revenues, but legislators couldn't muster the votes for a higher tax or fee. This question passed by a large majority two years ago and needs to pass only one more time before becoming part of the Constitution. We urge voters to be cautious on this issue."

After the elections, the media raised questions about all the money being spent by Nevada candidates. Republican John Ensign, for example, raised $1.7 million for his reelection campaign. Ensign's Democratic opponent Bob Coffin, in comparison, raised only a paltry $475,000. In the Second

> Despite the Las Vegas *Sun* advice, both Question 17 and 11 were passed by Nevada voters. What does this fact suggest about the "power of the press?"

District race, Republican Jim Gibbons spent $577,000 to win over Spike Wilson's $357,666. After the election, the media pointed out that the AFL-CIO spent over $550,000 for a 15-month campaign to defeat John Ensign, but failed. Interviewed after the election, Ensign said his victory would have been much larger if the AFL-CIO had kept its money out of Nevada.

Thanks to a ballot containing over 50 candidates and a total of 20 initiative and referendum questions, Clark County voters had to wait in lines for as long as three hours. One of these impatient voters was City Councilman Matthew Callister, who waited in line for two hours to vote. Angered by the delay, Callister criticized Clark County Registrar of Voters Kathryn Ferguson for the long lines saying, "That broad ought to be shitcanned."

> Should Councilman Callister have been sued for using the word "broad" to describe Kathryn Ferguson? Why or why not?

After the controversial election, Commissioner Erin Kenny mailed a flyer to Clark County voters explaining that despite delays the Electronic Ballot is more safe, secure and secret than paper ballots. According to the flyer, "Paper ballots can be spoiled through manipulation interpretation and destruction. Through electronic balloting, voters cannot vote for more than the legal number of candidates, offices, questions and amendments." ✫ What do you think? Should the Clark County Commission continue to use the AVC machine or go back to the paper ballots?

By now the Florida debacle of 2000 is well known. That state's 25 electoral votes won the election for George W. Bush, but the obsolete punch card voting machines used in Florida almost caused a constitutional crisis and required a U.S. Supreme Court decision. Meanwhile, back in Nevada, the electronic ballots worked fine and the over 300 voting locations kept lines down and voters were very satisfied.

Many candidates on Nevada's voting machines are designated "nonpartisan." In reality, most elected officials in the state are Democrat or Republican. As of July 1, 2001, Nevada had 378,754 registered Republicans and 381,400 registered Democrats. Which party did the better job of "getting out the vote."

> When the final 2000 Nevada popular votes were counted, George Bush had 301,575 and Al Gore had 279,978. So who won Nevada's four electoral votes in 2000?

Besides Democrats and Republicans, Nevada's electronic ballots carried the names of these political parties: Nonpartisan, Reform, Natural Law, Independent-American, Libertarian, and Green Party. One of these parties ran Ralph Nader for its presidential candidate in 2000. Which party was it? How many popular votes did Nader win nationwide? How many electoral votes did he have?

Nevada currently casts its four electoral votes on the customary "winner-take-all" basis. Each of the state's two Representatives is elected winner-take-all from the two congressional districts. Nevada's two U.S. Senators are also elected winner-take-all during separate elections. All 63 members of the Nevada Legislature are elected winner-take-all. Despite Nevada's reputation as a maverick state, every member of the state legislature is either a Republican or a Democrat.

One compelling virtue (or vice) of the winner-take-all custom is that it truly discourages third party candidates. To have a chance in Nevada or any other state for that matter, candidates must be nominated by a political party with the membership, resources, and talent to win. This unfair rule weeds out candidates with weak financial support, unpopular ideas, and abrasive personalities. Though sometimes chaotic, the nation's two-party system is more democratic than a one party system and more stable than a multiparty system. In a multiparty system, eight or ten parties without discipline, strong leadership, or carefully moderate platforms can contend passionately and illogically for the favor of voters who have a wild passion for a favorite idea. Sound too harsh? Check out those nation's with several viable political parties and decide if what works in Italy, Israel or France will work here.

Try to imagine an election in Nevada where every faction has its own favorite candidate. Consider the impact on the state's economy if every election became a moral-value mandate over issues like gambling, prostitution, and lap dancing.

In *Federalist 10*, James Madison wrote that mankind has a strong propensity to fall into mutual animosities and to form factions over religion, property and popular demagogues. How would Nevada fare if we had weak political parties and strong factions?

A demagogue is a political agitator who appeals to the lowest instincts of the mob. Where did this word originate, and why?

Judging by a typical Nevada Legislature, this state would be a prime candidate for factional discord. In 1981, for example, of the 42 members of the Assembly, there were 8 Catholics, 6 Protestants, 4 Episcopalians, 4 Mormons, 3 Lutherans, 3 Presbyterians, 2 Jewish, 2 Christians, 2 Methodists, and 6 members whose religion was not listed. Among the 21 state senators, there were 8 Catholics, 4 Mormons, 2 Protestants, 1 each Jewish, Episcopalian, Presbyterian, Lutheran, and Christian Scientist. Two did not list their religion. In a typical legislative session these religious differences would be mixed in with gender, race and ethnic differences. There would also be over 350 lobbyists representing a typical mixture of economic interests. These lobbyists would represent diverse interests ranging alphabetically all the way from the "Academically Talented Parents Organization of Clark County" to the "Wine & Spirits Wholesalers of Nevada."

It has been over two hundred years since James Madison warned us that factions were dangerous if not controlled. The Founding Fathers used republicanism, federalism, separation of powers, and checks and balances to make it extremely difficult for factions to run amuck. Because government needs responsible majorities, a two party system evolved. Despite having substantial freedom, a strong economy, and electronic miracles, many Americans despise their politicians and hunger for a brave new world where history books are banned and ignorant licentiousness is the norm. Isn't it about time for Americans to show some respect for the system which our Founders designed and which our ancestors improved?

Conventional wisdom holds that textbooks should avoid making moral-value judgments and leave that job to parents. Your authors, however, keep preaching the virtues of a two-party system where factions exist but are controlled. Is this wrong?

Nevada Customs & Rules

Anyone who has ever gambled in a Nevada casino understands the importance of being civil. Blackjack players, for example, usually ask for additional cards with signals or soft words. The player who yells or grabs extra cards gets dirty looks from the mature players, and might be asked to leave the casino.

Like other gamblers who know their customs, Blackjack players sometimes place a bet for the dealer. This small gratuity is known as the "tip." The initials t.i.p. once appeared on offering boxes in 18th century British coffeehouses and supposedly meant "to insure promptness." Like most customs, however, the tip is under siege. In Nevada, workers whose incomes are mostly from tips have been on the IRS list for many years. Since 1982 Congress has tried to clamp down on people who dodge taxes by hiding tips. The fact that tip income often went unrecorded led to laws that now require restaurants to monitor waiters' tips for the IRS.

About 10 years ago there was strong support for replacing tips with a mandatory "service charge." In restaurants like Del Frisco's Steak House in New Orleans, tipping was replaced by a 15% service charge. As often happens, however, customers resist service charges because they prefer the idea of a voluntary gratuity given for good service. In a 1989 survey conducted for *Time*, 77% of those polled said they opposed a mandatory service charge. One reason for the opposition, said *Time*, is the fact that a service charge is usually more than the average 14% tip left by customers. For their part, customers who oppose the service charge idea say they don't want to be hit for a fixed charge at restaurants where service is bad.[11]

For generous customers, Las Vegas tipping can be expensive. They end up tipping the valet, bellman, waiter, cocktail waitress, change persons, and *maitre d'*. The last named used to get the largest tip for two reasons: ☺ He decided where you sat in the showroom, and ☺ He has a French title. Now major strip resorts use a reserved seat policy, and the *maitre d'* is going the way of the dinosaur. Is the reserved seat policy an improvement over tipping?

Why don't casinos replace all tips, and simply raise the price of entertainment, cocktails, and the games? Then this extra charge can be added to the salaries of casino employees and taxed properly. Are there any compelling reasons to continue the tipping custom? Would there be any unintended consequences if a poker machine player had to pay $2 for a beer delivered by the cocktail waitress?

> **On September 18, 1965, Agent Maxwell Smart (Don Adams) made his debut on the NBC series "Get Smart." In this spoof of James Bond movies, Agent 86 (Smart) is a secret agent employed by CONTROL to stamp out the criminal organization CHAOS. Test your Las Vegas cultural literacy: What does the number 86 mean?**

In June 1947, Congress overrode a Harry Truman veto and passed the controversial Taft-Hartley Act. This law contains in Section 14B words that make labor leaders cringe: "Nothing in this act shall be construed as authorizing the execution of application of agreements requiring membership in a labor organization as a condition of employment in any state or territory in which such execution or application is prohibited by state or territorial law."

These 44 words mean that after a state passes a "right to work law" any employee of a firm within that state may not be compelled to join a union as a condition of employment. This provision in effect gave states the authority to outlaw "union shop" agreements, under which new employees must join the company's union within a certain number of days after being hired. Then and now organized labor considered Section 14B to be anti-union.

In 1952 Nevada joined several states by passing a right to work law. This was done through an initiative supported by powerful business groups and opposed by labor. Despite repeal attempts made in 1954 and 1956, the law remains on the books as a symbol of Nevada's generally pro-management attitude.

Under current laws, Nevada casinos can fire employees "at-will." The state's at-will firing law has inspired casino employees to try to change the rules through the initiative process. In June 1992, Tony Badillo, president of the Nevada Casino Dealers Association, announced that his group had collected 24,000 signatures for an initiative petition to ban "at-will firing" in the Nevada Constitution. The group, however, needed 32,595 names of registered voters and 10% of the voters in 13 of the state's 17 counties. Did the dealers get their quota of signatures in time, and thus repeal the state's Right to Work law?

In the matter of job tenure, should college professors and blackjack dealers be treated the same? Why or why not?

Nevada is unique. Casino workers are often hired because they have important friends; also known as "juice." These same employees, however, could be fired at-will by management. In the public sector, however, it is difficult to fire state employees. This is especially true of college and university faculty members who have tenure. Tenure is often portrayed in the mass media as a guaranteed job for faculty members who are lazy, incompetent, and unethical. In their defense, the professors say tenure is a necessary protection for a profession which must pursue knowledge and the truth.

Notes

1. "What is Tuff?" U.S. Department of Energy (October, 1985).

2. Keith Rogers, "Quake Rattles Nuke Dump's Future," Las Vegas *Review Journal* (June 30, 1992), pp. 1A, 3A.

3. Anne Peirce, "Students' Minds Latest DOE Target," Las Vegas *Sun* (June 24, 1992), p. 7B.

4. Mark Twain, "Flush Times in Virginia City," in Edmund Fuller (ed.), *Mark Twain: A Laurel Reader* (New York: Dell Publishing Co., Inc., 1958), pp. 155-163.

5. Russell R. Elliott, *History of Nevada*, 2d ed. rev., (Lincoln: University of Nebraska Press, 1987), pp. 69-89. James W. Hulse, *The Nevada Adventure*, 5th ed., (Reno: University of Nevada Press, 1981), pp. 83-104.

6. "DUI Ruling Criticized," Las Vegas *Sun* (May 13, 1992), p. 3A.

7. "High Stakes," *Time* (November 27, 1995).

8. William Graham Sumner, "What Social Classes Owe to Each Other," in Michael B. Levy (ed.), *Political Thought in America* (Homewood, Illinois: The Dorsey Press, 1982), p. 261.

9. "North Angers Feminists, Gay Rights Supporters," Las Vegas *Review Journal/Sun* (July 26, 1992), p. 9B.

10. Ned Day, "There's Only One Hitch to Laxalt's Presidential Bid," Las Vegas *Review Journal* (April 20, 1986), p. 7B.

11. "Leaving Tips," *Time* (Feb. 27, 1989), p. 54.

The Constitution of the United States of America

We the People of the United States, in Order to form a more perfect Union, establish Justice, insure domestic Tranquility, provide for the common defence, promote the general Welfare, and secure the Blessings of Liberty to ourselves and our Posterity, do ordain and establish this Constitution for the United States of America.

Article. I.

Section. 1. All legislative Powers herein granted shall be vested in a Congress of the United States, which shall consist of a Senate and House of Representatives.

Section. 2. The House of Representatives shall be composed of Members chosen every second Year by the People of the several States, and the Electors in each State shall have the Qualifications requisite for Electors of the most numerous Branch of the State Legislature.

No Person shall be a Representative who shall not have attained to the Age of twenty five Years, and been seven Years a Citizen of the United States, and who shall not, when elected, be an Inhabitant of that State in which he shall be chosen.

Representatives and direct Taxes shall be apportioned among the several States which may be included within this Union, according to their respective Numbers, which shall be determined by adding to the whole Number of free Persons, including those bound to Service for a Term of Years, and excluding Indians not taxed, three fifths of all other Persons. The actual Enumeration shall be made within three Years after the first Meeting of the Congress of the United States, and within every subsequent Term of ten Years, in such Manner as they shall by Law direct. The Number of Representatives shall not exceed one for every thirty Thousand, but each State shall have at Least one Representative; and until such enumeration shall be made, the State of New Hampshire shall be entitled to chuse three, Massachusetts eight, Rhode-Island and Providence Plantations one, Connecticut five, New-York six, New Jersey four, Pennsylvania eight, Delaware one, Maryland six, Virginia ten, North Carolina five, South Carolina five, and Georgia three.

When vacancies happen in the Representation from any State, the Executive Authority thereof shall issue Writs of Election to fill such Vacancies.

The House of Representatives shall chuse their Speaker and other Officers; and shall have the sole Power of Impeachment.

Section. 3. The Senate of the United States shall be composed of two Senators from each State, chosen by the Legislature thereof, for six Years; and each Senator shall have one Vote.

Immediately after they shall be assembled in Consequence of the first Election, they shall be divided as equally as may be into three Classes. The Seats of the Senators of the first Class shall be vacated at the Expiration of the second Year, of the second Class at the Expiration of the fourth Year, and of the third Class at the Expiration of the sixth Year, so that one third may be chosen every second Year; and if Vacancies happen by Resignation, or otherwise, during the

Recess of the Legislature of any State, the Executive thereof may make temporary Appointments until the next Meeting of the Legislature, which shall then fill such Vacancies.

No Person shall be a Senator who shall not have attained to the Age of thirty Years, and been nine Years a Citizen of the United States, and who shall not, when elected, be an Inhabitant of that State for which he shall be chosen.

The Vice President of the United States shall be President of the Senate, but shall have no Vote, unless they be equally divided.

The Senate shall chuse their other Officers, and also a President pro tempore, in the Absence of the Vice President, or when he shall exercise the Office of President of the United States.

The Senate shall have the sole Power to try all Impeachments. When sitting for that Purpose, they shall be on Oath or Affirmation. When the President of the United States is tried the Chief Justice shall preside: And no Person shall be convicted without the Concurrence of two thirds of the Members present.

Judgment in Cases of Impeachment shall not extend further than to removal from Office, and disqualification to hold and enjoy any Office of honor, Trust or Profit under the United States: but the Party convicted shall nevertheless be liable and subject to Indictment, Trial, Judgment and Punishment, according to Law.

Section. 4. The Times, Places and Manner of holding Elections for Senators and Representatives, shall be prescribed in each State by the Legislature thereof; but the Congress may at any time by Law make or alter such Regulations, except as to the Places of chusing Senators.

The Congress shall assemble at least once in every Year, and such Meeting shall be on the first Monday in December, unless they shall by Law appoint a different Day.

Section. 5. Each House shall be the Judge of the Elections, Returns and Qualifications of its own Members, and a Majority of each shall constitute a Quorum to do Business; but a smaller Number may adjourn from day to day, and may be authorized to compel the Attendance of absent Members, in such Manner, and under such Penalties as each House may provide.

Each House may determine the Rules of its Proceedings, punish its Members for disorderly Behaviour, and, with the Concurrence of two thirds, expel a Member.

Each House shall keep a Journal of its Proceedings, and from time to time publish the same, excepting such Parts as may in their Judgment require Secrecy; and the Yeas and Nays of the Members of either House on any question shall, at the Desire of one fifth of those Present, be entered on the Journal.

Neither House, during the Session of Congress, shall, without the Consent of the other, adjourn for more than three days, nor to any other Place than that in which the two Houses shall be sitting.

Section. 6. The Senators and Representatives shall receive a Compensation for their Services, to be ascertained by Law, and paid out of the Treasury of the United States. They shall in all Cases, except Treason, Felony and Breach of the Peace, be privileged from Arrest during their Attendance at the Session of their respective Houses, and in going to and returning from the same; and for any Speech or Debate in either House, they shall not be questioned in any other Place.

No Senator or Representative shall, during the Time for which he was elected, be appointed to any civil Office under the Authority of the United States, which shall have been created, or the Emoluments whereof shall have been encreased during such time; and no Person holding any Office under the United States, shall be a Member of either House during his Continuance in Office.

Section. 7. All Bills for raising Revenue shall originate in the House of Representatives; but the Senate may propose or concur with Amendments as on other Bills.

Every Bill which shall have passed the House of Representatives and the Senate, shall, before it become a Law, be presented to the President of the United States; If he approve he shall sign it, but if not he shall return it, with his Objections to that House in which it shall have originated, who shall enter the Objections at large on their Journal, and proceed to reconsider it. If after such Reconsideration two thirds of that House shall agree to pass the Bill, it shall be sent, together with the Objections, to the other House, by which it shall likewise be reconsidered, and if approved by two thirds of that House, it shall become a Law. But in all such Cases the Votes of both Houses shall be determined by yeas and Nays, and the Names of the Persons voting for and against the Bill shall be entered on the Journal of each House respectively. If any Bill shall not be returned by the President within ten Days (Sundays excepted) after it shall have been presented to him, the Same shall be a Law, in like Manner as if he had signed it, unless the Congress by their Adjournment prevent its Return, in which Case it shall not be a Law.

Every Order, Resolution, or Vote to which the Concurrence of the Senate and House of Representatives may be necessary (except on a question of Adjournment) shall be presented to the President of the United States; and before the Same shall take Effect, shall be approved by him, or being disapproved by him, shall be repassed by two thirds of the Senate and House of Representatives, according to the Rules and Limitations prescribed in the Case of a Bill.

Section. 8. The Congress shall have Power To lay and collect Taxes, Duties, Imposts and Excises, to pay the Debts and provide for the common Defence and general Welfare of the United States; but all Duties, Imposts and Excises shall be uniform throughout the United States;

To borrow Money on the credit of the United States;

To regulate Commerce with foreign Nations, and among the several States, and with the Indian Tribes;

To establish an uniform Rule of Naturalization, and uniform Laws on the subject of Bankruptcies throughout the United States;

To coin Money, regulate the Value thereof, and of foreign Coin, and fix the Standard of Weights and Measures;

To provide for the Punishment of counterfeiting the Securities and current Coin of the United States;

To establish Post Offices and post Roads;

To promote the Progress of Science and useful Arts, by securing for limited Times to Authors and Inventors the exclusive Right to their respective Writings and Discoveries;

To constitute Tribunals inferior to the supreme Court;

To define and punish Piracies and Felonies committed on the high Seas, and Offences against the Law of Nations;

To declare War, grant Letters of Marque and Reprisal, and make Rules concerning Captures on Land and Water;

To raise and support Armies, but no Appropriation of Money to that Use shall be for a longer Term than two Years;

To provide and maintain a Navy;

To make Rules for the Government and Regulation of the land and naval Forces;

To provide for calling forth the Militia to execute the Laws of the Union, suppress Insurrections and repel Invasions;

To provide for organizing, arming, and disciplining, the Militia, and for governing such Part of them as may be employed in the Service of the United States, reserving to the States respectively, the Appointment of the Officers, and the Authority of training the Militia according to the discipline prescribed by Congress;

To exercise exclusive Legislation in all Cases whatsoever, over such District (not exceeding ten Miles square) as may, by Cession of particular States, and the Acceptance of Congress, become the Seat of the Government of the United States, and to exercise like Authority over all Places purchased by the Consent of the Legislature of the State in which the Same shall be, for the Erection of Forts, Magazines, Arsenals, dock-Yards, and other needful Buildings;--And

To make all Laws which shall be necessary and proper for carrying into Execution the foregoing Powers, and all other Powers vested by this Constitution in the Government of the United States, or in any Department or Officer thereof.

Section. 9. The Migration or Importation of such Persons as any of the States now existing shall think proper to admit, shall not be prohibited by the Congress prior to the Year one thousand eight hundred and eight, but a Tax or duty may be imposed on such Importation, not exceeding ten dollars for each Person.

The Privilege of the Writ of Habeas Corpus shall not be suspended, unless when in Cases of Rebellion or Invasion the public Safety may require it.

No Bill of Attainder or ex post facto Law shall be passed.

No Capitation, or other direct, Tax shall be laid, unless in Proportion to the Census or Enumeration herein before directed to be taken.

No Tax or Duty shall be laid on Articles exported from any State.

No Preference shall be given by any Regulation of Commerce or Revenue to the Ports of one State over those of another: nor shall Vessels bound to, or from, one State, be obliged to enter, clear, or pay Duties in another.

No Money shall be drawn from the Treasury, but in Consequence of Appropriations made by Law; and a regular Statement and Account of the Receipts and Expenditures of all public Money shall be published from time to time.

No Title of Nobility shall be granted by the United States: And no Person holding any Office of Profit or Trust under them, shall, without the Consent of the Congress, accept of any present, Emolument, Office, or Title, of any kind whatever, from any King, Prince, or foreign State.

Section. 10. No State shall enter into any Treaty, Alliance, or Confederation; grant Letters of Marque and Reprisal; coin Money; emit Bills of Credit; make any Thing but gold and silver Coin a Tender in Payment of Debts; pass any Bill of Attainder, ex post facto Law, or Law impairing the Obligation of Contracts, or grant any Title of Nobility.

No State shall, without the Consent of the Congress, lay any Imposts or Duties on Imports or Exports, except what may be absolutely necessary for executing it's inspection Laws: and the net Produce of all Duties and Imposts, laid by any State on Imports or Exports, shall be for the Use of the Treasury of the United States; and all such Laws shall be subject to the Revision and Controul of the Congress.

No State shall, without the Consent of Congress, lay any Duty of Tonnage, keep Troops, or Ships of War in time of Peace, enter into any Agreement or Compact with another State, or with a foreign Power, or engage in War, unless actually invaded, or in such imminent Danger as will not admit of delay.

Article. II.

Section. 1. The executive Power shall be vested in a President of the United States of America. He shall hold his Office during the Term of four Years, and, together with the Vice President, chosen for the same Term, be elected, as follows

Each State shall appoint, in such Manner as the Legislature thereof may direct, a Number of Electors, equal to the whole Number of Senators and Representatives to which the State may be entitled in the Congress: but no Senator or Representative, or Person holding an Office of Trust or Profit under the United States, shall be appointed an Elector.

The Electors shall meet in their respective States, and vote by Ballot for two Persons, of whom one at least shall not be an Inhabitant of the same State with themselves. And they shall make a List of all the Persons voted for, and of the Number of Votes for each; which List they shall sign and certify, and transmit sealed to the Seat of Government of the United States, directed to the President of the Senate. The President of the Senate shall, in the Presence of the Senate and House of Representatives, open all the Certificates, and the Votes shall then be counted. The Person having the greatest Number of Votes shall be the President, if such Number be a Majority of the whole Number of Electors appointed; and if there be more than one who have such Majority, and have an equal Number of Votes, then the House of Representatives shall immediately chuse by Ballot one of them for President; and if no Person have a Majority, then from the five highest on the List the said House shall in like Manner chuse the President. But in chusing the President, the Votes shall be taken by States, the Representation from each State having one Vote; A quorum for this Purpose shall consist of a Member or Members from two thirds of the States, and a Majority of all the States shall be necessary to a Choice. In every Case, after the Choice of the President, the Person having the greatest Number of Votes of the Electors shall be the Vice President. But if there should remain two or more who have equal Votes, the Senate shall chuse from them by Ballot the Vice President.

The Congress may determine the Time of chusing the Electors, and the Day on which they shall give their Votes; which Day shall be the same throughout the United States.

No Person except a natural born Citizen, or a Citizen of the United States, at the time of the Adoption of this Constitution, shall be eligible to the Office of President; neither shall any Person be eligible to that Office who shall not have attained to the Age of thirty five Years, and been fourteen Years a Resident within the United States.

In Case of the Removal of the President from Office, or of his Death, Resignation, or Inability to discharge the Powers and Duties of the said Office, the Same shall devolve on the Vice President, and the Congress may by Law provide for the Case of Removal, Death, Resignation or Inability, both of the President and Vice President declaring what Officer shall then act as

President, and such Officer shall act accordingly, until the Disability be removed, or a President shall be elected.

The President shall, at stated Times, receive for his Services, a Compensation, which shall neither be encreased nor diminished during the Period for which he shall have been elected, and he shall not receive within that Period any other Emolument from the United States, or any of them.

Before he enter on the Execution of his Office, he shall take the following Oath or Affirmation:--"I do solemnly swear (or affirm) that I will faithfully execute the Office of President of the United States, and will to the best of my Ability, preserve, protect and defend the Constitution of the United States."

Section. 2. The President shall be Commander in Chief of the Army and Navy of the United States, and of the Militia of the several States, when called into the actual Service of the United States; he may require the Opinion, in writing, of the principal Officer in each of the executive Departments, upon any Subject relating to the Duties of their respective Offices, and he shall have Power to grant Reprieves and Pardons for Offences against the United States, except in Cases of Impeachment.

He shall have Power, by and with the Advice and Consent of the Senate, to make Treaties, provided two thirds of the Senators present concur; and he shall nominate, and by and with the Advice and Consent of the Senate, shall appoint Ambassadors, other public Ministers and Consuls, Judges of the supreme Court, and all other Officers of the United States, whose Appointments are not herein otherwise provided for, and which shall be established by Law: but the Congress may by Law vest the Appointment of such inferior Officers, as they think proper, in the President alone, in the Courts of Law, or in the Heads of Departments.

The President shall have Power to fill up all Vacancies that may happen during the Recess of the Senate, by granting Commissions which shall expire at the End of their next Session.

Section. 3. He shall from time to time give to the Congress Information of the State of the Union, and recommend to their Consideration such Measures as he shall judge necessary and expedient; he may, on extraordinary Occasions, convene both Houses, or either of them, and in Case of Disagreement between them, with Respect to the Time of Adjournment, he may adjourn them to such Time as he shall think proper; he shall receive Ambassadors and other public Ministers; he shall take Care that the Laws be faithfully executed, and shall Commission all the Officers of the United States.

Section. 4. The President, Vice President and all civil Officers of the United States, shall be removed from Office on Impeachment for, and Conviction of, Treason, Bribery, or other high Crimes and Misdemeanors.

Article. III.

Section. 1. The judicial Power of the United States, shall be vested in one supreme Court, and in such inferior Courts as the Congress may from time to time ordain and establish. The Judges, both of the supreme and inferior Courts, shall hold their Offices during good Behaviour, and shall, at stated Times, receive for their Services, a Compensation which shall not be diminished during their Continuance in Office.

Section. 2. The judicial Power shall extend to all Cases, in Law and Equity, arising under this Constitution, the Laws of the United States, and Treaties made, or which shall be made, under their Authority;--to all Cases affecting Ambassadors, other public Ministers and Consuls;--to all Cases of admiralty and maritime Jurisdiction;--to Controversies to which the United States shall be a Party;--to Controversies between two or more States;--between a State and Citizens of another State;--between Citizens of different States,--between Citizens of the same State claiming Lands under Grants of different States, and between a State, or the Citizens thereof, and foreign States, Citizens or Subjects.

In all Cases affecting Ambassadors, other public Ministers and Consuls, and those in which a State shall be Party, the supreme Court shall have original Jurisdiction. In all the other Cases before mentioned, the supreme Court shall have appellate Jurisdiction, both as to Law and Fact, with such Exceptions, and under such Regulations as the Congress shall make.

The Trial of all Crimes, except in Cases of Impeachment, shall be by Jury; and such Trial shall be held in the State where the said Crimes shall have been committed; but when not committed within any State, the Trial shall be at such Place or Places as the Congress may by Law have directed.

Section. 3. Treason against the United States, shall consist only in levying War against them, or in adhering to their Enemies, giving them Aid and Comfort. No Person shall be convicted of Treason unless on the Testimony of two Witnesses to the same overt Act, or on Confession in open Court.

The Congress shall have Power to declare the Punishment of Treason, but no Attainder of Treason shall work Corruption of Blood, or Forfeiture except during the Life of the Person attainted.

Article. IV.

Section. 1. Full Faith and Credit shall be given in each State to the public Acts, Records, and judicial Proceedings of every other State. And the Congress may by general Laws prescribe the Manner in which such Acts, Records and Proceedings shall be proved, and the Effect thereof.

Section. 2. The Citizens of each State shall be entitled to all Privileges and Immunities of Citizens in the several States.

A Person charged in any State with Treason, Felony, or other Crime, who shall flee from Justice, and be found in another State, shall on Demand of the executive Authority of the State from which he fled, be delivered up, to be removed to the State having Jurisdiction of the Crime.

No Person held to Service or Labour in one State, under the Laws thereof, escaping into another, shall, in Consequence of any Law or Regulation therein, be discharged from such Service or Labour, but shall be delivered up on Claim of the Party to whom such Service or Labour may be due.

Section. 3. New States may be admitted by the Congress into this Union; but no new State shall be formed or erected within the Jurisdiction of any other State; nor any State be formed by the

Junction of two or more States, or Parts of States, without the Consent of the Legislatures of the States concerned as well as of the Congress.

The Congress shall have Power to dispose of and make all needful Rules and Regulations respecting the Territory or other Property belonging to the United States; and nothing in this Constitution shall be so construed as to Prejudice any Claims of the United States, or of any particular State.

Section. 4. The United States shall guarantee to every State in this Union a Republican Form of Government, and shall protect each of them against Invasion; and on Application of the Legislature, or of the Executive (when the Legislature cannot be convened) against domestic Violence.

Article. V.

The Congress, whenever two thirds of both Houses shall deem it necessary, shall propose Amendments to this Constitution, or, on the Application of the Legislatures of two thirds of the several States, shall call a Convention for proposing Amendments, which, in either Case, shall be valid to all Intents and Purposes, as Part of this Constitution, when ratified by the Legislatures of three fourths of the several States, or by Conventions in three fourths thereof, as the one or the other Mode of Ratification may be proposed by the Congress; Provided that no Amendment which may be made prior to the Year One thousand eight hundred and eight shall in any Manner affect the first and fourth Clauses in the Ninth Section of the first Article; and that no State, without its Consent, shall be deprived of its equal Suffrage in the Senate.

Article. VI.

All Debts contracted and Engagements entered into, before the Adoption of this Constitution, shall be as valid against the United States under this Constitution, as under the Confederation.

This Constitution, and the Laws of the United States which shall be made in Pursuance thereof; and all Treaties made or which shall be made, under the Authority of the United States, shall be the supreme Law of the Land; and the Judges in every State shall be bound thereby, any Thi shall be made, under the Authority of the United States, shall be the suprem

The Senators and Representatives before mentioned, and the Members of the several State Legislatures, and all executive and judicial Officers, both of the United States and of the several States, shall be bound by Oath or Affirmation, to support this Constitution; but no religious Test shall ever be required as a Qualification to any Office or public Trust under the United States.

Article. VII.

The Ratification of the Conventions of nine States, shall be sufficient for the Establishment of this Constitution between the States so ratifying the Same.

Done in Convention by the Unanimous Consent of the States present the Seventeenth Day of September in the Year of our Lord one thousand seven hundred and Eighty seven and of the Independence of the United States of America the Twelfth IN WITNESS whereof We have hereunto subscribed our Names,

G. Washington:	Presidt. And deputy from Virginia
New Hampshire:	**John Langdon, Nicholas Gilman**
Massachusetts:	**Nathaniel Gorham, Rufus King**
Connecticut:	**Wm. Saml. Johnson, Roger Sherman**
New York:	**Alexander Hamilton**
New Jersey:	**Wil. Livingston, David Brearly, Wm. Paterson, Jona. Dayton**
Pennsylvania:	**B. Franklin, Thomas Mifflin, Robt. Morris, Geo. Clymer. Thos. FitzSimons, Jared Ingersoll, James Wilson, Gouv Morris**
Delaware:	**Geo. Read, Guning Bedford jr, John Dickinson, Richard Bassett, Jaco. Broom**
Maryland:	**James McHenry, Dan of St Thos. Jenifer, Danl Carroll**
Virginia:	**John Blair, James Madison Jr.**
North Carolina:	**Wm. Blount, Richd. Dobbs Spaight, Hu Williamson**
South Carolina:	**J. Rutledge, Charles Cotesworth Pinckney, Charles Pinckney, Pierce Butler**
Georgia:	**William Few, Abr Baldwin**

Amendments to the Constitution of the United States

Amendment 1 (1791)

Congress shall make no law respecting an establishment of religion, or prohibiting the free exercise thereof; or abridging the freedom of speech, or of the press; or the right of the people peaceably to assemble, and to petition the Government for a redress of grievances.

Amendment 2 (1791)

A well regulated Militia, being necessary to the security of a free State, the right of the people to keep and bear Arms, shall not be infringed.

Amendment 3 (1791)

No Soldier shall, in time of peace be quartered in any house, without the consent of the Owner, nor in time of war, but in a manner to be prescribed by law.

Amendment 4 (1791)

The right of the people to be secure in their persons, houses, papers, and effects, against unreasonable searches and seizures, shall not be violated, and no Warrants shall issue, but upon probable cause, supported by Oath or affirmation, and particularly describing the place to be searched, and the persons or things to be seized.

Amendment 5 (1791)

No person shall be held to answer for a capital, or otherwise infamous crime, unless on a presentment or indictment of a Grand Jury, except in cases arising in the land or naval forces, or in the Militia, when in actual service in time of War or public danger; nor shall any person be subject for the same offence to be twice put in jeopardy of life or limb; nor shall be compelled in any criminal case to be a witness against himself, nor be deprived of life, liberty, or property, without due process of law; nor shall private property be taken for public use, without just compensation.

Amendment 6 (1791)

In all criminal prosecutions, the accused shall enjoy the right to a speedy and public trial, by an impartial jury of the State and district wherein the crime shall have been committed, which district shall have been previously ascertained by law, and to be informed of the nature and cause of the accusation; to be confronted with the witnesses against him; to have compulsory process for obtaining witnesses in his favor, and to have the Assistance of Counsel for his defence.

Amendment 7 (1791)

In Suits at common law, where the value in controversy shall exceed twenty dollars, the right of trial by jury shall be preserved, and no fact tried by a jury, shall be otherwise re-examined in any Court of the United States, than according to the rules of the common law.

Amendment 8 (1791)

Excessive bail shall not be required, nor excessive fines imposed, nor cruel and unusual punishments inflicted.

Amendment 9 (1791)

The enumeration in the Constitution, of certain rights, shall not be construed to deny or disparage others retained by the people.

Amendment 10 (1791)

The powers not delegated to the United States by the Constitution, nor prohibited by it to the States, are reserved to the States respectively, or to the people.

Amendment 11 (1798)

The Judicial power of the United States shall not be construed to extend to any suit in law or equity, commenced or prosecuted against one of the United States by Citizens of another State, or by Citizens or Subjects of any Foreign State.

Amendment 12 (1804)

The Electors shall meet in their respective states, and vote by ballot for President and Vice-President, one of whom, at least, shall not be an inhabitant of the same state with themselves; they shall name in their ballots the person voted for as President, and in distinct ballots the person voted for as Vice-President, and they shall make distinct lists of all persons voted for as President, and of all persons voted for as Vice-President, and of the number of votes for each, which list they shall sign and certify, and transmit sealed to the seat of the government of the United States, directed to the President of the Senate;--The President of the Senate shall, in the presence of the Senate and House of Representatives, open all the certificates and the votes shall then be counted;--The person having the greatest number of votes for President, shall be the President, if such number be a majority of the whole number of Electors appointed; and if no person have such majority, then from the persons having the highest numbers not exceeding three on the list of those voted for as President, the House of Representatives shall choose immediately, by ballot, the President. But in choosing the President, the votes shall be taken by states, the representation from each state having one vote; a quorum for this purpose shall consist of a member or members from two thirds of the states, and a majority of all the states shall be necessary to a choice. And if the House of Representatives shall not choose a President whenever the right of choice shall devolve upon them, before the fourth day of March next following, then the Vice-President shall act as President, as in the case of the death or other constitutional disability of the President.--The person having the greatest number of votes as Vice-President, shall be the Vice-President, if such number be a majority of the whole number of

Electors appointed, and if no person have a majority, then from the two highest numbers on the list, the Senate shall choose the Vice-President; a quorum for the purpose shall consist of two thirds of the whole number of Senators, and a majority of the whole number shall be necessary to a choice. But no person constitutionally ineligible to the office of President shall be eligible to that of Vice-President of the United States.

Amendment 13 (1865)

Section 1. Neither slavery nor involuntary servitude, except as a punishment for crime whereof the party shall have been duly convicted, shall exist within the United States, or any place subject to their jurisdiction.

Section 2. Congress shall have power to enforce this article by appropriate legislation.

Amendment 14 (1868)

Section 1. All persons born or naturalized in the United States, and subject to the jurisdiction thereof, are citizens of the United States and of the State wherein they reside. No State shall make or enforce any law which shall abridge the privileges or immunities of citizens of the United States; nor shall any State deprive any person of life, liberty, or property, without due process of law; nor deny to any person within its jurisdiction the equal protection of the laws.

Section 2. Representatives shall be apportioned among the several States according to their respective numbers, counting the whole number of persons in each State, excluding Indians not taxed. But when the right to vote at any election for the choice of electors for President and Vice-President of the United States, Representatives in Congress, the Executive and Judicial officers of a State, or the members of the Legislature thereof, is denied to any of the male inhabitants of such State, being twenty-one years of age, and citizens of the United States, or in any way abridged, except for participation in rebellion, or other crime, the basis of representation therein shall be reduced in the proportion which the number of such male citizens shall bear to the whole number of male citizens twenty-one years of age in such State.

Section 3. No person shall be a Senator or Representative in Congress, or elector of President and Vice-President, or hold any office, civil or military, under the United States, or under any State, who, having previously taken an oath, as a member of Congress, or as an officer of the United States, or as a member of any State legislature, or as an executive or judicial officer of rebellion against the same, or given aid or comfort to the enemies thereof. But Congress may by a vote of two thirds of each House, remove such disability.

Section 4. The validity of the public debt of the United States, authorized by law, including debts incurred for payment of pensions and bounties for services in suppressing insurrection or rebellion, shall not be questioned. But neither the United States nor any State shall assume or pay any debt or obligation incurred in aid of insurrection or rebellion against the United States, or any claim for the loss or emancipation of any slave; but all such debts, obligations and claims shall be held illegal and void.

Section 5. The Congress shall have power to enforce, by appropriate legislation, the provisions of this article.

Amendment 15 (1870)

Section 1. The right of citizens of the United States to vote shall not be denied or abridged by the United States or by any State on account of race, color, or previous condition of servitude--

Section 2. The Congress shall have power to enforce this article by appropriate legislation.

Amendment 16 (1913)

The Congress shall have power to lay and collect taxes on incomes, from whatever source derived, without apportionment among the several States, and without regard to any census or enumeration.

Amendment 17 (1913)

The Senate of the United States shall be composed of two Senators from each State, elected by the people thereof, for six years; and each Senator shall have one vote. The electors in each State shall have the qualifications requisite for electors of the most numerous branch of the State legislatures.

When vacancies happen in the representation of any State in the Senate, the executive authority of such State shall issue writs of election to fill such vacancies: Provided, That the legislature of any State may empower the executive thereof to make temporary appointments until the people fill the vacancies by election as the legislature may direct.

This amendment shall not be so construed as to affect the election or term of any Senator chosen before it becomes valid as part of the Constitution.

Amendment 18 (1919 - repealed 1933)

Section 1. After one year from the ratification of this article the manufacture, sale, or transportation of intoxicating liquors within, the importation thereof into, or the exportation thereof from the United States and all territory subject to the jurisdiction thereof for beverage purposes is hereby prohibited.

Section 2. The Congress and the several States shall have concurrent power to enforce this article by appropriate legislation.

Section 3. This article shall be inoperative unless it shall have been ratified as an amendment to the Constitution by the legislatures of the several States, as provided in the Constitution, within seven years from the date of the submission hereof to the States by the Congress.

Amendment 19 (1920)

The right of citizens of the United States to vote shall not be denied or abridged by the United States or by any State on account of sex.

Congress shall have power to enforce this article by appropriate legislation.

Amendment 20 (1922)

Section 1. The terms of the President and Vice-President shall end at noon on the 20th day of January, and the terms of Senators and Representatives at noon on the third day of January, of the years in which such terms would have ended if this article had not been ratified; and the terms of their successors shall then begin.

Section 2. The Congress shall assemble at least once in every year, and such meeting shall begin at noon on the third day of January, unless they shall by law appoint a different day.

Section 3. If, at the time fixed for the beginning of the term of the President, the President elect shall have died, the Vice-President elect shall become President. If a President shall not have been chosen before the time fixed for the beginning of his term, or if the President elect shall have failed to qualify, then the Vice-President elect shall act as President until a President shall have qualified; and the Congress may by law provide for the case wherein neither a President elect nor a Vice-President elect shall have qualified, declaring who shall then act as President, or the manner in which one who is to act shall be selected, and such person shall act accordingly until a President or Vice-President shall have qualified.

Section 4. The Congress may by law provide for the case of the death of any of the persons from whom the House of Representatives may choose a President whenever the right of choice shall have devolved upon them, and for the case of the death of any of the persons from whom the Senate may choose a Vice-President whenever the right of choice shall have devolved upon them.

Section 5. Sections 1 and 2 shall take effect on the 15th day of October following the ratification of this article.

Section 6. This article shall be inoperative unless it shall have been ratified as an amendment to the Constitution by the legislatures of three fourths of the several States within seven years from the date of its submission.

Amendment 21 (1933)

Section 1. The eighteenth article of amendment to the Constitution of the United States is hereby repealed.

Section 2. The transportation or importation into any State, Territory, or possession of the United States for delivery or use therein of intoxicating liquors, in violation of the laws thereof, is hereby prohibited.

Section 3. This article shall be inoperative unless it shall have been ratified as an amendment to the Constitution by conventions in the several States, as provided in the Constitution, within seven years from the date of the submission hereof to the States by the Congress.

Amendment 22 (1951)

Section 1. No person shall be elected to the office of the President more than twice, and no person who has held the office of President, or acted as President, for more than two years of a term to which some other person was elected President shall be elected to the office of the President more than once. But this Article shall not apply to any person holding the office of President when this Article was proposed by the Congress, and shall not prevent any person who may be holding the office of President, or acting as President, during the term within which this Article becomes operative from holding the office of President or acting as President during the remainder of such term.

Section 2. This article shall be inoperative unless it shall have been ratified as an amendment to the Constitution by the legislatures of three fourths of the several States within seven years from the date of its submission to the States by the Congress.

Amendment 23 (1961)

Section 1. The District constituting the seat of Government of the United States shall appoint in such manner as the Congress may direct:

A number of electors of President and Vice-President equal to the whole number of Senators and Representatives in Congress to which the District would be entitled if it were a State, but in no event more than the least populous State; they shall be in addition to those appointed by the States, but they shall be considered, for the purposes of the election of President and Vice-President, to be electors appointed by a State; and they shall meet in the District and perform such duties as provided by the twelfth article of amendment.

Section 2. The Congress shall have power to enforce this article by appropriate legislation.

Amendment 24 (1964)

Section 1. The right of citizens of the United States to vote in any primary or other election for President or Vice-President, for electors for President or Vice-President, or for Senator or Representative in Congress, shall not be denied or abridged by the United States or any State by reason of failure to pay any poll tax or other tax.

Section 2. The Congress shall have power to enforce this article by appropriate legislation.

Amendment 25 (1967)

Section 1. In case of the removal of the President from office or his death or resignation, the Vice-President shall become President.

Section 2. Whenever there is a vacancy in the office of the Vice-President, the President shall nominate a Vice-President who shall take the office upon confirmation by a majority vote of both houses of Congress.

Section 3. Whenever the President transmits to the President pro tempore of the Senate and the Speaker of the House of Representatives his written declaration that he is unable to discharge the powers and duties of his office, and until he transmits to them a written declaration to the contrary, such powers and duties shall be discharged by the Vice-President as Acting President.

Section 4. Whenever the Vice-President and a majority of either the principal officers of the executive departments, or of such other body as Congress may by law provide, transmit to the President pro tempore of the Senate and the Speaker of the House of Representatives their written declaration that the President is unable to discharge the powers and duties of his office, the Vice-President shall immediately assume the powers and duties of the office as Acting President.

Thereafter, when the President transmits to the President pro tempore of the Senate and the Speaker of the House of Representatives his written declaration that no inability exists, he shall resume the powers and duties of his office unless the Vice-President and a majority of either the principal officers of the executive department, or of such other body as Congress may by law provide, transmit within four days to the President pro tempore of the Senate and the Speaker of the House of Representatives their written declaration that the President is unable to discharge the powers and duties of his office. Thereupon Congress shall decide the issue, assembling within 48 hours for that purpose if not in session. If the Congress, within 21 days after receipt of the latter written declaration, or, if Congress is not in session, within 21 days after Congress is required to assemble, determines by two-thirds vote of both houses that the President is unable to discharge the powers and duties of his office, the Vice-President shall continue to discharge the same as Acting President; otherwise, the President shall resume the powers and duties of his office.

Amendment 26 (1971)

Section 1. The right of citizens of the United States, who are eighteen years of age or older, to vote shall not be denied or abridged by the United States or any state on account of age.

Section 2. The Congress shall have power to enforce this article by appropriate legislation.

Amendment 27 (1992)

No law, varying the compensation for the services of Senators and Representatives, shall take effect until an election of Representatives shall have intervened.